Praise for *Saving Leonardo*

"Nancy Pearcey's books have been an enormous help to me as I've tried to figure out what it means to be a Christian writer in a culture that sometimes appears to have gone insane. In *Saving Leonardo*, she traces out the various secular worldviews that are sucking the blood out of Western Civilization, and reveals the one characteristic they all have in common: their demonstrable inferiority to a Christian worldview that unites heaven and earth, knowledge and faith. That is such good news, we should share it with the people who are educating our children."
— John R. Erickson
   Author, *Hank the Cowdog*

"*Saving Leonard* is a feast for the mind and for the eye. Nancy Pearcey not only is a trustworthy guide for a nuanced discussion on the relationship between culture and the gospel, but she is a gifted teacher as well. I pray that this book will open many eyes to the enormous riches of our visual arts heritage. May we become confident emissary into today's cultural pluralism. *Saving Leonard* is a rare, precious gift to the churches and universities alike."
— Makoto Fujimura
   Artist and author of *Refractions:*
   a journey of faith, art and culture

"When Nancy Pearcey to speak at Mackenzie Presbyterian University in São Paulo, Brazil for the first time we were not ready for what we heard. In a clear, passionate and convincing way Nancy argued from the history of science that the Christian faith is the very soul of science. The concepts that she expounded and defended strengthened the Christian witness within our University and encouraged Christian faculty and students to pursue these concepts further. I am sure that *Saving Leonardo* will continue and advance Nancy's vision, this time examining the arts as impacted by secularism and its destructive power. As with *Total Truth* and *How Now Should We Live?*, this book will do much to strengthen and encourage Christian witness within academic circles."
— Augustus Lopes
   Chancellor, Mackenzie Presbyterian
   University

"Nancy Pearcey is an intellectual prophet in our day and one of Evangelicalism's foremost cultural observers. *Saving Leonardo* is a tour de force. In it, Pearcey provides a penetrating analysis of the nature of contemporary secularism, a helpful exposition of how we got to the present situation, and a well-crafted strategy for changing the situation. This is her best effort yet, and it is a must read for believers who want to make a difference in our world."
— J. P. Moreland
   Distinguished Professor of Philosophy, Biola
   University and author of *The God Question*.

"Nancy Pearcey helps a new generation of evangelicals to understand the worldview challenges we now face and to develop an intelligent and articulate Christian understanding that can be communicated in today's context of cultural engagement.

Saving Leonardo should be put in the hands of all those who should always be ready to give an answer – and that means all of us."
— R. Albert Mohler, Jr.
   President, The Southern Baptist
   Theological Seminary

"Nancy Pearcey is unsurpassed in the current generation of Christian thinkers in articulating the need for Christianity to stand as a counterforce to trends in contemporary American society. The magic continues with this book. Pearcey's virtues as a writer and thinker are once again fully evident in the range of material that she has mastered, the encyclopedic collection of data that she presents, and the analytic rigor with which she separates truth from error in worldviews. Nancy Pearcey is a prophetic voice for contemporary Christians. In *Saving Leonardo* she illuminates a path by which Christians can forge the right worldview and avoid an unthinking drift into non-Christian worldviews."
— Leland Ryken
   Clyde S. Kilby Professor of English,
   Wheaton College

"Nancy Pearcey has done it again and better than ever. She has taken the complex sophistication of the best cultural analysis and laid it out for any person to grasp, enjoy and use to live out their daily lives honoring Christ. An astounding accomplishment!"
— James W. Sire,
   Author of *The Universe Next Door*

"G.K.Chesterton said 'the danger when Men stop believing in God is not that they'll believe in nothing; but that they will believe in anything.' Nancy Pearcey understands where believing in anything leads and in this book she reveals where a secular philosophy is taking us. A balanced, fair, and impacting work! Even secularists should read it. While they may think they are on the right road, they won't like where it leads. By the time they wake up, it will be too late for them and for America."
— Cal Thomas
   Syndicated and *USA Today* columnist

"Brilliant . . . wide-ranging and illuminating . . . As she does in *Total Truth*, Pearcey turns the 'fact/value' distinction that has become a commonplace of modern thought into a powerful and sharp-edged tool by which she dissects both anti-Christian ideas and ineffectual Christian responses. Whereas *Total Truth* illustrated her points by concentrating on science, *Saving Leonardo* does so by concentrating on the arts. The effect is to bring complex, abstract ideas down-to-earth—or, rather, down-to-life—and to help Christians recognize non-Biblical thinking in the culture and in themselves. . .*Saving Leonardo* bridges the gaps between the arts and the sciences, the theoretical and the practical. The book not only argues for the unity of Christian truth but exemplifies that unity and shows it in action."
— Gene Edward Veith
   Provost, Patrick Henry College

978-1-4336-6927-9

Published by B&H Publishing Group
Nashville, Tennessee

Dewey Decimal Classification:
Subject Heading:

Published in association with Yates & Yates, www.yates2.com.

Unless otherwise noted, Scripture quotations are from the Holy Bible, New International
Version, copyright © 1973, 1978, 1984 by International Bible Society.

Also used: The Holy Bible, English Standard Version® (ESV®)
Copyright © 2001 by Crossway, a publishing ministry of Good News Publishers.
All rights reserved. ESV Text Edition: 2007

Roy Lichtenstein, *Sweet Dreams Baby*, 1965 © Estate of Roy Lichtenstein
Leonardo da Vinci, *Mona Lisa*, 16th Century
Lyubov Sergeyevna Popova, *Two Figures*, 1913-14
Maxi Posters, *Pulp Fiction*

1 2 3 4 5 6 7 8 9 10 • 15 14 13 12 11 10

SAVING
LEONARDO

*A Call to Resist the Secular Assault on
Mind, Morals, & Meaning*

NANCY PEARCEY

Author of Total Truth: Liberating Christianity from Its Cultural Captivity

PUBLISHING GROUP

NASHVILLE, TENNESSEE

Leonardo da Vinci

Hence the anguish and the innermost tragedy
of this universal man,
divided between his irreconcilable worlds.

(Giovanni Gentile, Leonardo's Thought)

TABLE OF CONTENTS

Stealth Secularism—Blindsided by CBS—Secularism Go Global—Da Vinci in the Big Apple
March on the English Department—Co-Opting Christian Culture—When in Rome, Conquer
The Simple Gospel Is Not Simple—Questions Children Ask
Beyond Paintball and Whipped Cream—De-Coding Worldviews
What the Media Ignores—Reversing Secularism—No "Born" Christians
Where the Action Is

Easy Marks—Resisting Rome—Hamlet and Harry Potter—Spirituality in Secularville
Relativists for Jesus—Are Christians Bigots?—Is Christianity Exclusive?
C. S. Lewis: We Can't All Be Right—The Liberal Cave-In—Why Liberal Churches Fail
Kicking the Bible out of Class—Protecting Children from Religion—Good Cop/Bad Cop
Oppressive Tolerance—Secular Pharisees—Socrates' Slogan—Getting Through to Secularists

INTRODUCTION

Why Americans Hate Politics

During the 2008 presidential campaign, a troubling trend emerged—one that signals a crisis far broader than politics. Polls revealed that many young people feel alienated from the political process. They have grown disillusioned with a style of political debate that seems shrill, harsh, and irresolvable.

Of course, people in every age have complained that politics is stained by corruption and wheeler dealing. But today's disillusionment runs deeper. It is the tragic fruit of a secular worldview, which has decoupled politics from morality. And by recognizing how it happened, we can shed new light on the destructive impact of secularism across all of life. Politics is a microcosm that concentrates the forces at work through the rest of society.

A secular approach to politics first took root in the universities, the seedbed where worldviews are planted and nurtured. As William Galston of the Brookings Institution explains, in the modern age, scholars decided that the study of politics must be "scientific"—by which they meant value free.[1] As a consequence, political theory was no longer animated by a moral vision. It became purely pragmatic.

This represented a radical departure from the heritage of the American founders. At the birth of our nation, politics was assumed to be a profoundly moral enterprise—the pursuit of moral ideals such as justice, fairness, and the common good. James Madison, principal author of the U.S. Constitution, said the goal of government was to secure "the public good." As a recent article explains, the founders assumed that "government is not simply about securing individual rights and interests but some more substantial and transcendent good."[2]

But today, after decades of treating politics as value free, many political scientists reject the very concept of a transcendent good.

How did such a dramatic reversal occur? Through much of the twentieth century, American academia was dominated by the philosophy of empiricism, the doctrine that all knowledge is derived from the senses—what we see, hear, touch, and feel. Even moral statements were reduced to feelings. According to empiricism, we call things *good* when they give us pleasure. We call them *bad* when they cause pain.

Thus was born the fact/value split—the idea that humans can have genuine knowledge only in the realm of empirical facts. Morality was reduced to subjective preferences. The term *values* means literally whatever the individual happens to value.

This was a crucial turning point in the American mind. For if values are subjective, then they have no place in the university where we pursue objective research. In every field of study, knowledge claims were surgically separated from moral claims. Political thinkers decided that statements about the public good were nothing but masks for private taste. As Galston explains, they concluded that saying, "X is in the public interest" was merely a covert way of saying, "I like X."

Today we are reaping the bitter harvest of that cynicism. For when moral convictions are reduced to arbitrary preferences, then they can no longer be debated rationally. Persuasion gives way to propaganda. Politics becomes little more than marketing. Political operators resort to emotional manipulation, using slick rhetoric and advertising techniques to bypass people's minds and "hook" their feelings. Sound familiar?

Finally nothing is left but sheer force. Economist Lionel Robbins voiced the view of most social scientists: When we disagree over values, he said, "it is a case of thy blood or mine."[3]

No wonder American voters are disillusioned. In a book called *Why Americans Hate Politics,* E. J. Dionne says, "Americans hate politics as it is now practiced because we have lost all sense of the public good."[4] Without the conviction that there exists an objective good, public debate disintegrates into a cacophony of warring voices.

The disillusionment is so widespread that a book came out in Britain with nearly the same title: *Why We Hate Politics.* "Politicians are assumed today not to be selfless representatives of those who elected them, or benevolent guardians of the public good," the author says. How could they be, if there *is* no public good? "They are, instead, self-serving and self-interested rational utility-maximizers," advancing only those policies that benefit themselves.[5] Secular political philosophies inevitably end in sheer pragmatism and utilitarianism.

Because the word *secular* is the opposite of *religious,* many people assume that secularism is a problem for religious groups only. Not so. When politics loses its moral dimension, we all lose. When political discourse is debased, the entire society suffers. The reason Christians should be concerned is not to protect their own subculture, but to protect the democratic process for all people.

The same secular forces have exerted a destructive impact in every area of life. In the following chapters, you will learn to recognize and resist secular ideas in science, philosophy, ethics, the arts and humanities. We will examine the concepts and events, the thinkers and artists who led the way step by step in creating worldviews that undermine human dignity and liberty. And we will demonstrate that the only hope lies in a worldview that is rationally defensible, life affirming, and rooted in creation itself. As the Declaration of Independence puts it, human rights are unalienable only when a society regards them as endowed by the Creator. When Americans recover a message of liberty, justice, and the public good, then idealistic young people will no longer have reason to hate politics.

Part 1: The Threat of Global Secularism

The book is divided into two parts. Part one describes the growing threat of international secularism and how it affects us all. Sociologists inform us that secularism is going global, radiating out from urban centers on every continent. It is a monolithic worldview we must now all engage, no matter where we live or work. Chapter 1 asks: Are we up to the task?

Chapter 2 zooms in on the concept at the core of modern secularism: the polarization of facts from values. This affects far more than politics, cutting to the concept of truth itself. The fact/value split was a major theme in my earlier book *Total Truth*. But this chapter takes the concept into new areas, showing that it is not only a view of truth but also a strategy for gaining power—and ultimately for imposing political control. Those who fail to recognize this central strategy will continue to lose ground both culturally and personally. And society as a whole will continue to suffer. Secular ideologies preach liberty but practice tyranny.

The fact/value dualism is only the tip of the iceberg, however. Chapter 3 widens the lens to reveal its connection to controversial issues that threaten the dignity of human life itself—abortion, euthanasia, genetic engineering, and the destruction of human embryos. These practices rest on a dualistic view of the human being. In science, humans are viewed as nothing but complex biochemical mechanisms (the fact realm), while in ethics, the individual is treated as an autonomous self, making ungrounded choices (the value realm). The same dualism drives sexual practices such as homosexuality, transgenderism, and "hooking up." This chapter gives you the conceptual tools you need to respond to today's cutting-edge ethical issues.

Part 2: Two Paths to Secularism

Ideas are far easier to understand, however, if we go up for a bird's eye view to see how they developed over time. Part 2 widens the lens still further to trace the historical rise of secularism. Virtually all modern worldviews cluster into two major groups, originating in the clash between the Enlightenment and the Romantic movement. Once again, we encounter the same dualism: The Enlightenment focused on the fact realm; Romanticism sought to protect the values realm. We might think of them as two paths to secularism. By tracing these parallel paths running side by side through modern history, we will gain surprising new insights into the worldviews that shape our world today.

Chapter 4 starts off with a crash course in how to detect worldviews in the arts and culture. The common stereotype is that art is merely a matter of personal expression. But the truth is that artists interact deeply with the thought of their day. They translate worldviews into stories and images, creating a picture language that people often absorb without even thinking about it. Learning to "read" that language is a crucial skill for understanding the forces that are dramatically altering our world. This chapter ends with an overview of the two paths to secularism, setting us up to explore them in detail over the remaining chapters.

Chapters 5 and 6 explore one path to secularism—the cluster of worldviews that are offshoots of the Enlightenment. You probably remember terms like *Enlightenment* from high school history courses. You may even have studied worldviews such as empiricism, rationalism, naturalism, and materialism. But now these worldviews come to life as you see them expressed artistically in styles like impressionism, cubism, and those angular metallic structures that have sprouted up in our cities under the rubric of "public art." Writers and novelists played a role as well, crafting stories that portray humans as Darwinian organisms in the struggle for existence. As we walk through these chapters, you will "see" worldviews unfold before your eyes through painting, poetry, and novels.

We typically think of artists as Romantics, so chapters 7 and 8 turn to worldviews rooted in Romanticism. This path to secularism takes us through some of the most controversial worldviews of our time—existentialism, Marxism, postmodernism, deconstructionism, and New Age spirituality. Artists and writers make these worldviews tangible, helping us to experience them "from the inside" in styles such as expressionism, surrealism, and abstraction. Images and stories bring the ideas to life in a way that a purely abstract discussion could never do.

Chapter 9 identifies worldviews as they filter down to popular culture, where they have mass impact. This is the area that concerns parents the most, of course. They are eager to find ways to equip themselves and their children to counter the destructive impact of secular doctrines conveyed through music and movies. This chapter offers tips and tools for critiquing worldview themes preached by Hollywood.

The epilogue offers an inspirational vision of how each individual can become a culture-shaping influence. Those best qualified to understand the arts are those who genuinely love them, and who are striving to weave their own lives into a work of art that will attract others to the beauty of truth.

Part 1

The Threat of Global Secularism

Chapter One

"Through art we can know another's view of the universe."
—Marcel Proust

Are You an Easy Mark?

Hank the Cowdog is a humorous, homespun yarn for kids. Or it was, until the forces of political correctness got hold of it. Children's author John Erickson has created a dog character with a comic tough-guy swagger, the "Head of Ranch Security" living on a cattle ranch in West Texas. Over the years, I came to know Hank like an old friend because my son Michael is an auditory learner, which drove me to the library shelves in search of books on tape that would appeal to him.

The Hank stories, with their corny humor and mock macho tone, proved to be perfect. Michael would listen by the hour to tapes of Erickson spinning out tales about Hank and his run-ins with a caricatured cast of critters—a stub-tailed sidekick named Drover, an uncouth coyote clan, and a couple of backwoods buzzards. The action is centered on a family ranch owned by High Loper and his wife Sally May, with their son Little Alfred. Working for them is a ranch hand who lives down the road, a bachelor cowboy named Slim Chance (modeled on Erickson himself in younger years).

Stealth Secularism

The down-home rural story proved unacceptable, however, to big-city television executives. Several years ago CBS selected *Hank the Cowdog* for its "Storybreak" program, a video series based on children's books to air during Saturday morning cartoons. Initially, Erickson

1-1 John Erickson
Hank the Cowdog

Imposing a secular ideology

felt honored. When the video was broadcast for the first time, his entire hometown of Perryton, Texas, threw a celebration for its local author. But as Erickson sat down with two hundred schoolchildren to watch the video, he noticed that the story rang false at several points. For one thing, High Loper and Sally May were no longer married. Instead Sally May had been promoted to ranch boss. Loper had been *de*moted to a ranch hand who worked for her, along with Slim. In fact, all three adults lived together in a kind of bunkhouse.

What had happened to the family home? For that matter, what had happened to the *family*? Little Alfred had disappeared completely. Apparently a child was an unwanted nuisance on the CBS version of the ranch. Did I say ranch? No, the cattle ranch had been converted into a chicken farm. And the location was no longer west Texas but Arizona, set against a backdrop of saguaro cacti.

Erickson was puzzled by the drastic changes. "At first I thought someone had made a mistake," he told me. "Then I realized that at such a high level of professionalism, people don't make mistakes. The changes had to be intentional."[1] He was right. But it took several years for Erickson to figure out what that intention was.

When he began to read books on Christian worldview, he finally realized what had happened: He had been caught in the crossfire of clashing worldviews. His humorous little story had been subverted by the forces of political correctness. Marriage? A trap for women. Family? An outmoded and oppressive social institution. Children? A barrier to women's career aspirations. Cattle ranch? A scourge on the environment. So a revised script had been scrabbled together in which Sally May was transformed from ranch wife to ranch boss, ordering around the hired hands instead of raising Little Alfred.

"They had taken the family out of my story!" Erickson was stunned as the implication sank in. "They had removed all traces of the kind of home life that had been a source of strength to me, my parents, my grandparents, and back as far as we could trace our family history." And for what reason? "Because someone at the network had decided to use a Saturday morning cartoon series—and my *Hank* book—as a platform for their own ideology."

Blindsided by CBS

Stories and images can be powerful means for conveying ideas. Every time we read a book or watch a movie, we enter into an imaginative expression of the artist's worldview. It may be present subtly as a background belief, or expressed overtly as an intentional agenda. But it is there.

Writers and artists do not go home at night and study systematic philosophy. Yet they are whole persons who bring their basic assumptions about life into the study or the studio. "Stories offer meaning to the 'facts' of life," writes Robert K. Johnston in *Reel Spirituality*. They always "have an informing vision, or worldview, embedded in them."[2]

When the CBS producers imposed their politically correct worldview on the *Hank* video, they did not request Erickson's permission. They did not even notify him. He was simply blind-sided. "I am embarrassed that it took me so long to recognize what happened," Erickson told me. "I don't like getting whipped. I was an easy mark because I didn't know I was in a fight."

What about you? Do you know you are in a fight? Worldviews do not come neatly labeled. They do not ask permission before invading our mental space. Do you have the tools to detect the ideas competing for your allegiance in movies, school textbooks, news broadcasts, and even Saturday morning cartoons? Are you equipped to teach your children, students, and colleagues to recognize the most powerful worldviews of our age?

Or are you an "easy mark"? If so, your work and accomplishments could well be co-opted and redirected by others with their own ideological agenda to impose, as *Hank* was. And you won't even know how it happened.

Secularism Goes Global

Among the worldviews competing in America's pluralistic society, there is one that we all encounter in some form. It has become nearly universal, crossing ethnic, racial, and national boundaries. Sociologists describe it as an emerging global secularism. "There is, without question, a globalized *elite* culture," writes sociologist Peter Berger, "an international subculture composed of people with Western-type higher education." They tend to congregate in large metropolitan areas, so that elites in New York City have essentially the same secular mind-set as their counterparts in London, Tokyo, and Sao Paulo.

These urban elites exert power far out of proportion to their numbers. As Berger writes, "They control the institutions that provide the 'official' definitions of reality," such as law, education, mass media, academia, and advertising.[3] In short, they are society's gatekeepers. People who have the power to control the "'official' definitions of reality" are in a position to impose their own private worldview across an entire society.

As a consequence, global secularism is an international worldview that we all need to engage, no matter where we live or work. Political scientist Benjamin Barber dubbed it "McWorld," a homogenous global culture dominated by McDonalds, Macintosh, and MTV. "Common markets demand a common language," he explains, "and they produce common behaviors of the kind bred by cosmopolitan city life everywhere."[4]

That cosmopolitan lifestyle spills over into small towns and rural areas through television, advertising, music, movies, and fashion. Young people are most likely to be drawn in. Today teenagers in small towns often have more in common with teenagers in big cities than with their own parents, pastors, and teachers. In the words of Timothy Keller, pastor of Redeemer Presbyterian Church in New York City, "It is the culture/values set of world-class cities that is now being transmitted around the globe to every tongue, tribe, people, and nation."

What does that mean practical terms? It means that "kids in Iowa or even Mexico are becoming more like young adults in L.A. and New York City than they are like adults in their own locales."[5] The sobering implication is that adults in those locales must get up to speed on big-city metropolitan culture if they hope to communicate with *their own* kids.

The goal of this book is to equip you to detect, decipher, and defeat the monolithic secularism that is spreading rapidly and imposing its values on your family and hometown. We will trace its historical development and analyze its impact on some of the most controversial issues of our day. Because it is propagated through "Western-type higher education" (Berger's phrase) the best way to get a handle on it is to ask what the universities are teaching. What is taught in the science department, the philosophy department, and the art department shapes a society's "official definition of reality." Over time it filters down to the courtroom, the public school classroom, and the Hollywood production studio. Just ask John Erickson.

Da Vinci in the Big Apple

I discovered first hand how the global urban culture filters down when I shared a cab with a young unmarried couple in Manhattan. They were quintessential New Yorkers. He was a financial manager and Jewish. She was a lawyer and Asian. At first she acted aloof and business-like, tapping out messages to clients on her Palm Pilot as the cab plowed into

1-2 Dan Brown
The Da Vinci Code

Fiction as biblical criticism

traffic. Eventually, however, we struck up a conversation, and when she learned that I was in New York City to teach for a Christian summer program (World Journalism Institute) she immediately went on the offensive.

"What do you think of Dan Brown's *The Da Vinci Code*?" (The book had been out about a year.) "All my friends are losing their faith because of that book. What about you?"

I decided to leave details aside and take aim at the book's core claim—that the Bible is historically unreliable. Over the blaring horns of New York City traffic, I explained that the New Testament can be tested by exactly the same methods that scholars use to test any other ancient document. For example, historians can compare manuscripts in different languages from all around the Mediterranean world—Egypt, Syria, Turkey, Greece—to see how widely the texts diverge from one another. If variations are minor, then the texts were copied accurately and the version we have today is close to the original. And that is exactly what historians *do* find. Consequently, they have been able to reconstruct the original text with about 99.5 percent accuracy. There is no evidence that the New Testament texts were doctored or that legendary material was added later.

The young lawyer was intrigued. Then there's the age of the texts, I explained. We have fourteen thousand fragments of the New Testament, many of them dating from mere decades after it was first written. Compare that to other ancient texts. We have only about ten copies of Caesar's *Gallic Wars,* and the earliest is from about one thousand years after it was first written. With Plato and Aristotle, we have even fewer copies, and the time gap is even longer. Yet no one doubts the authenticity of the classical writers. By normal objective standards of historical scholarship, the New Testament text is incredibly accurate. There is nothing else like it in the ancient world.[6]

What about the Gnostic Gospels? In the novel, Dan Brown claims that the Gnostic Gospels give an earlier (and hence more authentic) account of Jesus' life, a view that has become widely popular. But professional historians say the Gnostic Gospels were written about a century *after* the New Testament, not before.

We continued talking all the way to the airport. By the time we arrived forty-five minutes later, the young woman had dropped her Big-City-Lawyer persona and was thanking me warmly. She confided that she had been raised in a church but had never heard Christianity defended by reasons and evidence.

As I stepped out of the cab, it struck me that our conversation had been sparked by a novel, a work of fiction. Yet should that be surprising? After all, where do most people wrestle with the big questions of life—about God, morality, and the meaning of life? Today's most influential worldviews are born in the universities, but they touch all of us through the books we read, the music we listen to, and the movies we watch. Ideas penetrate our minds most deeply when communicated through the imaginative language of image, story, and symbol. It is crucial for Christians to learn how to "read" that language and to identify worldviews transmitted through cultural forms.

An evangelical radio commentator once advised his audience to take *The Da Vinci Code* and "throw it away!" But putting on blinders is not the way to develop critical thinking. Nor is it the way to show love and compassion for the millions of people who were influenced by the book and who need answers to its false claims. Artists and writers are the most important conduit of worldviews. As philosopher William Barrett wrote, an age sees itself "in the looking glass of its art."[7] Anyone who wants to "understand the times and know what to do" (1 Chron. 12:32) must learn to interpret the images in that looking glass.

March on the English Department

Yet that radio commentator was expressing a view far too common in the church. The arts are often dismissed by Christians as mere entertainment, a leisure activity. Aren't there more pressing issues calling for our attention—such as what's happening in the White House?

Secular people know better. Consider a much-quoted line by Todd Gitlin, former president of the radical Students for a Democratic Society (SDS). After the 1960s student protests, Gitlin said, the Left began "marching on the English Department while the Right took the White House."[8] Today we must ask ourselves: Which was the more effective strategy? The 1960s radicals who avoided the draft with student deferments made their way up through the universities, became professors, and inculcated their radical ideas into the minds of generations of young people—ideas that shape the way they now vote.

This explains why Christians and other moral conservatives continue to lose ground culturally, in spite of a huge increase in political activism in recent decades. Sociologist James Davison Hunter, author of *Culture Wars,* says evangelicals have grown adept at mobilizing money and manpower to reach political goals. But they overlooked one crucial fact: that America's secular elites had already reached an *intellectual* consensus on the legitimacy of things like abortion and homosexual rights "far earlier than any kind of legislation or court decision that would ratify that consensus."[9]

In short, what came first was a shift in worldview. Ideas are born, nurtured, and developed in the universities long before they step out onto the political stage.

That is true today more than ever because politics itself is dominated by the Ivy League. Through most of America's history, the nation has had a reputation for being pragmatic, not ideological—focused on building gadgets and making money. As Calvin Coolidge famously said in the 1920s, "The business of America is business." Many of the nation's presidents have been military heroes. Despite exceptions like Franklin Roosevelt's Brain Trust, intellectuals have not been at the center of political power.

That changed with the 2008 election of Barack Obama. *Newsweek* welcomed his presidency by announcing, "Brains Are Back." The *New Scientist* hailed him as "the intellectual president," "a former academic who is deeply familiar with the world of thought." Indeed the entire Obama administration is filled with graduates from Ivy League universities. A *New York Times* article dubbed them "Achievetrons," listing the leading university each one graduated from.[10]

What this means is that the controlling force in politics is no longer business but ideology. Those who marched on the English department are now in the White House, bringing with them the radicalized secular ideologies they learned in the classroom. This is a trend that will continue long after the current president leaves office. Modern societies are knowledge-based societies, where information and expertise are as critical as economic resources. Those with the authority to define what qualifies as knowledge wield the greatest power.

Co-Opting Christian Culture

John Erickson discovered just how strategically that power can be wielded. The television network did not reject his *Hank* story outright. Instead it co-opted the tale to convey a message that he himself rejected. "When I made my deal with CBS," Erickson told me, "I never dreamed they would use my story as a vehicle for mocking the values of my parents, church, and community." His audience was co-opted as well. They were deceived into thinking they were getting a story from an author they trust, about characters they had grown to love. Instead the television producers distorted the story to convey their own elite secular worldview.

This gives a clue to the way society has been secularized over the past centuries. Throughout Western history, Christians have founded vast numbers of charities, orphanages, hospitals, YMCAs, schools, and universities—many of which were later co-opted and taken over by secular forces. The scientific enterprise itself arose out of a biblical view of nature (a topic covered in later chapters) but is now often deployed as a weapon to attack Christianity. You might even think of the family. Demographic studies show that religious families consistently have more children. The question is: Can they *keep* them? Parents invest enormous amounts of time, money, and emotional energy into raising their children, only to lose them to secular worldviews pounded into their minds through public education and the entertainment culture. A study in Britain found that non-religious parents have a near 100 percent chance of passing on their views to their children, whereas religious parents have only about a 50/50 chance of passing on their views.[11] The Erickson story is a microcosm of a broad pattern of secularization.

The process of co-option is so successful that Christians themselves no longer recognize their own heritage. Because it was the dominant worldview in Western culture for nearly two millennia, many of its tenets came to be regarded as simple common sense—like wallpaper that we no longer even notice. As a result, one of the most important steps in recovering a Christian worldview is simply to recognize it, reclaim it, and reconnect it to its biblical roots.

For example, our family had been reading Erickson's *Hank* books for years before we discovered that he is a Christian. Michael excitedly relayed the news to his friends. (He had prodded them into reading the books.) One boy replied, "I don't see anything particularly Christian about the *Hank* stories." Perceiving a teachable moment, I told the boys about the CBS rewrite, explaining how the editors had deleted the very concept of family from the story. "We do not typically think of such foundational moral concepts as respect for marriage and family as distinctively Christian," I explained, "because in the past virtually everyone in America agreed. But today a monolithic secularism is challenging the basic social ethics once taken for granted." Western societies no longer share a moral consensus broadly informed by a biblical worldview. We should not be surprised, then, that the singular freedoms and democratic institutions built upon that consensus are disappearing before our eyes.

It is becoming clear that much of what used to be considered common sense is not common at all. Instead it is a product of the West's distinctively Christian heritage. Today it can no longer be simply assumed. It has to be intentionally articulated and defended.

When in Rome, Conquer

The challenge faced by Christians today is parallel to that faced by the early church. The Roman Empire encompassed a vast variety of ethnic groups, each with its own gods and rituals. Then there was the intellectual class, which took over the philosophers of ancient Greece—thinkers so influential that we still know them today: Pythagoras, Socrates, Plato, Aristotle, the Stoics, the Epicureans. Virtually every major philosophical position that would arise in later centuries was already prefigured among the ancient Greeks. Any person brave enough to consider and accept the claims of Christ faced a pluralistic society with a wide diversity of secular and religious options—just as we do today.

How did the early church supplant those diverse and often hostile ideas? It studied, critiqued, argued against, sometimes adapted, and finally overcame them.[12] Individuals also demonstrated their commitment by authentic living, to the point of sacrifice and even death. One of the most amazing success stories in history is the way Christianity supplanted classical religions and worldviews to emerge as the leading influence on Western culture.

What does this suggest about the best strategy for engaging global secularism today? We often hear Christians speak about recovering the vitality of the early church. But which aspect of the early church are they thinking about? It's a safe bet they are *not* thinking about the way the early church went on the offensive against the dominant intellectual systems of the age. Today's churches pour their resources into rallies, friendship evangelism, and mercy missions that distribute food and medicine. And these are all vital. Yet if they aspire to the dynamic impact of the early church, they must do as it did, learning to address, critique, adapt, and overcome the dominant ideologies of our day.

To use a biblical metaphor, all Christians are called to be missionaries, responsible for learning the language of the society they are addressing. Within the boundaries of their native land, they may not face a literal language barrier. But they do face a *worldview* barrier as they seek to communicate with people whose thinking differs from their own. And they need training in how to overcome that worldview barrier. They must learn how to frame the biblical message in ways that connect with people's deepest convictions.

To use another biblical metaphor, Christians are called to be ambassadors for Christ (2 Cor. 5:20). Living in the Washington, DC, area, I often meet graduate students preparing to be ambassadors and diplomats, and they are very familiar with the concept of worldview. Their graduate courses teach that the critical factor in engaging a foreign culture is not learning the language but learning the worldview.

After all, the first rule of effective communication is *Know Your Audience.* To get a message across to people, you must address their assumptions, questions, objections, hopes, fears, and aspirations. In short, their worldview.

The Simple Gospel Is Not Simple

In the middle of a conversation, a friend suddenly burst out, "What's all this talk about *worldview?* Suddenly it seems that everywhere I look in Christian books and magazines, everyone is talking about *worldview.* What's wrong with just preaching the Word of God?" My friend, a strikingly beautiful Jamaican, had grown up in a fundamentalist home and found it incomprehensible that Christians would devote time to analyzing worldviews. Isn't it better to just preach the simple gospel?

The answer is that the ultimate goal *is* to preach the gospel. But the gospel is not simple to those whose background prevents them from understanding it. Today's global secular culture has erected a maze of mental barriers against even considering the biblical message. The goal of worldview analysis is to knock down those barriers—to "demolish strongholds," as the apostle Paul puts it (2 Cor. 10:4–5), so the Word of God can be heard in all its fullness. The term *stronghold* in the original Greek literally meant a castle or fortress. Paul used it as a metaphor for the arguments and ideas that build walls around people's minds and prevent them from knowing God: "We demolish arguments and every pretension that sets itself up against the knowledge of God."

This explains why the great theologian J. Gresham Machen could write, "False ideas are the greatest obstacle to the reception of the gospel."[13] Not pop culture. Not consumerism. Not moral temptation. False ideas.

Christians are called to tear down mental fortresses and liberate people from the power of false ideas. This process is sometimes called pre-evangelism because its purpose is to prepare people to hear and understand the gospel message. Once the walls are torn are down, then the message of salvation is the same for everyone—scientist or artist, educated or uneducated, urban or rural.

Questions Children Ask

Traditionally, churches have responded to fortresses not by demolishing them but by building counter-fortresses—with thick, high walls to shut out the world. They adopted an isolationist strategy to shield people from false ideas.

While visiting our home, a teenage boy went to wash his hands for dinner and came back with a suppressed grin and a sidelong glance at me as though he had just seen something naughty. "I can't *believe* you have a book on *Marxism* in your bathroom!" he exclaimed. Apparently in this teen's home, the message was that Christians don't read that sort of thing. They don't expose themselves to worldly ideas. But if we do not read and analyze Marx, then how will we demolish the Marxist stronghold that has enslaved millions of people over the past century? How will we teach our children to discern Marxist ideology—and a host of other secular ideologies angling for their allegiance on the college campus and in the entertainment culture?

An isolationist strategy ultimately backfires. A recent study by Fuller Seminary found that when teens graduate from high school, they often "graduate from God" as well. But the researchers also discovered one factor that proved most effective in helping young people retain their Christian convictions. What would you expect it to be? More prayer? More Bible study? As important as those things are, surprisingly, the most significant factor was whether they had a safe place to wrestle with doubts and questions *before* leaving home. The study concluded, "The more college students felt that they had the opportunity to express their doubt while they were in high school, the higher [their] levels of faith maturity and spiritual maturity."[14]

In other words, the only way teens become truly "prepared to give an answer to everyone who asks" (1 Pet. 3:15) is by wrestling personally with the questions.

This runs contrary to the typical approach in most Christian homes and churches. When I taught an apologetics course for homeschoolers, one mother confided that she hesitated to sign up her son. "I'm not sure I *want* him to know about people who don't believe in God," she said. Many people operate as though the definition of faith were, Don't ask questions, just believe. They quote Jesus himself, who taught his followers to have the faith of a child (Mark 10:15). But I once heard Francis Schaeffer respond by saying, "Don't you realize how many questions children ask?" The Fuller study shows that students actually grow more confident in their Christian commitment when the adults in their life—parents, pastors, teachers—guide them in exploring questions and grappling with the challenges posed by prevailing secular worldviews. By the time these teens leave home, they have learned how to practice Paul's maxim: "Test everything. Hold on to the good" (1 Thess. 5:21).

Paintball and Whipped Cream

That may sound like a challenging agenda for teenagers. But young people are attracted by a challenge. That's the message of *Do Hard Things* by Alex and Brett Harris.[15] The book blasted up the best-seller lists, giving ample evidence that teens are hungry for richer fare than the typical church youth group offers.

Sadly, many churches simply mirror the pop culture that youngsters are already immersed in. When our sons were younger and attended Vacation Bible School, we were disappointed that the programs offered very little teaching. Instead they tried to draw kids in by using loud music, silly skits, and slapstick games—lots of paintball and whipped cream. There's nothing wrong with good clean fun. But the force of sheer emotional experience will not equip teens to address the ideas they will encounter when they leave home and face the world on their own. Young people whose faith is mostly emotional are likely to retain it only as long as it is making them happy. As soon as a difficult crisis comes along, it will evaporate.

That's exactly what happened to a journalist named John Marks, author of *Reasons to Believe: One Man's Journey among the Evangelicals and the Faith He Left Behind*. "In my experience as a teenager, I never had a strong adult mentor who represented the faith in any mature way," Marks writes. "Most of my 'pastors' were Young Life leaders or youth group leaders who were decent people but didn't have much intellectual or theological wattage."[16] As soon as he faced a serious tragedy he could not make sense of with his limited theological knowledge, he abandoned his "journey among the evangelicals" and left his faith behind.

My own journey began in 1971 when I visited L'Abri Fellowship founded by Francis and Edith Schaeffer. I am deeply grateful that God led me to a ministry that did actively engage with ideas and culture. And yet, after only a month I packed my bags and left. Why? Because I found L'Abri so intensely attractive that even there I was afraid of being drawn to Christianity for emotional reasons instead of genuine conviction. Eventually I went back, but at the time I knew instinctively that an emotional experience was not enough. I wanted to build my life on the conviction of truth.

Voddie Baucham, a former all-American football player, offers a catchy athletic metaphor. "Sending young people into the world without a biblical worldview," he says, "is like sending a ballplayer onto the field without a playbook."[17] Team spirit is not enough. An athlete needs to comprehend the game's strategy.

De-Coding Worldviews

What's the best way to make sure young people are equipped with a biblical playbook, so they can apply biblical strategies to their lives? In recent years, the evangelical world has been swamped with books and conferences devoted to worldview teaching. The typical approach is to compare and contrast using grids and charts: existentialism, naturalism, Marxism, postmodernism, and so on. When I first became a Christian, I pored over books like these, eager to learn how to defend my new convictions. I worked hard to memorize the tenets of all the *isms* that I was encountering on the university campus.

Today I am still convinced that Christians need to understand worldviews. But I am *not* convinced that memorizing charts is the best method. It treats worldviews as isolated, disconnected, ahistorical snippets, reduced to thumbnail summaries to be memorized instead of genuinely understood.

What's worse, consuming prepackaged, predigested material can foster intellectual pride and laziness. It is all too easy to stick a label on an idea, slot it in the correct category, and then dismiss it without actively thinking it through. One of my students had already taken several worldview courses before signing for my class. But she had grown disillusioned. "I had pages and pages of notes and diagrams," she told me. But "I realized I had become very proud, placing everyone in neat philosophical categories. I had stopped listening to people because my knowledge trumped all. Communication became a matter of proving I was right." The study of worldview and apologetics can descend into little more than a game of *Gotcha!* where winning the argument is all important.

A biblical motivation for studying worldviews should be the same principle that motivates *all* authentic discipleship: The goal is to "love the Lord your God with all your heart and with all your soul and with all your mind," and to "love your neighbor as yourself" (Matt. 22:37–39). Loving requires knowing the person well. We nurture love for God by studying a biblical worldview to become more deeply acquainted with his truth, his character, his purpose in history and in our lives. And we demonstrate love for others when we study *their* worldview to get inside their thinking and find ways to connect God's truth with their innermost concerns and questions.

To adapt Baucham's metaphor, Christians should not only know their own playbook, they should also know the other side's playbook. As the apostle Paul wrote, we must become "all things to all people" in order to win them over (1 Cor. 9:22 ESV). The phrase does not mean merely dressing like the natives and learning their customs. Above all, it means becoming familiar with their interpretation of the world, so that we can enter empathetically and compassionately into their experience of life.

What the Media Ignores

The need to grapple with secular worldviews is growing more urgent than ever as secularism goes global. But we can be encouraged in the task by knowing that Christianity is going global as well. In terms of sheer numbers, the center of gravity in the Christian world has already shifted to Asia, Africa, and South America. According to historian Philip Jenkins, in a few decades, white western Christians will be only one in five compared to black and brown Christians. (Islam is growing too, but not as fast. "By 2050," Jenkins says, "there should still be about three Christians for every two Muslims.")[18]

The rise of global Christianity has come as an unwelcome surprise to the Western media and intelligentsia. In fact, until recently, they refused to take it seriously. Their assumption was that religions are always an expression of culture—and therefore Christianity is an expression of *Western* culture, imposed on Asia and Africa only through the coercive force of colonialism. As the colonial age ended, surely Christianity would die out while indigenous religions would revive. Better yet, the Third World would become modern and secular. Neither prediction has come true. Instead Christianity has exploded. South Korea now has five of the world's ten biggest churches. China has probably close to one hundred million Christians. More Chinese attend church each Sunday than are members of the Communist Party. In Africa at the start of the twentieth century, Christians were only 9 percent of the population; today they are 44 percent.[19]

Third World Christians typically wed their biblical commitments to strong tribal beliefs in the reality of the supernatural world. This means that they can sometimes meld pagan and biblical teachings in a wildly syncretistic mix. It also means, however, that they have no trouble believing that God acts supernaturally in history—both in biblical miracles and in modern miracles, such as healing. They are also firmly committed to biblical morality in areas such as marriage and sexuality.

Why did non-Western people suddenly discover God? During the colonial period, becoming a Christian meant selling out to foreign invaders. But when the imperial powers retreated, for the first time Africans were free to read the Bible in their own language and appropriate it for themselves. And that's just what they did, in huge numbers. Africans discovered that Christianity is not inherently Western but universal. It is "translatable" into any cultural idiom. As a result, it does not destroy indigenous cultures but actually affirms what is best in each one. We might say there have been repeated re-enactments of the day of Pentecost when people from multiple nations heard the gospel "in their own language" and were converted (Acts 2:8). According to Lamin Sanneh, a former Muslim from Gambia who now teaches at Yale University, "Christianity is the religion of over two thousand different language groups." There are more Christians who "pray and worship in more languages than in any other religion in the world."[20]

This Third World Pentecost is producing social benefits as well. Even critics are beginning to take notice. "As an atheist, I truly believe Africa needs God," writes journalist Matthew Parris. Why? Because Christianity liberates people from the "crushing passivity" created by African worldviews: "fear of evil spirits, of ancestors, of nature and the wild, of a tribal hierarchy." Freeing people from such deeply rooted fears takes much more than material help or technical know-how. A worldview can be replaced only by another worldview. Having grown up in Africa, Parris witnessed first hand how those who became Christian gained a sense of dignity and confidence. "They approached you direct," he says. "They walked tall."[21]

The same benefits are coming back full circle to the West as immigrants flood in from Asia, Africa, and South America. "On a typical Sunday, half of all churchgoers in London are African or Afro-Caribbean," Jenkins reports. "Of Britain's ten largest megachurches, four are pastored by Africans." In France, the city of Paris has two hundred fifty ethnic Protestant churches, most of them black African.[22]

In America, over the past fifteen years, more than one hundred new churches were started in New York City alone by African immigrants from countries like Nigeria, Ghana, Congo, and Ethiopia. In these churches, reports the *New York Times,* you are likely to see people playing conga drums, dressed in brightly colored kente cloth with head wraps. Moreover, these new arrivals are "overwhelmingly highly educated and professional."[23] Global urban secularism is being met by global urban Christianity.

Reversing Secularism

Even among native Europeans, who are more secularized than any other people group, there are signs of a reversal. "Italy is no longer a completely secular country," lamented a philosopher of science at the University of Milan. This was after a survey revealing that almost two-thirds of Italians want schools to cover scientific evidence for both evolution and creation.[24] In Holland, a quiet revival is taking place through lay ministries such as workplace prayer meetings. A survey by the Dutch Central Bureau of Statistics found that between 2003 and 2004, church attendance among under-twenties rose from 9 percent to 14 percent. When the study was published, commentators were skeptical. Not Holland! Not young people! The pattern was confirmed, however, by other government research.[25]

The turning of the tide is reflected in news headlines. In 1966 the cover of *Time* magazine asked, "Is God Dead?" In 2009 the cover of a new book announced, *God Is Back.* A major factor in the reversal was the fall of totalitarian regimes with their state-enforced atheism. Around the world there is now a trend toward self-rule and democracy, says a *Foreign Policy* article, and it has opened the door to religious groups seeking a greater public impact. "Democracy is giving the world's peoples their voice, and they want to talk about God."[26]

Why has this religious revival come as such a surprise to secular pundits? Ever since the Enlightenment, social scientists have accepted the secularization thesis—the idea that as societies modernize, they secularize. This was treated as an automatic, inevitable process. The more advanced, the less religious. The founder of sociology, Auguste Comte, proposed that all societies progress through three stages—from religious to metaphysical to scientific. This was the application of evolutionary concepts to culture: Cultures evolve from simple and primitive beliefs to ever more enlightened and sophisticated beliefs.

The secularization thesis relied on several assumptions, however, that proved false. For example, it assumed that religion survives only in protected enclaves like the rural villages of past ages. In such a homogeneous setting, religion had a taken-for-granted quality. No one questioned it, just as modern people don't question the law of gravity. But what happens when diverse religions clash and compete in the mixing bowl of pluralistic, multi-cultural urban areas? Then, according to the theory, religions lose their plausibility. In *The Secular City,* Harvey Cox writes that societies secularize when the "cosmopolitan confrontations of city living exposed the relativity of the myths and traditions men once thought were unquestionable."[27]

Yet religion has refused to die out despite the "cosmopolitan confrontations of city living." The secularization thesis has been debunked—tossed on the graveyard of failed theories.

Why were the experts so wrong? It turns out that, historically, Christianity has *not* been a religion of rural villages. In the Roman Empire, Christianity first took hold in the cities—so much so that the word *pagan* actually means someone from the countryside.[28] Even here in America, Christianity has been centered in the cities. In *The Churching of America,* two sociologists show statistically that during the rapid urbanization of the late nineteenth and early twentieth centuries, both Protestants and Catholics actually predominated in cities more than in rural areas. So it should not be surprising that today Christianity continues to thrive precisely in large, pluralistic urban areas.

No "Born" Christians

The secularization thesis relied on a second faulty assumption—that when people's convictions are challenged, they grow weaker. In reality, they grow stronger. In past generations, many people simply "inherited" their religion, following the tradition of their family and ethnic group. I was raised Lutheran because my ancestors on both sides were Scandinavian. But in today's large urban centers, it is no longer possible to remain Christian out of tradition. People face too much opposition and have too many alternatives.

To use sociological labels, traditional societies are "ascription" cultures where an individual's identity is derived largely from family, tradition, class, and social role. By contrast, modern societies are "achievement" cultures where individuals make their own choices about what job to take, who to marry, and what to believe. They are more likely to treat worldview commitments as something they seek out, investigate, weigh, compare, and adopt as a matter of intentional commitment and practice. As a result, says sociologist Christian Smith, those commitments are actually stronger.

And because large numbers of people are concentrated in major metropolitan areas, there is also a greater probability of finding like-minded people to form supportive subcultures. Thus, surprising as it may sound, "rather than being a source of secularization and religious decline, pluralism strengthens religion."[29] Just as the early church thrived in the diversity of the urban setting, so modern churches have the resources to thrive in pluralistic metropolitan areas. As East meets West, and North meets South, global Christianity has an unprecedented opportunity to challenge the global secular culture at its core.

Where the Action Is

The resurgence of religion is becoming evident even on secular university campuses. At Harvard, students are increasingly "churchgoing, Bible-studying, and believing," says Jay Harris, the dean who administers the General Education program. "We have a very strong evangelical community."[30]

Law professor Stanley Fish is witnessing the same trend. "Announce a course with 'religion' in the title, and you will have an overflow population," he writes. "Announce a lecture or panel on 'religion in our time' and you will have to hire a larger hall." A reporter once asked Fish what would come next on campus after the current fad of multiculturalism. What would replace "the triumvirate of race, gender, and class as the center of intellectual energy in the academy?"

"I answered like a shot: Religion," Fish writes.

Moreover, he adds, students are no longer interested in studying religion the way an anthropologist studies an ancient culture, treating it is a quaint custom of bygone ages. Instead they are looking to religion for viable answers and guidance for life. They are treating it as a genuine "candidate for the truth."

"Are we ready?" Fish asks his fellow professors. Are we prepared to discuss religious questions with students on those terms? "We had better be, because that is now where the action is."[31]

Are *you* ready? The Christian community has an unprecedented opportunity to be where the action is. People are hungry for alternatives to the dominant secular worldviews. The door is wide open to make a compelling case for Christianity as a positive agent of individual and cultural renewal. We must determine never again to get whipped because we didn't know we were in a fight. Never again be blindsided by a secular agenda. Never again allow schools and charities and ministries to be co-opted to serve a secular ideology. We must educate ourselves in a biblical worldview to maintain the integrity of our lives and our work, becoming a living alternative to the secular juggernaut.

The first step is to identify and counter the key strategies used to advance the global secular worldview. Let's get started.

Chapter 2

"Reason defines one kind of reality (what we know);
faith defines another (what we don't know)."
—Lisa Miller, religion editor, Newsweek

Truth and Tyranny

During the 2008 presidential campaign, ABC News published a disturbing article about young evangelicals. The reporter had interviewed several teens attending a Christian youth rally in New York City. The good news was that they expressed a strong commitment to biblical ethics. Most were pro-life, with some even ranking abortion as their number one political issue. But then there was a strange disconnect: Many of the *same teens* said their favorite political candidates were pro-choice. To the reporter, that sounded like a contradiction, a case of cognitive dissonance. "Doesn't that bother you?" he asked.

"Maybe a little bit," one teen replied, "but it's all personal preference. I mean, you can't really pass judgment on someone because that's their belief."[1]

Moral convictions are *all personal preference?* Where had these teens picked up such a relativistic view of morality? These were young people who were attending a religious rally, who embraced biblical ethics, who probably went to church regularly. Yet they had accepted a secularized view of truth that reduces Christianity to a subjective preference, draining it of any spiritual or cultural power. They had absorbed the central tenet of global secularism.

Easy Marks

The key to understanding modern secularism is its view of truth. Think of it this way: Before you decide what you believe, you must first decide what the credible options are. That list is determined by your definition of truth—what philosophers call your epistemology. It functions as a grid or sieve that allows only certain ideas through. Any idea sifted out becomes something you won't even bother considering.

By the same token, a society's view of truth functions as the intellectual gatekeeper in the public arena. It determines which ideas are taken seriously and which never even make it to the table.

Where did the young evangelicals interviewed by ABC News get *their* epistemology? The idea that morality is nothing more than personal preference arose in the West in the aftermath of the scientific revolution. Many thinkers were so impressed by its achievements that they elevated empirical science to the sole source of truth. Empiricism is the doctrine that all knowledge is derived from the senses—what we see, hear, hold, weigh, and measure. Obviously, moral truths cannot be stuffed into a test tube or studied under a microscope. As a result, moral statements were no longer considered truths at all, but merely expressions of emotion.

The most radical of the empiricist philosophers was David Hume, and he reasoned this way: If knowledge is based ultimately on sensations, then morality too must derive from sensations—pain or pleasure. We call things *good* when they give us a certain kind of pleasure. We call them *bad* when they cause pain. As Hume put it, morality is a matter of "taste and sentiment."

In reducing morality to personal taste, Hume took a step that altered the course of Western thought. He split traditional philosophy into two opposing categories. Traditionally, truth had been conceived as a comprehensive whole, covering both the natural order and the moral order. But Hume tore those two things apart. The natural order is something we perceive through the senses, so according to empiricism *that* qualified as genuine knowledge. But the moral order is not perceived through the senses, so *that* was reduced to subjective feelings. The great moral principles that people had thought were transcendent truths were not truths after all but only preferences.

Religion, the ultimate source of morality, was likewise discredited. For centuries, people had thought of religion as an explanatory system like any other philosophical system. They might not be certain that their own views were completely correct. But they were certain that there *was* a correct answer and that continued inquiry was worthwhile. God's existence was held to be an objective question—something you could be right or wrong about, based on rational reasons. With the rise of empiricism, however, religion was reduced to private feelings. Emotional comfort. The concept of truth as a unified, coherent worldview was shattered.

The division of truth is often referred to as the fact/value split (see Introduction). It is the assumption that objective knowledge is possible only in the realm of empirical facts, while morality and religion are merely values. The term literally means whatever I value. Whatever is important to me. My likes and preferences.

This concept of values seems to be the unspoken assumption in the young evangelicals' response to the ABC News reporter. Did they realize they were being influenced by a philosophy called empiricism? Had they consciously accepted its premise that nothing exists except what we can see, hear, weigh, and measure? Of course not. As Christians they acknowledged the existence of an invisible spiritual realm. Yet they had absorbed the divided concept of truth *derived from* empiricism.

In short, they were taken in by a secular worldview without even realizing it. And it robbed them of the strength and courage of their moral convictions. To use a phrase from chapter 1, these young evangelicals were getting whipped because they did not even realize they were in a fight. They had been sent out into the world without a playbook.

Plato said philosophers should rule the world, and they do—hundreds of years after they die. Elements of Hume's empiricist philosophy have filtered down to become the core of the global secular worldview. The strict separation of facts from values is *the* key to unlocking the history of the modern Western mind. We will survey its debilitating effects within the church, and then its secularizing effects in American public life.

Resisting Rome

The secular view of values is common among adults as well as teenagers. A neighbor I'll call Vickie is active in her church and teaches Sunday school. Yet she has been taken in by the same subjectivism. In a conversation I once happened to mention a mutual friend who was outspoken in expressing secular views. Surprisingly, Vickie's response was, "Whatever works for you." She refused to assert that her own commitment to Christianity was rooted in truth. It worked for her. It might not work for others.

Vickie affirmed the major biblical doctrines: the deity of Christ, the virgin birth, the resurrection, and so on. But she did not recognize that in addition to *individual truths*, the Bible also teaches a view of *the nature of truth*. Because all things were created by a single divine mind, all truth forms a single, coherent, mutually consistent system. Truth is unified and universal.

In New Testament times, the Greeks had a term for the underlying principle that unifies the world into an orderly cosmos, as opposed to randomness and chaos. They called it the *Logos*. The Stoic philosophers conceived it as a pantheistic mind pervading the universe. But the apostle John applied the term to Christ. "In the beginning was the Word"—*Logos* (John 1:1). Every Greek who heard John's gospel understood that he was claiming that Christ himself is the source of the order and coherence of the universe. As Paul put it, "in him all things hold together" (Col. 1:17). Creation has a rational, intelligible order that reflects God's creative plan.

From the beginning, however, this New Testament concept of truth came under fire. The Roman Empire did not regard religion as the search for truth about reality. *That* was the province of philosophers, not priests. The Romans defined religion solely in terms of ritual, ceremony, and cult practices. The empire was perfectly willing to accept Christianity if it would take its place as just another set of religious practices. What the empire would *not* accept, says Catholic theologian Lorenzo Albacete, was Christianity "as a source of truth about this world."

How did the early church respond? It resolutely refused to reduce Christianity to Rome's relativistic definition of religion. As Albacete writes, Christianity "would not accept a place with the religions of the empire" as merely another set of rituals and practices. It "saw itself as a philosophy, as a path to knowledge about reality, and not primarily as a source of spiritual or ethical inspiration."[2] The message of Christ's resurrection—in a physical body, in historical time—did not allow for any dualism that shoved religion off into a separate sphere of life concerned only with spiritual rules and rituals. The early church insisted that biblical truth is a comprehensive unity, encompassing the realms of *both* priest and philosopher. Truth is a unified whole.

Today Christians have largely lost that conviction. When they read verses like "the fear of the LORD is the beginning of wisdom" (Ps. 111:10), they interpret it to mean only spiritual wisdom. When they read that Christ is the one "in whom are hidden all the treasures of wisdom and knowledge" (Col. 2:3), they limit the term to spiritual knowledge. Yet these verses do not restrict their range. True wisdom consists in seeing every field of knowledge through the lens of God's truth—government, economics, science, business, and the arts. When Christians speak of a *worldview*, they are simply using modern terminology to restate the Bible's comprehensive claim.

Hamlet and Harry Potter

The fact/value dichotomy thus directly contradicts the biblical view of truth. Francis Schaeffer was among the first in the evangelical world to identify the problem. Although he did not use the terms *facts* versus *values,* clearly he was getting at the same idea. Using the metaphor of a building, he warned that truth had been split into two stories. The lower story consists of scientific facts, which are held to be empirically testable and universally valid. The upper story includes things like morality, theology, and aesthetics, which are now regarded as subjective and culturally relative.[3] Essentially the upper story became a convenient dumping ground for anything that an empiricist worldview did not recognize as real. Schaeffer used a simple graphic, which we can adapt like this:

The two-story concept of truth

VALUES
Private, subjective, relative

FACTS
Public, objective, universal

This dichotomy has grown so pervasive that most people do not even realize they hold it. It has become part of the cultural air we breathe. Consider two prominent examples:

Martin Luther King Jr.—"Science deals mainly with facts; religion deals mainly with values."

Albert Einstein—Science yields facts but not "value judgments"; religion expresses values but cannot "speak of facts."[4]

Of course, people have always known that there is a distinction between *is* and *ought,* between what you are and what you should be, between descriptive statements and normative statements. In earlier ages, however, people thought both types of statement dealt with questions of truth. If you made a moral statement about what someone *ought* to do, it was either true or false. What makes the fact/value split new is the epistemological status of the values realm. Values are not considered matters of truth but only personal perspectives and preferences.

Books on values education used in public schools make the point by throwing together questions of sheer preference with questions about genuine moral issues. For example, they might start by asking teens what their ideal summer vacation is or what kind of music they like and then, without skipping a beat, ask what they think about premarital sex or God and spirituality. The implicit message is that there is no essential difference—that there is no basis for decision-making beyond what you as an individual choose to value.

Because the term *values* is so widespread today, even Christians often use it when what they really mean is *biblical morality.* This creates a significant communication gap. To grasp the difference, think of a movie or a novel. Reading a novel can engage and inspire you. But you do not ask whether it really happened.

In fact, that's exactly the analogy used by Cambridge philosopher Peter Lipton, who has a Jewish background. In an interview, Lipton once said, "I stand in my synagogue and pray to God and have an intense relationship with God, and yet I don't believe in God."

Journalists were puzzled by Lipton's paradoxical confession. What could he possibly mean? Well, he explained, religion is like reading a novel—you can get pleasure and meaning from the experience *even though you know it is not literally true.*[5] Though most people do not state it quite so bluntly, this is a widespread view of religion today. If you suggest that Christianity deals with reality, that is regarded as a category mistake—as if someone were to talk about Hamlet or Harry Potter as a real person.

The upper-story view of religion has even filtered down to the comics. In a *Non Sequitur* strip, a father asks his young daughter, "Did you really tell your teacher that math is against our religion?"

"No," the little girl replies, "I said it was against *my* religion."

"Danae," the father scolds, "you can't arbitrarily make up a religion just to suit your needs."

2-1 Wiley Miller
Non Sequitur, March 31 2006
Upper-story view of religion

"Oh?" she asks. "So how did other religions get started?"

The next frame shows the father completely befuddled. Obviously he is thinking, *She's right.* In the final frame, the father is sitting with his drinking buddy who asks, "You've converted to *what?*"

"Danaeism," he answers. "At least it's a religion that's honest about staying ignorant."

The cartoonist's message is clear: religion is a social construction made up to meet people's emotional needs and wishes. Of course, this fails to explain the origin and call of Christianity, which often requires people to do things that go *against* their wishes, to the point of sacrifice and death. Nevertheless, it shows that the upper/lower story division has percolated from the global elites down to comic strip writers.

Spirituality in Secularville

Once we get a handle on the divided concept of truth, it clears up a host of puzzles and suggests more effective ways to communicate the gospel. Take, for example, the church's strategy for teaching teens. Many teachers and youth leaders argue that young people are postmodern—that they no longer think in a rational, linear fashion—and that schools and churches must overhaul their programs to focus on visual media and personal experience, or risk becoming irrelevant.

Before we lower the bar, however, and stop even trying to teach young people to think clearly, let's ask whether the diagnosis is accurate. How postmodern are young people really? William Lane Craig, a Christian apologist who speaks frequently on university campuses, has a good read on how students think. "Frankly, I don't confront many students who are postmodernists," he said. "For all the faddish talk, I think it's a myth. Students are not generally relativistic and pluralistic *except* when it comes to ethics and religion."[6] In short, their postmodernism is selective.

The reality is that modernism remains firmly entrenched in the fact realm—the hard sciences, finance, and industry. No one designs an airplane by postmodern principles. Postmodernism is typically held only in the values realm—theology, morality, and aesthetics. Think of it this way: We are often exhorted not to impose our values on others. But we never hear people say, "Don't impose your facts on me." Why not? Because facts are assumed to be objective and universal.

How postmodern are we really?

POSTMODERNISM
Religion and morality (Values)

MODERNISM
Science and industry (Facts)

The upshot is that most people function as modernists *and* postmodernists, depending on the context. Choosing a religion, says philosopher Ernest Gellner, has become akin to choosing a wallpaper pattern or menu item—an area of life where it is considered acceptable to act on purely personal taste or feelings. Most people do not look to spirituality for an explanatory system to answer the cosmic questions of life. Instead they choose their spirituality based on what meets their emotional needs and helps them cope with personal issues, from losing weight to gaining self-confidence. But, when "serious issues are at stake" like making money or meeting medical needs, Gellner says, then people want solutions based on "real knowledge."[7] They want to know the tested outcomes of objective science and research.

What this means is that most people live fragmented lives. In the private world of home, church, and friendships, they operate on view of truth (subjective values) that is completely contrary to the one they employ in the public world of work, business, and politics (objective facts). The opposition between facts and values has become the main obstacle to living as whole persons with a consistent, coherent philosophy of life.

Relativists for Jesus

The split view of truth has also become the main obstacle to living a consistent biblical worldview. Recently I talked to a graduate student in chemistry who converted to Christianity in high school, yet retained a divided concept of truth for several years afterward. "I operated on the assumption that what I learned in school and science was *really* true," she said, "while church was a kind of support group that provides a nice story to help you cope with reality."

How many other high schoolers operate by the same two-tiered concept of truth? Brett Kunkle of Stand to Reason devised a short test to find out. Talking to a typical church youth group, he first explained the difference between subjective and objective. To say that something is objective does not mean that everyone agrees, or that you know it for certain. It only means that it is capable of being true or false. If you are working on a complex mathematics problem, you may not be certain you have the right answer. But you are certain that there *is* a right answer, not merely personal preference.

After carefully defining terms, Kunkle started the test. That guy's shirt is red." Objective. "Red is the coolest color." Subjective. "2 + 2 = 4." Objective. And so on.

Then Kunkle said, "God exists." A full 75 percent of the teens said that statement was subjective.

Finally he said: "Premarital sex is wrong." All but one of the teens said *that* was subjective.

Clearly these Christian youngsters had absorbed the fact/value dualism. As a result they no longer grasped the comprehensive character of biblical truth. One teen said, "As a Christian, I think premarital sex is wrong," but other groups may have "their own opinion about the matter and it's alright for them."[8]

In other words, even Christian teens have absorbed the idea that something can be *true for you but not true for me.* The very meaning of the word *true* has been distorted. It no longer means that a statement matches what really exists in the world but only that it matches my inner experience. The sobering lesson is that it is possible to go to church, study the Bible, and attend youth group, yet still absorb a secular view of truth from the global secular culture.

Should we then be surprised that so many Christian teens adopt secular lifestyles? The divided concept of truth produces young people who are double-minded, unstable in all their ways (James 1:8). Tim Sweetman, a seventeen-year-old journalist and blogger, observes that many of his peers behave as "double agents." They "are Christians in church . . . but have a completely secular mind view. It's as if they have a split personality." Sweetman concludes that these church-going teens illustrate "the story of our culture—the 'dichotomy' of public and private, heart and mind."[9] Their divided lives are a mirror reflecting the divided concept of truth.

You can try Kunkle's test yourself. I corralled a couple of junior high kids and instead of asking about premarital sex, because they were younger, I said, "Stealing is wrong."

"That's subjective," one of them promptly declared.

"Why?"

"Someone just made *that* up!" he replied.

I arched an eyebrow. "Ever heard of the Ten Commandments?"

"Oops."

These were homeschooled youngsters raised in committed Christian homes. They had accepted biblical teachings cognitively, but their automatic, reflexive responses had been shaped by a postmodern sensibility from the surrounding pop culture. They put biblical truths in the upper story as social constructions—things that "someone just made up."

Kunkle began illustrating his test to church leaders to illustrate the mentality they are up against when working with double-agent teens. But to his astonishment, the adults *could not see what the problem was.* Their response was almost identical to that of the teens.[10] How can Christians rightly handle the Word of truth (2 Tim. 2:15) if they do not hold a biblical view of truth itself?

Are Christians Bigots?

The two-story view of truth also shapes the way most non-Christians respond when they hear the gospel today. Josh McDowell has been giving evangelistic talks on university campuses for decades. Over the years, he has noticed a striking difference in the way students respond. It used to be that when he spoke about the existence of God or the deity of Christ or the resurrection, he would be challenged (and sometimes heckled) with statements like these: "I don't believe it. Prove it. How can you say a man was raised from the dead? Give me some evidence."

Over roughly the past fifteen years, however, students have stopped asking those questions. Instead they typically respond with statements like these: "What right do you have to say that? You're intolerant! You're a bigot! Who do you think you are? What right do you have to judge anyone's moral life?"[11]

What changed? In the past, students treated the gospel as a genuine truth claim that could be supported by giving reasons and citing evidence—just like any other set of propositions. But today students put Christianity in the upstairs where it is reduced to personal choice and preference. Of course, if any group *did* try to impose its own personal preference on others, that *would* be oppressive, coercive, bigoted, and intolerant. This explains why so many people today treat Christian claims as veiled attempts at coercion. When talking about religion or morality, any truth claim is dismissed as a cover for a power play.

That's why it is crucial for Christians to address the crack-up of truth itself. Before they can make the case that Christianity is true, they first have to clarify what they mean by *truth*. This was the central question I wrestled with personally when I was an agnostic. When I went to L'Abri for the first time, my mind was thoroughly drenched in relativism. As a result, I had to grapple with the question whether there was such a thing as objective truth at all—before I could even consider whether Christianity was that truth. In his writings, Schaeffer insisted that the fracturing of truth is "the most crucial problem . . . facing Christianity today."[12]

Of course, like anyone else, Christians *can* be bigots at times. But ironically, even that often stems from a deficient view of truth. When church leaders lose the conviction that Christianity is about objective truth, they are left with trying to coax and cajole young people into believing and doing the right things. Generations of churched youngsters have been encouraged to shore up their religious commitment by sheer will power, closing their eyes and ears to contrary ideas. This explains why so many churches are full of people who are closed-minded, dogmatic, harsh, and judgmental. Only people who understand that Christianity is true to the real world are capable of the relaxed confidence that allows them to be open, patient, and loving toward those who differ from them.

Is Christianity Exclusive?

Understanding the two-story division provides new tools for responding to the most common objections against Christianity. There is probably nothing that offends the modern sensibility more than the affirmation that the Bible is true in a unique, exclusive, universal sense. We hear it all the time: How can you impose your personal views on everyone else? Of course, Christians recognize that other religions and worldviews contain *elements* of truth, and therefore they can be open and generous in affirming truth wherever it may be found. Nevertheless, they maintain that the overarching *system* of truth that fits reality is based on information from the Creator in Scripture and the person of Jesus Christ. To many modern people, that sounds incredibly exclusive and arrogant. Why? Because they automatically, unreflectively place all religious claims in the upper story, where they are not matters of truth but merely ethnic tradition or social glue or ineffable experience.

Think of it this way: If something genuinely *is* a matter of taste or tradition, then it *would be* wrong to impose it on others. If I root for the New York Giants while you root for the Chicago Bears, then it would be silly and even intrusive for me to insist that you should cheer for the same team I do. I grew up in a Swedish family where we celebrated Saint Lucia Day. Maybe you grew up with different traditions. It would be arrogant and exclusive for me to insist that you must celebrate only Swedish holidays.

The fact/value split has taught most people to put religion in the same category. This explains why Christians are often accused of imposing their views, no matter how gentle and polite they may be in person. Christians *intend* to communicate life-giving, objective truths about the real world. But their statements are *interpreted* as attempts to impose personal preferences. For the secularist, then, Christians are not merely wrong or mistaken. They are violating the rules of the game in a democratic society.

Once we recognize this misunderstanding, the common objections to Christianity become more understandable. They also become easier to debunk. After all, no one is offended that scientific theories claim exclusive truth. No one accuses scientists of being narrow and arrogant when they propound the laws of genetics or physics. These laws may not be in their final form yet; they may end up being changed with further research. But no one doubts that the answer, when we find it, will be exclusive. There are not a variety of different systems of science from which we can pick and choose, according to our personal taste or ethnic background. So why assume that theology and morality are completely different from everything else we know? Why assume that there is an absolute gulf separating scientific knowledge from theological and moral knowledge?

Take another example: The two-story dichotomy explains why so many modern people deplore the idea of sending missionaries to other countries. I was once reading the web site of a missionary organization, and in the comments section I saw that a critic had written, in essence, Why don't you Christians respect other people's beliefs and cultural traditions? Why do you think yours are superior? You have practiced cultural genocide, wiping out entire cultures in your imperialistic ambition to remake everyone in your own image.

Again, this common objection makes sense once we grasp the dynamics of the upper/lower story divide. If Christianity really were nothing but ethnic tradition or social glue, then imposing it on other societies *would* be imperialistic. But no one raises the same objection when we export scientific knowledge, such as sanitation, farming techniques, or medical care. In that case, it is understood that truth trumps mere custom—that societies benefit from gaining access to knowledge. Why put theological knowledge in a completely different category?

Ironically, those who pride themselves on being open and tolerant often end up merely practicing a different type of intolerance. They resist the idea that any one religion is true, because that implies the others are false—which they take to be disrespectful. It seems more respectful to say that all religions are symbolic ways of describing a mystical experience, or giving emotional comfort, or motivating people to be moral, or some such. In other words, in the case of religion, the actual teachings do not matter, only the social and emotional effects.

But is this relativistic view really tolerant? To say that the teachings do not matter is to say that all religions are wrong—because all religions claim that their teachings *do* matter. The relativistic view insists that Hindus are wrong; Buddhists are wrong; Muslims, Jews, and Christians are wrong—and that only the postmodern, upper-story view of religion is right. As philosopher Alvin Plantinga comments, "I find it hard to see how this attitude is a manifestation of tolerance or intellectual humility: it looks more like patronizing condescension."[13] The relativistic view of religion is just as exclusive as the claims of any traditional religion.

C. S. Lewis: We Can't All Be Right

Surprisingly, even defenders of religion sometimes accept the fact/value split. This is how you can tell that secularists have won the turf war for intellectual dominance—when people cave in to the secularist definition *of their own views*. Typically this represents a form of cognitive bargaining: The assumption is that if you place religion beyond the reach of reason and rationality (that is, in the upper story), then you render it immune to disproof.

But the bargain comes with a steep hidden cost. For if something cannot be tested in any way and shown to be *false*, by the same token it cannot be tested and known to be *true*. It can only be blindly believed.

An extreme example comes from an article by journalist Lee Siegel responding to the New Atheists. "The existence of God is undemonstrable, unverifiable, and the object of an impractical leap of faith, faith in the absurd," he declares. "Your willingness to stake your life on the possibility of an impossibility makes a fact out of a fantasy."[14] Can you imagine any other area of life where we would be willing to stake our lives on an impossibility, hoping to make "a fact out of a fantasy"?

Such an irrational strategy ultimately backfires. Any benefit that people get from religion—any power it has to fulfill them emotionally or motivate them morally—comes from the conviction that it is first of all *true.* We often hear people say that you can believe whatever you want as long as it meets your needs, as long as it works for you. The problem with this pragmatic view is that, ironically, it doesn't work. If you accept a religion just to meet an emotional need, then you will never be able to shake the unnerving sense that it is nothing but a projection of your own mind. And therefore it will never have the power to change you—to overcome your guilt, fears, compulsions, dysfunctions, addictions, and emotional wounds. The only God who can change us is a God who is "greater than our hearts" (1 John 3:20). Paradoxically, what humans need most is a God that is not the product of their own need.[15]

That's why the strategy of stripping religion of its truth claims to render it safe from disproof is self-defeating. To use the fiery language of J. S. Bezzant, "immunity from proof can secure nothing whatever except immunity from proof, and [let's] call nonsense by its name."[16] His point is that if your religion is so insulated from reality that you cannot adduce reasons *against* it, then it's not the sort of thing you can give reasons *for* either. You can only take that leap into the absurd. There is a terrible despair in staking one's entire life on something that cannot be known or reasoned about, but only blindly believed.

The only way out of that despair is to recover a robust confidence in the possibility of moral and theological truth. C. S. Lewis once said, "The Christian and the Materialist hold different beliefs about the universe. They can't both be right. The one who is wrong will act in a way which simply doesn't fit the real universe."[17] That is, moral and theological statements either fit the real universe or they do not. In this sense, we can even speak of moral and theological facts. Today a phrase like *moral facts* raises eyebrows. It strikes most people as an oxymoron. Which may be a good reason to start using it. It boldly brings back together what the fact/value dichotomy has split asunder.

The Liberal Cave-In

The cave-in to a secularist definition of religion can be seen everywhere, but most obviously in liberal theology. Liberalism is happy to cede to scientific naturalism the right to declare the truth about the universe (facts). It then treats religion as merely an overlay of meaning over whatever science decrees (values).

Consider a few examples. A rabbi writing about evolution in *USA Today* said, "Science explains *how* the world is. Religion explains *why* the world is."[18] I don't know which religion he was talking about. Certainly not his own tradition of Judaism, which is full of claims about "*how* the world is," both its creation and its history, especially the history of Israel.

Similarly, when Catholic priest Michael Heller received the 2008 Templeton Prize, he stated, "Science gives us Knowledge, and religion gives us Meaning."[19] But can those two things really be so neatly divided? When someone affirms that Christ rose from the dead, is that knowledge or meaning? The answer, of course, is that it is both. If the resurrection did not happen in history, then it can *have* no spiritual meaning.

Biblical Christianity refuses to separate historical fact from spiritual meaning. Its core claim is that the living God has acted in history, especially in the life, death, and resurrection of Jesus. Other religions tell people what *they* must do to achieve salvation, or become holy, or reach Nirvana, or connect with the divine. The burden of obligation is on the individual to perform the right ceremonies or perfect the right rituals. The Christian gospel is unique because it is the narrative of what *God* has done in history to accomplish salvation.

Liberal theologians typically give up the historical claims of Christianity for what they say is some deeper spiritual or ethical core. But if you strip away the history, there is no core left. If God has *not* acted in history to accomplish salvation, then there is no "good news" to tell (the literal meaning of the word *gospel).* As Paul told first-century audiences, if Jesus was not resurrected from the dead, if the tomb was not empty, then the Christian faith is based on a lie and is worthless (1 Cor. 15:17). He even urged his listeners to confirm the claim by seeking out the five hundred eyewitnesses who had seen the risen Christ. Paul was using a legal term, which means he was treating the resurrection like any other event that could be tested for its veracity. The central claim of Christianity is a stubborn historical fact, which was open to empirical investigation and knowable by ordinary means of historical verification.

The apostles were treating the resurrection in a way akin to what scientists today call a crucial experiment—an event that confirms or disconfirms an entire theory (or an entire theology). In their minds, historical facts and spiritual truths must cohere. Facts and faith must agree. Truth is a unity.

Why Liberal Churches Fail

Today this view of truth is the single overriding factor in whether a church grows or dies. A 1994 study sought to explain why theologically liberal churches are in decline, even though conservative churches are on the rise. Many church leaders think the way to attract people into the sanctuary is by using skits, pop music, and video clips in the worship service. But surprisingly, the study found that real church growth has nothing to do with tricks or techniques. Instead the central factor is a church's view of truth. The study found that the more strongly people affirmed orthodox Christian doctrines as objectively true—for everyone, everywhere—the more likely they were to be actively involved in a church. The reason liberal churches are declining is their "rejection of the claim that Christianity . . . is the only true religion."

Yet the problem in liberal churches runs even deeper than simply rejecting Christianity as the only true religion. Many reject even the *categories* of true and false. Some of the liberal Christians interviewed in the study said they did not care whether their children became Buddhists "as long as they believed in something."[20] In the upper-story view of religion, it does not matter what you believe as long as it meets your emotional needs. The study concluded that "liberals have no compelling truth, no 'good news,' to proclaim."[21]

Another study, done in 1998, uncovered similar results. When a mainline Lutheran was asked how he knew that his faith was true, he told researchers, "Nobody really knows if Christian faith is true." Another said, "Whether or not my faith is true is not an issue for me . . . . Truth is ephemeral, it's changing: what is true today is not true tomorrow." He summed up his creed by saying, "Whatever trips your trigger is fine with me."[22] No wonder liberal churches fail to inspire commitment. They have reduced their faith to Christianity Lite.

The key to the power of the biblical message is the conviction that it is actually true—objectively, universally, cosmically true. It is not merely a psychological coping mechanism. It is not a sociological product of Western culture. It is truth about the universe itself. This conviction is what sets orthodox Christianity off from Christianity Lite. And it is the source of genuine church growth.

Of course, knowing God goes far beyond mere mental assent to the Bible's message. That would be like a starving person who sits before an extravagant banquet and says, "Yes I believe there's such a thing as food," but then does not eat a bite. We are meant to experience God's truth and presence with our whole being. I realized that one of my students had the wrong impression when she wrote in her study guide, "Nancy Pearcey thinks we should not be so emotional in our worship." I quickly clarified that once a person is grounded in a biblical concept of truth, then the emotions can soar. As John Stott says in *Your Mind Matters,* "I am not pleading for a dry, humorless, academic Christianity, but for a warm devotion set on fire by truth."[23] Knowing God is a love relationship that engages the whole person: heart, soul, mind, and strength (Mark 12:30). To maintain that rich balance, however, Christians must always lean against the predominant error of their age. And the most characteristic error today is the break-up of truth.

Kicking the Bible out of Class

The fact/value divide is also the main strategy used to marginalize and disempower Christians in the public arena. In a nutshell, it allows secularists to dismiss opposing views not by marshalling good arguments against them, but by simply transferring them to the upper story of noncognitive values. Why bother to argue that Christianity is false when it's so much easier to take it out of the realm of true and false altogether? In this way, a theistic worldview can be dismissed as nothing but personal preference and bias. And private bias has no place in the public realm—areas such as government policy or public education.

This explains, for example, the process by which American public education was secularized. Until the 1930s, American universities were committed to "the unity of truth," says Harvard historian Julie Reuben. They held "the conviction that that all truths agreed and ultimately could be related to one another in a single system." This conviction rested ultimately on a biblical worldview. "Because the Christian God was a single, unified mind and the source of all truths, the curriculum was unified," explains philosopher J. P. Moreland. "Every discipline was expected to shed light on and harmonize with every other discipline."[24]

What marks the modern age is the shattering of the ideal of the unity of truth. In Reuben's words, universities came to accept the idea that "only 'science' constituted true knowledge." Theology and ethics were moved to the upper story where they "could be 'true' in an emotional or nonliteral sense, but not in terms of cognitively verifiable knowledge."[25]

Eventually they came to be regarded as outright harmful to the academic enterprise. For if values were purely subjective, then they threatened to contaminate objective research. Thus the idea arose that scholarship must be "value free."

For example, in the social sciences, Max Weber argued that in order to render sociology truly scientific, researchers must stop evaluating social arrangements by moral standards of justice or fairness. Instead they must simply describe them factually, without moral comment. In economics, Lionel Robbins argued that economics should no longer serve an ethical vision of creating a humane and equitable social order. "Economics deals with ascertainable facts; ethics with values and obligations."[26] In the Introduction, we traced the same trend in political theory. You might say that scholarship was defined as value free because values were first defined as "fact free"—no longer rooted in the objective world.

The secularization of American education was also driven by personal and professional motivations. Under the ideal of the unity of truth, scholars felt an obligation to find ways to harmonize the findings of science with the truths of theology. In *Value-Free Science?* historian Robert Proctor says scholars began to argue for the "autonomy" of their research because they wanted to render it "immune to religious or moral criticism."[27] In other words, the idea of value-free scholarship let them off the hook. If theology and ethics could be quarantined in the upper story, then scholars no longer needed to ask whether their theories harmonized with a Christian worldview. They no longer needed to concern themselves with the moral implications of their work. Instead they were free to view their study as an amoral arena for satisfying their own ambition for academic prestige, power, or material gain.

Historians often treat the rise of secularism as an inevitable, automatic byproduct of modernization. But there was nothing inevitable about it. It was pursued intentionally and aggressively by those who thought it served their personal advantage.

Protecting Children from Religion

And they were right. The fact/value dualism has proved remarkably effective for advancing secularists' social and political power, while stripping the public square of moral and theological perspectives. That's because it allows secularists to claim a monopoly on truth. They do not need to outlaw ideas or use coercive measures. All they have to say is, "*Our* secular views are based on objective science and facts. But *your* theologically based views are personal and private. And while we certainly respect them, you have no right to apply your private preferences to the public square—to politics or education or health care."

The concept of tolerance has thus been redefined to mean that moral and theological convictions are fine, as long as they are kept in the private sphere. The implication is that anyone who brings a Christian perspective into the public sphere will *not* be tolerated. As Stanley Fish puts it, under the regime of secular tolerance, religious adherents are compelled to live double lives—to suppress their deepest convictions when they enter the workplace or civic space. In public they are required to support ideas like "individualism, progress, profit, and secularism," even if at home they are committed to alternate ideals such as community, altruism, and transcendence.[28]

Thus ironically the term *tolerance* is used to justify *intolerance* toward Christianity. It is even treated as something socially harmful that must be carefully contained, like pornography. Francis Crick of DNA fame once said Christianity is all right between consenting adults, but it should not be taught to children.[29]

This dynamic explains why American institutions of power—law, media, academia, entertainment—are highly secularized, even though the nation has a largely Christian cultural history, and even though the American populace remains the most religious among the industrialized nations. Peter Berger offers a striking metaphor for this strange schism. Statistically, in terms of the sheer number of religious adherents, he says, the most religious country in the world is India. The most secular country in the world is Sweden. So how could we characterize America? It is a nation of "Indians" *ruled* by "Swedes." That is, the populace is as religious as the Indians, while the power elites are as secular as the Swedes.

Let's take that analogy a step further. How do the "Swedish" elites establish and maintain their power? How do they successfully ward off all challenges by the "Indians"? The fact/value split does the work for them. The "Indians'" view is put in the upper story, where it is treated as a harmless personal pastime instead of a serious contender for truth. As Yale law professor Stephen Carter complains, elite culture treats religion as private and trivial, "like building model airplanes, just another hobby," not something that ought "to be mentioned in serious discourse."[30]

A striking example appeared in the documentary film "Expelled." Biologist P. Z. Myers, an aggressive polemicist for atheism, said he looks forward to the day when religion is treated as a pastime that people do for fun on the weekend "like knitting"—something "that really doesn't affect their life."

Of course, when theologically based perspectives are locked into the private realm, then only secular perspectives will be operative in the public realm. This explains the common complaint voiced by the American populace that "Washington is not listening." Their ideas never make it past the intellectual gatekeeper. The fact/value dichotomy has the effect of depriving targeted groups of social and political power. They may be accommodated for a while out of political expediency. But their ideas are not taken seriously, and they will be dismissed as soon as the political climate makes it safe to do so.

A recent news clip illustrates how the practice works. In May 2008 the British parliament approved the creation of animal/human hybrids in the laboratory. The *Times* science editor hailed it as "a watershed for British science" and "free scientific inquiry." He then praised Parliament for overriding opposition from what he called "a religious minority."[31] The point is that once the opposing sides had been labeled *scientific* versus *religious,* no further argument was felt to be needed. All moral, ethical, philosophical, and metaphysical objections to animal/human hybrids were simply ignored.

The *Newsweek* religion editor labeled the two opposing sides even more starkly: "Reason defines one kind of reality (what we know); faith defines another (what we don't know)."[32] In any public debate, *what we know* is obviously going to win out over *what we don't know* every time. In the words of Phillip Johnson, former law professor at UC Berkeley, "Agnostics rule America . . . because their metaphysics (i.e., scientific naturalism) rules the universities, and the universities control the social definition of knowledge."[33] That is, the universities define "what we know."

Todd Gitlin was right: Whoever marches on the English department—and the rest of the university—will end up wielding political power.

Good Cop/Bad Cop

Talking about a culture's view of truth may sound abstract, but the payoff is highly practical. You might think of the fact/value divide as a variation on the good cop/bad cop strategy. On one hand, when secularists are feeling confident, they will assert bluntly that science has disproved Christianity, and that it is time for mature people to face the facts and discard the false comforts of religion. That's the bad cop stance. When I was a university student, it was the typical stance of most of my professors. Today it is the rhetoric of New Atheists like Christopher Hitchens, who says, "I think religion should be treated with ridicule, hatred, and contempt."[34]

However, when the public protests the atheistic takeover of society vigorously enough, then secularists will adopt the conciliatory demeanor of the good cop. They will assure everyone that there really is no conflict, and that they respect everyone's "cherished values" or "deeply held beliefs." But the use of emotive language is a sleight of hand. It quietly slips theologically based views upstairs where they have no impact on the "real" world of science, politics, education, or business, or health care. And once the public has been lulled back into complacency, then the bad cop can resume his attacks.

Consider an example. Back in 1998, Paul Kurtz, founder of the Council for Secular Humanism, was functioning in the bad cop mode. He asserted that Darwinism had decisively disproved the existence of a Creator.[35] A few years later, however, noting a rise in "religiosity" across America, Kurtz recommended a more conciliatory strategy. In the *Skeptical Inquirer,* he continued to insist that all religions "traffic in fantasy and fiction." Nevertheless, he urged fellow skeptics to soften the blow when talking to the public. "I think that religion and science are compatible," he wrote, "depending of course on what is meant by religion."

Well, what did *he* mean by the term? "Religion presents moral poetry, aesthetic inspiration, performative ceremonial rituals," he wrote. "The creative religious imagination weaves tales of consolation and of expectation. They are dramatic expressions of human longing, enabling humans to overcome grief and depression."[36] This is the language of the good cop. Under the heavy rhetorical draping, Kurtz is saying that religion can be tolerated only if treated as a form of therapy—consoling and inspiring perhaps, but still essentially "fantasy and fiction."

As long as Christianity is treated as "moral poetry" and "tales of consolation," it poses no threat to the sovereignty of secularism. It is tame and safe. But it also falls far short of the Bible's robust and full-bodied definition of truth. Christianity does have rich expressive and emotional impact, but only because it is first of all true to reality.

In short, secularists propose that religion and science need not conflict so long as religion is defined *their* way. Essentially they are saying, "Render to Caesar the things that are Caesar's, and to God the things that Caesar says he can have."[37]

This is the core of the good cop/bad cop strategy. The doctrine of separate spheres is portrayed as a peacekeeping device. But when you read the fine print, you discover that the peace treaty relegates Christianity to the reservation, where it is forbidden to make any factual claims that might conflict with a materialistic version of science. It is a strategy designed to pacify religious people without giving any quarter to religious truth claims.

Sports teams would give anything if they were allowed to see their opponents' playbooks. But Christians *have* their opponents' playbook. The details may differ, but the strategy will be some version of the two-story division of truth.

Oppressive Tolerance

Yet the breakup of truth is not a problem only for Christians. It has corrosive consequences across the board. After all, secular people are just as eager to promote the moral causes *they* care most about—women's rights, environmentalism, abortion rights, homosexual rights, whatever. The problem is that *by their own definition of values*, their moral views have no cognitive standing.

This explains why there is so much pressure for political correctness—because there is no other form of correctness.[38] If moral knowledge is impossible, then we are left with only political and legal measures to coerce people into compliance.

As a result, the same people who aspire to be liberated from what they call oppressive moral codes are actually paving the way for new forms of oppression. As literary theorist Terry Eagleton explains, "'Value' is a transitive term: It means *whatever is valued* by certain people in specific situations." There is no universal yardstick to measure values. They are merely matters of private taste. And private taste is not open to rational persuasion. All that remains is power and coercion—each group seeking to impose its own preferences on others. As Eagleton says, values are merely "the assumptions by which certain social groups exercise and maintain power over others."[39]

Exactly. Young people like the teens at the rally in New York City often accept moral relativism because they want to be tolerant and non-judgmental. But in reality they are opening the door to a politics of manipulation and coercion. The loss of objectivity in moral thought does not lead to liberation. It leads to oppression. Secular ideologies preach liberty, but they practice tyranny.

Recognizing the problem, some secularists are searching for ways to salvage an objective status for morality. The favored strategy is to invoke evolutionary psychology. Hardly a week goes by without an article appearing in the popular press claiming that natural selection has explained the origin of this or that moral trait. Typically the argument goes something like this: You Christians claim that it is impossible to have morality without God. Well, we've solved *that* problem. Evolutionary forces can produce empathy, cooperation, mutual aid, and all the other forms of social bonding. These behaviors are selected for because they help secure genetic fitness and promote survival.

Voilá, evolution becomes the basis for moral realism. And evolutionary biologists become the new priests. As a *New York Times* article says, if "morality grew out of behavioral rules shaped by evolution," then "it is for biologists, not philosophers or theologians, to say what these rules are."[40]

But does evolutionary psychology really succeed in providing an objective basis for morality? Far from it. For when morality is redefined in terms of *non-moral* behavior, such as passing on one's genes, then it is no longer genuinely *moral* behavior, choosing right from wrong.[41]

Goodness becomes an illusion programmed into the human organism by natural selection because it makes groups cooperate better and survive longer. Evolutionary psychologist Michael Ruse puts it bluntly: "Morality is a collective illusion of humankind put in place by our genes in order to make us good cooperators."[42]

In short, an evolutionary account of morality relies on an equivocation of terms. It speaks of *good* and *evil* but they are no longer moral categories. In his 1838 notebooks Darwin scribbled, "Our descent, then, is the origin of our evil passions!!—The Devil under [the] form of [the] Baboon is our grandfather!" That is, what we call *evil* is merely inherited animal passions. The baboon genes made me do it.

But if what we call evil is a natural product of evolutionary forces, then we have no basis for opposing it—which means we will end up colluding with oppression and injustice. In a provocative article, two philosophers argue that Darwinists really ought to be complete nihilists (from the Latin *nihil,* meaning *nothing).* They should be *metaphysical* nihilists who deny "that there is any meaning or purpose to the universe." And they should be *ethical* nihilists who deny any "intrinsic values and obligations." Why? Because morality makes sense only in a world imbued with meaning and purpose.[43] Morality is a way of stating what humans are designed to do—their purpose for living. And if there is no Designer, then there *is* no design or purpose. Therefore there can be no genuine morality.

When Darwinian evolution is accepted in the lower story as fact, then morality is inevitably shifted to the upper story of noncognitive value. Which means there is no way to avoid the oppression of some group imposing *its* values on the rest of us.

For the sake of genuine tolerance and freedom, it is urgent to challenge the two-zone division of truth. Those who hold to the divided concept of truth typically consider themselves open-minded and tolerant. But in reality, they are imposing their own narrow, limited, culturally conditioned, secular view of truth on the rest of society. Recovering the unity of truth is the key to renewal, both in the church and in the culture.

Secular Pharisees

What is the best strategy to help people overcome the two-story divide? The most powerful critique is simply to point out that no one really adheres to it in practice. The division of truth has created two contradictory domains that are exaggerated to the point of being unrealistic and unliveable.

Starting with the lower story, many historians and philosophers of science today acknowledge that science is *not* the pursuit of purely objective, neutral facts. Scientists are driven as much as anyone else by personal interests, professional ambitions, political commitments, and metaphysical worldviews. The dominant worldview in academia today is evolutionary naturalism, which goes far beyond mere facts. It is an explanatory system that attempts to *interpret* the facts.

In a candid article, a science journalist admits, "I believe a material explanation will be found [to the origin of life], but that confidence comes from my faith that science is up to the task of explaining, in purely material or naturalistic terms, the whole history of life." He concludes, "My faith is well founded, but it is still faith."[44]

Unfortunately, most scientists are not so self-aware. The fact/value split blinds them to the faith status of their own views. As a result, secular worldviews get away with claiming to be objective and unbiased. It's time to call their bluff.

The upper story is equally unrealistic and unliveable. No one is a consistent moral relativist. Most people are painfully aware of the injustice and oppression in the world, and they are quite certain that it is wrong—not just unpleasant or personally offensive but genuinely wrong. They do not treat their own opposition to injustice as merely an upper-story private value.

And I would suggest that no one really can. All human beings are made in the image of God, hardwired with an intrinsic moral sense. As Romans 2 says, even those who do not know God's revealed law nevertheless have the moral law "written on their hearts." As a result, they are constantly making mental judgments. *He shouldn't do that. She's so insensitive.* People cannot function for even a few hours without making moral evaluations.

This holds true even for those who insist that morality is relative. The famous atheist Bertrand Russell once expounded his theory that *good* and *bad* have no objective validity—then minutes later fiercely denounced someone for being "such a *scoundrel!*"[45] Ironically, moral relativists often even pride themselves on being morally superior to others. After all, *they* are tolerant and non-judgmental. *They* are not like other people who are insufferably bigoted and closed-minded and deserve the harshest condemnation. Every group draws a line in the sand somewhere that allows them to feel morally superior, like the Pharisee in Jesus' parable who thanked God he was not like other people (Luke 19:11). Moral relativism may claim to be about tolerance and humility, but in reality it often fosters a highly moralistic, condemning attitude.

The upshot is that no one functions in real life on the basis of the fact/value split. Though many people imbibe its morally relativistic language, it fails to match the way they actually live. It fails to match who they truly are. They have been co-opted by an empiricist view of truth—one that they cannot follow in practice without violating their own humanity.

Socrates' Slogan

At the same time, most people long for a unified vision of life. After *Total Truth* was published, I was interviewed on a radio program located in the Pacific Northwest, devoted to the topic of spirituality. As the program opened, the host's first question was, "What do you mean when you write about a Christian worldview?"

Knowing that the audience was likely to be liberal and New Age, I decided to emphasize universal human concerns. "The question of worldview is really a question of integrity," I replied.

"To say people should be intentional about their worldview is like Socrates' dictum that the unexamined life is not worth living. It means we ought to examine our fundamental convictions about what is true, and then try to live consistently on that basis in every area of life."

This kind of integrity is probably more difficult today than in Socrates' day, I explained, because modern societies tend to be highly fragmented. The public/private divide creates pressure to leave our deepest convictions behind when we enter the public arena. This has created a crisis of integrity. The concept of worldview expresses the natural human longing for a life of integrity—a term that comes from the Latin word for *wholeness.*

The radio host was hooked. It made sense to her that Christians would want to bring their deepest convictions to bear on their public lives. That they would want their spirituality to have something to say about the environment and global issues, not just what they do in church on Sunday. That they would want to apply a moral perspective to business and public policy, not just their personal relationships. While my New Age audience might disagree with certain biblical principles, this approach defused their initial hostility. They, too, could connect with the goal of being whole persons free to express their core convictions across the whole of life.

The central challenge of our age, says Catholic philosopher Louis Dupré, is the lack of any integrating truth. "We experience our culture as fragmented; we live on bits of meaning and lack the overall vision that holds them together in a whole." As a result, people feel an intense need for self-integration. Christianity has the power to integrate our lives and create a coherent personality structure—but only if we embrace it as the ultimate, capital-T Truth that pulls together all lesser truths. "Faith cannot simply remain one discrete part of life," Dupré says. It must "integrate all other aspects of existence."[46] Anything less is neither beautiful nor compelling enough to ignite our passion or transform our character.

This is not a vision of a theocracy, as critics often contend. For the goal is not for the church *as an ecclesiastical institution* to take control of the other institutions of society. That was the mistake made in the Middle Ages when the church exerted its authority over the state, schools, arts, and professional guilds. The result was oppressive. In fact, when any single institution in society dominates the others, the result is a loss of freedom. The twentieth century taught that lesson through the extreme case of modern totalitarianism. In places like the former Soviet Union, the state absorbed and thereby destroyed the entire social infrastructure, at a horrific cost in terms of cruelty and coercion.

A distinctive insight of the Reformation was that Christian influence in society is primarily the work of individuals and lay organizations—nurtured and taught by the church, but accountable directly to God. This was the meaning of the Reformation principle of *coram Deo* (literally "before the face of God"). The church is a training ground to equip individuals with a biblical worldview and to send them out to the front lines to think and act creatively on the basis of biblical truth. The result is not oppression but a wonderful liberation of their creative powers.

Getting Through to Secularists

Getting secularists even to "hear" a biblical conception of truth may be the greatest communication challenge facing Christians today. Back in the 1940s, C. S. Lewis wrote, "Religion involves a series of statements about facts which must be either true or false."[47] Today those are fighting words. Most people no longer think religion is about facts, or that it is even an issue of true or false.

In *Reasons to Believe,* reporter John Marks tries to explicate the biblical concept of truth—somewhat like an anthropologist interpreting the customs of an obscure tribe. It takes Marks almost a page, in a rising crescendo of prose, to communicate what the Bible even means by truth.

"When a Bible-believing Christian talks about truth . . . he is not speaking about a thing conditioned by culture or crafted ultimately by language," Marks writes. (That is, truth is not a social construction.) It is not "affected by tides and times or rendered different from generation to generation." (Truth is not relative to time or place.) Scripture is "the explicit word of God." (It has a transcendent source.) It is "nothing more and nothing less than the ultimate fact of existence, raw and undiluted." (It is ultimate truth.) The gospel "does not dissolve in water or burn in fire. It is Truth. It is final."[48] You can almost imagine trumpets blaring as the text climbs to its concluding climax.

Marks' struggle simply to *explain* the biblical view of truth (which he does not accept) spotlights the challenge faced by Christians today. In order to persuade people that the Bible's message is true, they first must explain *what kind* of truth they mean. They must emancipate people's minds from the debilitating fact/value dualism. By analyzing the secularist playbook, Christians will be equipped to counter secularist strategies and communicate more effectively with secular people.

To accomplish this crucial task, we must now widen our scope to take in a bigger picture. The divided concept of truth is the core of the global secular worldview, yet it is still only one aspect. Every view of truth (epistemology) is linked to a view of reality (metaphysics). The dualism of fact and value has a corollary in a dualistic view of the human being—which has devastating consequences in areas like abortion, euthanasia, and sexuality. In the next chapter, we will learn how to respond to the most heart-rending ethical controversies of our day.

Chapter 3

"Men and women have a top storey as well as a ground floor;
and you can't have the one without the other."
—*George Bernard Shaw*

Sex, Lies, and Secularism

Anne Lamott, a favorite writer among Christian young adults, helped a man kill himself a few years ago. And she's not sorry.

"The man I killed did not want to die, but he no longer felt he had much of a choice," Lamott writes in *The Los Angeles Times*.[1] With his body wasting away from cancer and his mind beginning to waver, the man was open to Lamott's offer to acquire the lethal drugs needed to commit suicide. She first deceived a health care provider into giving her the drugs: "Through wily and underground ways, I came up with a prescription that would cover enough pills for a lethal dose." Then she crushed the pills with a mortar and pestle, mixed them with applesauce, and handed the deadly potion to her friend.

Hate Thy Neighbor

The friend "was sort of surprised that as a Christian I so staunchly agreed with him about assisted suicide," Lamott notes. To justify her stance, she does not reflect deeply on the data of Scripture or the history of Christian moral thought. In fact, she does not reflect on those things at all. Instead she compares life to a school, assuring her friend that it's okay to drop out early and get an incomplete. Though in her writings Lamott positions herself as a Christian, she essentially jettisons Scriptural principles regarding life as a gift from God. There is nothing distinctively Christian in her essay, even though it deals with an issue as serious as ending a person's life.

Lamott's views align in many ways, in fact, with the tenets of global secularism. She is ethically and politically liberal, not only on assisted suicide but also on abortion. In an earlier *Los Angeles Times* piece, she described a conference where she gave vent to an angry outburst against the pro-life position. "As a Christian and a feminist," she explained, I had to speak out for "women whose lives had been righted and redeemed by *Roe v. Wade*,"[2] the 1973 Supreme Court decision legalizing abortion.

"Righted and redeemed" by abortion? This is putting a veneer of biblical language over an essentially secular ethical stance. And it illustrates how even Christians can get drawn into a secularist worldview. To maintain their integrity, they must come to terms with the ethical outworkings of global secularism. They must stand against those who enable death and despair, while making a positive case for "loving thy neighbor."

In the field of bioethics, it is easy to get caught up in the latest controversy or news item. But current events are surface effects, like waves gliding on top of the ocean. The underlying worldviews are like tectonic plates whose movements *cause* the surface waves. A worldview approach enables Christians to move beyond merely denouncing social ills such as abortion, which can sound harsh, angry, and judgmental. And it equips them to demonstrate positively that biblical wisdom leads to a just and humane society. Protests and placards are not enough. To be strategically effective in protecting human dignity, we need to get behind the slogans and uncover the secular worldviews that shape people's thinking.

Death by Dualism

What *are* the worldview principles behind bioethical issues such as assisted suicide and abortion? Let's view them through the lens of one woman's personal story. British broadcaster Miranda Sawyer is blonde, beautiful, and a self-proclaimed liberal feminist. She had always been proudly pro-choice . . . until she became pregnant with her first child. Then she began to struggle.

"I was calling the life inside me a baby because I wanted it. Yet if I hadn't, I would think of it just as a group of cells that it was okay to kill." That did not make sense.

Yet Sawyer could not imagine herself becoming—horrors!—anti-abortion. "I spent some time thinking about the precise point when our baby came into existence. Was he there before I did the [pregnancy] test? Something was, or the test couldn't have come up positive. But what? A person? A potential person? Life? What was life exactly?"

What indeed? Sawyer met "Snowflake" children born from frozen embryos. "If an embryo can survive being artificially created [in a laboratory], being frozen, being FedExed hundreds of miles and then implanted into someone else's womb, then surely the anti-abortionists were right? Life does begin at conception." Yet she remained firmly opposed to any legal restrictions on abortion.

Finally she encountered a moral philosopher who proposed a crucial distinction: that an unborn child is *alive* but not a *person*. "In the end, I have to agree that life begins at conception," she concluded. "But perhaps the fact of life isn't what is important. It's whether that life has grown enough to start becoming a person."[3]

This distinction is widely accepted today. But notice what has happened to the concept of the human being: It has been ripped apart. For if life begins at one point in time, while the person comes into being sometime later, then clearly they are two different things. In ordinary conversation, we use terms like *human being* and *person* to refer to the same thing. But a wedge was driven between them in *Roe v. Wade* when the Supreme Court ruled that a fetus is human from the beginning, but not a person until some later point in time. This is a radically fragmented view of what it means to be human. And it has a dangerously dehumanizing effect on the way Americans view themselves—and others.

Ever since antiquity, of course, most cultures have assumed that a human being comprises both physical and spiritual elements—body and soul. What is novel in our day is that these two elements have been split apart and redefined in terms that are outright contradictory. As we will see, the human *body* is regarded as nothing but a complex mechanism, in accord with a modernist conception of science (the fact realm). By contrast, the human *person* is defined in terms of ungrounded choice and autonomy, in accord with a postmodernist conception of the self (the value realm). These two concepts interact in a deadly dualism to shape contemporary debates over abortion, euthanasia, sexuality, and the other life issues. Using our two-story image, we might visualize the dualism like this:

Liberal view of the human being

PERSON

An autonomous self (Postmodernism)

BODY

A biochemical machine (Modernism)

In the previous chapter, we diagnosed the divided concept of truth at the core of the global secular worldview. Its corollary is a divided concept of human nature. In the lower story, the human body has been reduced to a mechanism with no higher value than gadgets and gizmos—a view that clears the decks for unbridled experimentation with human life and DNA. At the same time, in the upper story, the postmodern self rejects all moral limits on its desires, denouncing them as a violation of its liberty. The floodgates have been flung open for unfettered refashioning of human nature itself.

Ghost in the Machine

To understand how body and self were ripped apart, we need to take a brief glance backward in history. Prior to the Enlightenment, nature was regarded as God's creation, imbued with his purposes. There was no two-story conflict between the natural and spiritual realms because both were the product of a single Mind. All of creation was coordinated in a unified whole. (The crucial division was love and loyalty to God versus sin and alienation from God.) To use a technical term, Christianity led to a *teleological* view of nature, from the Greek *telos,* which means a thing's goal, purpose, or ideal state. The ideal state for humans is the image of God. We were created to reflect God's own character. The moral law is the road map telling us how to reach that goal, the instruction manual for becoming the kind of person God originally intended us to be.

The most important source of information for that instruction manual is, of course, God's communication in Scripture. But another source is his communication in nature. We can read signs in nature that indicate God's original purpose—traces of God's image that remain even in a fallen world. For example, the biological correspondence between male and female is part of the original creation that God pronounced "very good"—morally good. Thus it provides a reference point for morality. Moral rules are not arbitrary; they are rooted in the way God created human nature.

With the rise of modern science, however, many Westerners began to embrace a mechanistic model of nature. By the fourteenth century, mechanical clocks had become common in Europe, and some were quite elaborate, featuring automated figures that marched around, bobbing in and out. The cathedral clock in Strasbourg, France, featured an automaton or robot shaped like a rooster, made of iron and copper. Every day at noon it would spread its wings, flap its beak, stick out its tongue, and crow three times (using a reed and bellows) to remind the townsfolk of Peter's denial of Christ. Then the three kings would emerge and bow before a figure of the baby Jesus carried in Mary's arms. These mechanical clocks and toys became a powerful metaphor for nature itself. Some thinkers began to argue that if toy figures can wag their heads and wave their arms because they are moved by hidden gears and wheels and springs, then surely the inner workings of living things could be explained in the same way.

The mechanistic model view was perfectly compatible with a biblical view of nature. The early proponents were mostly Christians, such as Robert Boyle and Isaac Newton. After all, a machine requires an inventor, a designer. If the universe is like a mechanical wind-up tool, then someone must have created

3-1 Cathedral clock
Strasbourg, France, 1354

Are living things robots too?

it and wound it up. Besides, tools are invented for a purpose, to fulfill a function. Thus the universe too was created for a purpose. As historian John Herman Randall writes, "The whole form of Newtonian science practically forced men, as a necessary scientific hypothesis, to believe in an external Creator."[4]

The mechanistic approach began to harden into a radical mind/body dichotomy, however, in the philosophy of Rene Descartes.[5] The human body he viewed as a kind of robot or wind-up toy. "I suppose the body to be nothing but a statue or machine made of earth," he wrote. Its motion follows "necessarily from the very arrangement of the parts," just as the motion of a clock follows "from the power, the situation, and the shape of its counterweights and wheels."

Because Descartes was Catholic, however, he also wanted to salvage the concept of a mind or spirit capable of surviving the body after death. Thus he defined the mind as a free, self-sufficient consciousness connected somehow to the robot body—in his words, a "rational soul united to this machine." As one philosopher explains, Cartesian dualism "appeared to effect a compromise and reconciliation between the Church and the scientists." The rule was: "to each its own jurisdiction—to the scientists, matter and its mechanical laws of motion; to the theologians, mental substance, the souls of human beings."[6]

Cartesian dualism was irreverently dubbed the "ghost in the machine." And it created enormous difficulties for Western thinkers. For how could two such opposing substances form a single interacting unity? How could a robotic body and thinking mind function as an integrated whole? These two substances are not just different (like the biblical concept of body and soul) but mutually exclusive. "Cartesian dualism breaks man up into two complete substances," says philosopher Jacques Maritain: "on the one hand, the body which is only geometrical extension; on the other, the soul which is only thought." The human being was "split asunder."[7]

To use our two-story image, downstairs was the body operating by the blind, mechanical laws of nature. Upstairs was the independent, autonomous ego. As a Christian philosopher puts it, Descartes "splits the world of our total experience into two halves."[8]

Disenchanting Nature

Eventually Western thought itself was split into "two halves." We will delve into the details of this split in later chapters, but to grasp the most pressing issues in bioethics we need to cover the highlights. With the growth of secular worldviews, many thinkers decided that the universe-machine no longer needed a designer to create it, or a celestial mechanic to wind it up. They substituted the image of the universe as a self-creating dynamo, operating by automatic, undirected physical forces. Never mind that a self-creating universe is a contradiction in terms. (Before an object exists, there is no *self* to do the creating.) The concept of a self-evolving universe served to eliminate any need for a transcendent Creator.

This secularized worldview had profound moral implications. For if nature was not the handiwork of a personal God, then it no longer bore signs of God's good purposes—which meant it no longer provided a basis for moral truths. Nature became "a mechanistic system of extended matter without religious or moral significance," explains philosopher David West. Things such as purpose and design were no longer thought to be categories for explaining nature, but only mental concepts in the human mind.

The next step is crucial: Because nature did not reveal *God's* will, it became a morally neutral realm upon which humans may impose *their* will. As West explains, when nature was considered "a manifestation of God's will," then the goal of knowledge was "to fulfill God's design" and live in harmony with his purposes. But according to secularism, nature does not reveal God's purpose. Therefore the only goal of knowledge is to improve "our ability to predict and control nature" to serve our own needs and preferences. [9]

To use the language of the fact/value split, nature became the realm of value-neutral *facts,* available to serve whatever *values* humans may choose.[10] Theologian N. T. Wright puts it colorfully: The Enlightenment promoted the idea "that we have now come of age, that God can be kicked upstairs, that we can get on with running the world however we want to, carving it up to our advantage without outside interference."[11]

The value-free view of nature included the human body. It too became merely raw material subject to the choices of the autonomous self. In the words of Roger Lundin of Wheaton College, both nature and the body became "essentially amoral mechanisms to be used to whatever private ends we have."[12]

We can call this view *liberalism*, employing a definition by the self-described liberal philosopher Peter Berkowitz. In his words, "Each generation of liberal thinkers" focuses on "dimensions of life previously regarded as fixed by nature," then seeks to show that in reality they are "subject to human will and remaking."[13] In other words, previous generations thought there was a fixed, universal human nature that expressed a God-given teleology. For example, they thought heterosexual marriage was rooted in human nature. It was the way humans were created to function. By contrast, liberalism denies that there *is* any fixed or universal human nature. Humans are an accidental configuration of matter, a product of blind evolutionary forces that did not have us in mind.[14] Marriage is a social behavior that evolved because it was adaptive at some point in evolutionary history. But it is not intrinsic to human nature. We are free to redefine it at will. It is open to unlimited "human will and remaking."

You might say the human body has become almost a form of property that can be controlled and manipulated. Philosopher Daniel Dennett offers the analogy of driving a car: "Since Descartes in the seventeenth century we have had a vision of the self as a sort of immaterial ghost that owns and controls a body the way you own and control your car."[15] That is, the body is no longer regarded as an integral part of the human person but as "sub-personal," functioning strictly on the level of biology and chemistry—almost like a possession that can be used to serve the self's desires.

Splitting the Adam

This history throws surprising new light on the abortion debate. In the past, abortion supporters simply denied that the fetus is human: "It's just a blob of tissue." Today, however, due to advances in genetics and DNA, virtually no ethicist denies that the fetus is human: biologically, genetically, scientifically human. But this refers to the *fact* realm—where, as we have seen, human life is regarded as a product of the blind, mechanical forces of nature, with no intrinsic dignity or value (lower story). As a result, simply being human does not confer any moral status. Nor does it warrant legal protection. The turning point is said to be the stage at which the fetus becomes a "person," typically defined in terms of self-awareness, autonomy, and the ability to make choices (upper story).

This radical dualism is called personhood theory, and it prevails today among liberal bioethicists. For example, Hans Küng, a liberal Catholic theologian, writes that "a fertilized ovum evidently is human life but is not a person." Princeton ethicist Peter Singer acknowledges that "the life of a human organism begins at conception." But "the life of a person— . . . a being with some level of self-awareness—does not begin so early." Joseph Fletcher of situation ethics fame says, "What is critical is *personal* status, not merely *human* status." In his view, genetically defective fetuses and newborns do not attain the status of personhood. They are "sub-personal" and therefore fail to qualify for the right to life.[16] Adapting our earlier diagram, personhood theory could be represented like this:

Personhood theory

PERSON
"Persons" have freedom and moral dignity

BODY
"Humans" are disposable machines

A flaw in this theory is that once personhood is separated from biology, no one can agree how to define it. Some ethicists say personhood emerges when the developing organism begins to exhibit neural activity, or feel pain, or achieve a certain level of cognitive function or consciousness. For example, Singer says, "I use the term 'person' to refer to a being who is capable of anticipating the future, of having wants and desires for the future."[17] Anyone who lacks these functions he labels a "nonperson."

Other ethicists focus on the desire to live (on the assumption that life is valuable only if someone wants it). John Harris defines a person as "a creature capable of valuing its own existence." Killing is wrong only in the case of someone who is cognitively developed enough to harbor an explicit, conscious desire to live. "Nonpersons or potential persons cannot be wronged in this way because death does not deprive them of anything they can value," Harris argues. "If they cannot wish to live, they cannot have that wish frustrated by being killed."

These conflicting definitions demonstrate how tricky it is to define personhood once it is cut off from the sheer fact of being biologically human. Miranda Sawyer concluded that personhood begins sometime before birth: "Once an embryo has developed enough to feel pain, or begin a personality, then . . . ending that life is wrong." But Harris scoffs at that idea: "Nine months of development leaves the human embryo far short of the emergence of anything that can be called a person."[18] James Watson, co-discoverer of the DNA double helix, recommended waiting until after birth and giving a newborn baby three days of genetic testing before deciding whether it should be allowed to live. For Singer, personhood remains a "gray" area even at three years of age.[19] After all, how much cognitive functioning does a toddler have?

The upshot is that once the concept of personhood is detached from biology, it becomes subjective and arbitrary—opening a door to inhumanity and oppression. Anyone at any stage of life could be demoted to the status of "non-person" and denied the right to live.

Pro-Abortion Is Anti-Science

This background equips us to counter the most common arguments for abortion. It is often said that pro-choice ethicists base their views on science, while pro-lifers appeal to religion—which is why their views have no place in public policy. For example, in *First Things* Stanley Fish wrote, "A pro-choice advocate sees abortion as a decision to be made in accordance with the best scientific opinion as to when the beginning of life, as we know it, occurs." By contrast, "a pro-life advocate sees abortion as a sin against a God who infuses life at the moment of conception."[20]

But this stereotype has things precisely backward. During the 2008 presidential campaign, it was pro-abortion candidates who treated it as a religious issue. Asked when human life begins, Barack Obama said, "I don't presume to be able to answer these kinds of theological questions." Joseph Biden said he spoke "as a Roman Catholic" but that "Jews, Muslims, and others" might differ.

By contrast, pro-life leaders consistently appeal to science. Yuval Levin, a member of former president Bush's Council on Bioethics, states: "The question of when a new human life begins is not fundamentally a theological question but a biological question . . . Human life has a straightforward scientific definition."[21] And that scientific definition begins at conception. From that moment on, nothing substantially new appears. The individual merely unfolds the capacities that are intrinsic to the kind of organism it is—whether a hummingbird or a human being.

Of course, people are much *more* than biological organisms. Yet biology gives an objective, universally detectable marker of human status. By contrast, when disconnected from biology, liberal definitions of personhood float vaguely in postmodern space with no objective criteria. *Which* abilities or functions count in deciding whether a person has moral worth? And how developed do they have to be in order to count? Every liberal ethicist draws the line at a different place, depending on his or her own personal choice and values.

Ironically, although pro-lifers are criticized for bringing private values into the public realm, it is actually the pro-choice position that is based on private views and values.

Even Fish had to eat his words. Two years after writing the *First Things* article quoted earlier, he had to retract what he said. "Nowadays, it is pro-lifers who make the scientific question of when the beginning of life occurs the key one," he admitted, while "pro-choicers want to transform the question into a 'metaphysical' or 'religious' one."[22]

Because science supports the pro-life position so unequivocally, some pro-choicers are now actually repudiating science. "The question is not really about life in any biological sense," intones Yale professor Paul Bloom in the *New York Times*. "It is instead asking about the magical moment at which a cluster of cells becomes more than a mere physical thing." And what "magical" force has the power to convert a "mere physical thing" into a person with a dignity so profound that it is morally wrong to kill it? Bloom replies: That "is not a question that scientists could ever answer."[23]

Similarly, Jennie Bristow, editor of *Abortion Review*, does her best to dismiss science as a red herring. "With anti-abortionists pushing 'scientific evidence' on fetal viability, it is time to restate the *moral* case for a woman's right to choose." Her article is titled, "Abortion: Stop Hiding behind the Science."[24]

In short, liberals are admitting that *their* position is anti-science. Put bluntly, abortion supporters have lost the argument on the scientific level. They can no longer deny that an embryo is biologically human. As a result, they have shifted their argument to a vague upper-story concept of personhood—defined ultimately by nothing beyond their own personal choice. And when their view is codified into law, then their private values are imposed on everyone else.

The Bible and the Body

As a sociological fact, of course, many pro-lifers are members of religious communities. But that does not mean their arguments depend on theological teachings about the spirit or soul. One could even say that the real issue at stake is the status of the *body*. Abortion is defended by arguments that identify moral worth solely with mental capacities such as self-awareness and self-consciousness. The body is denigrated to the level of the sub-personal. It is trivialized as a form of raw material that can be tinkered with, manipulated, experimented on, or destroyed with no moral significance. Human life is reduced to a utilitarian calculus, subject only to a cost-benefit analysis.

This is a far *lower* view of human life than anything taught in biblical Christianity. According to the Bible, the material world has intrinsic value because God created it, and God will ultimately redeem it. At the time of the early church, these were revolutionary claims. Ancient pagan culture was permeated by world-denying philosophies such as Platonism and Gnosticism. These dualistic philosophies defined salvation as the liberation of the soul from the prison-house of the body.

In that cultural context, the early church's claim of the incarnation—that God himself took on human flesh (John 1:14)—was an astounding concept. So was its claim that Jesus rose bodily from the dead. In fact, these teachings were so astounding that, in the second century, the Gnostics denied them altogether. They taught that Jesus was an avatar from a higher, spiritual plane who entered the physical world temporarily to bring enlightenment and then returned to a higher state of being. As N. T. Wright explains, they "translated the language of resurrection into a private spirituality and a dualistic cosmology."[25]

Just as today, a dualistic view was far more socially acceptable. As a case in point, the Gnostics were not persecuted by the Roman Empire as the Christians were. Why not? Because a privatized spirituality poses no threat to power, no matter how brutal or corrupt it may be. It was Christians who were burned at the stake and thrown to the lions. They understood that when Jesus was raised from the dead and given a new, resurrection body, God was inaugurating the promised new creation, in which all injustice and corruption will be wiped out. They were energized to reject dualism and take a stand against injustice here and now.

In the Apostle's Creed, the church boldly affirms that all God's people will share in that new creation through "the resurrection of the body." In other words, they will not be saved *out of* the material creation but will be saved *together with* the material creation. At the end of time, God is not going to scrap the idea of a physical world in time and space, as though his first creation was just a mistake. The biblical teaching is that God is going to restore, renew, and recreate it into a new heaven and new earth. At death humans do undergo a temporary splitting of body and soul, but that's why death is called "the last enemy" (1 Cor. 15:26)—because it separates what God intended to be unified. And in the new creation, they will be re-unified. Eternally. The doctrine of the physical resurrection means that the physical world matters. It matters to God and it should matter to God's people.[26]

Today these doctrines are just as astounding as they were in the ancient world. Western culture is regressively falling back into a dualism that denigrates the material realm, just as paganism did. In an unexpected twist, it is orthodox Christians who are arguing against liberals to defend a high view of the human body.

Liberals sometimes say, "If you're against abortion, don't have one. But don't impose your views on others." At first, that might sound fair. But what liberals fail to understand is that every social practice rests on certain assumptions of what the world is like—on a worldview. When a society accepts the practice, it absorbs the worldview that justifies it. That's why abortion is not merely a matter of private individuals making private choices. It is about deciding which worldview will shape our communal life together.

Personhood theory is a radically dualistic view of the human being that reduces the body to an exploitable commodity. And when that worldview is absorbed, it has life-and-death consequences not only for the fetus but ultimately for everyone. Its dehumanizing effect puts all of us at risk. When Christians argue for the truth of the biblical worldview, they are seeking to protect human rights and dignity for everyone across the board.

Targeting Terri

The same dualistic worldview is at the root of euthanasia. Supporters of voluntary euthanasia, or assisted suicide, often argue that human dignity consists in the ability to exercise conscious, deliberate control over our lives (upper story). If that mental control is lost or threatened because of disease or injury, then personhood itself is lost. All that remains is organic life (lower story). And, as we have seen, the human organism is regarded as a biochemical machine with no intrinsic value of its own.

The reasoning is highlighted in an opera written in 2002 by minimalist composer Steve Reich. The libretto juxtaposes quotations by two scientists. First zoologist Richard Dawkins asserts that humans are nothing but "machines created by our genes." Then biologist Robert Pollack draws the logical conclusion: "I have no sense of guilt pulling the plug on any machine."[27]

What about *in*voluntary euthanasia? Not surprisingly, if individuals are not even capable of giving informed consent, that itself is taken to mean that they are no longer persons. The best-known example was the 2005 Terri Schiavo case. The media presented it as a right-to-die case, but Terri was not dying. She was not terminally ill. So that was not actually the heart of the debate. The core issue was personhood theory.

In a television debate, a bioethicist from the University of Florida was asked point blank, "Do you think Terri is a person?"

"No, I do not," he replied. "I think having awareness is an essential criterion of personhood."[28]

Whatever you think of the specifics of Terri's case, that statement captures its broader significance. According to personhood theory, a mentally disabled individual is no longer a *person*, even though she is obviously still *human*.

Those who favored cutting off Terri's food and water included neurologist Ronald Cranford, who has defended the same policy even for disabled people who are conscious and partly mobile. A California case involved a brain-damaged man who could perform logical tests with colored pegs and even scoot along hospital hallways in an electric wheelchair (like the famous physicist Stephen Hawking). Nevertheless, Cranford argued that the man should have his feeding tube removed and should be left to die.[29]

We are not talking here about cases where medical professionals must make a practical judgment between saving life and merely prolonging death. When all organ systems are shutting down despite the best medical treatment, then intervention may accomplish nothing except prolong the dying process. By contrast, personhood theory is a philosophy used to justify actively ending a life.

According to personhood theory, just being part of the human race is not morally relevant. Individuals must earn the status of personhood by meeting an additional set of criteria—the ability to make decisions, exercise self-awareness, and so on. Those who do not make the grade are demoted to non-persons. Many ethicists have begun to argue that non-persons may be used for utilitarian purposes such as research and harvesting organs. Wesley Smith, author of *Culture of Death,* calls this a proposal for "human strip-mining"[30] and warns that it would reduce human life to a marketable commodity.

Embryo Plantation

Human embryos are already being treated as a marketable commodity. In the two-story paradigm, human embryos are merely biological entities, not persons. Therefore they can be destroyed without moral significance, if a utilitarian calculus suggests some benefit to society. Many Americans have come to accept the idea that in the search for new medical cures, human embryos can be sown, harvested, patented, and sold—as though they were just another natural resource.

If we reject the two-story dualism, however, then personhood is inextricably linked to being biologically human at every stage of development. Destroying an embryo is morally akin to killing an adult.

Moreover, embryo research typically involves creating human life in order to destroy it. Even those who are uncertain whether the embryo is fully a person often find this troubling. A fundamental principle of ethics is that people should be treated as intrinsically valuable, not valuable only as a means to some extrinsic end. As we say in ordinary conversation, it is wrong to *use* people. As Wesley Smith writes, there something deeply dehumanizing about "treating human life—no matter how nascent—as a mere natural resource to be harvested like a soy bean crop."[31] Such a utilitarian view of human life inevitably exerts a coarsening and brutalizing effect across the entire society.

Darwinstein

Ironically, embryo research is not even necessary. Research using adult stem cells is *not* morally problematic and has produced excellent results. For some scientists, the real agenda behind embryo research is that it offers a first step toward full-scale genetic engineering. Today many scientists embrace the philosophy of naturalism or materialism, which reduces humans to material products of their genes. In that case, it is logical to conclude that the way to improve the human race is simply to adjust their genes. And embryo research is providing the tools.

A movement calling itself transhumanism urges society to take charge of evolution through gene modification. Transhumanists argue that human life as it exists today has no inherent value or dignity. It is merely one step in an endless evolutionary chain—a chance configuration of cells that will be surpassed in the next stage of evolution. Waxing poetic, philosopher John Gray writes that humans are "only currents in the drift of genes."[32]

The implications are not so poetic, however. Nick Bostrom, a leading transhumanist at Oxford, writes that human nature is "a work-in-progress, a half-baked beginning that we can learn to remold in desirable ways."[33] But who decides what is desirable? Who will have the power to remold human nature?

And why stop there? If humans are just a chance collection of cells, why not mix in cells from other species, creating human-animal hybrids? Transhumanists argue that the species *Homo sapiens* is no higher (and sometimes lower) on the cognitive scale than other species, and thus there is no ethical barrier to splicing animal DNA into human DNA. These transgenic technologies (*trans-genic* means "across species") are proposed as means to enhance human capabilities and create a post-human race.

The same technologies might also be used to enhance animals' capabilities. Futurist author James Hughes advocates what he calls "uplifting" chimpanzees genetically to give them human intellectual capacities—not because that would be good for chimps but because it would prove that they deserve the legal status of persons. "Persons don't have to be human, and not all humans are persons," Hughes says [34]—which reveals just how undefined and open-ended the concept of personhood has become.

The assumption that drives all these futurist scenarios, says embryologist Brian Goodwin, is the Darwinian claim there is no such things as species—that what we call species are merely temporary groupings in the ever-shifting populations of evolving organisms, eddies in the genetic stream. Because of this Darwinian assumption, Goodwin explains, "we've lost even the concept of human nature." As a result, "life becomes a set of parts, commodities that can be shifted around" to suit some geneticists' vision of progress.[35]

Using a literary metaphor, biologist Thomas Eisner says a species is not "a hard-bound volume of the library of nature" but instead "a loose-leaf book, whose individual pages, the genes, might be available for selective transfer and modification of other species."[36] This is a highly revealing metaphor. It suggests that if there is no author of the book of life, then there is no basis for regarding organisms as integrated wholes. When an author tells a story, all the segments are held together by a common theme or purpose. But if life is an accident produced by blind, material forces, then there is no unifying theme. Organisms can be treated as random collections of genes and other spare parts to be mixed and matched at will.

Humanist Hell

Transhumanists often speak in euphoric tones as though a technology-created utopia were just around the corner. We are on "the cusp of a new Enlightenment," enthuses Adrian Woolfson of Cambridge University. We can finally "entertain the possibility of modifying our own nature and creating artificial life."[37] But this utopian vision is an illusion. What counts most in producing a truly humane society is not the level of technology but the prevailing worldview. And a worldview that says human life has no inherent value or dignity will never lead to utopia, no matter how advanced the tools and gadgets.

To prove the point, we do not even have to cite high-tech examples such as genetic engineering. Once personhood is up for grabs, the power to decide who should live or die can be exercised through low-tech measures. For example, the pragmatist philosopher Richard Rorty has seriously suggested that rich nations may end up engaging in "economic triage" against poor nations. After all, throughout history, societies have come up with various ways to exclude certain groups from the human family by labeling them *subhuman*—groups belonging to a different tribe, clan, race, or religion. The idea that human rights are universal, Rorty notes, was a completely novel concept ushered in by Christianity. It rests on the biblical teaching "that all human beings are created in the image of God."

Because of Darwin, Rorty states, we no longer accept creation. And therefore we no longer need to maintain that everyone who is biologically human has equal dignity. We are free to revert to the pre-Christian attitude that only certain groups qualify for human rights.

What criterion should we use in selecting which groups qualify? The most logical would be an economic criterion, Rorty argues. Any concept of mutual obligation "has to be one which takes money into account." It has to ask: Do we actually have the economic resources to help these people? When that question is raised, then the idea that everyone should have the same rights "is obviously unfeasible." For "no foreseeable application of technology could make every human family rich enough to give their children anything remotely like the chances that a family in the lucky parts of the world now takes for granted." Thus, Rorty concludes, there is no meaningful way to state that "the poorer five billion citizens of the member states of the United Nations" have the same human rights as the rich nations.

What then? Should the rich nations decide they have no moral obligation to help the world's poor? Should they, like some pre-Christian tribe, declare poorer nations to be subhuman? Rorty declines to answer the question directly, but the logic of his argument certainly points in that direction.[38] Once moral obligation is not based simply on being human, then it is completely logical—albeit brutal—to choose economics as the criterion for personhood. For that matter, any criterion could be chosen. Any category of humans is fair game to be excluded or even eliminated.

The stakes in this debate are very high. "If human life does not matter simply and merely because it is human, this means that moral worth becomes subjective and a matter of who has the power to decide," Smith warns. "History shows that once we create categories of differing worth, those humans denigrated by the political power structure as having less value are exploited, oppressed, and killed."[39] The totalitarian systems of the twentieth century—Nazism and Communism—give evidence of the morally horrific consequences of treating humans as mere things to be manipulated to create someone's vision of utopia. Utopianism linked to power leads to gulags and death camps.

What NPR Can't Handle

The debate on the life issues is often portrayed as a conflict pitting those who think the state should remain neutral on moral issues against those want to "impose" their beliefs on others. Yet as we have seen, a secular liberal view is far from neutral.

A few years ago I was invited to speak at a Christian worldview conference hosted by an Ivy League university, and quickly noticed a pattern emerging. After each speaker, invariably the students would raise the same question in some form: *But if we talk about a Christian worldview, aren't we imposing our views on others?* Clearly, even highly educated, Ivy League students have absorbed the secular doctrine that it is illegitimate to speak from a Christian perspective in the public arena—that to do so violates ideals of neutrality and objectivity.

When the same question came up after my lecture, as it inevitably did, I was ready with a counter-question: Is the *liberal* position neutral? Is *it* unbiased and objective? Of course not. It rests on a highly contentious, dualistic view of human nature, that involves a subjective definition of the person (upper story) and a crassly utilitarian view of the body (lower story). There's nothing neutral about any of that. And when the government mandates policies based on that worldview, it is imposing a secular liberal ideology on an entire society.

The problem is that worldviews do not come neatly labeled. No one says bioethical controversies involve two conflicting views of human nature. Instead people typically speak of a conflict of science versus religion—facts versus faith. When we hear that kind of language, we should press everyone to put their worldview cards on the table. Only then will Americans engage in a genuinely free and open debate.

I was once invited to be a guest on a National Public Radio program in San Francisco. But before going on the air, the producer first wanted to know my stance on abortion. The accepted view, he commented, is that abortion is acceptable "until the fetus becomes a person."

"That phrase carries enormous philosophical baggage," I explained. "Personhood theory assumes a *fragmented* view of human nature, which treats the body as expendable." By contrast, "those who oppose abortion hold a *holistic* view of human nature as an integrated unity. They insist that the body has intrinsic value and worth."

The producer seemed surprised by this argument. I went on: "The pro-choice position is *exclusive*. It says that some people don't measure up, don't make the cut. They don't qualify for the rights of personhood." By contrast, "the pro-life position is *inclusive*. If you are a member of the human race, you're 'in.' You have the dignity and status of a full member of the moral community."

A few days later the producer contacted me to say the program had been canceled. It can be difficult for liberals to accept the dehumanizing implications of their views. I had used some of the most venerated liberal buzzwords (*inclusive, holistic*) to demonstrate that a biblical worldview actually fulfills the highest ideals of liberalism far better than any secular worldview.

Hooking Up, Feeling Down

Let's move now to the most contentious sexual issues of our day, such as homosexuality, transgenderism, and the hook-up culture. Understanding the two-story dualism is a powerful tool to respond to these cutting-edge issues and to offer a humane and holistic biblical alternative.

As we saw earlier, the biblical worldview is teleological. The biological structure of our bodies is not some evolutionary accident. It signals a divine purpose for male and female to form covenants for mutual love and the nurturing of new life. Biblical morality reflects the purpose for which we were created.

By contrast, a secular materialistic view of nature has no room for purpose or teleology. Our bodies are products of blind, material forces. Therefore they are morally neutral. The implication is that what we do with our bodies has no moral significance. We could call this the Proverbs 30 view of sexuality, with its picture of someone who has committed adultery: "She eats and wipes her mouth, and says, 'I have done nothing wrong'" (Prov. 30:20). In other words, sex is just a biological appetite, like eating. When you feel the need, you satisfy it. No big deal. What we do with our bodies is separate from who we are as persons.

How does this fragmented view of sexuality work out in practice? A survey by the Institute for American Values found that 40 percent of college women engage in "hooking up," purely physical encounters with no expectation of any personal relationship. "What makes hooking up unique is that its practitioners agree that there will be no commitment, no exclusivity, no feelings," explains the *Washington Post*. Hookup partners are referred to as "friends with benefits" but that's a euphemism because they are not really even friends. The unwritten etiquette is that you never meet to just talk or spend time together, explains a *New York Times* article. "You just keep it purely sexual, and that way people don't have mixed expectations, and no one gets hurt."[40]

Except, of course, that people *do* get hurt. The same article quotes a teenager named Melissa who was depressed because her hookup partner had just broken up with her. People are not machines and they cannot surgically separate their emotions from what they do with their bodies.

Rolling Stone magazine interviewed a college student who captured the thinking of the hook-up culture neatly. In her words, people "assume that there are two very distinct elements in a relationship, one emotional and one sexual, and they pretend like there are clean lines between them."[41] Do you recognize the language of dualism? Young people are trying to live out the fragmenting philosophy that they have been taught. They assume that sexual relationships can be solely physical (lower story), disconnected from the mind and emotions (upper story)—with "clean lines" between them.

The "hook-up" culture

PERSONAL

Mental and emotional relationship

PHYSICAL

Sexual relationship

George Bernard Shaw diagnosed the problem in his play *Too True to Be Good.* "When men and women pick one another up just for a bit of fun, they find they've picked up more than they bargained for, because men and women have a top storey as well as a ground floor," says one of the characters. "You can't have the one without the other. They're always trying to; but it doesn't work." Today's young people are still desperately trying to. But it still doesn't work.

Of course, the fact that it does not work ought to tell us something. It means the hook-up culture rests on an inadequate conception of human nature. People are trying to live out a worldview that does not fit who they really are.

Because humans are created in God's image, their experience will never quite "fit" a secular view of human nature. In practice, non-Christians will always run into some point of contradiction between their secular worldview and their real-life experience. That contradiction provides an opening to make the case that the secular worldview is flawed. It fails to explain human life and experience. Young people like Melissa are trying to live out a worldview that does not match their true nature—and it is tearing them apart with its pain and heartache.

When Adults Aid and Abet

Tragically, some adults are actually complicit in pressuring teens to keep the top story separate from the ground floor—that is, to engage in casual sexual activity. Scarleteen, a sex-ed web site, includes a Sex Readiness Checklist that includes this item under the heading of emotional readiness: "I can separate sex from love." (You are mature if you are emotionally detached.) The magazine *Cosmopolitan* advises women that the way to "wow a man after sex" is to ask for a ride home. (Make it clear you have no intention of hanging around hoping for a relationship.) *Seventeen* magazine warns teen girls to "keep your hearts under wraps" or boys may find you "boring and clingy."

These examples were collected by Wendy Shalit in her book *Girls Gone Mild*.[42] On her web site, Shalit posts letters from readers, some of them heartrending. The day I checked the site, there was one from sixteen-year-old Amanda lamenting that in a typical high school, "the more detached you can be from your sexuality, the cooler you are." She added that even adults—teachers, books, magazines, television, parents—often urge teens to adopt a "no big deal" attitude toward sexuality.

As though to prove the point, some reviews of Shalit's book actually defended loveless sexual encounters. The *Washington Post* suggested that it is healthy when teenage girls "refuse to conflate" love and sex: "Sometimes they coexist, sometimes not." The *Nation* asked defiantly, "Why should sex have an everlasting warranty of love attached to it?"[43] Why indeed, if the body is just a piece of matter that can be stimulated for pleasure with no moral significance?

The same bleak view of sexuality is inculcated in young children's minds by the public school system. A video put out by Children's Television Workshop defines sexual relations as simply "something done by two adults to give each other pleasure."[44] No hint that sexuality has any moral or social significance. No suggestion that it has a richer purpose than sheer sensual gratification, such as bonding husband and wife together to create a safe haven for raising children. Instead sexuality is portrayed an exchange of physical services between two autonomous, disconnected individuals. It's sex as commodity.

To use a punchy phrase from John Kavanaugh, "commodification splits *sexuality* from *selfhood*."[45] Sexuality is treated not as the embodied expression of our full selfhood, but merely as an instrument for physical release and recreation.

PoMoSexual Alienation

The same fragmented approach to sexuality drives the liberal view of homosexuality as well. The Children's Television Workshop video quoted above defines homosexuality as simply "two people of the same gender giving each other pleasure." If a sexual encounter is just an exchange of physical services, why does it really matter which gender you are?

In fact, the cutting edge today is the idea that gender itself is a social construction—and therefore it can be *de*constructed. In her influential book *Gender Trouble,* Judith Butler argues that gender is not a fixed attribute but a fluid, free-floating variable that shifts according to personal preference. Gender is a "fiction," a "fabrication," a "fantasy" that can be made and re-made at will.[46]

Butler's theory has become popular on college campuses, especially among transgender students—"trannies," for short. These are students who reject the binary male/female system as a mere social construction, and an oppressive one at that. A *New York Time* article reports that some colleges now offer separate bathrooms, housing, and sports teams for students who do not identify themselves as either male or female. At Wesleyan, the campus clinic no longer requires students to check "male" or "female" on their health forms. Instead, they are asked to "describe your gender identity history."[47] In other words: Which genders have you been over the course of your lifetime?

This fluid view of gender is typically presented as liberating—a way to create your own identity instead of accepting one that has been culturally assigned. As a magazine for homosexuals explains, people today "don't want to fit into any boxes—not gay, straight, lesbian, or bisexual ones." Instead "they want to be free to change their minds." The article was addressed to people who had come out of the closet as homosexuals, but later found themselves attracted to heterosexual relationships again. So what *am* I, they wondered? Not to worry, the author reassured them. The idea that one is born with a certain gender that cannot be changed is so *modernist*. Society is moving to a *postmodern* view in which you can choose any gender you want, at any time.[48] Call it a pomosexual view.[49]

Gender has become a postmodern, upper-story concept—undefinable, manipulable, completely detached from physical anatomy.

To some degree, of course, this trend is driven by a reaction against the narrow gender roles inherited from the Victorian age. In traditional societies, most work was done on family farms and homesteads, allowing both fathers and mothers to participate in productive work while raising their children. But after the Industrial Revolution, work was moved from the home to factories and offices. The scope of both sexes grew narrower and more confining. Women at home no longer had access to income-producing work, while men virtually dropped out of child-rearing compared to earlier ages. Gender roles likewise grew one-sided and constricting. It is understandable that many would protest the damage caused by restrictive gender stereotypes.[50] But it's quite another thing to reject the idea of defined gender altogether.

Liberal Christians tend to follow the lead of secularists on these issues instead of offering a genuine alternative. When a female United Methodist minister underwent a sex change operation to become a male, she explained, "My body didn't match what I am."[51] Clearly she did not regard her body as *part* of "what I am." Physical identity was irrelevant. In a book titled *Omnigender,* former evangelical writer Virginia Mollenkott argues that all sexual identities are now up for grabs. A reviewer wrote, with no apparent sense of irony, "Arguments against women's ordination need wholesale revamping since we do not know for sure now what a woman is."[52]

The body has become a morally neutral piece of matter that can be manipulated for whatever purposes the self may impose on it—like stamping Lincoln's profile on a copper penny.

Today this pomosexual view is acquiring the force of law. Several states have already passed laws requiring employers to accommodate transgenders in the workplace. In 2007 California passed a law requiring schools to accommodate transgender students by allowing them to use the restroom or locker room of their preferred gender, regardless of their anatomical sex. Up to this time, the state education code had defined sex in biological terms: "'Sex' means the biological condition or quality of being a male or female human being." The new law defined sex as socially constructed gender: "Gender means sex and includes a person's gender identity and gender related appearance and behavior *whether or not stereotypically associated with the person's assigned sex at birth.*"[53]

Note the assumption that your sex is "assigned" to you, as though it were purely arbitrary instead of an anatomical fact. The law is being used to impose a secular liberal worldview that dismisses physical anatomy as insignificant, inconsequential, and completely irrelevant to gender identity.

Bodies Matter

This is a devastatingly disrespectful view of the physical body. The two-story dichotomy alienates people from their own bodies, treating physical anatomy as having no intrinsic dignity or significance.

Pomosexual alienation

GENDER
Psychological identity and sexual desire

BIOLOGY
Physical identity and anatomy

It may seem surprising to say that Western society debases the physical body, given the ridiculously high value people place on physical appearance—the obsession with cosmetics, diets, plastic surgery, botox. And yet it is true. In the two-story divide, no respect is given to the intrinsic good or *telos* (purpose) of the human body. No dignity is accorded to the unique capabilities inherent in being male or female. Interestingly, Butler herself came to recognize the problem. Critics of her book argued that by divorcing gender from anatomy, she was ignoring and even denigrating "the materiality of the body."[54] Eventually she agreed, and wrote a follow-up book titled *Bodies That Matter.*

Just so. Bodies do matter. A genuinely biblical view honors and respects our biological identity as part of who we are as whole persons. Psalm 139 says God "knits" together our bodies in the womb. Masculine or feminine identity is a gift from God to be enjoyed in gratitude.

The irony is that Christians are often accused of being prudes and Puritans who hold a negative view of the body and its functions, such as sex. During one college debate over abortion, the pro-choice students shouted at the pro-life students, "You're just anti-sex." But the truth is that Christianity has a much more respectful view of our psycho-sexual identity.

The Bible's treatment of the subject begins in Genesis 2, the account of God's creation of the two sexes. When Adam recognizes Eve as kindred to himself, he exclaims, "This at last is bone of my bones and flesh of my flesh" (Gen. 2:23 ESV). Was he referring only to the bodily correspondence between the two sexes? Clearly not. The reference to physical unity was intended to express a joyous unity on all levels—including mind, emotion, and spirit. Jesus' commentary on the same verse is that "they are no longer two but one flesh" (Matt. 19:6 ESV). Scripture offers a stunningly high view of physical union as a union of whole persons across all dimensions. The deepest level of physical intimacy is meant to express the deepest level of personal intimacy— whole persons committed to one another. When sex is torn apart from that union, we are in essence telling a lie.

Liberalism treats sex as instrumental to *extrinsic* goals, such as physical pleasure or expressing affection. That's why liberals do not object to any form of sexual relation as long as it meets those extrinsic goals—as long as involves mutual pleasure or affection. By contrast, a biblical worldview treats sex as *intrinsically* good in constituting the one-flesh relationship. Humans are an image of God not only as individuals but also in their relationship with one another—and most intensely in the intimate sexual–emotional–spiritual unity of marriage.

This explains why marriage is used throughout Scripture as a metaphor for the intimate relationship God aspires to have with his people. In the Old Testament, Israel is the unfaithful wife. In the New Testament, the church is the bride of Christ. The marital metaphor means that our sexual nature possesses a "language" that is ultimately meant to proclaim God's own transcendent love and faithfulness.

Metaphysically Lost

In dealing with such contentious moral issues, it is most effective to address the worldview level. Every social practice is the expression of fundamental assumptions about what it means to be human. When a society accepts, endorses, and approves the practice, it implicitly commits itself to the accompanying worldview—and all the more so if those practices are enshrined in law. The law functions as a teacher, educating people on what society considers to be morally acceptable. If America accepts practices such as abortion, euthanasia, homosexual "marriage," and so on, in the process it will absorb the worldview that justifies those practices—the two-story fragmentation of the human being. And the negative consequences will reach into every aspect of our communal life.

When the former pope John Paul II was a young man struggling against Marxism, he concluded that the most damaging aspect of Communism (and indeed all atheistic ideologies) is a low view of human life. "The evil of our times" consists in a denigration of human dignity, he wrote. "This evil is even much more of the *metaphysical* than of the *moral* order."[55] To use a biblical term, there is more than one way to be lost. The Bible speaks of people being morally lost without Christ. But it is also true that people are metaphysically lost when they live according to nonbiblical worldviews. When talking with secular people, Christians should make the case that the secular liberal view of human nature does not fit who they are. It does not match the real world. As a result, it is inevitably destructive, both personally and socially.

At the skating rink where my son was taking lessons, a "woman" showed up one day with long hair and heavy make-up, wearing a shiny ice-skating costume with a short skirt and colorful tights. But something was wrong with her build. She was tall with a rugged profile, broad shoulders, and knobby knees. In short, "she" was obviously male—probably in the process of a sex change operation. Christians must show compassion to people who are pressured by a pomosexual society to despise their own bodies and reject their anatomical identity. Loving God means loving those who bear his image in the world.

Christians should speak out on moral issues *not* because they feel "offended" or because their "cherished beliefs" are threatened, but because they have compassion for those who are trapped by destructive ideas. Their motivation should be that they are compelled by the love of Christ (2 Cor. 5:14).

The Church's Alienated Youth

Sadly, the love of Christ is not the motivation most churches succeed in communicating—even to their own youth. A 2007 Barna survey of churchgoers in the under-thirties age group found that about 50 percent—half!—said "they perceive Christianity to be judgmental, hypocritical, and too political."[56]

These are not critics from outside the church but young people sitting in the pews. Nor are they merely expressing the normal idealism of youth, which always finds fault with established institutions. The study found that this generation exhibits "a greater degree of criticism toward Christianity than did previous generations."

What this means is that precisely in the decades when evangelicals became more activist in the public arena, they grew more alienated from their own youth in the private arena. Nowhere is this more true than on hot-button issues such as abortion and homosexuality. During the 2008 presidential campaign, dozens of news articles came out announcing that young evangelicals were breaking from issues associated with the Religious Right to embrace issues typically associated with the Left, such as poverty, environmentalism, and social justice. ABC News asked, "Are Young Evangelicals Skewing More Liberal?"[57]

It's not that young people are no longer concerned about moral issues like abortion, explains John Green of the Pew Research Center. "If anything, some of our surveys show younger evangelicals are a little more pro-life than their elders."[58] Why, then, have they grown so disillusioned? Because they are tired of seeing moral issues turned into political footballs.

Christians who entered the public arena in recent decades typically employed standard political tactics and strategies—but they did not know how to address the underlying worldview issues. And when a political approach did not work, they simply raised the decibel level and pushed harder. To rally the troops and raise money, activist groups typically use rhetoric geared to stir up fear and outrage—until even their own children found them shrill and strident. A new book titled *American Grace: How Religion Is Reshaping Our Civic and Political Lives* reports that young Americans are dropping out of religion at an alarming rate of five to six times the historic rate (30–40 percent have no religion today versus 5–10 percent a generation ago). Many of them harbor an image of Christians as angry, unloving, and moralistic.[59]

Before the church can hope to win over the surrounding society, it must first win over its own youth. Young people do not just need rules, they need reasons. It's time for the church to regroup, rethink, and recast its strategy for social and political engagement. Christians must learn to engage the secular worldviews that drive the public debate. They must learn to articulate a worldview rationale for biblical morality. And most importantly, they must back up their message with authentic living before a watching world.

To learn how to recognize secular worldviews and their impact on our daily lives, we need to dig deeper and ask where they came from. In part 1 we have diagnosed the division of truth and the fragmentation of the human being. In part 2 we will discover that this is just the tip of the iceberg. Western thought itself has divided into two separate streams—two paths to secularism. To be effective in offering genuine alternatives to global secularism, we must map out those two paths, reading the signposts along the way to identify the major worldviews that shape our world today.

Part 2

Two Paths to Secularism

Chapter 4

"Art and science . . . become rivals
about who owns the truth."
—*Jacques Barzun*

Crash Course on Art and Worldview

When I was growing up, families did not watch *Frosty the Snowman* during the Christmas holidays. They watched opera. Seriously. All across America, families made a tradition of tuning in to *Amahl and the Night Visitors,* the first opera composed for television. Written in 1951, it was broadcast every Christmas season for years, and continues to be performed widely in churches and concert halls to this day.

The story line is widely known: The three kings on their way to Bethlehem stop at the hut of a poor, lame shepherd boy. As the kings describe the divine infant they are seeking—"On love alone he will build his kingdom"—the boy longs to send a gift of his own. When he offers his only possession, a handmade crutch, he is miraculously healed. Walking and leaping, the boy joins the three kings on their journey to Bethlehem to give thanks to the Christ child in person.

The Magic of Amahl

What is *not* widely known is that the plot reflects a miraculous healing in the composer's own life. As a child growing up in Italy, "I was lame for a while," recalls Gian-Carlo Menotti. On his right ankle, a tumor swelled up so large that he could not walk. Doctors were mystified. But his nanny Maria knew of a church not far away where, it was said, God worked miracles.

"Gian-Carlo," Maria asked him earnestly, "do you believe God can heal you?" With a child's firm conviction, the boy nodded his head, and together they made their way to the church.

4-1 Gian-Carlo Menotti
Amahl and the Night Visitors, 1951

The scandal of beauty

While there, Menotti recalls, "I was given a blessing. . . . and I suddenly walked."[1] That childhood memory was the inspiration for Amahl, a ragged little boy leaning on his crutch, in need of his own miracle.

And the three kings? They were based on the Italian custom of giving gifts not on Christmas but on January 6, the feast of Epiphany, which commemorates the visit of the wise men to the baby Jesus. As a youngster, Menotti struggled to stay awake long enough to see the three kings coming with their gifts of incense, myrrh, and gold. Though he never succeeded in catching a glimpse of them, he imagined he could hear floating from afar the solemn strains of their singing, the heavy rhythm of the camels' hooves, the jingle of the silver bridles. These were the memories he wanted to recapture in the opera. In one of the most moving scenes, the kings sing about the child they are seeking:

Have you seen a child . . . ?
His eyes are mild,
His hands are those of a king,
as King He was born.

Have you seen a child . . . ?
His eyes are sad,
His hands are those of the poor,
as poor He was born.

Incense, myrrh, and gold we bring to His side,
and the Eastern Star is our guide.[2]

I heard the opera for the first time when I was four years old. But it was not the televised version. It was a live concert, with my mother playing violin in the orchestra. I was entranced by the set, the costumes, the singing—and especially by watching my mother contribute to the creation of such beauty and magic.

Beauty Despised as a Beast

Despite the opera's popularity, not everyone was so entranced. Menotti's compositions proved to be controversial—not because they were avant-garde but precisely because they were so beautiful. The leading classical composers of the twentieth century were producing atonal music that was highly discordant and jarring to the ear—pieces the public did not like and could not understand. Anyone who composed music that people actually enjoyed was accused by fellow musicians of selling out for the sake of money. Music critic Henry Pleasants wrote at the time that the classical composer "dare not be popular, for popular music is assumed to be synonymous with light or easy music, and therefore inferior." Mentioning Menotti as an example, Pleasants wrote: "Those who have courted the public have enjoyed some measure of popular success but little esteem in the profession. . . . They are not thought of as significant contributors to musical history."[3] The composer who aspired to be taken seriously as a cutting-edge artist felt obliged to shock, repel, and scandalize.

Menotti knew what the critics were saying, and he was puzzled by it. Among critics, he commented, "to say of a piece that it is harsh, dry, acid, and unrelenting is to praise it. While to call it sweet and graceful is to damn it." Nevertheless, he said, "I have dared to do away completely with fashionable dissonance, and . . . to rediscover the nobility of gracefulness and the pleasure of sweetness."[4]

It is safe to say that Menotti's puzzlement is shared by the public. Why has dissonance become so fashionable? Why is art praised primarily when it is harsh and offensive? Why have many artists rejected the very concept of beauty? The problem comes down to the personal level when parents can no longer allow their children to watch television or listen to the latest music CD without monitoring for bad language and objectionable content.

If the arts reflect a culture's worldview, what does all this say about today's secular worldview? Artists are society's barometers, sensitive to new ideas as they percolate through the cultural atmosphere. They are also gifted at using stories and images to flesh out those ideas. Learning to interpret the arts can be a powerful strategy for understanding the monolithic secularism that is spreading around the globe today.

In part 1 we diagnosed the divided concept of truth and its corollary, the divided concept of the human being. But ideas are far easier to understand if we go up for a bird's eye view to see where they came from. In part 2 we will discover that Western thought itself has split into two streams. We might think of them as two divergent paths to secularism, running side by side through modern history. We will explore those paths not only in words but also in images and stories, through the arts and literature. The rich texture of this tale will bring ideas alive, equipping you to engage in discussion with real people seeking livable answers in a world that is falling apart.

To start off, we need a crash course in how to detect worldview themes in the arts. Then we will lay out an aerial map of the two paths to secularism. This will prepare you to recognize the most significant turns in the road as we descend to details in the chapters that follow.

Artists as Thinkers

At the outset we need to debunk the stereotype that art has nothing to do with ideas or worldviews. Drama critic Eric Bentley once published a book called *The Playwright as Thinker* that proved highly successful—once people got over the shock of the title. The initial response by reviewers was to protest: That can't be right. "How can playwrights be thinkers, when everyone knows that they're *feelers?* They deal in emotions, not ideas—don't they?"[5]

The truth is that artists interact deeply with the thought of their day, translating worldviews into stories and images. Fortunately, scholars are beginning to recognize this fact. Meyer Schapiro led the way in a ground-breaking essay in the 1950s noting that "unsuspected levels of meaning" were uncovered when critics began "to explain styles as an artistic expression of a world view." In the 1960s Finley Eversole wrote that every culture has its own "world-view," and that "the artist gives us concrete images of this world-view." Dutch art historian Hans Rookmaaker said, "Art tries, literally, to picture the things which philosophy tries to put into carefully thought-out words." The contemporary architect David Gobel says that in art "a worldview is made tangible."[6]

At a 2006 conference of the International Arts Movement, I had the honor of sharing a podium with the poet Dana Gioia, who at the time was chairman of the National Endowment for the Arts. "All art is a language—a language of color, sound, movement, or words," Gioia said. "When we immerse ourselves in a work of art, *we enter into the artist's worldview.* It can be an expansive and glorious worldview, or it can be cramped, dehumanizing worldview."[7]

Of course, none of these scholars is saying that a work of art can be reduced to the cognitive level alone. Aesthetic elements—style, color, texture, tone, plot, characterization—are the artist's essential tools and have an impact all their own. The composer Gustav Mahler once said, "If I could condense my experience into words, I certainly would not compose music about it." Yet ordinary people are rarely equipped to evaluate the technical qualities of a work of art. In the words of John Walford of Wheaton College, non-artists are interested mostly in the way art connects with "larger human issues and concerns."[8] An artist creates an imaginary world and then invites us to enter that world, to experience what life looks and feels like from a particular perspective. The audience does care so much about the technical skills used to accomplish the trick. Their central concern is the conception of the world that the artist is fleshing out.

Moreover, as we will discover, even aesthetic elements grow ultimately out of worldviews. This can be a difficult concept to grasp. In popular music, for example, most people readily recognize that the *lyrics* express the songwriter's perspective and experience. But they tend to assume that the musical *style* is neutral. That is a mistake. Artistic styles develop originally as vehicles for expressing particular worldviews. As painter Louis Finkelstein says, "The sense of all stylistic change is that the underlying view of the world changes."[9]

What this means is that we can "read" the history of ideas through the history of changing artistic styles. This opens up a uniquely engaging means of interpreting worldviews—one that involves the whole person: mind and imagination, intellect and emotion.

New Way to "Read" Art

There are many good books that discuss Christian aesthetics or a biblical justification for the arts. That is not my purpose here. The question I am asking is not whether these art works are beautiful or well executed, but how they give pictorial expression to a worldview. In a book review, philosopher Jean-Paul Sartre once commented that he enjoyed the novel, but disagreed with the novelist's worldview. In his words, "I like his art, but I do not believe in his metaphysics."[10] In the following pages, you may or may not like the art. The goal, however, is to determine whether you agree with the artists' worldview.

To quote painter Anthony Toney, "Different approaches in painting or art generally are manifestations of different views of reality." For a brief primer on how to detect those different views of reality, let's take a walk through a virtual art museum.

The Geometric Greeks

Beginning with the ancient Greeks, a major thread in the fabric of Western thought has been the conviction that ultimate truth is found in mathematics and geometry. At the time, this was a completely novel idea. Earlier civilizations, like the Egyptians and Babylonians, had treated geometry as a grab bag of practical tools for calculation—rules of thumb discovered by trial and error, useful for carpenters and surveyors. It must have been tremendously exciting when the Greek philosophers first discovered that geometric laws were not merely practical tools but demonstrable truths that could be stated in formulas and justified by logical, deductive proofs. If you were bored in high school geometry, it's probably because no one explained what a novel breakthrough this kind of rigorous reasoning was. The Greeks were so awed by it that many venerated geometry as *the* gateway to logically certain knowledge.

Think, for example, of Pythagoras whose name is familiar because of the theorem named after him. He discovered that even musical harmonies depend on geometric proportions. Two tones are an octave apart when the higher tone has a frequency exactly twice as fast as the frequency of the lower tone—a ratio of 2 to 1. The two sound waves fit together so closely that the pitches sound extremely consonant. In fact, we consider them essentially the same note: An octave above the note C is likewise called C. A ratio of 2 to 3 produces a harmonic fifth, which creates a clear, open tone. A ratio of 3 to 4 produces a harmonic fourth. Pythagoras concluded that number was the divine force that holds the cosmos in a perfectly harmonious order. He even founded a mystery religion teaching that spiritual illumination could be achieved through the study of music and mathematics. Having once traveled to Persia, Pythagoras would don a Persian robe and turban to make dramatic appearances on a curtained stage, where he would astonish the public with demonstrations of geometric proofs.

Pythagoras influenced Plato, who believed that geometry was the means to draw the mind up to the realm of eternal truths. Over the gate to his school was carved the inscription, "Let none ignorant of geometry enter here." He even thought the divine mind had nothing better to do than to eternally contemplate geometry: "God always geometrizes."

CLASSICAL GREECE

4-2 Apollo Belvedere   4-3 Venus de Milo

Art of mathematical ideals

These ideas spilled over into art as well. If beauty reflected the underlying order of the cosmos, then beauty itself must be a matter of mathematics. Sculptors worked out precise mathematical rules governing the ideal proportion of fingers to hand, hand to arm, thigh to leg, head to body, and so on. In the fifth century BC, the sculptor Polykleitos said that "Apollo was beautiful because his body conformed to certain laws of proportion and so partook of the divine beauty of mathematics."[11] For the Greeks, explains Walford, "the proportions of the human body and the mathematical structure of the universe were related."[12]

The principle illustrated here is that "all art is founded on faith," says art historian Kenneth Clark. "The Greek faith in harmonious numbers found expression in their painting and sculpture."[13] It gave rise to a style marked by clarity, restraint, balance, and mathematical proportion.

No living human body is as perfectly proportioned as a Greek statue. That's because these statues do not represent particular individuals but universal ideals or types. Philosophers of the classical age gave priority to the ideal over the real, the universal over the individual. They did not assign any dignity or value to the features that make each person unique. What mattered were the shared features that made up universal human nature. Individuality was regarded as nothing more than an aberration, an irregularity, a departure from the ideal.[14] Consciously or not, classical *art* was reflecting classical *philosophy*.

Byzantine Icons

Jump now to the Byzantine era, a period that began about AD 330 when Constantine moved the capital of the Roman Empire to Byzantium. (He changed its name to Constantinople.) In Byzantine icons, the figures tend to be formal, highly stylized, and two-dimensional. Turn the page and you will see that the effect is almost like a piece of Christmas wrapping paper stuck to the wall. What was this style saying? Did Byzantine painters really think the air was gold? What were they communicating through this style?

The main philosophical influence on Byzantine culture was neo-Platonism, which mixed Greek thought with Eastern mysticism. The result was a sharp dualism that regarded the material world as the realm of death, decay, evil, and corruption. The path to wisdom was to withdraw from the physical world known by the senses, in order to contemplate the realm of ideals or universals known by the inner eye of reason. The ultimate goal of life was to escape from the prison house of the physical body and ascend to the spiritual realm.

Elements of neo-Platonic dualism filtered into the thinking of Christian theologians such as Augustine, Origen, Boethius, and the Cappadocian fathers. We see its impact, for example, in the monastic movement. Because the material world was regarded as the source of evil and corruption, the monk withdrew into the monastery to contemplate spiritual ideals. Because nature was thought to have little value, the monk did not own property. Because the physical body was a source of sin, the monk suppressed bodily desires through ascetic practices—simple food, coarse clothing, the rejection of sex and marriage. Christians began to divide the created world into two spheres, sacred versus secular. They recast morality in terms of negative rules, as though holiness could be achieved simply by avoiding certain parts of creation. They lost the biblical teaching that all of created reality comes from God's hand and is intrinsically good.

Around the fifth century we see the impact of neo-Platonism on the arts, as artists lost interest in portraying the ordinary world. In Byzantine icons, the emphasis was not on Jesus' humanity but on his divinity. He was typically portrayed as the all-powerful Judge and Ruler of the universe. And Mary was never a poor peasant girl from Galilee but the Mother of God who (according to Catholic and Orthodox theology) was already exalted on high.

BYZANTINE

4-4 Mosaic of Jesus Christ
Hagia Sofia Church, Istanbul, Turkey, ca. 12th c.

4-5 Mosaic of Virgin Mary and Jesus Christ
Hagia Sofia Church, Istanbul, Turkey, ca. 12th c.

Neo-Platonic Christianity

Note that the figures are not embedded in any narrative setting. There is no backdrop of trees or cityscapes. Instead the gold background was meant to draw the mind up to eternal truths (which, like gold, neither rust nor decay). The reds are rich scarlet and the blues are clear sapphire, almost as though they too were precious jewels. The solemn splendor tells the spectator that something sacred or miraculous is being portrayed. Typically the subject makes eye contact with the viewer in order to create a sense of personal confrontation—an exhortation to stop and heed the sacred message. The icon was a visual sermon.[15]

Byzantine artists were not striving to express personal feelings. On the contrary, they followed strict rules and formulas laid down precisely to *eliminate* any personal perspective. Icons were revered as "windows" leading the worshipper to a transcendent spiritual realm.

First Manger Scene

The thirteenth century was the century of the friars—the Franciscans and Dominicans. These were monks who left the monasteries to teach, preach, and practice charity out in the world. And the reason they cared so much about the world was that they developed a more biblical view of it.

The Dominicans were founded around 1226, about the time Aristotle's philosophy was rediscovered. They labored to adapt it to Christian theology. Unlike Pythagoras and Plato, Aristotle was not interested in geometry but in biology. He taught that we gain access to universal truths not by turning away from the natural world to a realm of abstract ideals, but by observing natural objects perceived through the senses. He argued that natural processes are *good* because they are the means by which things attain their true nature—their *telos*. An acorn becomes an oak. An egg becomes an eagle. Under Aristotle's influence, Dominicans such as Thomas Aquinas began to argue that creation is good because it is the handiwork of a good Creator.[16]

The Franciscans were founded at around the same time by Francis of Assisi. Francis is credited with creating the first Nativity scene, complete with a live baby in a manger surrounded by oxen and donkeys. Up to this time Easter, not Christmas, had been celebrated as the pre-eminent Christian holiday. What motivated Francis to shift the focus to Jesus' birth? A new interest in Christ's humanity. Meditation on the incarnation had led theologians to insist that we do not have to withdraw from nature in order to contemplate God. For God himself took on a physical body in the person of Jesus Christ. He made himself known in and through the created world. As Jesus said, "Anyone who has seen me has seen the Father" (John 14:9). And because God himself became flesh, physical life could not be intrinsically bad or evil. We do not need to reject the material world in order to be spiritually minded.

The Greek preference for the universal began to be balanced by an appreciation of the concrete individual. For God himself—the ultimate universal—had become a unique individual. Individuality was no longer merely an arbitrary aberration from the universal ideal. It had worth and dignity in its own right.[17]

These theological trends had enormous impact on the arts. "The focus on Christ's humanity altered the course of art," writes one historian. "Artists strove to make the figures they painted as real as possible and the depicted surroundings as natural as they could."[18] Fra Angelico was a Dominican, and Giotto was influenced by the Franciscans. Comparing their paintings to Byzantine icons, what differences do you detect? The figures are no longer flat and formal. They possess genuine weight, bulk, and volume. They stand in real, three-dimensional space, within a physical setting. Both paintings have a narrative line;

MIDDLE AGES

4-6 Fra Angelica
Annunciation, 1438

4-7 Giotto
Lamentation, 1305

Nature as God's good creation

they tell a story or recount an event. In Giotto's *Lamentation* the figures express their sorrow through intense facial expressions and dramatic hand gestures. Even the angels grimace in grief. The emotional drama is enhanced by the diagonal line of the stone wall pitching down toward Jesus' head, symbolizing the theme of descent (cf. Phil. 2:5–8).

"Giotto's worldview is fundamentally different" from that of the Byzantines, explains one scholar. Giotto has discarded the "dualistic, ascetic theology" inspired by neo-Platonism, and has replaced it with "an incarnational theology." The physical world is no longer a prison to be escaped from. Instead it is the locus for "the meeting of the human and the divine, the physical and the spiritual, the temporal and the eternal."[19]

To enhance the incarnational theme, artists began to include elaborate and realistic details that matched the architectural features of the surrounding room or courtyard. This explains Fra Angelico's pillars and arches. The goal was to create the optical illusion that the painting was part of the room—as though we could actually walk over and meet the biblical characters and witness the events. The use of perspective thus underscored the message that these events happened in *our* world—that the spiritual realm has entered deeply into ordinary life.

The most famous example is Leonardo da Vinci's *Last Supper,* which was ingeniously devised to appear as an extension of the dining hall where it was originally hung. The monk who sat at the table some five centuries ago, breaking bread and sipping wine, saw the solid wall give way and felt personally swept up into that dramatic moment of confrontation when the disciples asked, "Is it I, Lord?" And as Bach says in his *St. Matthew's Passion,* for each person the answer must be, Yes, it *is* I and my sins that put Jesus on the cross. It is I who should have suffered what he is about to suffer out of love for me.[20] The painting thus conveyed profound spiritual truths, not through words but through visual images.

You Shall Be as Gods

To mention Leonardo is to bridge into the next historical period. During the Renaissance, the Platonic Academy in Florence revived neo-Platonism. Philosophers such as Marsilio Ficino regarded it as a "perennial" wisdom given by God to the Gentiles, parallel to the Old Testament given to the Hebrews. As a result, they were convinced that they could harmonize this perennial wisdom with Christianity. What they really did was transform it into Renaissance humanism.

Recall that for neo-Platonism, the source of evil and suffering was dualism. The spirit was trapped within matter (the body), which was subject to death and corruption. Ficino's philosophy thus began with the question: How can we overcome dualism? His answer was that humans must *rule over* matter. Created in the image of God, the human being must become a "terrestrial god." He is "god of the animals" because he governs them; he is "god of all materials" because he uses them to manufacture the things he needs. Instead of calling for a monastic retreat *from* the world, Renaissance humanism called for mastery *of* the world. The old-age dichotomy of spirit and matter would be overcome as spirit conquers matter. In this way, writes one historian, Renaissance thinkers hoped to overcome "the impediments and limitations resulting from man's dualistic nature."[21]

RENAISSANCE

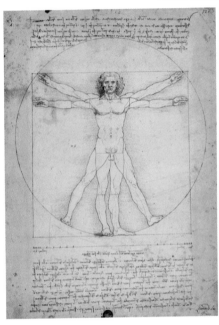

4-8 Leonardo da Vinci
Vitruvian Man, 1487

4-9 Michelangelo Buonarroti
Isaiah, the Sistine Chapel, 1509

Human mastery of nature

This explains the ideal of the Renaissance Man, the individual who masters a wide range of fields in both the arts and sciences. And the supreme instance was Leonardo da Vinci—scientist, inventor, mathematician, engineer, and above all, artist. For Leonardo, the painter was a "god" capable of creating images at will. His *Vitruvian Man* (named after a Roman architect who calculated the body's ideal proportions) expresses the neo-Platonic idea that the human being is a microcosm uniting the two realms of spirit and matter. "In the iconography of the day," explains a historian, "the square was generally taken as symbolic of the earth while the circle was representative of the eternity of heaven." In Leonardo's image, then, the ideal human is "both of this earth and heaven . . . the unifier of the universe."[22]

Did this polymath fulfill the Renaissance goal then of overcoming "man's dualistic nature"? Sadly no, says philosopher Giovanni Gentile. As an engineer and mathematician, Leonardo anticipated the mechanistic worldview that arose soon afterward in the scientific revolution—a vision of nature "ordered in a closed and fixed system, necessary and mechanically invariable." Yet as an artist, Leonardo never stopped seeking to capture the ideal or the universal. In a poignant passage, Gentile speaks of "the anguish and the innermost tragedy of this universal man, divided between his irreconcilable worlds."[23] Standing at the threshold of modernity, Leonardo is a symbol of the modern mind and its tragic inability to find a unified truth.

The World as Book

By contrast, the Reformation did have the resources to overcome dualism and recover a unified worldview. When Martin Luther left the Catholic Church, he rejected the dualism of the monastic mindset. He argued that a priest or nun is not the least bit superior to a merchant, farmer, miller, or homemaker. The Protestant doctrine of vocation insisted that any honest work can be a calling from God, a way to fulfill the cultural mandate (the Genesis command to cultivate the earth). Reformation-inspired artwork typically showed ordinary people plying their trade. The paintings shine with a quiet intensity to convey the biblical concept that ordinary life is infused with spiritual dignity and significance.[24]

The Reformation inspired a fresh interest in portraying nature as well. Ever since the church fathers, theologians had spoken of "two books" of revelation—the book of God's Word (Scripture) and the book of God's world (creation). Paraphrasing the first chapter of Romans, the Netherlands Reformed Confession says, "The world is before our eyes like a beautiful book, in which all created things, great and small, are like letters, which give us the invisible things of God to behold." The Dutch landscape painters, like Jacob van Ruisdael, sought to portray nature as "God's second book of revelation"[25]

BAROQUE (PROTESTANT)

4-10 Jan Vermeer
Kitchen Maid, 1658

4-11 Jacob van Ruisdael
Mill at Wijk, 1670

The sanctity of ordinary life and work

4-12 Rembrandt van Rijn
The Denial of St. Peter, 1660

A better image of God

Finally, the Reformers argued that a living human person is a better image of God than the carvings of wood or stone typical of Catholic churches. This explains why artists like Rembrandt produced so many studies of human character. In his exquisite portrayal of Peter, we can "read" the conflicting fears that cross his face as the servant girl asks if he is one of Jesus' disciples. Rembrandt is highlighting the world-shaping significance of each individual's spiritual struggles and choices. In the background on the right, Jesus looks back at Peter with an expression that is both anguished and gentle, hinting at future forgiveness and restoration. In Peter's darkest moment of temptation and betrayal, Rembrandt includes a foreshadowing of redemption.

Matter Is Spiritual

The Catholic Church had its own Reformation (sometimes called the Counter-Reformation). One regrettable result of the Protestant Reformation was a surge in iconoclasm—the smashing of statues and images. This had nothing to do with opposition to art *per se,* but had everything to do with concerns over theology. In the visual arts, the Reformers charged that imagery had slid over into idolatry, just as the brass serpent in ancient Israel had become an idol (2 Kings 18:4). In the verbal arts, they charged that allegorical interpretations of Scripture made use of excessive symbolism and metaphor, obscuring the core gospel message. In the end, they rejected the entire panoply of medieval devotional practices: relics, stained glass, confessions, indulgences, pilgrimages, processions, holy water, and the mass itself. These rituals struck them as akin to magic, as though spiritual powers inhered in material objects where they could be controlled and manipulated by human beings.

Many Reformers—especially the Calvinists—sought an austere, uncluttered form of worship focused on the Word instead of image or ritual. To emphasize God's transcendence, they whitewashed over religious paintings on church walls, leaving them plain and unadorned. Instead of cultivating elegance and eloquence in their sermons, they preferred plain speech. The English

Reformer Thomas Cranmer said he aspired to make his words "so plain, that the least child . . . may understand them."[26]

The challenge facing Catholic theologians, then, was to defend the use of images. Like the iconoclasts, their arguments had nothing to do with art *per se*. They reached back to earlier debates over images that had raged in the seventh and ninth centuries. (Yes, the same debate had erupted in the church before.) And they revived the same defense that had been successful then—the doctrine of the incarnation. Images were acceptable, they argued, because Christ "is the image of the invisible God" (Col. 1:15). The Word had become flesh. Therefore the material world has the dignity of being an avenue of divine presence. As one historian explains, "God Himself through Christ had taken on human form and thus revealed the earthly world to be capable of bearing the Divine." With this justification, "the Christian use of images sought to lift the visible and earthly to the dignity of reflecting the invisible or eternal."[27]

Thus Catholic art of the Baroque era sought to convey the idea that God's presence and power is immanent in and through the material world. Notice below how this conviction is expressed even in the style itself. Baroque painters like Peter Paul Rubens are known for their solid, massy, tangible

BAROQUE (CATHOLIC)

4-13 Michelangelo Carravagio
The Deposition, 1604

4-14 Peter Paul Rubens
The Raising of the Cross, 1611

The world reveals the "weight" (kabod) of glory

figures. When we think of traditional art museums, we often have a mental image of heavy, fleshy nudes, very different from contemporary ideals of feminine beauty. We might call that the Rubens look. What was he saying with this style? A devout Catholic, he was expressing the biblical concept that creation carries the weight of spiritual glory. The Hebrew word for *glory* is *kabod,* which literally means weight or substance (as when we say someone has a weighty presence). Thus the style itself was saying that the material world has the dignity of being the dwelling place of God.

Enlightened Control

The next stop in our virtual museum is the Enlightenment. Most people remember terms like *Enlightenment* from high school history courses. Launched by the rise of modern science, its

ENLIGHTENMENT

4-15 Thomas Gainsborough,
Mr. and Mrs. Andrews, 1750

4-16 Jean-Antoine Watteau
Assembly in a Park, 1720

Nature as property

leading metaphor was nature as a great machine. The hope was that by learning the laws by which the machine operates, humans would be able to control it.

The art of the Enlightenment period expresses an attitude of confidence in human dominion over nature. Watteau treats nature as a pleasure park for the amusement of fashionable members of high society (see facing page). Gainsborough treats nature as property. Notice that the hay field has been plowed in neat, parallel rows, which indicates the use of the newly invented seed drill—a sign that the young couple is wealthy and anxious to be scientific and up-to-date. In the background, the sheep are securely fenced in; the enclosure of livestock was likewise an innovation of the time. The man holds his hunting rifle at a casual angle in the crook of his arm. He knows he can get *what* he wants from nature *when* he wants it. Husband and wife proudly position themselves angled at the side to showcase their property. They have even placed a bench outdoors as though to turn all of nature into their own backyard. Nature has been domesticated. The tone of these paintings is one of confidence, pride, even complacency.[28]

Romantic Reaction

There was a dark side, however, to the Enlightenment worldview. For if nature was a machine running by natural laws, the implication was determinism—the doctrine that everything is controlled by the implacable laws of nature. There is no freedom, no creativity, no moral responsibility. Nature seemed cold and dead. The Romantics proposed to replace the mechanistic metaphor with an organic metaphor—nature as alive, growing, free, imbued with spiritual force or life.

ROMANTICISM

4-17 John Kensett
Lake George, 1869

4-18 Sanford Robinson Gifford,
October in the Catskills, 1880

Quasi-pantheistic view of nature

They revived medieval myths of fairies, sprites, and elves. The term *Romanticism* itself reflects an older usage referring to a quest or adventure, like the romance of King Arthur.

Many Romantics replaced orthodox Christianity with a quasi-pantheistic philosophy, in which God was not the transcendent Creator of nature but a spiritual presence immanent within nature. Ralph Waldo Emerson spoke of God as the Oversoul: "the soul of the whole . . . the eternal ONE."[29] This was expressed artistically by a pervasive glow that seems to emanate almost from within nature itself. (Light has traditionally been used as a symbol of divine presence.) The paintings on the previous page are from a movement called luminism, a product of transcendentalism, which was an American form of Romanticism. In luminism, explains Gene Edward Veith, "individual details are often effaced as everything blends into a harmonious unity"— dissolving into the universal One, the All.[30]

4-19 Jasper Francis Cropsey
Autumn on the Hudson River, 1860

A transcendent Creator

For contrast, consider the Hudson River School painters. Like the other Romantics, they looked to nature as a source of religious experience. However, they tended to retain a more orthodox conception of divine transcendence. (Jasper Cropsey was a member of the Dutch Reformed Church.) In their paintings, details are clear and objective. Sunlight often comes from above, "shining down from a heavenly source," with rays of light slashing down through the landscape. It was a visual means of emphasizing that God is not an immanent spirit *within* nature but the transcendent Creator *of* nature.[31]

Two Paths to Secularism

What do we learn from this quick sampling of art works—this hop-skip-and-jump through art history? Clearly, art is never just a copy of nature. Artists always select, arrange, and order their materials to offer an interpretation or perspective. This is not to say that a work of art can be reduced to a verbal summary. Art communicates on many levels. Many of the artist's deepest convictions may not even be conscious. Nevertheless, artists do not mechanically record what they see. They also communicate what they believe on the deepest level to be *true*.

As we move forward into the modern age, then, we will find that the crack-up of truth diagnosed in earlier chapters had a deep impact on the arts. The effect was put in a nutshell by cultural critic Martha Bayles in *Hole in Our Soul: The Loss of Beauty and Meaning in American Popular Music*. The modern age has been a period of "intense self-consciousness about the meaning and purpose of art," she writes. And it all started when art "began having radical doubts about its relationship with the truth."[32]

That sentence is *the* hermeneutical key for understanding what happened to art in the modern age: It became disconnected from the concept of truth.

How did that happen? When historians say "modern," they generally mean the period beginning with the Enlightenment. Many thinkers were so impressed by the scientific revolution that they began to regard science as the sole source of truth. Whatever could not be known by the scientific method was not real. Science was no longer merely one means for investigating the world. It was elevated into an exclusivist worldview—*scientism* or *positivism*.

As we just saw, the Enlightenment provoked a reaction in the Romantic movement—and the two have been at loggerheads ever since. To use the language of the fact/value split, Enlightenment thinkers laid claim to the realm of empirical *facts*. Many of them embraced philosophical naturalism or materialism, the doctrine that fundamental reality consists of matter. By contrast, the Romantics wanted to protect the realm of *values*. They proposed philosophical idealism, the doctrine that fundamental reality consists of mind or spirit. The term *idealism* is used not in the ordinary sense of having high ideals but in the philosophic sense that the ultimate causal reality is not material but mental—the realm of *ideas*.

Borrowing a metaphor from novelist Walker Percy, we could say that every philosophy proposes some ultimate category and seeks to explain all of reality in terms of that one category—a little like trying to stuff the entire universe into a single box. Materialism stuffs everything into the "box of things," while idealism puts everything into "the mind box."[33]

The division in western thought

ROMANTICISM
Box of mind (Idealism)

ENLIGHTENMENT
Box of things (Materialism)

Let's run through a quick inventory of what is contained in each box, and how they developed historically. Then we will describe the impact the two boxes had on the arts. This gives a bird's eye view of the terrain we will cover in greater detail through the rest of part 2.

Exorcising the Ghost from the Machine

The pivotal thinker in the division of truth was the eighteenth-century philosopher Immanuel Kant. On one hand, his philosophy offered support for the Enlightenment. He decreed that human reason is not capable of knowing anything beyond the natural world investigated by empirical science—the "box of things." Our mental constitution is simply not equipped, he said, to know anything about the realm of religion, morality, or metaphysics.

This was a momentous turning point. By cutting off every form of knowledge except science, Kant was dismissing virtually the entire history of Western thought. In the ancient world, it would never have occurred to Plato or Aristotle that our reasoning powers were incapable of drawing out any truths beyond the realm of nature. In the Middle Ages, vast monuments to rational inquiry were constructed, such as Thomas Aquinas' *Summa Theologica,* using reason to investigate supernatural truths. As a result, when Kant limited knowledge to empirical phenomena, he was taking a radical step. He practically sneered at anyone who "believes himself capable of soaring so far above all possible experience on the wings of *mere ideas.*"[34]

Kant's philosophy overlapped neatly with the by-then familiar Cartesian dualism that had split the human being into a "ghost in the machine." Because the "ghost" could not be observed empirically, it soon proved easy to exorcise. Those inclined to materialism or naturalism reduced humans to nothing but complex physical mechanisms within a closed nexus of cause and effect. "Let us conclude boldly then," said la Mettrie in 1749, "that man is a machine." That "bold" conclusion meant there was no such thing as a mind distinct from the physical brain. Beliefs, feelings, desires, goals, and intentions were ultimately only products of the physical mechanisms of the nervous system—the activation of neurons. Humans were said to be essentially robots or automatons.

This view is still very much with us today. A columnist for the scientific journal *Nature* recently announced that genetics and neuroscience "are verging on drawing the ultimate materialist picture of human nature"—a picture in which humans are "all machine and no ghost." And if there is no ghost, then freedom is an illusion. Even consciousness is unreal. "Humans think they are free, conscious beings," writes philosopher John Gray, but "they are deluded animals." Even the sense of being a unique individual self is a "chimera." Some neuroscientists, like Steven Pinker of MIT, even suggest that humans are essentially zombies, akin to the movie monster "who acts just like you or me but in whom there is no self actually feeling anything."[35]

In ordinary life, of course, it is impossible to function without believing that we are self-aware, choosing beings—that we do something because we *want* to or because we *think* it's the best course. What cognitive scientists are saying is that inner states such as *wanting* or *thinking* do not actually exist. They are illusions. Natural selection has programmed humans to accept such illusions because life is much easier if we can explain people's behavior in terms of their thoughts and choices. As Woolfson writes, evolution has endowed us with "genes that make us believe in concepts like the soul," but those concepts are illusory. "One day such irrational tendencies might be removed by adjusting the relevant brain circuitry." In the meantime, "We will have to resign ourselves to the unpalatable fact that we are nothing more than machines."[36]

The fatal flaw in this theory is that it undercuts itself. If consciousness is an illusion, then who is conscious of that fact? And why should we trust the thinking of scientific reductionists who tell us there is no such thing as thinking? More significantly, if the real world forces "illusions" upon us such as the concept of consciousness, then perhaps they are not illusions after all. The starting point of any *worldview* should be the ideas that are indispensable for functioning in the real *world*.

Despite these flaws, a radical form of reductionism continues to grow in popularity. The book *What We Believe but Cannot Prove* features one hundred scientists and philosophers, hardly any of whom accepts the reality of consciousness or a unified self.[37]

The Romantics Revolt

Obviously this one-sided picture of the person radically undermines human dignity and significance. When it was first proposed, the Romantics were appalled. For them, the "ghost" in the machine was the real hero of the cosmic drama, and they were determined to move it to center stage. Freedom and consciousness were precisely the things they cared most about.

Paradoxical as it may seem, like their Enlightenment rivals, the Romantics turned to Kant's philosophy for support. According to Kant, reason proves things by tracing them back to the laws of nature—which means it cannot prove things like God, morality, and freedom because they are not reducible to natural forces. By same token, however, reason cannot *disprove* those things either. Kant concluded that humans belong to "two worlds." On one hand, they are part of *nature*, by which he meant the deterministic, mechanistic system known by science. On the other hand, they also operate in the world of *freedom* as free agents who make moral choices.

These two worlds are clearly contradictory. Freedom is impossible in a materialist world in which all actions are determined by natural forces. Kant never did find a way to resolve this contradiction. Thus his philosophy never coheres into a unified whole. "Kant left a gaping abyss between his conception of knowledge and his theory of morals," writes philosopher Robert Solomon, "and so left the human mind as if cleft in two."[38] Philosophers describe this gaping abyss as Kant's nature/freedom dichotomy. In the lower story, humans are part of the Newtonian world machine. In the upper story, they are autonomous selves.

When a worldview contains an outright contradiction, one side inevitably comes to dominate. For Kant, the winner was the world of *nature*. After all, it could be tested and verified by empirical science. By contrast, the world of *freedom* could be defended only on the grounds of moral necessity. Humans are compelled to act *as if* they were free, because moral responsibility makes no sense unless we can make genuine choices. They are compelled to act *as if* there were a God, because a universal moral law requires a transcendent lawgiver. And they are compelled to act *as if* there were an afterlife, when cosmic justice will be established, because otherwise moral laws have no ultimate significance.

For Kant, we cannot actually know that any of these things exist. We can only believe they do because they function as incentives for morality. In his terminology, metaphysical concepts are not *constitutive*, telling us what exists in the world. They are only *regulative*, functioning as ideals to regulate our behavior. Essentially Kant agreed with David Hume (chapter 2) that morality and theology are cognitively meaningless—that is, they have no meaning in regard to what really exists. Nevertheless he hoped to salvage them by insisting that they are necessary for morality. In his words, they are "*impossible* to know" but "*morally necessary* to suppose."[39]

Kant's dualism

FREEDOM
Unknowable ideals

NATURE
Knowable facts

Even in Kant's own lifetime, however, critics accused him of turning the upper story into nothing but a collection of useful fictions. As one philosopher writes, Kant was "forced into the embarrassing position of postulating the existence of something of which, by definition, we can know nothing at all."[40]

In practice, when conflicts arise, what is regarded as *knowable* will trump what is *unknowable* every time. To give a concrete example of the impact of Kant's dichotomy, any time the claims of scientific materialism contradicted Scripture, theologians were told that it was their interpretation of Scripture that must adapt and adjust, never the other way around. They were even told that it was illegitimate for Christianity to make statements about the natural world at all. Christianity was permitted to tell Sunday school stories as object lessons to inspire morality, but it was not allowed to claim that those stories were true. This explains the rise of theological liberalism. "Under Kant's influence," writes Stanley Hauerwas, "Christian theologians simply left the natural world to science," and began to treat theology as little more than window dressing for morality.[41]

At the time of the Romantics, however, the fact that Kant countenanced an upper story at all seemed to provide a haven for precisely those essential human qualities that were under attack by materialism—consciousness, creativity, spirituality, love, altruism, and moral freedom. As a result, the Kantian dualism exerted enormous influence. We see it expressed, for example, in these words by poet W. H. Auden: "As a biological organism Man is a natural creature subject to the necessities [determinism] of nature; as a being with consciousness and will, he is at the same time a historical person with the freedom of the spirit."[42] For the Romantics, the two-story division was a strategy for protecting the freedom of the spirit.

The Sovereign Self

Kant gave the Romantics yet another gift. He proposed that even the lower story—the world of nature—is ultimately a creation of the human mind. The raw materials of knowledge are sense impressions, he said, which flood in through our eyes and ears in a jumbled chaos. How are these perceptions organized into a coherent, ordered conception of the universe? By the action of the human mind. It is the mind that supplies the necessary ordering principles: before and after, cause and effect, space and time, number, and so on. The world appears to be lawful and ordered only because the human mind *creates* that order, like pressing clay into a mold.

Instead of teaching that we live in a world structured by God, Kant proposed that we live in a world structured by human consciousness. In his words, "Mind is the law-giver to nature." This is philosophical idealism—the box of mind.

For the Romantics, it was a short step from there to saying that there must also be a Transcendental Mind—not only a ghost in the machine of the human *body* but also a ghost in the machine of the *world*, a World Spirit or Absolute Mind. The individual ego was somehow part of a Transcendental Ego. The material universe itself was the emanation of a mental or spiritual substance.

After the Romantic era, however, the idea of the Absolute eventually collapsed under the weight of sheer mystical vagueness. Philosophical idealism gave way to existentialism, in which the Transcendental Ego disappeared and all that was left was the individual ego, alone in a non-personal universe. In existentialism, humans could no longer look to any transcendent reality to confirm their deepest longings for meaning and significance. The solitary self was alienated in a mechanistic universe that was coldly indifferent or outright hostile to human aspirations. All humans had left was Kant's realm of *as if*—they must try to live *as if* their moral choices mattered, *as if* life had meaning.

In our own day, existentialism has given way to postmodernism, in which the self is immersed in the constant flux of evolution. Nothing is stable; all is open to re-interpretation. (Recall the discussion of postmodern gender in chapter 3.) Thus the lasting legacy of the upper-story stream of philosophy is a conviction that the self is the creator of its own universe. The postmodern self surveys the world and is free to impose upon it whatever mental or moral construction it chooses.[43]

Zen and the Crack-Up of Philosophy

What do we learn from this highly telescoped view of the crack-up of Western thought? After Kant, philosophy split into two opposing streams: heirs of the Enlightenment versus heirs of Romanticism. In twentieth-century philosophy, these two streams were labeled the analytic versus the continental tradition.

Twentieth-century philosophy

CONTINENTAL TRADITION

Heirs of Romanticism

ANALYTIC TRADITION

Heirs of the Enlightenment

Each tradition extended one side of Kant's nature/freedom dualism.[44] Analytic thinkers were defenders of the Enlightenment—Kant's lower story. They agreed with Kant that genuine knowledge is possible only of the natural world. Eventually they declared that because the great metaphysical questions of God and morality were unknowable, they were outright meaningless. The only proper role for philosophy was to serve as a handmaid to science. Its task was to analyze and clarify the concepts and methods used in science.

Today analytic philosophy is deeply entrenched in philosophy departments all across America. Brian Leiter, professor of law and philosophy at the University of Chicago, says, "*All* the Ivy League universities, *all* the leading state research universities, *all* the University of California campuses, most of the top liberal arts colleges, most of the flagship campuses of the second-tier state research universities boast philosophy departments that *overwhelmingly* self-identify as 'analytic': it is hard to imagine a 'movement' that is more academically and professionally entrenched than analytic philosophy." [45] In a recent survey of philosophers at leading universities, mostly in the English-speaking world, 91 percent reported belonging to the analytic tradition.[46] It is sometimes even called Anglo-American philosophy.

By contrast, continental thinkers were defenders of Romanticism—Kant's upper story. In American universities, continental thought is rarely found in philosophy departments. But it has virtually overrun the humanities: theology, art history, literary criticism, cultural studies, and political theory. That's because it never gave up asking the "Big Questions" about the meaning of life, good and evil, oppression and justice, the nature of art and beauty. From the beginning, however, its tone has been defensive—for those are the very questions that, according to Kant, reason cannot answer since they are beyond the empirical realm.[47]

Continental philosophy continues to seek a more expansive view of reason that *would* be able to answer those questions.

In our own day, the gulf dividing analytic from continental philosophy is so wide that one philosopher complains they have become "two philosophical worlds." Another worries that "we have reached a point at which it is as if we're working in different subjects" and "shouting across the gulf." Still another says "it sometimes appears as if analytic and continental philosophy are really two separate disciplines with nothing much in common."[48] Kantian dualism has become a major parting of the ways in Western thought and culture—two divergent paths to secularism.[49]

Clearly, worldviews are not a scattershot of disconnected ideas to memorize, master, and slot into a grid. They form ongoing traditions that move along the same path, in the same basic direction, following the same map—either the Enlightenment map or the Romantic map. Alternately, you might think of them as two genealogical lines connected by family resemblances. To make sense of any particular worldview, the first step is to identify the family lineage it belongs to and the common themes it shares.

Lest you be tempted to dismiss this discussion as abstract, abstruse, and of interest only to small coterie of intellectuals, let me remind you that the topic we just covered is the theme of the one of the best-selling books of the past quarter century. Robert Pirsig's *Zen and the Art of Motorcycle Maintenance* has sold more than four million copies in twenty-seven languages and is often described as the most widely read book on philosophy ever. Its theme? The irreconcilability of the analytic and Romantic outlooks. Both contain elements of truth, and therefore both correspond to modes of thinking that we all share. "The Romantic mode is primarily inspirational, imaginative, creative, intuitive," Pirsig explains, whereas the analytic mode "proceeds by reason and by laws." In the modern world, these two are so divided that we feel torn between two "separate worlds."[50]

4-20 Robert Pirsig
Zen and the Art of Motorcycle Maintenance, 1974
Real questions by real people

Pirsig's search for a resolution led him on a motorcycle quest across America, jotting down his musings between tinkering with his engine and sleeping under the stars. (In case you wondered, Zen is Romantic, while maintaining a motorcycle engine is strictly analytic.) The book's astonishing popularity banishes all doubt that the technical terms used by philosophers reflect real questions raised by ordinary people.

Art under Siege

Artists likewise give expression to the experience of ordinary people—not in technical terms but in stories and images. How were the arts affected by the crack-up of philosophy? Again we will lay out the roadmap, then go into detail in later chapters.

We return to the Enlightenment. Most people know that the Enlightenment was an age when Christianity was put on the defensive. For the first time in centuries, it became socially acceptable to attack Christianity publicly or to publicly declare oneself an atheist. Think: the age of Voltaire.

But what most people do *not* know is that at the same time the Enlightenment put the arts and humanities on the defensive. Rationalist critics began to insist that art should be stripped of anything that does not exist in the ordinary, everyday world. They attacked the use of poetic elements, such as the Greek myths with their gods and goddesses. They debunked fantasy and fairy tales with their giants, witches, winged horses, enchanted forests, and magic swords. They even criticized figurative language—the use of symbol and metaphor. Why? Because it is not the factual, literal language of science.[51]

At best, critics said, art is merely decorative. Ornamental. Entertaining. Isaac Newton called poetry "ingenious nonsense." (At the time *poetry* meant the arts in general—from Greek *poiein,* to make.) Hume denounced poets as "liars by profession." Philosopher Jeremy Bentham agreed: "All poetry is misrepresentation." He believed words should be used for nothing but "precise logical truth." Thomas Sprat, historian of the Royal Society (the first professional association of scientists) said the time had come when even metaphor and figurative speech ought to be banished "out of all *civil Societies,* as a thing fatal to Peace and good Manners." Prose became the vehicle of facts and enlightened thought. Poetry was demoted to a vehicle of fiction and feelings.

Who Owns the Truth?

All this added up to a staggering assault on the arts. Until this time the goal of art had been to express *truth* of some kind. Even though it made use of fiction and fantasy, its purpose was to communicate enduring truths about the human condition. From ancient times, various definitions of art had been proposed, but all of them had included the idea that art is a mirror or reflection or representation of the world. The main test of art was thus its truthfulness—its ability to portray life faithfully. Aristotle even said that poetry is *truer* than history. Why? Because history deals with individual facts, while poetry communicates universal truths.

But now, in a startling turnaround, Enlightenment thinkers began to deny that art had anything to do with truth. As one historian explains, "Before the eighteenth century, art had been considered a form of knowledge, an aspect of objective truth." But "beauty does not exist as an objective quality in a universe of atomic motions."[52] Atoms belonged to the realm of objective facts. Beauty was relegated to the realm of subjective values.

By the late nineteenth century, the philosopher George Santayana could assert the fact/value divide as an accepted axiom: "Intellectual judgments are judgments of *fact*," he writes, while "aesthetic and moral judgments are . . . judgments of *value*."[53]

Certain artists continued to stand against this radical reductionism—especially Christian artists. For the biblical concept of truth is holistic. It accepts scientific methodology as one avenue to truth *without* reducing truth to what we can study in test tubes. "It is an insight of Christian aesthetic theory that bona fide art presents reliable, specific knowledge," writes Calvinist philosopher Calvin Seerveld. Art employs a different idiom from science or philosophy—an idiom of color and shape, shade and texture, sound and rhythm. Nevertheless it is "a vehicle for real knowledge," which is "as valid and sure" as other forms of knowledge.[54]

In a similar vein, Catholic novelist Walker Percy insists that art is "a serious instrument for the exploration of reality." It is "as scientific and as cognitive as, say, Galileo's telescope or Wilson's cloud chamber."

Yet this position has become rare. As Percy himself notes, today most people assume that "natural science has the truth, all the truth," and that art is merely "icing on the cognitive cake."[55] Similarly, Jeremy Begbie, director of Duke University's Initiatives in Theology and the Arts, says, "It is the natural sciences which are thought to grant us publicly verifiable truth, while the arts are concerned with matters of private taste."[56] Public truth/private taste. Clearly the fact/value split in all its implications has eroded the status and esteem that the arts once enjoyed.

Artists' Survival Strategies

As art was stripped of its traditional status as a source of truth, artists were put on the defensive. Scientism tolerated no other avenues to truth. Art critic Donald Kuspit offers an eloquent summary of the challenge that artists faced. The pressing issue, he says,

> . . . was whether artistic creativity could hold its own against scientific and technological creativity. *They* contributed a great deal to human welfare. What did art contribute? . . . *Science* understood the workings of nature . . . What did art understand? The desperate modern question is . . . what place art has in modern life.[57]

How did artists respond to this desperate question—this challenge from scientific culture? The answer is that they had two options: In a phrase, they could either fight 'em or join 'em. Some artists chose to fight 'em. By that I mean they turned art into a protest against the Enlightenment. That was the Romantics' strategy. They decided that art would function as "as the repository and refuge of the spirituality [which] the material world repudiated and shunned."[58] In short, it would become virtually a substitute religion.

Other artists decided the best strategy was to join 'em. If truth was defined by science, then it seemed that the only way art could *regain its connection to the truth* was by imitating science. Art could recover its traditional status as a source of truth by reflecting Enlightenment worldviews, such as empiricism and naturalism.

Thus art itself split into two steams. Art historians sometimes refer to them as the idealist versus the naturalist stream (each stream encompassing several artistic movements).[59] Artists in the naturalist stream *portrayed* the scientific worldview, while artists the idealist stream *protested* it.

Two streams in modern art

IDEALIST
Protests the scientific worldview

NATURALIST
Portrays the scientific worldview

In the twentieth century, it became more common to use the terminology of expressionism versus formalism. Expressionism defined art as the outpouring of inner feelings. Formalism dictated that art should *not* express subjective experience or tell a story, but should consist solely in the investigation of objective formal elements—line, color, space, volume, and so on.[60]

Twentieth-century terminology

EXPRESSIONISM
Expression of subjective feelings

FORMALISM
Analysis of objective form

Clearly the break-up of art mirrors the breakup of modern philosophy into the analytic and continental traditions. Through the rest of part 2 we will track these two paths to secularism. By taking a holistic approach that includes both art and ideas, we will get a fuller picture of the worldviews that confront and challenge us today.

Christian Freedom

There are obvious parallels between the fate of art and the fate of religion in the modern world. Beginning in the Enlightenment, both were stripped of their traditional status as avenues to truth. Both were put on the defensive and reduced to private, subjective experience. Both were kicked out of the *fact* realm and relegated to the *value* realm. As educator Douglas Sloan says, "The arts, almost as much as religion, were themselves caught in the modern dualism of objective fact and subjective meaning."[61]

Put bluntly, both were reduced to the status of private fantasy. As literary critic M. H. Abrams writes, when science was given a monopoly on truth, "the statements of traditional religion become no less fictions and illusions than those of traditional poetry."[62]

Given that both art and religion have been marginalized by Western culture's love affair with science, you might expect that Christians would naturally reach out to artists and sympathize with their plight. Right? Well, no. As a rule, modern evangelicals do not have a great reputation for encouraging artists. Generally they fall into two camps. Typical churchgoers tend to take the moralistic approach. They condemn immoral content in the arts and turn it off, tune it out. This is the fortress mentality: Don't let your kids watch it or listen to it. Other Christians are so concerned to show that *they* are not narrow or fundamentalist—that *they* are cultured and sophisticated—that they find something "redemptive" in virtually everything.

A worldview approach offers an alternative to this dilemma. It encourages Christians to enjoy the aesthetic qualities of art, while at the same time providing them with tools for critical analysis of the motivating ideas. As we proceed, we will discover that Christian artists have worked in virtually all artistic styles. Biblical truth is so rich and multi-dimensional that it can affirm what is true in every worldview, while at the same time critiquing its errors and transcending its limitations. In this way, Christianity makes possible the greatest intellectual and artistic freedom.

In the following chapters, we will locate worldviews within an ongoing conversation carried out not only by philosophers and scientists, but also by artists, writers, and composers. As Gene Edward Veith writes, in the arts, "abstract ideas find expression in tangible forms, so that we see more clearly their human implications."[63] Let's allow the arts be our teacher as we learn about the ideas that have shaped the world we live in.

Chapter 5

"Art tries, literally, to picture the things
which philosophy tries to put into carefully thought-out words."
—Hans Rookmaaker

Beauty in the Eye of the Machine
(The Enlightenment Heritage)

What happens to a boy who is raised to be little more than a thinking machine? That's how philosopher John Stuart Mill described his own childhood. Born in 1806, young John was the object of an experiment run by his father and the philosopher Jeremy Bentham. In the first half of the nineteenth century, these two men led a British political movement called the Philosophical Radicals. What was distinctive about the Radicals was their commitment to social and political reform strictly according to reason. And by "reason" they meant the principle of utilitarianism, the greatest good for the greatest number. (Bentham is considered the founder of utilitarianism.) When little John was born, they determined to rear him up to become an intellectual prodigy, a prophet for their utilitarian creed.

At the age of three, John Mill began lessons in Greek from his father. By eight, he was also learning Latin and could study the classical thinkers—Plato, Aristotle, Virgil, Cicero—in their original languages. By eleven, he was studying Newton, logic, mathematics, history, and political economy. As a teenager, he was reading philosophers like Hobbes, Hume, and of course his mentor Bentham. The experiment seemed to be working. Young John was years ahead of his peers, heralded as the crown prince of the Philosophical Radical movement. He had already founded several intellectual societies and had begun to contribute articles to journals.

John Stuart Mill's Crisis

Success came at a steep price, however. At the age of twenty, Mill suffered a mental crisis. It came crashing in on him that he had been turned into little more than a "reasoning machine." He realized that even if he achieved his goals of rational political reform, he would not be happy. "The whole foundation on which my life was constructed fell down," he wrote in his *Autobiography*. "I seemed to have nothing left to live for."[1] So intense was his depression that he compared himself to someone on the threshold of a religious conversion. Because in Britain most evangelicals were Methodist, he described his mental condition as that "in which converts to Methodism usually are, when smitten by their first 'conviction of sin.'"

Yet Mill did not find a resolution to his crisis in religion. Instead he found it in poetry. His depression lifted when he discovered the poetry of Wordsworth, Coleridge, and the other Romantics.

As a result of his crisis, Mill began to question the Enlightenment thinking in which he had been steeped. For example, the doctrine of determinism: "I felt as if I was scientifically proved to be the helpless slave of antecedent circumstances; as if my character and that of all others had been formed for us by agencies beyond our control." If that was true, however, then social and political reform was impossible. For if people really are helpless slaves of their circumstances, then how can they change those circumstances? The puppet cannot rise up against the puppeteer.

Mill was caught in a tug of war. On one side was the Enlightenment worldview in which he had been indoctrinated. On the other side was the social reform he wanted to promote. In his words, he felt trapped between "thinking one doctrine *true*" (that human behavior is determined) while thinking "the contrary doctrine *morally beneficial*"[2] (that moral reform is possible). In short, he was personally experiencing Kant's nature/freedom dualism—the opposition between the lower story of rationalism and determinism, versus the upper story of moral freedom. Because the two were contradictory, they could not both be true. Yet he could not deny either one.

The young man's mental struggle reveals the personal tension created by the conflict between the Enlightenment and Romantic modes of thinking. In fact, it was Mill who first used the rubric *continental philosophy* to describe Romantic idealism.[3] Clearly, this was not merely some abstract subject he read about in textbooks. It was an inner struggle waged within his own mind and soul.

Most people seek relief from the tension by tilting toward one side or the other. And that's exactly what Mill did. Despite his delight in poetry, he remained committed to the Enlightenment worldview. In his mind, the scientific method was the only route to genuine knowledge. No matter how inspirational he found poetry, he did not regard it as a vehicle for truth. Mill did not say that art and poetry consisted of outright falsehood, as his mentor

Bentham did (see chapter 4). But to rescue it from the charge of being false, he proposed that it is neither true *nor* false. It does not offer any assertions about the world at all, but merely expresses the artist's feelings. Poetry may *appear* to describe some aspect of the world (for example, a ferocious lion) but in reality it is only describing the poet's state of mind (his "awe, wonder, and terror" before the lion). In short, Mill demoted art to the status of pseudo-statements—statements that have the *form* of truth claims but in reality are merely expressions of subjective emotion.[4]

This was a novel and ultimately destructive view of the arts. Up to this time, most people had assumed that art was concerned with truth. Its goal was to represent or reflect reality in some way. Thus Mill and other Enlightenment thinkers were posing a direct challenge to the traditional view of the arts. In this chapter and the next, we will trace one way artists responded to that challenge—what we dubbed the "join 'em" strategy in chapter 4. These were artists who decided that the way to regain art's cognitive status was to follow the lead of science. Art would recover its connection to the truth by reflecting a scientific worldview. This is what historians call the naturalist stream in art (lower story). Because it denied any transcendent realm, it would contribute to a deadly, dehumanizing image of humanity.

Other artists responded to the challenge with the "fight 'em" strategy. They formed the idealist stream in art (upper story). These two broad streams run parallel to one another, and if we were to follow them strictly by dates, the account would flip back and forth between them. To avoid that jerky pattern, we will not take a strictly chronological approach but will trace each stream separately. We will begin with the Enlightenment heritage and follow the analytic tradition all the way through the twentieth century. Then we will start over with Romanticism and follow the continental tradition to the twentieth century. By untangling the two strategies and giving each one a sharper profile, we will find them far easier to recognize. And we will gain the skills needed to recognize and resist the two paths to secularism.

Stars of Science

Before the Enlightenment, people rarely considered science to be antagonistic to either art or religion. Most of the major figures who jump-started modern science were devout Christians—Copernicus, Kepler, Galileo, Boyle, Newton. In a 2003 study, sociologist Rodney Stark identified the fifty-two top "stars" who did groundbreaking work to launch the scientific revolution. Turning then to biographical documents, he discovered that all but two of them were Christian.[5]

Does that surprise you? Today many people assume that science and religion are inherently in conflict. But historians of science have turned that assumption upside down. Today most historians agree that the scientific outlook actually rests on fundamental concepts derived from a biblical view of nature.

Consider, for example, the idea of "laws" in nature. Today that idea is so familiar that we consider it common sense. But historians tell us that no other culture—East or West, ancient or modern—has ever come up with the concept of laws in nature. It appeared for the first and only time in Europe during the Middle Ages, a period when its culture was thoroughly permeated with biblical assumptions. As historian A. R. Hall notes, the use of the word *law* in the context of natural events "would have been unintelligible in antiquity, whereas the Hebraic and Christian belief in a deity who was at once Creator and Lawgiver rendered it valid." Moreover, the concept of laws was not considered metaphorical, a mere figure of speech, but literally true. As Randall writes, "Natural laws were regarded as real laws or commands, decrees from the Almighty, literally obeyed."[6]

Of course, all societies have recognized cause-and-effect patterns in nature, which enabled them to construct buildings, bridges, and weapons. Yet they typically considered these to be merely practical rules of thumb. The intrinsic order of nature itself was thought to be inscrutable to the human mind. And when people do not believe there *are* rational laws behind natural phenomena, then they will not go looking for them—and science will not get off the ground.

For example, many ancient societies were animistic. Nature was thought to be full of gods or spirits ready to inflict disaster—storms, floods, droughts, famines—unless they were placated by the correct performance of the correct rituals. In these societies, says historian Carl Becker, nature seemed "intractable, even mysterious and dangerous."[7] It did not seem at all orderly or predictable.

By contrast, the Bible rejects any religious status for nature. In the opening lines of Genesis, the sun, moon, and stars are not gods. Nor are they emanations of a divine essence. They are created objects. As a result, they do not have ultimate power over humans. The biblical teaching of a transcendent God liberated people from fear of spiritual forces within nature. As divinity professor Harvey Cox writes, "however highly developed a culture's powers of observation, however refined its equipment for measuring, no real scientific breakthrough is possible until man can face the natural world unafraid."[8] By exorcising the gods of nature, biblical monotheism freed humanity to investigate it without fear. It taught them to think of nature as regular, predictable, and open to systematic study.

In the biblical worldview, theologian Thomas Derr says, "man did not face a world full of ambiguous and capricious gods who were alive in the objects of the natural world." Instead there was "one supreme creator God whose will was steadfast." Thus "nature exhibited regularity, dependability, and orderliness. It was intelligible and could be [scientifically] studied."[9]

In short, the idea of an intelligible order in nature was not derived from scientific observation. It was derived from biblical theology *prior* to observation. And it was what made the scientific enterprise possible in the first place.

Ode to a Spinning Machine

The application of science to technology was likewise motivated by a biblical world-view. Many Christian theologians were eager to use science to restore humanity's steward-ship over the rest of creation, which had been damaged by the fall into sin. In the words of theologian Ernst Benz, "the founders of modern technology" appealed to "the destiny of man as *imago dei* and his vocation as the fellow worker of God . . . to share God's dominion over the earth."[10]

A frequently cited example is Francis Bacon, a founder of the scientific method. In the seventeenth century, he wrote that man "fell at the same time from his state of innocency and from his dominion over creation." Yet "both of these losses can, even in this life, be in some part repaired; the former by religion and faith, the latter by arts and science." By *arts* Bacon meant the technical arts, and his point was that the scientific study of nature, applied through technology, could be used to reverse the effects of the fall.

Thus from the beginning, science was suffused with the humanitarian goal of alle-viating the toil and suffering caused by the fall. According to historian Lynn White, the development of industry and technology was inspired by the "spiritual egalitarianism" of the Bible, which engendered "a religious urge to substitute a power machine for a man where the required motion is so severe and monotonous that it seems unworthy of a child of God."[11]

Given this biblical and humanitarian context, it is no surprise that the scientific revo-lution was welcomed as benign and beneficial. Many artists were happy to function as cheerleaders for science. Read this section from John Dyer's 1757 ode to the new spinning machines (if you can imagine a poem exalting spindles and cylinders):

A circular machine, of new design,
In conic shape: . . . the carded wool,
Is smoothly lapp'ed around those cylinders,
Which, gently turning, yield it to yon cirque
Of upright spindles, which, with rapid whirl,
Spin out, in long extent, an even twine.[12]

As long as science and its technological spin-offs were driven by a religious humanitarianism, artists were happy to celebrate them.

5-1 Anonymous
Spinning Machine, 19th c.

Inspired by Christian humanitarianism

Empiricism's Brush-Off

Over time, however, a secular approach began to crowd out the biblical worldview. The stunning new scientific theories were co-opted by Enlightenment ideologues who stripped them of their Christian context. A biblically informed respect for empirical facts, which had inspired science to begin with, was replaced by empiric*ism*, a philosophy that elevates the senses to the sole source of truth. Whatever could not be known by empirical methods was rejected as myth or metaphor.

We can witness the transition in the writings of poets such as Abraham Cowley in the mid-seventeenth century. Cowley was proud to be nicknamed "the Poet of Natural Philosophy" (an early term for *science*). He composed odes in honor of several early scientists and their discoveries. In Cowley's poems, however, we already detect the encroachment of science into other areas of life. He reduced love to a natural force akin to magnetism. He explained away biblical miracles as products of natural forces. (A poem alluding to Sodom and Gomorrah speculates that the biblical fire and brimstone were nothing but unusual thunder and lightning.) Though Cowley considered himself a Christian, clearly he had begun to narrow down the definition of truth to fit the limited categories permitted by empirical science. One scholar described him as a poet who "no longer pretends to create worlds transcending this one but rather reports on the material facts of this world."[13]

The idea that art should simply "report on the material facts of this world" entailed a radical shift in subject matter. Up to this time, artists had felt perfectly comfortable giving *visible* expression to *invisible* realities. They might use personifications to depict abstract ideals, such as a blindfolded woman to represent Justice. Or they might portray figures from Greek myths and legends. Often they depicted spiritual realities, such as God and angels. Under the influence of empiricism, however, artists began to insist that they could paint only visual sensations—only what the eye sees.

That's what Francisco Goya meant when he declared, "There is no reason why my brush should see more than I do." In other words, I can *paint* only what I *see*. So he portrays the terrible massacre of five thousand Spanish peasants by French soldiers, but refuses to impart any theological meaning to the scene (see facing page). In fact, Goya was deliberately subverting "a long tradition of martyrdom pictures," says biographer Fred Licht.[14] Compare it to the painting by Gamborino that is thought to have served as Goya's source. In martyr paintings, the victim looks up to heaven, confident that God will ultimately bring justice. But Goya's victim appeals hopelessly to his murderers. In traditional Christian art, the martyr is a spiritual hero, suffering for the cause of Christ. But Goya's victim is just one of "the anonymous millions whose death is irrelevant" shuffling in an apparently endless line stretching into the distance. Christian art typically shows the heavens opening and angels preparing the martyr's crown. But for Goya, the heavens are closed—dark and silent. The church is in the dark background as well, which implies that Christianity has no answers. Art critic John Canaday says, "No other painter has seen the world more naked of saving grace."[15]

EMPIRICISM
REALISM

5-2 Francisco Goya
The Third of May, 1814

5-3 Miguel Gamborino
Assassination of Five Monks from Valencia, 1813

The heavens are closed

Goya was an early representative of realism, typically defined as a movement that aims at an objective or value-free depiction of events. Yet compare his painting to a later one by Edouard

5-4 Edouard Manet
Execution of Emperor Maximilian of Mexico, 1867

The visual equivalent of a newspaper report

Manet that is obviously modeled on it. Manet's approach is much more consistent with the empiricist program of offering nothing but a visual report.

What differences do you see between his painting and Goya's? Most obviously, it is missing the sense of tragic outrage. Goya highlights the faces of the victims to emphasize the injustice being done to them. But in Manet's version you can hardly even make out their faces. Goya's soldiers are stiff, stylized, and faceless, as though to represent mechanized cruelty.

But Manet's soldiers are just doing their job—especially the officer on the side, who is casually preparing his rifle for the coup de grace. Are the onlookers peering over the wall horrified? No, they are merely curious.

Clearly Goya had not yet broken from the long-standing view that art should convey a theme, a statement of the inner truth or significance of events. His painting is an impassioned protest. Its theme might be called something like *the horror of injustice* or *the inhumanity of man to man*. He was still following Aristotle's dictum that "the aim of art is to represent not the outward appearance of things, but their inward significance."

By contrast, Manet depicts only the surface of things. He drains all the tragic drama from his painting and gives us the visual equivalent of a value-free report. As one art historian writes, Manet's "presentation of the scene lacks rhetorical devices—gestures, facial expressions, accessories—that would make the moral or meaning clear." Indeed, "it is completely devoid of a moral." Manet merely records the event as a historical fact, a temporal event.[16]

Manet's piece is thus a much more consistent example of the naturalist stream in art. "The classicist sought to create images in which eternal and universal values are summarized," Canaday writes. "But naturalism is *amoral* . . . the naturalist deals with the moment only, even at its most ephemeral."[17]

The Show-Me Artist

The term *realism* was originally coined to describe the work of Gustave Courbet. He professed the empiricist program in these words: "The art of painting should consist only in the representation

5-5 Gustav Courbet
Burial at Ornans, 1850

"Show me an angel."

of objects which the artists can see and touch."[18] Once when Courbet was preparing a painting for a church, he was asked to include angels. "I have never seen angels," he famously retorted. "Show me an angel, and I will paint one." His point was: If I can't *see* it, I can't *paint* it.

Courbet's painting of his great uncle's funeral sparked fierce controversy (above). A funeral is typically an occasion that evokes sorrow, grief, perhaps reflections on our own morality. Yet, as one art historian notes, Courbet's painting "is not organized around the evocation of a powerful emotional response." In fact, it is not organized around any theme at all. Critics at the time "complained that the old women were ugly, that some of the male figures were coarse and obviously drunk, that the priest was singularly unspiritual."[19] The unsympathetic treatment and haphazard composition, the bleak sky and barren cliffs, all imply that this is an event with no particular significance—just a local event with local townspeople. Yet the painting is huge, on a scale devoted at the time only to heroic, world-historical events thought to impart some uplifting lesson. Courbet was intentionally subverting the idea that art *should* be about grand events with a moral lesson.

Realist painters treated religion as a strictly human phenomenon—an interesting sociological fact, a quaint ritual, nothing more. Even when the treatment is sympathetic, as in the painting on the right by Wilhelm Leibl, the focus is on the worshippers, not on the objective existence

5-6 William Leibl
Three Women in a Village Church, 1881

**Religion as a
picturesque custom**

of what (or Who) they are worshipping. Leibl does not show a cross or altar or any other indica-
tion of the object of these women's devotion. The eye is not led upward to any higher horizon.
Christianity is portrayed sentimentally, as a picturesque rural custom.

Scripture and Sense Data

In every worldview there is a grain of truth. And the truth in empiricism is that the Creator
did fashion our senses to give us access to the world he created. The gospel itself has an important
empirical element. The apostle John insists that the message of Christ's death and resurrection
is based on that "which we have heard, which we have seen with our eyes, which we looked
upon and have touched with our hands" (1 John 1:1). When Paul addressed the Roman rulers,
he pointed out that the events of Jesus' life, death, and resurrection "were not done in a corner"
(Acts 26:26). They were public events witnessed by many people who were still alive at the
time—and who could therefore potentially refute the apostles' claim, if they had any contrary
evidence to present. The four Gospels claim to be public truth, based on eyewitness testimony
and open to cross-examination and testing.[20]

Motivated by the gospel's respect for empirical data, scholars have developed an empirically
based form of apologetics that investigates the historical evidence for the events of the New
Testament, from Nathaniel Lardner's *Credibility of the Gospel History* in the 1700s to the most
up-to-date scholarship in books such as Gary Habermas's *The Historical Jesus: Ancient Evidence
for the Life of Christ* and N. T. Wright's *The Resurrection of the Son of God*. This is not to say that
the resurrection can be proved from some neutral standpoint. Ultimately, worldviews are at
stake. Nevertheless, it is possible to offer a historically based challenge to secular accounts of the
New Testament events—and in doing so, to challenge the secular worldviews from which those
accounts arise.

Even modern science, with its empirical methodology, owes much to the biblical worldview. Prior to the rise of Christianity, the Greeks had defined science primarily in terms of
logic. In classical philosophy, things were composed of matter and form. Science was defined
as knowledge of the forms. Since the forms were rational and eternal (like numbers), science
was logically necessary (like mathematics). Its truth depended strictly on logic, not on empirical
findings.

The obvious problem with this definition is that it undercuts the need for empirical investigation. Once you grasp the essence of any object, then you do not have to examine it. You can
spin out all the important information about it by sheer deduction. Take, for example, a saucepan: Once you know that the purpose of a saucepan is to boil liquids, then you can deduce that
it *must* have a certain shape to hold the liquid, that it *must* be made of material that will not melt
when heated, and so on. This deductive method was made into the model for all knowledge. As
a result, classical thinkers had little use for detailed experiments and observations.

Over the centuries, however, as Christian theologians reflected on the biblical text, they began to question the Greek definition of science. In the Middle Ages, theologians reasoned that because God is omnipotent, he could have made the world in any number of different ways. He was free to choose the kind of universe he would create. The ordered patterns in nature are not logically necessary. They are contingent on God's will. The implication for science is that we cannot sit in our ivory towers and simply deduce what *must* happen. Instead we have to go out into the world to discover what *does* happen—what kind of order God has in fact chosen to create. In short, we must observe and experiment. The new view was stated in the seventeenth century by Newton's friend Roger Cotes, who wrote that nature arose from "the perfectly free will of God," and for that reason we must learn about it "from observations and experiments."[21]

To give just one example, Aristotle had argued that the earth *must* be at the center of the cosmos, because in his cosmology, elements seek their "natural" place. But such deductive reasoning was anathema to the French monk and mathematician Marin Mersenne. "For Mersenne there was no 'must' about it," writes historian John Hedley Brook. "It was wrong to say that the center was the earth's natural place. God had been free to put it where He liked. It was incumbent on us to find to where this was."[22]

Thus the experimental methodology of modern science owes its origin to the biblical concept of a Creator. The early scientists rejected Aristotle's definition of science as logically certain knowledge based on deduction. They substituted a new definition of science as probable knowledge based on empirical evidence. As philosopher Richard Popkin notes, theologians were as significant as scientists and philosophers in creating "the so-called British empiricism that has played so great a role in Western thought ever since."[23]

Peasants and Banjos

The same biblical respect for the empirical world was expressed by Christian artists. In fact, some historians say it was Christianity that gave rise to realism in the first place. In classical and neo-classical culture, art was expected to be about grand historical or mythological subjects. Important events took place only among gods and heroes, kings and warriors. By contrast, the working classes and the peasantry were usually portrayed as comic yokels. Realism broke with this prevailing tradition by emphasizing the dignity of ordinary, even humble, people. Where did this new style come from? From the biblical doctrine of the incarnation.

"It was the story of Christ" that broke down the classical rules of style, writes literary critic Erich Auerbach, through its "mixture of everyday reality and the highest and most sublime tragedy." The world-changing events of the gospel took place among everyday, ordinary people. Jesus welcomed sinners and prostitutes. He invited humble fishermen to be his disciples and ate with tax collectors (despised collaborators with the Roman occupation forces). These were characters who would never be considered suitable for representation in classical art. But amazingly, their lives became the locus of the great climax in God's plan of salvation. As a result, for the first time in history, it became "possible in literature as well as the visual arts to represent the most everyday phenomena of reality in a serious and significant context." Moreover, because Christ died the ignominious death of a condemned criminal, Auerbach adds, it became possible to portray in a sympathetic way "even the ugly, the undignified, the physically base."[24]

Thus Jean Francois Millet, a devout Catholic, became "the first to give peasants a Michelangelesque grandeur," according to art historian Frederick Hartt. "Before his time peasants had been portrayed as stupid or even ridiculous."[25] They could be used in comedy or genre painting, but not in serious art. Initially people were shocked by Millet's paintings because they accorded such dignity to humble figures. He broke new ground because of his Christian perspective. As one historian puts it, Millet gave "daily life a biblical gravity," painting the human being as "the lifelike icon of the invisible God."[26]

The American painter Henry Tanner was likewise a devout Christian, the son of a minister in the African Methodist Episcopalian Church. Tanner complained that "many of the artists who have represented Negro life have seen only the comic, the ludicrous side of it."[27] Even the banjo had become a caricature. The image of banjo-strumming slaves was a visual cliché. Tanner subverts the stereotypes with an image of profound tenderness.

CHRISTIAN REALISM

5-7 Jean Francois Millet
The Sower, 1850

5-8 Henry O. Tanner
The Banjo Lesson, 1893

Granting dignity to the poor and outcast

Clearly the Christian realists harbored a deep sympathy for the poor. They were not painting just what the eye sees, but seeking to express their subjects' inner dignity and significance.

Finding God in Nature

A school among English artists called the Pre-Raphaelites went even further, seeking to paint with precise, scientific accuracy. In the aftermath of the scientific revolution, there was a vast outpouring of books on natural theology—arguments for the existence of God based on the rational harmony in nature. The theme of these books was that nature, rightly interpreted, reveals spiritual and moral truths.

In the nineteenth century, it became all the rage to set up a nature cabinet in one's home, filled with fossils, rocks, gems, sea shells, and pressed flowers. In 1855 Charles Kingsley said he could see the reflection of God even in the crabs and sea anemones in a rock-pool on the beach. In his words, the lover of nature "acknowledges the finger-mark of God, and wonders, and worships."[28]

The Pre-Raphaelites hoped their paintings would likewise reveal the finger-mark of God, inspiring viewers to wonder and worship. Their name indicates that they wanted to recover the freshness of art prior to Raphael, whose style had been imitated so often that it had become a visual cliché. They urged artists to imitate nature instead. John Ruskin, a leader of the movement, thought it possible to train our eyes to see a leaf, for example, not just as part of a plant but as the embodiment of religious and moral truths. "The simplest forms of nature are strangely animated by the sense of Divine presence," he wrote; "the trees and flowers seem all, in a sort, children of God."[29]

For Ruskin, this suggested that artists should strive for a style that was empirically precise and scientifically accurate. By portraying nature in a way that took into account the latest findings of science, he thought, artists would reveal God's hand. One might say that the Pre-Raphaelites sought an aesthetic that would be a visual version of natural theology.

This explains why William Holman Hunt, whose paintings are featured on the next page, painted with such painstaking accuracy and sharp-focus detail. Even distant objects are not hazy but clear and hard-edged. *The Hireling Shepherd* alludes to Jesus' parable about the hired shepherd who neglects the sheep. Notice the sheep on the right wandering off into the fields. The lamb on the maiden's lap eats a green apple, which is poisonous to sheep. *The Scapegoat* refers to the Jewish Day of Atonement when a scapegoat was sent into the wilderness bearing the sins of the people (Lev. 16). The image was intended to bring to mind Jesus' suffering and atonement, which was prefigured by the Old Testament ritual. Hunt traveled to the Holy Land for a first-hand study of the Dead Sea, striving for exact accuracy in all details—scientific, geographical, archeological, and historical.

The goal of the Pre-Raphaelites' hyper-realism, explains art critic Peter Fuller, was to craft an aesthetic "rooted in the spiritual revelations of the new science."[30] They hoped to counter secular philosophies like empiricism and materialism through a symbolic realism, linking scientifically realistic details with complex spiritual references.

THE PRE-RAPHAELITES

5-9 William Holman Hunt
The Hireling Shepherd, 1851

5-10 William Holman Hunt
The Scapegoat, 1856

A visual version of natural theology

The linkage of natural and spiritual was the trademark of Christian realism. The Catholic apologist Frank Sheed once said, "The secular novelist sees what is visible; the Christian novelist sees what is there." Just so. On one hand, Christian realists affirmed the goodness of the empirical realm known by the senses. On the other hand, they regarded it as only one aspect of a richer, multi-dimensional reality created by God. In their worldview, Auerbach explains, the influence of God "reaches so deeply into the everyday that the two realms of the sublime and the everyday are not only actually unseparated but basically inseparable."[31] Truth was unified. Christian realists gave temporal things an eternal significance.

The Impressionists' Worldview

This was a far cry from the secular version of realism, which stripped away moral and spiritual meanings and aimed at a value-free depiction of factual reality—"only what the eye sees." Let's pick up that theme again. If art was supposed to depict only what the eye sees, what exactly *does* the eye see?

That question was taken up by the impressionists. They pored over scientific treatments of light and optics to better understand the process of vision—the physiological process by which we acquire knowledge of the world. This was the age of positivism, an extreme form of empiricism. Positivism says we cannot know the world as it really is. We can only report our sensations of the world. The impressionists turned art into a record of optical sensations.

The empiricist philosophers of the day were intrigued by case histories of patients who were born blind due to cataracts and then had their sight surgically restored (made possible for the first time in 1743). Here was the ideal experiment to test how knowledge is built up from sense experience. The leading spokesman for a scientific approach to art, Hippolyte Taine, reported that when post-operative patients looked on the world for the first time as adults, they did not even recognize objects as separate items. They were unable to perform such fundamental operations as distinguishing figure from ground. All they saw were streaks and planes of color. "The eye has only the sensation of different colored patches." The patients had to learn how to construct a coherent world out of a dazzle of color patches.[32]

And don't we *all* construct the world the same way? the positivists asked. For example, when you look at a wooden table, what do you really see? A patch of color: brown, flat, smooth, hard, rectangular. According to positivism, these direct sense impressions are the ultimate source of knowledge. And at that foundational level, we cannot be wrong or mistaken. Obviously, everyone does make mistakes at times, but that occurs in the process of *interpreting* sense data. Perhaps the brown rectangle is not a wooden table after all but a plastic crate. However, if we suspend all inference and interpretation to get in touch with raw, immediate sensation, *that* is something we can be absolutely certain about. Direct, unfiltered sense data would provide a foolproof, infallible foundation for knowledge. Even if we're not sure what the object is, we can be certain of that brown color patch.

POSITIVISM
IMPRESSIONISM

5-11 Claude Monet
Regatta at Argenteuil, 1872

5-12 Camille Pissarro
The Boulevard Montmartre at Night, 1897

Constructing the world from color patches

This explains why Claude Monet said, "When you go out to paint, try to forget what objects you have before you, a tree, a house, a field, or whatever. Merely think, here is a little square of blue, here an oblong of pink, here a streak of yellow." Color patches. Monet even added that he wished he himself had been born blind and received sight for the first time as an adult. That way, he would be able to paint colors "without knowing what the objects were that he saw before him." In other words, he would have no idea how to *interpret* what he was seeing. He would have access to the raw data of sensation without interpretation, the supposedly infallible foundation of knowledge.

"The term 'impression' had a very specific meaning in nineteenth-century theories of perception," explains art historian Robert Williams. The term was used to denote those raw, primal, pristine sensations where knowledge of the world begins.[33] Clearly, Monet was not interested just in painting pretty pictures. He was wrestling with the philosophical problem of knowledge (epistemology)—not in philosophical terms but in artistic terms.[34]

The typical art book says the impressionists were trying to simulate the effects of reflected light. But it does not explain *why* they thought that's what art should be about. When I was a university student, I took a yearlong course on modern philosophy where we engaged in endless classroom discussions about whether the ultimate source of knowledge consists in color patches. That is the question the impressionists were asking. Their style makes perfect sense once we realize that they were influenced by the struggle of positivism to build knowledge anew on the foundation of pure sense data. Art historian W. H. Janson summarizes their approach as "the revolution of the color patch."[35]

Da Vinci versus Degas

The idea that truth could be found by stripping the mind of all interpretation and starting over again from scratch was quintessentially modern. As a theoretical ideal, it represented a radical break with everything that had gone before. Ever since the ancient Greeks, the purpose of art had always been to convey some theme or interpretation of life. For all their differences, writes Canaday, no earlier art movements had "doubted the assumption that we are here for a *reason* and that our being is justified and *meaningful* . . . that there is a *harmony*, a discoverable *truth* . . . a meaningful *order* . . . a universal *plan* . . . some *purpose*."

What marks the modern age is the loss of this conviction. By the time of the impressionists, Canaday says, people no longer hoped "to achieve the expression of an ideal universal

5-13 Edgar Degas
Ballerina and Lady with Fan, 1885
A fragmented worldview

order . . . [or] universal knowledge." It seemed that all we really know is immediate experience—the "small and commonplace fragments of the infinitely complex world."[36]

Art began to reflect that sense of fragmentation. Turn back to Edgar Degas' *Ballerina and Lady with Fan* on the previous page. Note the arbitrary cropping, the off-center angle of vision, the figures cut off at the edges—some even with their heads sliced off—almost as though someone had taken a camera shot without aiming first.

Degas was in fact a talented amateur photographer. The haphazard look of his paintings was partly due to the way the camera taught people to "see" images that were not intentionally composed. After all, this is not the way we naturally view the world. We do not see people with their heads cut off. Photography taught artists how to portray what the world looks like without interpretation—without selecting, composing, arranging, aligning, balancing, framing, and so on.[37] This was a radically new approach to painting. Instead of telling a story or conveying a moral theme, the goal was to capture a fleeting moment, like a snapshot. When philosophers said the path to truth was to clear the mind of all interpretation, artists set about showing what an uninterpeted world looks like.

Another way to put it is that the impressionists began to abandon traditional rules of composition which bind the elements into a coherent whole. Consider, for example, Leonardo Da Vinci's

5-14 Leonardo da Vinci
Madonna of the Rocks, 1483

A unified composition

Madonna of the Rocks. Notice how he uses the traditional pyramid composition to draw the elements together and focus our attention on what's most important in the center. By contrast, in Degas' *Ballet Rehearsal* on the facing page, what's in the center? Well, nothing. Everything is incidental, happening on the side, partly chopped off by the picture frame. Even the ballet rehearsal (supposedly the theme of the painting) is partly obstructed by the staircase. Degas was striving for an unposed, unplanned effect—a chance point of view—as though someone just happened to come in at the back of the room at an arbitrary moment in time.[38]

Traditionally, an artist would use light and shadow to pull one part of the painting forward and make it the focal point—somewhat like the climax of a story—while the rest falls into background and is clearly secondary. But in Degas' painting, the light splotches do not highlight any figure. There is no focal point, no real distinction between foreground and background, no intelligible overall "shape" imposed on the subject matter. As modern people stopped believing that life itself had a coherent story line, artists stopped seeking to tell a coherent story in their paintings. They merely tried to capture a segment of the random flux of life. This was the slice of life effect.

SLICE OF LIFE

5-15 Edgar Degas
Ballet Rehearsal, 1874

5-16 Edouard Manet
The Railway, 1873

Random, fleeting moments

Manet's *The Railway* likewise lacks a focal point (see previous page). Despite the title, there is no train. The woman on the left glances up from her book as though a passerby had just interrupted her reading and taken a snapshot. As one art critic says, the painting "offers no story, no clear relationship between its figures, no centre of interest. It's like a slice of uninterpreted actuality."[39] A slice of life.

Doe a Discord

At the same time, impressionist composers began to abandon traditional rules of musical composition. They no longer felt the need to write music with a discernible shape or storyline: a beginning, a development, a climax, and a resolution. In an aria from a classical opera like Mozart's *The Marriage of Figaro,* you can count on hearing introductory material, then a period of development building on the musical theme, leading inevitably toward the climax on a high note, then finally ending with a conclusion that ties everything together. The piece begins and ends in the same tonality—for example, the key of C major—to impart a sense of departure and return. The narrative storyline is driven forward by structural elements such as contrast, repetition, and harmonic progression. If you play the guitar, think of the way the dissonance of a G7 chord creates a sense of forward movement that resolves into a C chord.

In the late nineteenth century, impressionist composers like Debussy and Ravel began to create music that abandoned any narrative storyline. To eliminate any sense of directed motion, Debussy used scattered fragments of melodies, chords that do not resolve (parallel chords), endings with no cadence signaling a conclusion. The result was a sense that the composition had no particular beginning or ending. It seemed almost like a fragment cut from some infinitely long piece of music that continues on indefinitely—like the flux of life itself.

In the words of musicologist Donald Grout, "Impressionism did not seek to express deeply felt emotion or tell a story but to evoke a mood, a fleeting sentiment, an atmosphere."[40] This is the slice of life effect in music.

Art for No One's Sake

Today most people define art in terms of personal expression. But that is a Romantic definition. The impressionists emphatically rejected it. Under the impact of empiricism, they declared that art should be merely a record of sensations—visual and auditory effects. As the American impressionist James Whistler put it, art should appeal only "to the artistic sense of eye or ear," without seeking to inspire "devotion, pity, love, patriotism, and the like."[41]

Edgar Allan Poe put the same idea more bluntly: Art "has no concern whatever either with Duty or Truth."[42]

Visual artists began to assign musical titles to their works to suggest that a painting did not represent anything but was merely an abstract harmony of colors. A case in point was Whistler's "Symphony in White No. 1." People debated endlessly who the woman was, what the white dress meant (was she a bride?), what the wolf skin rug signified, why she was holding a lily (a common religious symbol), and so on. After all, viewers at the time were used to the idea that the elements in a painting were supposed to *mean* something.

But the joke was on the public. "The story was that there *was* no story," writes art critic Robert Hughes. The woman was merely "a model posing in Whistler's studio to give him a pretext to paint shades of white with extreme virtuosity and subtlety."[43] The painting was to be evaluated solely in terms of formal elements—color, line, shape, texture, and so on.

The idea that the validity of a work of art rests on formal elements alone is called formalism. And it represents a major break with all traditional concepts of art. Up to this time, the purpose of art had been to convey a message or a moral. To arouse virtue and courage. To instruct and inspire. To enrich, elevate, uplift, and refine. When Handel's *Messiah* was first performed, a nobleman hailed the work as "a noble entertainment." Handel replied: "My Lord, I should be sorry if I only entertained them; I wished to make them better."

In the nineteenth century, however, artists began to attack the very idea of moral uplift and refine-

5-17 James Whistler
Symphony in White No. 1, 1862

Nothing but retinal and auditory effects

ment. They became what literary critic Lionel Trilling labeled an "adversary culture,"[44] deploying their art to undermine bourgeois society. In earlier ages, artists had been thoroughly embedded in their society, expressing its prevailing concerns and convictions. But now they proudly certified their superiority to the common folk by their defiance of established norms. "Until we come to the modern epoch, all art had a social significance and a social obligation," observes artist Suzi Gablik. But "*our* great art has been overtly hostile to the social order."[45]

This was the operational meaning of the nineteenth-century slogan "art for art's sake." It meant a rejection of art for the *public's* sake. Artists castigated the bourgeoisie for caring only about what was useful and profitable—for being crass, selfish, and utilitarian. It must be admitted that their accusations had some justification. The bourgeois spirit was informed by a liberal theology that had replaced biblical concepts of sin and salvation with a self-congratulatory doctrine of material and moral progress. Liberal Christians were respectable, civilized, moralistic, and self-righteous. Their Victorian Jesus was meek, mild, and sentimentalized. As Rookmaaker says, the bourgeois spirit did not wrestle honestly with the challenges posed by modernity, but merely "tried to cover up the fact that the old values had lost their hold."[46] As a result, artists disdained conventional society for being timid and reactionary. They prided themselves on their own courage in facing harsh truths.

This is when artists and writers began to go "slumming," hanging out at nightclubs and bordellos with criminals and prostitutes, portraying the seamy side of life. They were determined to shock the bourgeoisie into facing "real" life.

THE ADVERSARY CULTURE

5-18 Edgar Degas
Absinthe Drinker, 1876

5-19 Toulouse-Lautrec
Training of the New Girls, (Moulin Rouge), 1892

Artists go "slumming"

Despite their empiricist premise, many impressionist paintings and musical pieces are quite beautiful. They remain immensely popular with the public. The reason is that the impressionists continued to incorporate a great deal of the Western artistic and musical tradition. Typically it takes several generations for a worldview and all its implications to thoroughly permeate a society.

Moreover, like great artists in every era, they were masters of their craft. God's good gifts— including things like skill and insight—are given to everyone. This is the doctrine of common grace: that God "causes his sun to rise on the evil and the good, and sends rain on the righteous and the unrighteous" (Matt. 5:45). As a result, most artists' vision is better than their worldview. They are sensitive to dimensions of reality that go beyond what is strictly permitted within the cramped categories of their secular worldview. One might say that the more attuned artists are to actual human experience, the less restricted they are by their worldview, and the richer their vision of the world.

The Rationalist Reaction

Eventually a reaction set in against impressionism. Some artists felt that the definition of art as nothing but retinal effects was too superficial. "Monet is just an eye," Paul Cezanne complained—nothing but a walking eye. These artists wanted to revive the older ideal that art uncovers some deeper level of reality.

But they were still modern people. They still wanted to be "scientific." So in deciding *what* that deeper truth was, they turned from empiricism to its main rival—the philosophy of rationalism. As Rookmaaker explains, they wanted to "paint the structure of reality as understood by human rationality, the rationalistic principles 'behind' the thing seen."[47]

And what *was* the deeper "structure of reality"? According to rationalism, it was mathematical. To trace the source of this idea, we must turn once again to the beginnings of modern science. The early scientists proposed that the Creator, being a rational God, had made the universe with a mathematical structure. To uncover that structure was a way to honor the Creator. In the words of mathematician Morris Kline, "The search for the mathematical laws of nature was an act of devotion which would reveal the glory and grandeur of His handiwork."[48]

The roots of this mathematical view of the world reach back even further, of course, to Pythagoras and Euclid. In fact, the ancient Greeks are often given credit for the origin of modern science. But that is a mistake. The Greeks locked up mathematical truths in a kind of Platonic heaven of ideal forms—a realm of mental blueprints or templates for all the objects in the material world. The problem was that these blueprints did not match their objects except in a rough and approximate way. Why not? Because the Greeks regarded matter as eternal, not created. Therefore matter had its own inherent, independent properties, which did not necessarily line up with the blueprints in the ideal realm. Think of geometry: Its rules do not really refer to the smudged, uneven triangles we sketch with chalk or ink. They refer to the abstract ideal of a triangle.

As a result, classical philosophers did not expect to find mathematically precise relationships within nature. As historian Dudley Shapere explains, in Platonic thought the physical world "contains an essentially irrational element: nothing in it can be described *exactly* by reason, and in particular by mathematical concepts and laws."[49] Thus the idea that the material world follows mathematical laws did not come from the ancient Greeks.

Instead it came from the biblical concept of creation *ex nihilo*. Matter is not eternal. It is created. Therefore it does not have any inherent, independent properties of its own. It has whatever properties God wanted it to have. In practical terms, this meant that people began to expect matter to follow exact rational and mathematical laws. The Nobel prize-winning physicist C. F. von Weizsacker sums up the difference: "Matter in the Platonic sense . . . will not obey mathematical laws exactly." But "matter which God has created from nothing may well strictly follow the rules which its Creator laid down for it." In this way, he concludes, modern science is "a legacy, I might even have said a child, of Christianity."[50]

Today we take it for granted that science is a matter of formulating mathematical laws, and we fail to realize how novel this idea once was. As historian R. G. Collingwood points out, "*the very possibility* of applied mathematics is an expression . . . of the Christian belief that nature is the creation of an omnipotent God."[51] As I was growing up, my father taught applied mathematics at universities like Purdue and Texas Tech, so I like to remind him that the very existence of his field depends on a Christian worldview.

Galileo versus Aristotle

These ideas had enormous historical impact. For example, how did Johann Kepler discover that the planetary orbits are ellipses? Ever since antiquity, people had thought the planets moved in circular orbits. The idea went back to Aristotle. He had reasoned that the heavens are "perfect," and the circle is the "perfect" shape, ergo the heavenly bodies must move in circles. (This was an example of the Greeks' deductive approach to science.) How did Kepler succeed in breaking through a settled belief in circular orbits that had held sway for two thousand years?

It began when he had difficulty plotting the orbit of Mars. The most accurate circle he could construct based on observations was slightly wobbly. Had Kepler retained the Greek mentality, he would have shrugged off such a minor aberration. His thinking would have been that objects correspond to geometrical ideals, after all, only approximately. But Kepler was a devout Lutheran. He was convinced that if God wanted a line to form a circle, it would be exactly a circle. And if it was not exactly a circle, it must be exactly something else. It would not be merely an arbitrary departure from the ideal. This theological conviction sustained Kepler through six years of intellectual struggle and thousands of pages of scientific calculations before he finally hit upon the idea of ellipses.

Kepler later spoke gratefully of the minor mismatch in Mars' orbit as a "gift from God" because it spurred his greatest scientific breakthrough. The chief aim of science, he said, is "to discover the rational order and harmony which has been imposed on it by God and which He revealed to us in the language of mathematics."[52]

Galileo shared Kepler's conviction that God created the world with a mathematical structure. But not everyone did. This was the question at the heart of the famous Galileo controversy. The typical story is that Galileo was persecuted because he championed the heliocentric theory of Copernicus. But the truth is that no one at the time objected to Copernicanism—as long as it was used merely as a calculating device. There was not enough empirical data yet to decide between an earth-centered and a sun-centered system. Both systems worked equally well for navigation, which was the main practical use of astronomy at the time. Most people were willing to use whichever astronomical theory worked best, without worrying about whether it was physically true.

Galileo attracted controversy because he insisted that the Copernican system was not just a useful calculating tool but physically true. The central question at stake was thus the status of mathematical truth: Does mathematics tell us what is true in the physical world? This was a philosophical question, not a theological one. And Galileo's main opponents were not churchmen but the Aristotelian philosophers in the universities. For them, mathematics was not high on the list of what makes the world what it is. The essential feature of Aristotle's universe was not *quantity* but *quality*—hot and cold, wet and dry, soft and hard. In the universities, mathematics ranked much lower than physics. A mere mathematician was not supposed to dictate to the physicists what theory they could hold.

We get a fascinating glimpse into mindset of the time from the words of one of Galileo's opponents, a philosophy professor at the University of Pisa. "How far from the truth are those who wish to prove natural facts by means of mathematical reasoning," he wrote indignantly. "Anyone who thinks he can prove *natural* properties with *mathematical* arguments is simply demented, for the two sciences are very different."[53]

When I read that quotation in my lectures, inevitably the audience breaks into laughter. Today it seems obvious that science is about explaining nature using mathematical formulas. Not so in Galileo's day. When he declared that the book of nature is written by God in the language of mathematics, those were fighting words—a declaration of war on Aristotelian philosophy.[54]

The Galileo saga is typically told as a conflict between science and religion. But in reality it was a conflict among Christians over the correct philosophy of nature. Was it Aristotle's *quality* or Galileo's *quantity*? Galileo's victory was the triumph of the idea that the nature is constructed on a mathematical blueprint.

Stealing Newton

It was the work of Newton, however, that finally persuaded people of the power of mathematics to explain nature. His law of universal gravitation demonstrated that a vast range of natural phenomena could be described by a single mathematical formula—from the familiar motions on earth (the arc of a cannonball) to the far-distant motions in the heavens (the orbit of a planet). Such simplicity! Such elegance! No wonder Newton became the first scientific superstar.

His dramatic breakthrough came about through a biblical insight. Aristotle had drawn a sharp distinction between the earth—the realm of change and decay—and the heavens, which to the naked eye appeared unchanging and eternal. Aristotle decided that the two must be composed of completely different substances. He concluded that it was impossible to apply the principles of physics worked out on earth to things in the heavens, like stars and planets.

This Aristotelian picture of the cosmos remained virtually unquestioned for nearly two millennia. What finally undermined such a long-standing intellectual tradition? Reflection on the biblical concept of creation. As Kline explains, "God had designed the universe, and it was to be expected that all phenomena of nature would follow one master plan." It was natural to think that "one mind designing a universe would almost surely have employed one set of basic principles to govern related phenomena."[55] Operating on that assumption, Newton demonstrated that the heavens are not composed of a different substance after all. The universe is a unified cosmos. It can be described everywhere by the same mathematical laws.

Newton not only wove theology into his science, he also turned around and used science to support theology. "The main business" of science, he said, is to reason back along the chain

5-20 William Blake
Newton, 1795

One master plan

of mechanical causes and effects "till we come to the very first cause, which certainly is not mechanical"—namely, a personal Creator. Newton also gave examples of such reasoning. He argued that the intricate balance of the solar system could not be explained by natural causes alone, which are "blind or fortuitous," but only by an intelligent cause "very well skilled in mechanics and geometry."

Even Newton's most significant scientific discovery—the concept of gravity—he saw as evidence for God. Gravity could not be derived from the intrinsic properties of matter, such as mass and extension. Therefore Newton conceived the force of gravity as evidence of God's direct, active governance of the world.

Indeed for Newton, the most basic elements of the universe—time and space themselves—were actually properties of God. Absolute time was God's own duration "from eternity to eternity." Absolute space was God's omnipresence, "from infinity to infinity."[56] In Newton's physics, it is quite literally in God that we live, move, and have our being (cf. Acts 17:28).

Eventually, however, Enlightenment ideologues began to subject the new science to the corrosive process of secularization. Voltaire championed Newton's work on the European continent, but in the process he carefully omitted any mention of the great scientist's biblical perspective. Instead he co-opted Newton's physics to serve an Enlightenment agenda—the same pattern of secularization that has continued right to our own day, as we saw in the CBS rewrite of John Erickson's *Hank* story. Newton's concept of gravity was given a materialistic interpretation. It was no longer an avenue of the Creator's power holding the universe together, but merely a force inherent within matter itself. Newton's absolute time and space were reduced to merely logical categories. Eventually his theories were absorbed into the very materialistic worldview he had hoped to refute.[57]

The irony is that this came to be called the "Newtonian" worldview, though it was one that he himself would never have accepted. It pictured the universe as a vast machine, operating by inexorable mathematical laws. Mathematical models were applied not only in science but also in social, political, and moral thought. It seemed so simple: Galileo had observed a ball rolling down an inclined plane and discovered the mathematical law of acceleration for all moving bodies. Newton had observed a falling object (an apple, according to legend) and calculated the mathematical law of gravity for all matter. Shouldn't the same methodology apply to the social sciences? Shouldn't it be possible to observe a few simple cases and then discover universal laws governing all human behavior? In the eighteenth century, says one historian, "many believed that the time was near when all things would be explained by means of a universal physics."[58] The mathematical methods that worked in physics would surely work in every other field. They would provide the means to control not only nature but also human nature.

Picasso's Rationalist Lesson

This background explains why rationalist philosophers held up mathematics as the most certain path to true knowledge. Descartes decreed that all branches of knowledge must seek to "attain a certitude equal to that of the demonstrations of Arithmetic and Geometry." The philosopher Leibniz looked forward to the day when all human reasoning would be reduced to a kind of calculus—a set of operations that would resolve all conflicts of opinion. As he put it, we should strive to make our reasonings "as tangible as those of the Mathematicians," so that "when there are disputes among persons, we can simply say, Let us calculate, without further ado, to see who is right." Whereas empiricist philosophers tried to build the entire edifice of knowledge on sense impressions, rationalists tried to do the same thing with mathematics.

How was the rationalist vision expressed in the arts? When the early scientists spoke of mathematics, they meant primarily geometry. In his famous statement that the book of nature "is written in the language of mathematics," Galileo went on to say that its characters "are triangles, circles, and other geometric figures." In the arts, then, rationalism inspired the rise of geometric formalism.

This explains cubism, which sought to portray nature's underlying geometric blueprint. The springboard for cubism was a remark by Cezanne that artists should "interpret nature in terms of the cylinder, the sphere, the cone"—virtually a paraphrase of Galileo. In the words of art historians Lucy Adelman and Michael Compton, "Cubist pictures were made up largely of intersecting straight lines and arcs, the very stuff of schoolboy geometry as practiced by means of ruler and compass." The underlying structure was a flat grid of intersecting horizontal and vertical elements—the famous cubist grid.

As in science, mathematics represented human control over nature. To quote Adelman and Compton again, "Geometry was exploited as the expression of man's power to impose order on the world, to use his intellect to dominate and control nature."[59] The cubist grid represented the imposition of a rational, formal order.

RATIONALISM
CUBISM

5-21 Georges Braque
Woman with a Guitar, 1913

5-22 Pablo Picasso
Man with a Guitar, 1912

Nature's hidden geometric blueprint

Back in the eighteenth century, Kant had sought to unify the rival claims of empiricism and rationalism by proposing that the senses give the basic *data* of knowledge, while reason gives the rational *form* that knowledge takes. What interested the cubists was the rational form. Their faceted surfaces, geometric lines, and angled planes shifted the focus of painting. Art was no longer the *portrayal of a subject* but the *investigation of form.*

Perhaps the most famous example was Picasso's *Les Demoiselles d'Avignon,* which rendered five prostitutes in a brothel broken up into geometrical patterns. Picasso's painting was intended as a "rationalist lesson," writes Wendy Steiner. Its goal was to teach viewers to not see "sexualized women" but merely a problem in "space relations." Viewers were supposed to "look through" immoral subject matter in order to apprehend pure form.[60]

In fact, formalists insisted that the power of great art had *always* been due to its underlying geometry. A painting's subject or story was nothing but a distraction. What made it into a work of art was its abstract geometric structure. Picture in your mind, for example, a pietà (Mary mourning the crucified Christ). According to formalists, the impact of the painting had nothing to do with the theological meaning of the Savior's death.

5-23 Pablo Picasso
Demoiselles d'Avignon, 1907

Apprehending pure form

They seriously maintained that the "religious sentiment is evoked in the beholder not by the dead Christ or by the weeping Virgin, but by the specific angle created by their adjacent bodies."[61]

Art history books typically explain that the cubists sought to portray objects from several viewpoints simultaneously: top, bottom, left, and right.[62] But *why* were they motivated to break down objects into geometric shapes? Their geometric formalism makes much more sense once you realize that they were influenced by the philosophy of rationalism. As Schapiro explains, cubism "represents a commitment to scientific perspective," to "the philosophy of the Enlightenment, of rationalism."[63]

Machine Descending a Staircase

Related to cubism was a school called futurism, which celebrated the rise of the newly industrialized world. The early twentieth century was an era of rapid invention—the radio, the automobile, the airplane, the neon light. Many people were intoxicated by the new mechanical power and speed. They were convinced that nature was inferior to manufactured items—that moonlight, for example, had been supplanted by electric lamps. The founder of futurism wrote a provocative article titled "Let's Murder the Moonshine," in which he welcomed "the reign of holy Electric Light" and "the idea of mechanical beauty." He venerated machines as virtually alive: "We therefore exalt love for the machine," for motors "seem to have personalities, souls, or wills."[64]

If the machine was treated as virtually alive, that's because humans had been reduced to machines. The figures in futurist paintings were often mechanical and robotic-like. Marcel Duchamp's *Nude Descending a Staircase* caused a major scandal at the 1913 Armory Show in New York, the controversial exhibit that first brought modern art to America. But we can understand it if we think of it as cubism in motion, mimicking time-lapse photography. To portray motion, Duchamp explained, "we enter the realm of geometry and mathematics, just as if we were to build a machine." He dubbed this painting "the machine figure."

FUTURISM

5-24 Marcel Duchamp
Nude Descending a Staircase, 1912

5-25 Kasimir Malevich
The Knife Grinder, 1912

The "Machine Figure"

Francis Schaeffer once remarked that if "American theologians had understood the Armory Show of 1913" they would have had a head start in interpreting modern culture. Instead they "lagged behind," always reacting, always on the defensive.[65] If today's Christians hope to be pro-active, they must acquire artistic literacy. Only then will they get ahead of the cultural curve and learn how to speak God's truth anew to each generation.

Mathem-Artists

Eventually objects disappeared altogether, giving way to an abstract geometry of straight black lines and flat planes of color. It was the cubist grid, bare and unadorned. Geometric abstraction was one of "the logical consequences" of cubism, according to Piet Mondrian—art that was "more mathematical than naturalistic." His goal was to replicate in his art the underlying mathematical structure of the cosmos. He even believed that "the appearance of the universal-as-the-mathematical is the essence of all feelings of beauty."[66] Mondrian founded a school known as De Stijl, and though his estate did not give permission to include any of his paintings, his work has the distinctive characteristics shared by other members of the school (below).

GEOMETRIC ABSTRACTION

5-26 Theo van Doesburg
Simultaneous Counter Composition, 1929

5-27 César Domela
Neo-Pastic Composition, 20th c.

Reflecting the mathematical structure of the cosmos

If the cubists began to shift the focus of art to Kant's universal forms, the abstractionists completed the shift. Their goal was to turn art into a universal visual language. But "the universal cannot be expressed purely so long as the particular obstructs the path," as Mondrian wrote.[67] Thus geometric abstraction was seen as a means of "purifying" art by eliminating all traces of particular or individual objects. As we saw in chapter 4, ever since the ancient Greeks, rationalism has had a tendency to devalue individuality. Geometric formalism can be understood as the visual expression of a rationalist worldview that exalted the universal and the ideal, at the expense of the individual.

Tom Wolfe's Art Museum

A common critique of formalism is that it is too intellectual, driven more by philosophy than by aesthetics. In 1911 Guillaume Apollinaire, a prominent theoretician of cubism, admitted that the style is "more cerebral than sensual" because it seeks "to express the grandeur of metaphysical forms." And metaphysical forms appeal more to the mind than to the eye. After all, once art has been reduced to straight black lines and primary color blocks, it is difficult to create much visual variety. As Kuspit notes, a bare cube does not generate much interest. "There is no need to analyze it, to think about it," he writes. "One intuitively grasps its axiomatic character, and doesn't bother with it anymore (unless one is a mathematician)."[68] Geometric formalism seems more concerned with conveying a rationalist worldview than with reveling in visual beauty.

In *The Painted Word*, novelist Tom Wolfe complains that art has become so intellectual that museums have to post ever-larger plaques alongside works of art in order to explain what the point is. He jokes that in the galleries of the future, the sizes will be reversed: Instead of large paintings with small plaques alongside, museums will feature postcard-sized paintings with huge plaques alongside—because they require so much text to explain the worldview behind them.[69] Wolfe is pulling our leg, but he has a serious point. Today creating works of high artistic quality is considered less important than making an ideological statement. Hence the title of Wolfe's book: Paintings have become little more than "painted words." Worldview has trumped aesthetics.

Schoenberg Composes by Numbers

The same criticism—that it appeals more to the mind than to the ear—is often leveled against musical modernism. The towering figure of twentieth-century classical music was Igor Stravinsky. His style was starkly anti-Romantic—clear, hard-edged, unsentimental, non-expressive. His trademark pieces retained tonality, but just barely. He experimented with polytonality (two or more musical keys at the same time) and polyrhythm (two or more rhythmic patterns at the same time). For example, in his ballet *Petrushka,* there is a place where the first clarinet plays a melody in C major, while the second clarinet plays a variant of the same melody in F sharp major. When his ballet *The Rite of Spring* opened in Paris in 1913, it provoked a riot. It was difficult for the public to assimilate such dissonant-sounding works. Many historians say musical modernism was born that night.

5-28 Igor Stravinsky
The Rite of Spring, 1913

Birth of musical modernism

It was Arnold Schoenberg, however, who made a complete break with tonality. If you do not have a musical background, tonality refers to music that uses the major and minor scales. Think of the lyrics to "Doe a Deer" in *The Sound of Music*. In the key of C major, for example, the note C functions as "Doe," and a musical composition will revolve around that fundamental tone. This is what gives the piece its sense of tonal mooring, its home plate, its feeling of closure at the end. By contrast, atonal music does not make use of scales, musical keys, chord progressions, and so on. No tone is more important than any other.

Schoenberg started by composing completely free atonal music. But there were no guiding principles for atonality, so eventually he sensed a need for some new method to impose order and organization. In 1921 he introduced the twelve-tone system, a kind of musical formalism in which the order of pitches in a piece was predetermined by a mathematical calculation of intervals. (If you count both white and black keys on a piano keyboard, there are twelve tones in an octave.) The rule is that every tone within an octave must be used once before any note can be repeated. This serves to eliminate the auditory sense of a tonal center.

Here's how it works. The tones are assigned numerical values based on counting half steps, and are then arranged into a series—hence the label *serialism*. The initial series is manipulated up or down, forward or backward, and with a bit of math, you end up with a matrix like the one below. The matrix is then used to write the composition. Composing music is not a matter of personal expression but mathematical calculation. Just follow the formula. It was the cubist grid applied to music.

THE TWELVE TONE SYSTEM

	0	11	3	4	8	7	9	5	6	1	2	10
0	B	Bb	D	Eb	G	F#	G#	E	F	C	C#	A
1	C	B	Eb	E	G#	G	A	F	F#	C#	D	Bb
9	G#	G	B	C	E	Eb	F	Db	D	A	Bb	F#
8	G	F#	Bb	B	Eb	D	E	C	C#	G#	A	F
4	Eb	D	F#	G	B	Bb	C	G#	A	E	F	C#
5	Eb	Eb	G	G#	C	B	C#	A	Bb	F	F#	D
3	D	C#	F	F#	Bb	A	B	G#	G#	Eb	E	C
7	F#	F#	A	Bb	D	C#	Eb	B	C#	G#	G#	E
6	F	Eb	G#	A	C#	C	D	Bb	B	F#	G	Eb
11	Bb	A	C#	D	F#	F#	G#	Eb	E	B	C#	G#
10	A	G#	C	C#	F#	Eb	F#	Db	Eb	Bb	B	G
2	C#	C	E	F	A	G#	Bb	F#	G#	D	Eb	B

5-29 Serialism

Composing music by mathematical calculation

Music as Math

Once again, the cubist grid represented the imposition of mathematical order. Schoenberg's followers, Pierre Boulez and Milton Babbitt, took the compose-by-numbers scheme even further. While he had used twelve rows of pitches, they added twelve levels of volume, twelve rows of durations (the length of time each note sounds), and even twelve ways of striking the piano keys. The result was complete control: "the total organization of music."[70]

Boulez explained that his goal was to wipe his mind clean of everything he knew about music and begin anew. As he put it, his music was "an experiment in what one might call Cartesian doubt, to bring everything into question again, make a clear sweep of one's heritage, and start all over again from scratch." As we saw earlier, this was the trademark of modernism: to strip the mind of all interpretation and start over again. As Begbie comments, Boulez exemplifies "the arch-modernist view of the artist whose sovereign constructive intellect brings order and meaning to the sonic world."[71]

Unfortunately, the music created by this complex mathematical formalism was virtually impossible to listen to. Schoenberg called his rejection of tonality "the emancipation of dissonance" and most audiences do find it distressingly dissonant. This is not music that invites you to whistle or tap your feet. It has no melody line, no recognizable chord progressions, no repeated phrases that the listener can recognize and then "follow along" with the music. When a composer begins with a random series of sounds, no matter how much he manipulates it mathematically, the result still sounds random.

Serialism's defenders insisted that the music was not random but did have an order—one that was detectable not by the ear but by the eye. That is, you could see the mathematical relationships worked out on paper. But that was precisely the problem, critics say. Serialism was too cerebral. It did not treat music as an auditory phenomenon but as a mathematical construction. It was "intellectual through and through," Begbie writes. "Whether the music was pleasant to listen to or easy to play was quite secondary; what mattered above all was adherence to intellectually derived schemes."[72]

Serialists tried to boost their credibility by imitating scientific and mathematical jargon. Instead of speaking of chords, they spoke of "densities," "sets," and "classes." They composed in musical "laboratories" and adopted scientific-sounding titles like *Configurations* and *Structures.* They even dressed like scientists, wearing thick black glasses and button-down shirts with pens in the pocket.[73] As a *New York Times* music critic comments, "twelve-tone music and serialism were treated like scientific disciplines by composers working within universities."[74] And if that yielded music that was unpleasant to listen to, well, that was the price to pay for intellectual respectability in a scientific age. In an influential article, Babbitt compared composers to theoretical physicists whose work is likewise unintelligible to the public. The article was titled "Who Cares If You Listen?"

In short, serialist composers abandoned aesthetics—how the music *sounds*—in favor of imposing a rationalist schema. As Bayles writes, serialism became "a sterile, hypermathematical exercise" that was "ill suited to the human ear."[75] Once again, the worldview *behind* the music was more important than the music itself. A misguided worship of rationalism trumps the ideal of beauty.

Boulez said the goal of his mathematical approach was to write music in a way that "eliminates personal invention."[76] The use of mathematical calculation to predetermine the entire musical process left no room for personal creativity. Knowingly or not, he was expressing the logical consequences of a rationalist worldview that begins with blind, material forces. Logically, a cause must be adequate to account for its effect. Any worldview that posits a *non-personal* starting point does not have the intellectual resources to account for *personal* agents, like human beings. And therefore it inevitably ends by denigrating the person and squashing personal creativity.

Search for Secular Infallibility

To conclude the chapter, let's evaluate the two major Enlightenment worldviews we have covered so far—empiricism and rationalism. Applying biblical language, we might say that a worldview is a mental idol. An idol is a false god, a mistaken concept of the divine. It does not have to be religious in the traditional sense or involve formal worship ceremonies. Secular worldviews can play exactly the same role in a person's life as traditional religion does.

The Bible defines idolatry as the human tendency to elevate something in creation to the status of God. In Romans 1:25, the apostle Paul writes, "They exchanged the truth about God for a lie, and worshiped and served the creature rather than the Creator." Humans are inherently religious, and when they deny the Creator, they will fasten on something *within* creation and elevate it to an object of worship. In practical life, people who reject God will seek some substitute emotional fulfillment: power, profit, or pleasure. In intellectual life, they will seek some substitute to play the role of the divine in their thinking—the ultimate reality, the source of everything else.[77] Worldviews are idols of the heart (Ezek. 14:3).

A major task of worldview analysis is to unmask those idols and debunk their claims. As Timothy Keller writes, "Every human personality, community, thought-form, and culture will be based on some ultimate concern or some ultimate allegiance—either to God or to some God-substitute. . . . The best way to analyze cultures is by identifying their corporate idols."[78]

Modern secular idols arose when doubts were raised about the very nature of truth. It began with the Reformation, which unleashed a century of religious warfare. Countries were torn apart as Christians literally shed one another's blood in disagreements over religious truth. Then came the Renaissance, spurred by the rediscovery of classical texts—Plato, Aristotle, Democritus, Epicurus. And *they* all disagreed with one another as well. Thus the dawn of the modern age was a period of baffling intellectual conflict. The urgent question of day was, How can we be certain *which* of these competing truth claims is really true?

Enlightenment thinkers hit upon a strategy that they thought would cut through the intellectual chaos. They looked for a source of truth more foundational than all the conflicting claims and counterclaims. It would have to be a truth more immediate and more directly accessible than anything offered by the competing theologies and philosophies. That meant it had to be a truth located within the individual—*not* in any of the civic institutions that were engaged in armed warfare against one another, *not* in any of the theological authorities that were denouncing one another, *not* in any of the sacred books or ancient texts that were competing for acceptance. Not in any external source at all. The Enlightenment hope was to find a method that could be used by each individual to discover knowledge strictly on his or her own.[79]

What methods met those qualifications? The two major philosophical approaches that emerged were empiricism and rationalism. Philosophy books often discuss the rivalry between them. But I want to stress what made them alike. Despite their differences, they were blood brothers under the skin. Both were attempts to ground human knowledge on secure foundations apart from divine revelation. Both sought to replace revelation with some other source of knowledge that would be equally certain and equally universal. Both were looking for infallibility within individual consciousness.

They merely disagreed over what that source was.

Empiricists made an idol of the senses. Raw sense data would be the source of absolutely reliable knowledge. Francis Bacon has gone down in history as the originator of modern empiricism. The pursuit of knowledge, he said, must "begin anew from the very foundation."[80] We must clear away everything we think we know, strip away all inferences and interpretations, and get down to the bedrock foundation of knowledge. For Bacon, that foundation consisted of bare sense impressions. They were the avenue to knowledge in its simplest, most direct—and therefore infallible—form.

Rationalists took a different tack. They decreed that knowledge must be grounded on what we can know directly and solely by reason. Think of Descartes with his famous "I think, therefore I am." He proposed a method of systematic doubt (Cartesian doubt) to strip his mind of every fuzzy, unclear, or half-baked idea. Eventually he hoped to dig down deep enough to reach a truth so clear and certain that it could not be doubted.

And what was that bedrock certainty? What Descartes could not doubt was, well, his own mental process of doubting. Even if all my ideas are delusions, he said, there is still an "I" who is experiencing those delusions. He concluded that one can doubt the world of physical objects, but one cannot doubt the existence of one's self. That is the most certain and immediate knowledge possible. On this infallible foundation, Descartes hoped to start over from scratch and rebuild the entire edifice of knowledge.

Surprisingly, neither Bacon nor Descartes were secular thinkers. Both expressed at least some level of Christian commitment. Yet the philosophies they proposed ended up contributing to the secularization of Western thought. Both empiricism and rationalism implied that the path to truth was to start over again from scratch—to reject all teachings, all traditions, all received truths, all revelation claims like the Bible, and begin anew. This is the core of the modernist project, whatever shape it may take: the idea that if you strip away enough cultural debris like laws and customs and traditions—anything humans can be wrong or mistaken about—you would finally reach something you *cannot* be wrong or mistaken about. Why not? Because it was not known by inference or discursive reasoning, but by introspection into the immediate data of consciousness. It was something that cannot be doubted or debated, immune to any external criticisms or challenges. Like the foundation of a house, it would provide a solid, infallible foundation to build the edifice of knowledge.

In other words, it would function as a substitute for divine revelation, providing the same certainty and universality. This is why philosopher Karl Popper speaks of "the religious character of [Enlightenment] epistemologies." Baconian empiricism appealed to "*the authority of the senses,*" he explains, while Cartesian rationalism appealed to "*the authority of the intellect.*"[81] But their goal was the same: to replace divine revelation with an alternate authority.

Along the same line, Randall says Enlightenment thinkers were yearning for an absolute kind of knowledge attainable in reality only by divine revelation. "They were trying to arrive at that complete and perfect understanding and explanation of the universe that only a God could possess," he writes. "Their ideal was still a *system of revelation,* though they had abandoned the *method* of revelation."[82] That is, they had rejected the concept of divine revelation, but they were still seeking the kind of truth that only revelation from a living Creator can provide. Their goal was to find a method by which each individual could transcend his or her limited niche in time and space to achieve a "God's eye" view of reality. In short, they were seeking a God substitute.

God Substitutes

This explains why secularism is not neutral, though it often claims to be. In relation to the biblical God, secularists may be skeptics. But in relation to their own god substitutes, they are true believers. To adapt an observation from C. S. Lewis, their skepticism is only on the surface. It is for use on *other people's* beliefs. "They are not nearly skeptical enough" about their *own* beliefs.[83] And when they enforce secular views in the realm of law, education, sexuality, and health care, they are imposing their own beliefs on everyone else across an entire society.

The consequence of those secular views is inevitably dehumanizing. The reason is that secularism in all its forms is reductionistic. A worldview that does not start with God must start with something *less* than God—something within creation—which then becomes the category to explain all of reality. Think back to Walker Percy's metaphor of a box. Empiricism puts everything in the box of the senses. Rationalism puts everything into the box of human reason. Anything that does not fit into the box is denied, denigrated, or declared to be unreal. The diverse and multi-faceted world God created is reduced to a single category.

Humans, too, are stuffed into the box. Thus every idol is ultimately dehumanizing, leaving a wreckage of pain and alienation in its wake.

The best way to counter secular idols is by offering something better. To counter secular empiricism, there is what we might call a Christian empiricism that affirms the value of the sensory world *without* reducing reality to what the human eye sees. It does not deny the invisible realm of truth, goodness, beauty, and love. And to counter secular rationalism, there is a Christian rationalism that affirms the value of rationality *without* reducing truth to ideas that originate within finite, fallen human reason. A biblically based worldview is capable of affirming the best insights of secular philosophies without ever falling into reductionism. That's because it does not start with anything in creation but with the transcendent Creator. It does not *deify* any part of creation—and therefore it is not compelled to *deny* the other parts of creation. It recognizes and rejoices in the vast diversity and complexity of created reality.

This is genuinely good news. A biblical worldview liberates us from the cramped confines of any reductionistic scheme, freeing us to enjoy the richness and beauty of God's creation. We should refuse to allow good words like *empirical* and *rational* be taken over by secular worldviews. Instead we should work to fill these terms with balanced biblical content.

Concentration Camp Music

By the same token, Christian artists should refuse to allow artistic styles to be defined by secular art theories. The same stylistic elements can often be used in the context of a richer, more humane biblical vision.

5-30 Olivier Messiaen
Quartet for the End of Time, 1941

Christian modernism

Consider just one example: atonal music. One of Boulez's teachers was the French atonal composer Olivier Messiaen. During World War II, Messiaen was interned in a German prison camp. Among his fellow prisoners he found a clarinetist, a violinist, a cellist, and a pianist, so he composed a piece for that unusual combination of instruments. Titled *Quartet for the End of Time*, it was performed for the first time in prison camp Stalag VII for an audience of four hundred ragged fellow prisoners.

Messiaen was a devout Catholic who never shied away from making his convictions clear. At the head of the score he wrote an inscription from the book of

Revelation: "In homage to the Angel of the Apocalypse, who lifts his hand toward heaven, saying 'There shall be time no longer.'" The piece was an affirmation that no matter how powerful the Nazi regime appeared to be, its time would end. Two of the quartet's movements, "Praise to the Eternity of Jesus" and "Praise to the Immortality of Jesus," convey an ethereal serenity. Above one passage (where the composer usually instructs the musician to play fast or slow), Messiaen wrote to play *with love*. The power of this piece, says one music critic, comes from the fact that it was written while living under the inhumanity of the Nazi regime. "In the face of hate, this honestly Christian man did not ask, 'Why, O Lord?' He said, 'I love you.'"[84]

The *Quartet* is definitely a twentieth-century work. Messiaen eliminated any steady beat throughout the piece. (He had heard enough of the steady marching of jackboots.) Instead the rhythm expands and contracts in a fluid manner that contributes to a sense of transcendence. Messiaen combined tonal and atonal elements in a way that made him a target on all sides. The mid-century avant-garde criticized him for being too sweet and sentimental, while the more traditional listening public found him too austere and discordant. Today many composers look to Messiaen as a model of how to fuse the best of modernism with the best of tradition. Instead of confining atonal music to a reductionistic Cartesian framework as Boulez did, Messiaen found ways to use it to express the beauty of the world created by God.

In the next chapter we dare to question other idols in the pantheon of modern thought, as we continue tracing Enlightenment worldviews in the lower story. Our next idol is surely one of the most influential in the modern age. It is time to turn to the impact of Darwinism.

Chapter 6

*"You can learn more about a nation from
reading yesterday's novels than today's newspapers."*
—*James H. Billington*

Art Red in Tooth and Claw
(The Enlightenment Heritage)

All men must die. . . .

It was the law of all flesh. Nature was not kindly to the flesh. She had no concern for the concrete thing called the individual. Her interest lay in the species, the race. . . . Nature did not care.

It was the same everywhere, with all things. He remembered how he had abandoned his own father on an upper reach of the Klondike one winter . . . .

Koskoosh placed another stick on the fire and harked back deeper into the past. He remembered, when a boy, during a time of plenty, when he saw a moose pulled down by the wolves. . . . —the old bull moose—the torn flanks and bloody sides, the riddled mane, and the great branching horns, down low and tossing to the last. He saw the flashing forms of gray, the gleaming eyes, the lolling tongues, the slavered fangs. And he saw the inexorable circle close in till it became a dark point in the midst of the stamped snow. . . .

Hark! What was that? A chill passed over his body. The familiar, long-drawn howl broke the void, and it was close at hand. His hand shot into the fire and dragged out a burning faggot. A ring of crouching, jaw-slobbered gray was stretched round about. The old man listened to the drawing in of this circle.

Why should he cling to life? he asked, and dropped the blazing stick into the snow. It sizzled and went out. Again he saw the last stand of the old bull moose, and Koskoosh dropped his head wearily upon his knees. What did it matter after all? Was it not the law of life?

—Jack London, "The Law of Life," 1901

Jack London's God

With his square chin and dark tousled hair, Jack London was the perfect image of the rugged outdoorsman. It was an image he cultivated skillfully in order to boost book sales. As a result, he became the best-known representative of literary naturalism, a movement that fleshed out in fiction the tenets of *philosophical* naturalism. These were novelists and playwrights who portrayed humans as biological organisms with no real freedom, determined by their genetic heritage and social environment.

As a young man, London worked as a sailor, pirate, hobo, and prospector in the Alaskan gold rush—rough, demanding experiences that prepared him to take a Darwinian view of the world. Largely self-taught, London acquired his education by devouring books in the public library. There he came upon the works of Herbert Spencer, a British philosopher who was the most influential popularizer of evolution in nineteenth-century America. Immediately the young writer underwent what one historian calls "a conversion experience."[1] In Spencer, he found evolution projected onto a large screen, applied not only to biology but also to sociology, art, literature, commerce—evolution expanded into a complete worldview. It was Spencer who coined the phrase "survival of the fittest" (Charles Darwin borrowed it from him). And he saw the process at work everywhere, not only in nature but also in human society. Spencer, more than anyone else in the nineteenth century, brought evolution to America.

And London, more than anyone else, integrated an evolutionary worldview into American fiction. Through Spencer he discovered Darwin, whose works he read so thoroughly that he could quote entire passages by heart. He embraced other materialist thinkers as well, such as Karl Marx and Friedrich Nietzsche. Yet it was Spencer who remained his "god," the deity to whom "he would remain faithful for the rest of his life."[2]

The way he served his god was by writing stories expressing Spencer's evolutionary worldview. In "The Law of Life," Koskoosh is an old Eskimo, abandoned by the tribe and left to die in the falling snow. Weak, blind, and waiting for the wolves that will inevitably devour him, he reconciles himself to his fate by musing that, in the evolutionary scheme of things, the individual does not really matter anyway. Nature assigns the organism only one task: to reproduce so the species will survive. After that, if it dies, "what did it matter after all? Was it not the law of life?" The story pounds home the naturalistic theme that humans have no higher purpose beyond sheer biological existence.

Naturalism may be the most prominent Enlightenment worldview in our own day. One philosopher considers it the "deepest and most decisive" division separating analytic from continental philosophy.[3] In this chapter we will continue our analysis of the analytic tradition (the lower story). After an excursion into Darwinism and naturalism, we will pick up the threads from the previous chapter and show how they were woven together to form the fabric of twentieth-century analytic thought. Then in the following chapter, we turn to the rival tradition of worldviews that stem from Romanticism (the upper story) or the continental tradition.

Scarlett Johansson on Evolution

These two rival traditions—two paths to secularism—ran along parallel tracks, most of the time antagonistic to one another. By the end of the nineteenth century, when literary naturalism arose, Romanticism had degenerated into a faded, moralistic, sugar-and-spice Victorian sentimentalism. In literature it was referred to as the "genteel tradition."[4] It proved an easy target for the naturalists, who claimed to be introducing a more robust and realistic approach to literature. Naturalism was in fact an outgrowth of realism—but grittier, harsher, more pessimistic. It portrayed humans as nothing but biological organisms, products of evolutionary forces.

The literary naturalists were highly effective in communicating an evolutionary worldview to the general public. In our own day, that worldview has filtered down through all levels of society. In 2005 the London Zoo offered a provocative exhibit with a sign that read: "Warning: Humans in their Natural Environment." The exhibit featured men and women dressed in bathing suits with green fig leaves attached. The humans cavorted, posed on the rocks, and pretended to groom like baboons, picking parasites out of one another's hair. Several children were heard asking, "Why are there people in there?" That's exactly the question the zoo was hoping to spark, a spokeswoman replied: "Seeing people in a different environment, among other animals . . . teaches members of the public that the human is just another primate."[5]

What are the implications of seeing humans as "just another primate"? Even Hollywood actresses know the answer to that question. In an interview, Scarlett Johansson was once asked to respond to rumors that she had a reputation for being sexually promiscuous. Her reply was unfiltered naturalism: Humans are merely biological organisms and therefore the practice of monogamy—being sexually faithful to one person—is just not natural. "I do think on some basic level we are animals," Johansson said, "and by instinct we kind of breed accordingly."

Actress Sienna Miller was more caustic. "Monogamy is . . . an overrated virtue," she told *Rolling Stone,* "because, let's face it, we're f——animals."[6] Obviously, Darwinian evolution is not just a scientific theory. It has worldview implications that percolate from classic literature down to Hollywood and into our living rooms.

Aristotle Earns a Nobel Prize

How did Darwinian concepts come to prevail—first in biology and then in literature, art, and popular culture? Prior to Darwin's day, mechanistic theories had become common in fields like physics and chemistry. But they did not work well in biology. Living things were too complex to be explained by blind material processes.

Most importantly, living structures exhibit a goal-directedness (teleology) that has no place in mechanistic accounts. For example, if I were to give a detailed account of all the physical components of an eye—lens, iris, rods, cones—would that tell you what an eye is? Clearly not. What defines an eye is not its physical components but its goal or purpose. It is an organ for seeing.

In this regard, living things do not resemble the things studied by physics and chemistry—rocks and molecules—so much as they resemble human artifacts. If you had designed a tool or gadget and wanted to explain what it was, you would talk about what it does, its purpose. Imagine that space aliens land on earth and find a computer. They analyze it exhaustively in terms of the materials that make it up. They figure out that it is a collection of wires and silicon chips interacting by the laws of electromagnetism and mechanics. When the aliens are finished with their analysis, have they figured out what the computer is? Not at all. The most comprehensive physical-chemical analysis will not reveal the purpose for which a computer was made—to carry out calculations, keep records, play games, check e-mail, and so on. What defines a human artifact is its goal or purpose.

At the dawn of Western culture, Aristotle had already intuited that biological processes are directed by a built-in goal or teleology. Anticipating modern genetics, he observed that the development of living organisms must be directed by some internal program to ensure that chicks grow into hens, not horses, and that tadpoles become frogs, not dogs. Today biologists credit Aristotle with being right in principle, if not in detail. Zoologist Ernst Mayr writes that the discovery of DNA reveals that Aristotle was correct in maintaining "that something more than the laws of physics was needed" to explain living things. What was needed was a teleological principle, which modern biologists call the genetic code: "The blueprint of development and activity—the genetic program—represents the formative principle which Aristotle had postulated."

Geneticist Max Delbrück even playfully suggests that Aristotle ought to receive a posthumous Nobel Prize for discovering DNA. The Aristotelian concept of a teleological principle, he says, was remarkably similar to the modern concept of a genetic program—a "pre-imposed plan" that governs development from embryo to adult.[7]

No God of the Gaps

The idea of a plan or purpose governing living things clearly comports with a biblical worldview. In fact, most of the founders of modern biology were Christians, often clergy. "In the eighteenth and early nineteenth centuries," says Mayr, the study of biology "was almost completely in the hands of amateurs, particularly country parsons." The obvious evidence of design even inspired a form of apologetics known as natural theology (as we saw in chapter 5). The argument went like this: Natural processes acting on their own are blind. They cannot *foresee* the structures an organism will need and design them accordingly. Therefore living structures must be the "wise contrivances" of an intelligent Creator. The title of a book by botanist John Ray in 1722 sums up the theme of natural theology: *The Wisdom of God Manifested in the Works of the Creation.* The marvelous "fit" between an organism and its environment was taken as evidence of purposeful design. God had endowed birds with wings to fly, fish with fins to swim, and flowers with bright colors to attract insect pollinators.

Notice that natural theology was not a god-of-the-gaps argument. Critics sometimes accuse Christians of dragging God into science only to fill gaps in scientific knowledge. The charge is that instead of searching for an explanation, Christians simply throw up their hands and say, God did it—like the ancient Greeks who explained storms by saying Zeus was casting lightning bolts down to earth. But that is a caricature. Natural theology is not based on what we do *not* know. It is based on what we *do* know about living things. Life processes are goal-directed. But physical-chemical forces are undirected—blind and automatic. Therefore they are not adequate to account for the origin of life.

Because the argument from design is based on knowledge, not ignorance, it actually grew stronger as science advanced. The more scientists discovered about the *goal-directed* processes in living things, the more implausible it seemed that life could arise by *undirected* material causes. For two centuries, between roughly 1650 and 1850, natural theology was enormously popular, inspiring most of the fieldwork done in biology during that period. "It is difficult for the modern person to appreciate the unity of science and Christian religion that existed," writes Mayr. "The Christian dogma of creationism and the argument from design coming from natural theology dominated biological thinking for centuries."[8]

Meaningless Materialism

Against this background, we can understand why Darwin's 1859 theory of natural selection invoked a firestorm of controversy. The idea of evolution itself was not all that revolutionary. Various versions of evolution had already been proposed long before Darwin (as we will see in chapter 7). But these earlier versions had presumed a God or Mind behind the evolutionary process, providentially directing it according to some goal, plan, purpose, or design. The reason Darwin's theory was so controversial was that he denied any concept of design. As biologist Jerry Coyne explains, Darwin's ideas "imply that, far from having a divinely scripted role in the drama of life, our species is the accidental and contingent result of a purely natural process." A biography of Darwin puts it this way: "Where most men and women generally believed in some kind of design in nature—some kind of plan and order—and felt a deep-seated, mostly inexpressible belief that their existence had meaning, Darwin wanted them to see all life as empty of any divine purpose."[9]

The core of the evolution controversy can thus be phrased in simple terms: Did mind create matter? Or did matter give rise to mind? According to a theistic worldview, mind is primary. It is the fundamental creative force in the universe (whether God created the world quickly by fiat or slowly by a gradual process). Darwin reversed things. According to his theory, matter is the primary creative force, and mind emerged only very late in evolutionary history.[10]

To be more precise, mind does not exist at all. Only the brain exists. Our thoughts are merely the byproducts of neurons firing in the brain, driven ultimately by the need for survival. In the words of Harvard paleontologist Stephen J. Gould, "Darwin applied a consistent philosophy of materialism to his interpretation of nature," in which "mind, spirit, and God as well, are just words that express the wondrous results of neuronal complexity."[11] That is, they are merely concepts that appear in the human mind when the electrical circuitry of the brain has evolved to a certain level of complexity.

The problem with this view is that it undercuts itself. If ideas are merely the "results of neuronal complexity," then that applies to *all* ideas—including the idea of materialism itself. It too is the byproduct of neurons firing in the brain. In which case, why should we give it any credence?

Materialists like to single out views they disagree with and discredit them by applying evolutionary accounts of their origin. But in the process, they are cutting off the branch they are sitting on. In order to be logically consistent, they must apply the same evolutionary accounts to their *own* views—which makes their views just as meaningless as those they are trying to discredit. To borrow a metaphor from apologist Greg Koukl, materialism commits suicide. When caught in the noose of its own categories, it self-destructs.[12]

The only way for materialists to avoid suicide is to be logically *in*consistent and exempt themselves from their own categories of analysis. As one philosopher puts it, the materialist must function as though he were an "angelic observer" who is somehow able to float above the determinist cage in which he locks everyone else.[13] Whenever a philosophy has to exempt itself from its own categories of explanation, that is a clear sign it is logically flawed.

Blowing Religion to Bits

Despite its flaws, evolutionary materialism became the leading dogma in biology—and all of modern thought. To quote a widely used college textbook, "Darwin's theory of evolution was a crucial plank in the platform of mechanism and materialism," which "has since been the stage of most Western thought," including the arts and humanities.[14]

The literary naturalists used fiction to portray society as a product of evolution, subject to the law of tooth and claw. They proposed to rip away the façade of respectable society and uncover the animal nature at the heart of human nature—the "beast within." For example, Honoré de Balzac treated the novel as a "zoology" of human types formed by adaptation to their habitats. His goal was to tear away the hypocrisy of polite society to show the egoism, passion, and violence lurking beneath.[15]

If humans are mere beasts, then they have no real freedom but are determined by their biological heritage and cultural conditioning. The poet Edgar Lee Masters in *Spoon River Anthology* (1916) pictured humans as rats caught in a trap, struggling helplessly against the wires of the cage. The naturalists' credo is often summed up with a line from *An American Tragedy* (1925) by Theodore Dreiser: "All of us are more or less pawns. We're moved about like chessmen by circumstances over which we have no control."[16]

Dreiser's personal odyssey followed the same trajectory as London's. He too underwent a naturalistic rite of passage by reading Spencer and Darwin. As he later recalled, Spencer blew him "intellectually to bits," destroying the last vestiges of his Catholic upbringing. He concluded that all human "ideals, struggles, deprivations, sorrows, and joys" were nothing but products of chemical reactions in the brain. "Chemic compulsions," he called them.[17]

PHILOSOPHICAL NATURALISM
LITERARY NATURALISM

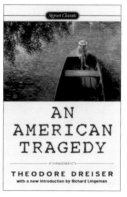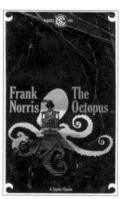

6-1 Edgar Rice Burroughs	6-2 Jack London	6-3 Theodore Dreiser	6-4 Frank Norris
Jungle Tales of Tarzan	*The Call of the Wild*	*An American Tragedy*	*The Octopus*

Humans at the mercy of evolutionary forces

Similarly, Frank Norris portrayed humans as animals under a thin veneer of civilization—brutes beneath the skin. In *The Octopus* (1901), nature is virtually a substitute deity, and a cruel one at that. "Nature was, then, a gigantic engine, a vast cyclopean power, huge, terrible, a leviathan with a heart of steel, knowing no compunction, no forgiveness, no tolerance; crushing out the human atom standing in its way." By the end of the novel, the main character gains brief insight into "the explanation of existence." He realizes that "men were nothings," that "FORCE only existed—FORCE that brought men into the world, FORCE that crowded them out of it . . . FORCE that made the wheat grow, FORCE that garnered it from the soil." The naturalists portrayed nature as immense, powerful, pitiless, indifferent. Its forces completely overshadow the puny, insignificant efforts of human beings.

Zola's Zoology

Like other lower-story artists, naturalist writers took their lead from science. They conceived the novel or play as a kind of laboratory. "The rise of the scientific worldview led to the idea that the stage . . . should become like an instrument of scientific inquiry into human behaviour," writes a theater critic. It would be "a laboratory in which the laws governing the interaction of human beings and social classes could be studied."[18] The naturalists even aimed at a tone suitable for scientific investigation—detached, clinical, and above all, value free. Events were to be presented without moral commentary.

In Gustave Flaubert's *Madame Bovary,* the main character engages in various adulterous affairs and suffers a gradual breakdown of character until she commits suicide. Yet the process is portrayed with clinical detachment—no sympathy, no redemption, no moral to the story. When Flaubert was charged with obscenity, his lawyer defended him by arguing that the book's scenes exhibit the same fidelity to fact as a camera. But that was precisely the problem. Events were described photographically, without moral comment. Flaubert once wrote that art should strive for "the exactness of the physical sciences." He treats his characters as somewhat repellent specimens that he picks up with tweezers to examine.

Today's readers are puzzled by the charge of obscenity, given that the book contains no explicit sexual descriptions. But nineteenth-century readers were far more sensitive to the shift in worldview. They were aghast at the novel's naturalistic worldview—its refusal to apply any kind of transcendent perspective or moral principle—which they recognized as reductionistic and dehumanizing.[19] The literary naturalists may have claimed to be scientific and objective, but they were not simply observing human experience. They were imposing a preconceived philosophical framework that reduced humans to biological organisms in the Darwinian struggle for existence.

The best-known theorist of naturalism was Emile Zola. He disliked the way earlier realists (like Charles Dickens) had laced their stories with moral themes. In Zola's view, the novelist should be an amoral observer—"a recorder who is forbidden to judge." Like a scientist, the novelist simply sets up the lab conditions, then reports on how his human specimens respond: "experiment tried in such and such conditions gives such and such results." The goal was to "dissect piece by piece this human machinery" until the novelist is able to explain human passions by "the fixed laws of nature."[20]

In Zola's *Thérèse Raquin,* a couple engage in an adulterous affair without love, driven by sheer animal drive, then conspire to murder the woman's husband. Afterward they destroy one another psychologically and finally commit suicide. When the book was first published, many readers thought the plot suggested a moral theme—crime and punishment. Outraged, Zola wrote a preface to the second edition making it clear that he had *no* intention of communicating a moral message or dealing with themes of sin and guilt. What he was doing in the book was conducting a scientific analysis of the human personality—dissecting the psyche in the same dispassionate

LITERATURE AS LABORATORY

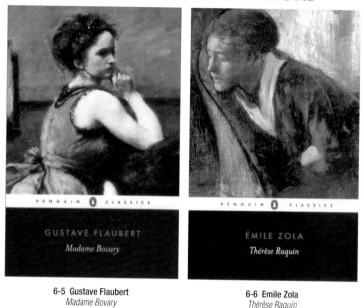

6-5 **Gustave Flaubert**
Madame Bovary

6-6 **Emile Zola**
Thérèse Raquin

"Human Animals, Nothing More"

way a scientist dissects a body. In his words, "I simply applied to two living bodies the analytical method that surgeons apply to corpses." I was portraying characters "without free will," governed by the inexorable laws of their physical nature. They "are human animals, nothing more."[21]

Why Atheism Is Boring

Portraying humans as sheer animals "without free will" was not entirely easy, however. It proved difficult to flesh out believable characters who made no decisions but were swept along by social and biological forces—puppets of fate. It also made for characters who were incredibly dull. There can be no real character development if they are helpless victims of their environment. A professor of film studies says naturalism was frankly "boring." When writers followed Zola's prescription simply to report on how humans react to the environment, it resulted in the loss of a strong narrative line, creating "dramas which meander and never quite reach a resolution."[22]

An example is Anton Chekhov's *The Three Sisters*. The sisters desperately want to escape their provincial town and move to

6-7 **Anton Chekhov**
The Three Sisters, 1901

Why realism is unrealistic

Moscow. But though they keep *talking* about it through all four acts of the play, they never actually do it. They cannot break free from the trap of family customs and social expectations. In
naturalism, explains a drama historian, "man has no freedom from the environment, of which he
is a product and helpless victim." Thus in naturalistic drama, "there is never a decisive beginning
or end, never a clear-cut climax or turn, because man is not expected to make a major decision."[23]
Audiences often find these plays frustrating and depressing.

More significantly, however, a deterministic worldview produces characters that are not true
to life. In reality, people do make genuine decisions. Much of the drama of human life stems from
wrestling with wrenching moral dilemmas. Though naturalism was an offshoot of realism, we could
say its greatest flaw was that it was *not realistic enough*. We all experience the moment-by-moment
reality of making choices. The experience of freedom is attested to in every human culture, in every
era of history, and in every part of the globe.

When naturalism declares freedom to be an illusion, it denies this universal human experience.
But that is not a valid move in the worldview game. After all, the purpose of a worldview is to
explain the basic data of human experience, not to *deny* it.

Even the novelists' own lives did not fit their professed naturalistic worldview. Historian
Cynthia Russett notes that the literary naturalists typically kept their intellectual life separate from
their lived experience. They accepted "determinism as a theory but not something to live by."[24] I
would go further and suggest that they *could* not live by it because it is contrary to human nature.

The test of any worldview is two-fold: 1) Is it internally logically consistent? 2) Does it fit the
real world? That is, can it be applied and lived out consistently without doing violence to human
nature? This second question suggests a biblical form of pragmatism. After all, the purpose of a
worldview is to explain the *world*—to provide a mental map for navigating reality. If the map does
not work in the real world, then it is not an accurate guide. Just as you test a scientific theory by
going into the laboratory to see what happens when you actually mix chemicals in test tubes, so you
test a worldview by seeing how well it works in ordinary life.

Because humans are created in God's image and live in God's world, at some point every non-
biblical worldview will fail the practical test. Adherents will not be able to apply it consistently in
practice—because it does not fit who they really are. Instead they will find themselves living as
though the biblical view of human nature were true—because *that* is who they really are. You might
say that the naturalists' map of reality is too "small." It covers only *part* of reality. As a result, they
cannot live according to its dictates. They keep walking off the map and into "terra incognita"—
terrain that their map does not account for.

Fawlty Reasoning

Consider a contemporary example. Richard Dawkins, who has been dubbed Darwin's
Rottweiler, argues that from a naturalistic perspective, we should not hold individuals responsible

for what they do. After all, he says, the human brain is merely an advanced computer. And when a mechanism malfunctions, we don't *punish* it, we *fix* it.

He presses the point with an illustration from the British comedy show "Fawlty Towers." When Basil Fawlty's car won't start, he first gives it fair warning, counts to three, and finally picks up a tree branch and starts thrashing it. The episode always gets a laugh. But Dawkins asks, "Why don't we laugh at a judge who punishes a criminal? . . . Doesn't a truly scientific, mechanistic view of the nervous system make nonsense of the very idea of responsibility?"[25] So much for the entire Western justice system.

In practice, however, Dawkins admits that he cannot live with the consequences of his professed worldview. A few years ago he was in Washington, DC, promoting his most recent book. A young man was in the audience who worked for a Washington think tank—and who had read *Total Truth*. During the question period, he asked Dawkins, "If humans are machines, and it is inappropriate to blame or praise them for their actions, then should we be giving you credit for the book you are promoting?"

Dawkins quickly backtracked. "I can't bring myself to *do* that," he responded. "I actually do respond in an emotional way and I blame people, I give people credit." We might say that in real life, Dawkins keeps walking off his own map. He acts in ways that his worldview does not account for.

The young man pressed the point further: "But don't you see that as an inconsistency in your views?"

Dawkins replied, "I sort of do, yes. But it is an inconsistency that we sort of have to live with—*otherwise life would be intolerable.*"[26] It was an astonishing admission that in practice no one can live by the naturalistic worldview he himself promotes—that its consequences would be "intolerable."

When your worldview does not work in the real world, that is a sign of something seriously wrong with your worldview. In this kind of pragmatic test, a Christian worldview wins hands down. It insists that humans are created in the image of a personal God, a supreme agent who thinks, chooses, and acts. Thus Christianity has the intellectual resources to explain why *humans* are personal agents, with the capacity to think, choose, and act. It gives a map "big" enough to cover all aspects of human experience. The biblical worldview fits the real world.

Christian Realism

It should not be surprising, then, that the historically Bible gave rise to realism in the arts. In the visual arts, as we saw in chapter 5, realism had its origin in a biblical worldview. And the same is true in literature. In classical literature, a high style was used for nobles and gods, while a low, comic style was used for peasants and farmers. In the ancient world, there *was* no style for portraying ordinary, everyday life seriously and compassionately.

Except in the Bible. Take the account of Peter's betrayal. Peter is a mere fisherman, and his denial takes place among common people—soldiers and serving maids. In classical literature, says Auerbach, such a humble event could have been treated "only as farce or comedy," with Peter portrayed as a comic sidekick or buffoon. Yet the New Testament portrays him as a full human being "in the highest and deepest and most tragic sense." Thus the Bible broke down the classical rules of style. "A scene like Peter's denial fits into no antique genre. It is too serious for comedy, too contemporary and everyday for tragedy, politically too insignificant for history." It is completely unique.

The same is true of virtually all the events in the New Testament. They take place within the lives of common people, yet they "assume the importance of world-revolutionary events." Each individual participates in a moral drama of cosmic importance. As a result, the Bible introduced a realistic style that would change literature for all time.[27] Unlike secular realism, it was not reductionistic. It did not reduce human life to a product of natural forces. On the contrary, it recognized the dignity of ordinary people and commonplace history—precisely because they were *not* merely ordinary and common, but were elements in God's unfolding plan of salvation.

Jane Eyre and the Bible

Biblical realism proposed that the key to a true reading of history was typology, recognizing events as types or foreshadowing. For example, the sacrifice of Isaac prefigures the sacrifice of Christ. The Exodus was a type of salvation, liberation from the slavery of sin. The crossing of the Red Sea was a type of baptism. The Israelites' wandering in the wilderness was a type of Christ's forty days in the wilderness. The manna in the wilderness was a type of the Lord's Supper. The sacrifices and offerings in Leviticus prefigure the sacrifice of Christ. The brass serpent on a pole was a type of Christ being lifted up on the cross. And Moses striking the rock prefigured Christ's suffering, the "Rock of Ages, cleft for me." (See 1 Cor. 10:4.)

In short, history was not a succession of brute facts. It was a work of art, a kind of poetry, filled with types and symbols. Typology revealed that humans live in two interwoven realms of meaning—the material and the spiritual. An event that is genuinely historical participates at the same time in additional levels of meaning. As the eighteenth-century hymn writer William Cowper wrote:

> Israel, in ancient days,
> Not only had a view
> Of Sinai in a blaze,
> But learn'd the Gospel too:
>   The types and figures were a glass
>   In which they saw a Saviour's face.[28]

Under the influence of the Bible, typology became a popular literary technique. As literary historian George Landow explains, it enabled poets and painters "to add another dimension of meaning which spiritually redeems the physical, the material, making it richer and more relevant."

Consider an example. In Charlotte Bronte's novel *Jane Eyre,* the main character realizes she is so madly in love that she "could no longer see God." She had "made an idol" of Mr. Rochester. When she learns that Mr. Rochester already has a wife, Jane uses scriptural imagery to describe her despair. "My hopes were all dead—struck with a subtle doom, such as in one night fell on all the first-born in the land of Egypt." Jane was placing the events of her own life within a spiritual context, recognizing that she was being stripped of her idols just as the Egyptians had been. (Each of the ten plagues invoked by Moses demonstrated God's power over one of the gods worshiped by the polytheistic Egyptians.)

6-8 Charlotte Bronte
Jane Eyre

Multiple layers of meaning

Mr. Rochester tries to persuade Jane to go away and live with him as his mistress, leaving his home, which he calls "this accursed place, this tent of Achan." By using this Old Testament type, he admits more than he realizes, for Achan was an Israelite who stole plunder that was not rightly his and tried to hide it from God—just as Mr. Rochester hopes to keep Jane, who is not rightfully his.

What nineteenth-century writers "acquired from years of meditating upon the Bible," explains Landow, "was a habit of mind, an assurance that everything possesses significant meaning," which "the sensitive eye can read in terms of type and symbol."[29] Biblical typology gave rise to an understanding of history in which ordinary and commonplace events are invested with multiple dimensions of meaning. They are infused with immense dignity as elements in the working out of divine salvation.

Typology is far more than a literary device, however. The New Testament writers speak of Christ's death and resurrection as cosmic events in which that any individuals in any age can participate. "I have been crucified with Christ" (Gal. 2:20). "We suffer with him in order that we may also be glorified with him" (Rom. 8:17 ESV). "Rejoice that you participate in the sufferings of Christ, so that you may be overjoyed when his glory is revealed" (1 Pet. 4:14). The pattern of Christ's life is a prototype that can explicate and give meaning to any individual's life, imbuing both suffering and joy with additional layers of spiritual significance. It provides the pattern by which your life and mine can be woven into the larger story of God's redemption history.

What Embarrassed Hemingway

It was precisely the idea that life has higher layers of meaning that the literary naturalists rejected. In fact, they rejected the idea that life has an intelligible story line at all. In a recent *New Yorker* article, a novelist says, "It is possible to conceive of the debate over evolution as a literary one. Does the universe have an author? Is natural history a story with a plot, or just a random accumulation of anecdotes? Do things reverberate with a secondary, higher meaning, or are they merely what they are?"[30]

The naturalists asserted that the universe does *not* have an author and therefore things do *not* have a secondary, higher meaning. Humans are trapped in a one-dimensional world of sheer biological existence. Nature is "red in tooth and claw." Life is a harsh, dog-eat-dog struggle for survival. This was a dark, gloomy picture of the world, and many naturalists responded by dismissing the very concept of beauty. "The time for Beauty is over," Flaubert stated bluntly. The public has a hard time understanding why many modern artists have rejected the ideal of beauty. But it is understandable when we realize that it was a consequence of a ruthless naturalistic worldview. Works by naturalist writers typically featured sordid settings, violent plots, coarse characters, and language laced with slang and obscenities.

6-9 Ernest Hemingway
A Farewell to Arms

Brute facts

Besides, the philosophy of naturalism taught that metaphysical ideals like beauty and goodness were not even real. They were not facts, only values—products of human subjectivity. And subjectivity introduces bias and distortion into science. It "spoils the data," Zola said. He insisted that novelists should toss out things like moral themes and "symbols of virtue and vice," striving instead to simply record facts like a scientist. "You start from the point that nature is sufficient, that you must accept it as it is, without modification or pruning," Zola wrote. "The work becomes a report, nothing more."[31]

And what *were* the facts that the novelist reports? Only the concrete facts acknowledged by empiricism or positivism—what can be seen, touched, weighed, and measured. This is the theme of a well-known passage in Ernest Hemingway's *A Farewell to Arms*. "I was always embarrassed by the words sacred, glorious, and sacrifice," says a character who clearly represents Hemingway himself.

Only the names of places had dignity. Certain numbers were the same way and certain dates . . . Abstract words such as glory, honor, courage or hallow were obscene beside the concrete names of villages, the numbers of roads, the names of rivers, the numbers of regiments and the dates.

What is this passage saying? That abstract ideals or concepts are unreal—empty rhetoric, pompous pieties, downright embarrassing. That reality consists solely of concrete facts like names, numbers, and dates. Brute facts.

In rejecting abstract concepts, the literary naturalists did not seem to notice that their own naturalistic worldview was itself an abstract concept. It was not an empirical fact but a metaphysical *interpretation* of the facts. As so often happens, their criticism was selective. It was for use on other people's worldviews, not their own.

Duchamp Throws It in Our Face

In the visual arts, the equivalent to Hemingway's brute fact was the found object (French: *objet trouvé*), sometimes called the ready-made. Artists would scrounge up odds and ends—wire, bolts, boards, nails—and present them as art, without adding anything from their own creative vision. This was dubbed the anti-art movement. The resulting works that resulted often struck the public as little more than adolescent antics. But they implied a serious theme—that brute facts are the sole reality, without any intelligible order imposed upon them. Artists were following Zola's naturalistic prescription: Accept reality "as it is, without modification or pruning."

ANTI-ART

 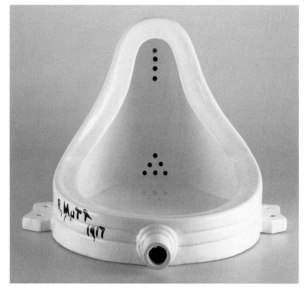

6-10 Man Ray
Gift, 1921

6-11 Marcel Duchamp
Fountain, 1917

Eliminating the hand of the artist

As the artists themselves often put it, the goal was to eliminate the hand of the artist. In selecting his ready-mades, Duchamp explained, his rule was that they "had to consist of something of no aesthetic value." Similarly Man Ray said, "I disregard completely the aesthetic quality of the object. I am against craftsmanship."[32] In other words, the goal was to offer something that had no beauty or design. When artists were persuaded that nature operates by blind, undirected processes—with no overarching purpose, order, or design—then consciously or unconsciously they began to express that worldview by refusing to impose any order or design on their starting materials.

Viewers sometimes try to be charitable by softening the revolutionary intentions of these controversial pieces, saying that artists were merely finding beauty in unusual places. I have read passages that speak admiringly of the smooth, gleaming lines of Duchamp's urinal (preceding page) comparing it to a Henry Moore sculpture. But we should give artists the respect of listening to what they themselves say about their work. Duchamp angrily repudiated those who tried to domesticate his anti-art objects. "I threw the urinal into their faces as a challenge," he growled, "and now they come and admire it as an art object for its aesthetic beauty."[33] We are not being charitable when we tame these artists' defiant gestures by saying, *Oh, how pretty.* To point out the naturalistic, even nihilistic, stance of the anti-art movement is not to impose an external judgment. It is merely to take the artists at their own word. If the universe does not have an author, if it was not created by a supreme artist, then what basis is there for humans to create works of art? This is an honest question, and it was a question raised by the anti-art movement.

Taking God out of Nature

Artists and writers adopted philosophies like naturalism and positivism because they had accepted Darwin's theory of evolution. But the influence also went the other way around. Darwin came to his theory of natural selection because *he* had already accepted naturalism and positivism.

In his *Autobiography* we learn that years earlier he had already embraced naturalism, rejecting the biblical concept of miracles: "The more we know of the fixed laws of nature the more incredible do miracles become."[34] Consequently when Darwin began to consider the origin of species, according to historian Neal Gillespie, "he did so as an evolutionist because he had *first* become a positivist, and only later did he find the theory to validate his conviction."[35] His scientific search was driven by the need to find a theory that would satisfy the philosophy he had already accepted.

The same was true for many of Darwin's supporters. We are often told that the reason his theory of evolution won the day was that it fit the facts. But according Gillespie, the real reason is that many people had already accepted the philosophy of positivism: "It was the prior success of positivism in science that assured the victory of evolution in biology." There was no need to attack Christianity directly, Gillespie adds. One only needed to adopt "positivism as the epistemological standard in science. And this eventually took God out of nature (if not out of reality) as effectively as atheism."[36] That is, once positivism was accepted in philosophy, then Darwinism—or something very much like it—was all but unavoidable in science.

Liberal Book-Burners

The next major philosophy we encounter was an extreme form of positivism called logical positivism. This reconnects with the themes of the previous chapter because logical positivism in a sense combines the two philosophies discussed there: empiricism and rationalism. We even return to David Hume. Logical positivism applies what is sometimes called Hume's fork. Reliable knowledge comes in two forms, Hume said: (1) ideas that are derived from sensation and (2) ideas that are logically necessary, like mathematics. The type of knowledge he had in mind was science. Nothing else was permitted into the category of knowledge—not metaphysics, theology, ethics, or aesthetics.

Hume urged people to use his two-pronged fork to purge books from the library shelves. Take each book in hand and ask: Does it contain experimental reasoning based on facts? Does it contain logical reasoning based on mathematics? If you find anything else—any metaphysics or theology—then "commit it to the flames," he cried. For "it can contain nothing but sophistry and illusion."[37]

Centuries later, in the 1920s and 30s, the logical positivists took Hume's radical program to heart. Their goal was to "purify" knowledge by paring it down to Hume's two elements: 1) sentences stating bare empirical facts and 2) logical connectives ("and," "or," "if . . . then," "if and only if"). The most notorious part of logical positivism was its so-called verification principle, a rule stating that anything that cannot be verified empirically is not merely false but outright meaningless. In the past, for example, atheists had argued that religious statements are false. But according to the logical positivists, religious statements are not so much false as meaningless. The phrase "God exists" may *appear* to be a proposition (a statement that is either true or false). But it is not a genuine proposition at all, they said. Why not? Because the existence of the supernatural cannot be directly verified or falsified by empirical science. They concluded that statements about God are disguised expressions of personal emotion.

The logical positivists applied the same reasoning to morality. When we say *This action is right,* most of us think we are giving information about that action. Not so, said the logical positivists. Making a moral evaluation is akin to saying "Hooray!" or "Right on!" And of course, "Hooray" is not capable of being true or false. It merely expresses approval or liking. If this sounds familiar, it should. It is a particularly virulent form of the fact/value split.

In our own day, the verification rule has retreated into well-deserved obscurity. For it got rid of too much—including logical positivism itself. Could the verification rule itself be empirically verified? No. It was not a statement of empirical fact verifiable by science. It was a metaphysical rule. Therefore it did not fulfill *its own* criterion for truth. As one philosopher comments, "Despite their professed elimination of all metaphysical claims, it seems that the positivists did in fact rely on one central metaphysical doctrine—the principle of verifiability itself."[38] Logical positivism was a philosophy that had to exempt itself from the rule it applied to everyone else, otherwise it would undercut itself. And ultimately that's what it did. It committed suicide.

Abandoning the Big Questions

In spite of the self-destruction of logical positivism, its spirit lives on. It has even redefined the role of philosophy itself. For, ironically, philosophy *as a whole* fails the test of Hume's fork—it is neither a branch of empirical science nor of mathematics. What role is left for it then? Many philosophers decided that the serious business of discovering truth was no longer the task of philosophy. *That* was now the task of science. Philosophy would merely help out by clarifying terms. It became a method for analyzing the concepts and language used in science.

This drastic reduction in the status of philosophy was called the linguistic turn, or linguistic analysis, or analytic philosophy. And a momentous turn it surely was. For the first time since the ancient Greeks, philosophy essentially denied that it had any distinctive subject matter of its own. It was merely a handmaiden to science. Its function was to clear up confusions and obfuscations that arise from the careless use of language. The hope was that once terms were clarified, many long-standing philosophical problems would simply dissolve away.

Analytic philosophy has dominated American philosophy departments through much of the twentieth century. Critics charge that it is not so much a philosophy as an anti-philosophy, for it has abandoned the Big Questions that humans have asked through the ages: Who is God? What does it mean to be human? What is justice? How do we distinguish good and evil? In short, analytic thought discarded the great metaphysical questions that lay at the heart of philosophy for twenty-five hundred years. Instead it proposed that many of those questions arose from muddled thinking, which could be clarified by a close analysis of language. Cut the verbal clutter! Clear away abstract terms and metaphysical speculations! Clean out the cobwebs of centuries! The goal of analytic philosophy was to reduce ordinary language to an ideal universal language couched in terms of formal logic.

Instead of making metaphysical assertions about the nature of reality, philosophy would simply analyze the logical structure of propositions. Philosophy books became studded with symbols of formal logic that look something like this:

$$\neg(\forall x \neg \varphi) \qquad \exists x\,(P(x) \wedge \forall y\,(P(y) \rightarrow (x = y)))$$

Logical formalism gave philosophy an aura of mathematical precision but rendered it unintelligible to ordinary people. Critics often denounced it as "empty formalism," charging that philosophy was no longer interested in finding truth but only in investigating the formal nature of propositions.

Cubist Buildings

The term *formalism* should be familiar because we have encountered it already in the arts (chapter 5). A famous group of logical positivists, who called themselves the Vienna Circle, included several members who were also artists or members of a formalist movement in architecture, which gave rise to the international style. As a result, this style can be considered a visual expression of logical positivism.[39] The movement included the Bauhaus (in Germany) and De Stijl (in Holland). Its bare glass-and-steel boxes are all too familiar in our cities today.

LOGICAL POSITIVISM
INTERNATIONAL STYLE

6-12 Walter Gropius
Bauhaus Building, Dessau, Germany, 1926

6-13 Mies van der Rohe & Philip Johnson
Seagram Building, New York City, 1958

The modernist mentality applied to architecture

The parallels are obvious: Just as philosophers wanted to strip ordinary language of its idiosyncrasies and reduce it to a universal formal language, so artists aimed to strip architecture of all ornamentation and reduce it to universal geometric forms. Even their slogans were similar: Cut the clutter! Clear away moldings, cornices, scrolls, and gingerbread! Toss out historical styles like Greek columns and Gothic spires! The result was flat roofs, smooth facades, and cubist shapes (influenced, in fact, by cubist painting). One of the founders of De Stijl said the goal

6-14 Charles Garnier
Paris Opera House, 1874

Ornate columns, statues, friezes

was to create a style based solely on "numbers, measurements, and abstract line."[40]

This was the modernist mentality applied to architecture: Toss the entire past onto the junk heap and start over again from scratch. The entire city was treated as "a tabula rasa on which one could inscribe totally new, functionalist ideas."[41] The resulting geometric formalism was so popular with architects that it prevailed even when the design did not work. In climates with heavy rain and snow, the flat rooftops were notoriously prone to leak. The reason the style exerted such a strong attraction, says Robert Hughes, was its ultra rationalism: It "seemed to be the epitome of reason—straight lines, rational thought."[42]

The international style is so familiar to us today that we need a bit of historical imagination to sense how shocking it was at first. An example of what was considered impressive architecture at the time was the Paris Opera House, with its ornate columns and winged statues. By contrast, Bauhaus buildings resembled box-like grids. It was the cubist grid applied to architecture.

Designers associated with the Bauhaus went on to apply geometric principles to items *inside* their buildings as well—to furniture and kitchenware. The style was dubbed "the machine aesthetic" because it sought to imitate the smooth, gleaming lines of machinery.

BAUHAUS IN THE HOUSE

6-15 Marcel Breuer
Laccio Table, 1925

6-16 Gerrit Rietveld
Schroeder Table, 1923

6-17 Marianne Brandt
Tea Pot, 1924 (replica)

The machine aesthetic

Bauhaus Bastille

The best-known apostle of the international style was a French architect who went by the nickname Le Corbusier (the crow). His goal, he said, was to "mass produce houses as efficiently as a factory assembly line," made of poured concrete and stripped of all ornamentation. The resulting buildings were standardized cubist structures that he called "machines to live in" because they had the functional efficiency of a machine. By implication, schools are machines to be taught in, and hospitals are machines to be cured in. In fact, Le Corbusier thought of the entire city as a large, efficient machine. His ideal city was constructed of simple, repetitive lines joined by right angles. It was the cubist grid on a huge scale. On the right is his plan for Paris. He wanted to raze most of the city to the ground and rebuild it from scratch. Corbusier called his approach "scientific architecture" and he offered it to city planners as a tool for rational planning and social control.

6-18 Le Corbusier
Paris City Plan, 1925

The grid as social control

Most of Le Corbusier's plans were never built. Yet they exerted an enormous influence, in part because he promised to eliminate dark, irregular areas of the city that were potential hotbeds of sedition and insurrection. As an example, Le Corbusier offered the growth of the early Christian church in ancient Rome. In that city, "the plebes lived in an inextricable chaos," so that "police activity was extremely difficult." Consequently "St. Paul of Tarsus was impossible to arrest while he stayed in the slums, and the words of his Sermons were passed like wildfire from mouth to mouth."[43] Christianity became an illustration of the dangers facing urban planners if they failed to practice rational planning by imposing the Corbusian grid.

Le Corbusier was not alone in his utopian dreams of architecture as a means of social transformation. Many modernist architects were convinced that they stood in the vanguard of social reform. By changing the material structures that shape the way humans *live,* they hoped to change the way humans *think.* The rationalism of modern architecture would make people think and live more rationally.[44] As Ludwig Mies van der Rohe declared in 1927, "The struggle for the new dwelling is but part of the larger struggle for a new social order."

Philip Johnson later recalled, somewhat tongue in cheek, the architects' utopian hopes: "We were thoroughly of the opinion that if you had good architecture, the lives of people would be improved . . . until perfectibility would descend on us like the Holy Ghost and we would be happy for ever after." This messianic vision, Johnson adds wryly, was "one of those illusions of the '20s."[45]

An illusion it certainly was. Ordinary people found the stripped-down buildings austere, utilitarian, and impersonal. The huge glass-and-concrete boxes had no softening materials to add warmth, no decorative touches, no quiet nooks or crannies, no quaint local styles like the half-timber of a Tudor home or the onion dome of an Austrian church. Instead all the buildings were subject to the same monolithic uniformity. Villagers living near the famous Bauhaus school found its stark style so inhumane that they turned it into a boogeyman. German mothers would warn their children, "If you don't behave, I'll send you to the Bauhaus."[46]

Despite the objections of ordinary folk, many cities erected huge housing projects in the uniform style thought to be so modern and functional. Apartments were conceived as cells mathematically calculated to give each citizen so many cubic meters of living space, air, and other necessities. City planners swallowed wholesale the premise of scientific rationalism, treating humans as complex mechanisms whose problems can be fixed simply by slotting them into a Corbusian "machine to live in." They hoped that the construction of decent housing would solve a host of social problems all at once, from poverty to crime to drug abuse.

6-19 Pruitt-Igoe housing development
St. Louis, 1972

Blowing up the Bauhaus

But humans are not merely material beings. They are also social, moral, and spiritual beings. And to ignore those dimensions is to court disaster. The buildings turned out to be high-rise cement prisons—dreary, depressing, depersonalizing. Many became seedbeds of crime and social pathology. Some were eventually dynamited to the ground, most famously the Pruitt-Igoe housing development in St. Louis in 1972. Former inhabitants cheered as it crumbled to dust.

The international style gave brick-and-mortar expression to a rationalist, functionalist worldview that stressed uniformity at the expense of individuality. In the words of social critic Theodore Dalrymple, the "bleak Corbusian functionalism expresses in concrete form the insignificance of man as an individual." The decaying housing projects still seen in cities around the world remain a visible expression of "the materialist and rationalist conception of human life."[47]

The lesson is that philosophical ideas do not stay contained in ivory towers. They affect the way people think and live—and even the kind of buildings they construct. This is not to deny that the geometric lines of the international style can be aesthetically pleasing. And some of us might enjoy having Bauhaus style furniture in our homes. Yet the materialism and rationalism that inspired these styles are not adequate worldviews. They have produced a harvest of damaged lives and desolated neighborhoods.

ABC Art

If logical positivism was given visual form by the Bauhaus, then linguistic analysis was given visual form by minimalism. Recall that linguistic analysis limited philosophy to an analysis of the formal structure of language. Likewise minimalism limited art to an analysis of *its* formal language. The "letters" of a work of art are things like line, color, texture, shape, volume, and space. These are the ABCs of art. Minimalism, with its stark, simple, geometric forms, has actually been dubbed ABC Art.[48] Critics sometimes charge that minimalism reduced art to little more than playing around with the painter's alphabet.[49]

ANALYTIC PHILOSOPHY
MINIMALISM

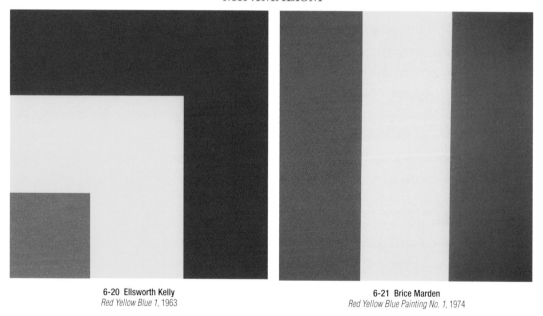

6-20 Ellsworth Kelly
Red Yellow Blue 1, 1963

6-21 Brice Marden
Red Yellow Blue Painting No. 1, 1974

Playing with the ABCs of art

Classical music had its own version of minimalism. It consisted of extremely simple scraps of melody organized in rhythmic patterns repeated over and over, seeming to go nowhere. Because of its near-mechanical repetition, minimalism has been criticized as the "emotionally blank soundtrack of the Machine Age."[50] Because of its simplicity, it has also been disparaged as a kind of ABC music. Music critic Harold Schonberg calls minimalism "a kind of baby music that went back to the classical triad [the three notes of a chord] and little more."[51]

Is it enough simply to play with the ABCs of art? At a L'Abri conference in the 1970s I attended a lecture by Hans Rookmaaker in which he discussed a painting consisting of two brightly colored rectangles side by side, red and green. Afterward a young artist, her voice angry and distressed, asked why he objected to that style of painting.

"What's *wrong* with just being excited about the interesting contrast of colors?" she asked.

"There's nothing wrong with it," Rookmaaker replied. "But that's the kind of thing you enjoy when playing around with colors on your palette. It is not a finished work of art." To call it *art* is to abandon art's traditional purpose of conveying some deeper vision of the human condition.

Colors alone can be visually stimulating, sometimes intensely so. As a result, minimalist paintings can be visually arresting and aesthetically pleasing. In the same way, chord progressions can produce fascinating harmonies. Alliteration and assonance can create arresting patterns of sound. These are all important tools in the artist's toolbox. However, just as philosophy was reduced to analyzing language, so art was reduced to analyzing the ABCs of its craft. As Seerveld comments, modern art "has refined a brilliant alphabet but has nothing to say."[52]

When I visited the Guggenheim Museum in New York City in the 1980s, I listened to a docent discuss a painting that consisted of a monochrome canvas with a small dot toward one side. The docent lectured at length about "the tension produced by the asymmetry" of the off-center dot. Well, certainly. When someone like Rubens paints a scene with the main subject off center, perhaps with sweeping diagonal lines, those elements do produce a sense of tension and movement. However, for a traditional painter like Rubens, these compositional elements were merely the painter's working materials. They were the alphabet used to tell the story. They did not take the place of the story.

Pile of Bricks

In the same way, minimalist sculpture consisted of simple structures repeated over and over. The hard-edged shapes were so simple and precise that they could be produced by anyone. In fact, they could be mass-produced. And typically they were. Minimalist works featured metal boxes and bricks that were not created by the artist but manufactured mechanically in factories. As Hartt explains, minimalist objects refuse "to show anything that might indicate the presence of the artist's hand." They are "standardized and industrial"—"anonymous"—"impersonal."[53]

If the universe is the product of non-personal natural forces, how is that worldview expressed in the arts? By the elimination of all traces of *personal* creativity. Uniqueness of individual expression is replaced by rational uniformity.

I once taught a homeschool course for high-schoolers, some of whom were not thrilled that their parents had signed them up for a subject as arcane as art history. On the first day of class, one of the teenage boys swaggered in with a challenge in his voice. "Are you going to tell us why a pile of bricks can be called art?" he asked.

MINIMALIST SCULPTURE

6-22 Donald Judd
Untitled, 1965

6-23 Sol LeWitt
Two Open Modular Cubes/Half-Off, 1972

Standardized, anonymous, impersonal

"Yes, I am," I said, matching his assertive tone. "By the time you leave this class you will understand what drives modern art. You may not like it, you may not think it is beautiful, but you will understand the worldview behind it."

Below is Carl Andre's notorious "pile of bricks," which sparked fierce controversy when it was first exhibited at the Tate in 1976. It is essentially a grid constructed of 120 bricks—"the number richest in factors," Andre explains. Arithmetic is "the scaffolding or armature of my work."[54] Not only were the bricks manufactured in a factory, they were even assembled by others. Andre did not take part in the construction of the sculpture.

In an interview Andre stated, "I am a materialist, an admirer of Lucretius," referring to the famous materialist philosopher of ancient Rome.[55] Whether or not he was making the connection intentionally, his refusal to invest personal creativity into his works reflected his philosophy that the universe is the product of non-personal material forces.

Of course, none of these artists wholly succeeded in eliminating the hand of the artist. With a little education, you can begin to recognize

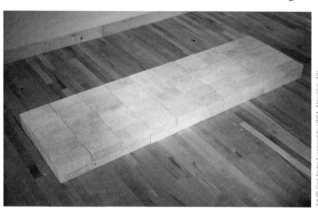

6-24 Carl Andre
Equivalent VIII, 1966

Mathematics and materialism

a Judd or an Andre. That is a clue that their worldview does not fit reality. Because all people were created by a personal God, they cannot completely obliterate personal expression. Even when they reject the biblical worldview in their *thinking*, inevitably it comes out in some way in their *lives*. They cannot help expressing their own nature as individuals created in the image of God.

Painting Is Just Paint

An offshoot of minimalism, color field painting, went even further. Under the impact of materialist philosophy, painting was finally defined solely in terms of its material constituents: paint and canvas. "Only the 'dictates of the medium'—pure paint and the flatness of the picture plane—were held to be worthwhile concerns for painting," Gablik explains. "The work is a painted surface, nothing more."[56]

MATERIALISM
COLOR FIELD

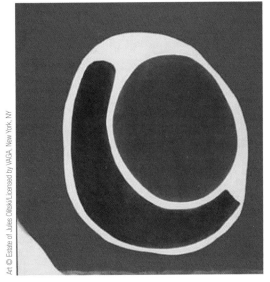

6-25 Jules Olitski
The Prince Patutszky-Red, 1962

6-26 Kenneth Noland
Number One, 1958

"A Painted Surface, Nothing More"

In the artists' own words, "What is of importance in painting is paint" (Jules Olitski). "It's all color and surface, that's all" (Kenneth Noland).[57]

Back in the Renaissance when painters worked out the laws of perspective, they transformed the canvas into a window through which we see the world. Standing in front of the canvas, your attention was not supposed to be focused on the material surface of the painting itself. You were to look "through" it to an illusion of three-dimensional space beyond. An example is the works of Jan van Goyen, who was a master at creating a sense of distance, with a definite foreground, middle ground, and background that seems to recede endlessly (below).

PAINTINGS ABOUT NOTHING

6-27 Jan van Goyen
Shipping on the Kil, 1645

6-28 Frank Stella
Single Consentric Squares, 1974

What You See Is . . . What You See

By contrast, formalists rejected the illusion of space. They treated the picture plane as an opaque surface. It was no longer a window to the world. They even spoke as though any kind of image or representation were "tainted" by association with the entire European artistic heritage. Frank Stella said, "I always get into arguments with people who want to retain the old values in painting . . . asserting that there is something there besides the paint on the canvas"—that is, something besides the sheer material elements. Stella then uttered a phrase that became the unofficial slogan of minimalism: "What you see is what you see."[58]

Stella's point was that painting should not be *about* anything. It should not say or express anything. It should just stand there as a material object in its own right. A painting should be completely self-contained and self-referential, judged solely by how it organizes line and color into a formal whole.

Loss of Transcendence

This view of art is completely unprecedented in human history. After all, "there is no known human society without some conception of a supernatural order," observes Gablik. And "traditionally, artists have used art as a material means of reaching spiritual ends." Only in the modern West has the idea appeared that art has nothing to do with spiritual or ethical truths—that art is merely a way of exploring the formal qualities of line, color, texture, volume, and so on.[59]

Formalism dominated art theory through most of the twentieth century. Artists were asked to jettison narrative, representation, and perspective—virtually the entire Western artistic tradition—and strip painting down to purely formal elements. The parallel with analytic philosophy is clear. Both have turned their backs on the big questions about transcendent realities. Philosopher Ernest Gellner observes that linguistic analysis could be termed "linguistic naturalism" in the sense that it recognizes no transcendent source of truth. It is exclusively "this-worldly"—a "dreary kind of philosophy done under a low and leaden sky."[60]

Formalism likewise represents a this-worldly approach to art. As Barrett writes, there was a time when art offered a ladder to a transcendent realm. But no longer.

> When mankind no longer lives spontaneously turned toward God or the supersensible [beyond the senses] world—when, to echo the words of Yeats, the ladder is gone by which we would climb to a higher reality—the artist too must stand face to face with a flat and inexplicable world.[61]

Gablik calls this an approach to art that has "no remnants of transcendence."[62]

Christian Common Sense

But that is not the end of the story. Just as Christianity offers a true empiricism that refuses to reduce the rich diversity of creation to what can be known by the senses alone; and just as Christianity offers a true rationalism that refuses to reduce knowable truth to the limits of human reason, so too Christianity makes use of the best of analytic thought without reducing it to a dreary, this-worldly perspective. Indeed, some of today's most prominent analytic philosophers are Christians. Their work demonstrates that the precise reasoning and logical rigor characteristic of analytical thought can be used to support biblical truth.

The best known of those philosophers is Alvin Plantinga, of Dutch Reformed background. Tall, lanky, with the typical Dutch chinstrap beard, Plantinga is the founder of what is called Reformed epistemology. About forty years ago, Plantinga's writings burst like fireworks on the world of analytic philosophy, which long ago had relegated theism to the museum of obsolete intellectual curiosities. It turned out that, like every other philosophy, analytic thought contains kernels of truth that make sense only within a Christian worldview.

In fact, its roots originally grew out of biblical principles. Though analytic thought arose in the early twentieth century, it was inspired in part by an earlier philosophy called common sense realism. The founder of common sense realism was Thomas Reid, an eighteenth-century Scottish Presbyterian clergyman. He was responding to his fellow Scotsman, the radical skeptic David Hume. Reid argued that the only way philosophy could avoid ending in Hume's skepticism was to begin with divine creation. The reason we are justified in trusting our minds is that God designed them to "fit" the world he created.

In common sense realism, the term *common* meant "held in common" or "shared by all." There seem to be certain concepts held by all people across all cultures and across all time—for example, that effects have causes, that the material world is real, that there is genuine good and evil, that we are free moral agents, that reason is a valid test for truth, and so on. These concepts are not only universal, they are also necessary for functioning in the real world. No matter how much we question them in theory, we cannot deny them in practice. Reid labeled them "self-evident."

In the eighteenth and nineteenth centuries, common sense realism was wildly popular throughout America. It was held by many evangelical Christians as well as by Deists, Unitarians, and Universalists.[63] When Thomas Jefferson drafted the Declaration of Independence with the phrase, "We hold these truths to be self-evident," he was influenced by common sense realism. It could be said, then, that Plantinga is reviving a classic American intellectual tradition—and returning it to its original theistic context. His technical writings are filled with modal logic and the letter formulas that make analytic philosophy so daunting to non-specialists. Yet his logical rigor has won the respect of even hostile critics. In the journal *Philo,* Quentin Smith, an advocate of philosophical naturalism, says Plantinga has demonstrated that Christians can match their secular colleagues in "conceptual precision, rigor in argumentation, technical erudition, and an in-depth defense of an original worldview." Plantinga's work is proof that Christians are capable of "writing at the highest qualitative level of analytic philosophy."[64]

Other forms of theistic realism, most of them influenced by Plantinga, have swept through the philosophical community. Christians now fill graduate programs, occupy key teaching positions, and write important books in the field of analytic philosophy. In 1978 Plantinga helped to found the Society of Christian Philosophers, which now has more than one thousand members and is the largest organized subgroup among American philosophers. As Quentin Smith observes, in other fields, Christians typically compartmentalize their religious convictions from their scholarly work out of fear of committing academic suicide. But "in philosophy, it became, almost overnight, 'academically respectable' to argue for theism."

The influx of Christians into philosophy has even attracted the attention of the popular press. In 1980 *Time* magazine ran an article titled "Modernizing the Case for God." It once seemed, the article said, that God had been chased out of heaven by Marx, banished to the unconscious by Freud, and driven out of the empirical world by Darwin. But today, "God is making a comeback." The most intriguing thing is that this is not happening in churches among ordinary churchgoers "but in the crisp intellectual circles of academic philosophers, where the consensus had long banished the Almighty from fruitful discourse."[65] Many of today's brightest philosophers are Christians, and they're using the best resources of analytic philosophy to argue in defense of theism.

In short, philosophy is being de-secularized. And that gives hope for reversing the process of secularization in other academic disciplines as well.

Holy Minimalism

It is too early to tell what impact this renaissance of Christian philosophy will have on the art world. There are hints in music, however, where a Christian version of minimalism has emerged. Because *any* return to melody is welcome to the public, minimalist recordings—with their repeating fragments of melody—have sold well. Among the best-selling are recordings by Christian composers who combine minimalism with elements from Byzantine chant and medieval polyphony, creating a haunting, meditative effect.

The style was quickly dubbed holy minimalism. Its best known representatives are Henryk Górecki (a Polish Catholic), Arvo Pärt (an Estonian Orthodox), and John Tavener (a British composer who converted to Russian Orthodoxy). In 1993 Górecki's *Symphony No. 3* reached the top of both the classical and the popular charts at the same time—an unprecedented accomplishment for a living composer. Tavener burst into public awareness in 1997 when his "Song for Athene" was performed at the funeral of Princess Diana. Audiences around the world rushed out to buy the CD.

Interestingly, it was Stravinsky who led the way back to medieval music. As with Pärt and Tavener, it began with a spiritual awakening. In 1925 Stravinsky developed an abscess on his finger, painful enough that he almost cancelled an upcoming piano concert. "Somewhat to his own surprise, he went to a church, got on his knees, and asked for divine aid."[66] The finger continued to fester, however, even as he walked out on the stage. He apologized to the audience for what he feared would be a poor performance and sat down at the piano—when suddenly the pain ceased. He removed the bandage and found that his finger was completely healed. Stravinsky took the sudden cure as a miracle. He returned to the Russian Orthodox Church and wrote several sacred compositions, many of which draw on medieval chant. At the top of the score for *Symphony of Psalms,* for the first time he wrote the same dedication that Bach attached to all his works: "To the glory of God."

Once again we see how Christian artists can borrow stylistic elements that were inspired by modern philosophies, but deepen and enrich them with elements from classical Christian traditions. They are creating works of art that are genuinely modern while expressing the beauty of a biblical worldview.

"Seeing" Worldviews

Through chapters 5 and 6, we have traced the Enlightenment stream of thought, the analytic tradition, through several worldviews—empiricism, rationalism, Darwinism, naturalism, logical positivism, and linguistic analysis. We have watched as these worldviews gradually stripped away all transcendent dimensions to human existence. In fact, every secular worldview is reductionistic in some way. It seizes on some fragment of creation and treats it as the whole story, while dismissing and denying everything that falls outside its prescribed categories. It proposes a box and then tries to fit the entire universe into that box.

Recognizing this dynamic provides a powerful tool for apologetics. You can be utterly confident that any non-biblical worldview will be too "small" to account for all of reality. There will be some things that do not fit into the box. At that point, the worldview fails. It does not have the resources to account for all of created reality.

By contrast, the biblical God is transcendent to creation. Therefore a biblical worldview does not need to divinize any part of creation—nor does it need to deny and denigrate any other part. As a result, Christians can affirm what is good wherever it is found. In these chapters we have been encouraged to see that Christians have not abandoned their posts as cultural creatives. They have wrestled with secular ideas and found ways to restate a humane biblical worldview in both words and images suitable for each age.

Most people are surprised to learn that a large number of artistic styles were inspired by Enlightenment worldviews. Typically we think of artists as Romantics. So let's turn to the Romantic movement and trace the history of the continental tradition. Art and literature help us "see" worldviews unfold before our eyes, so we can be better equipped to communicate biblical truth in our own generation.

Chapter 7

"Art is our religion, our center of gravity, our truth."
—*Franz Marc*

Romancing the Canvas
(The Romantic Heritage)

No one expressed the crisis of the modern age better than the early twentieth-century writer Henry Adams. A lean man with brooding eyes and a drooping moustache, Adams came face to face with the contrast between medieval and modern culture while traveling in France. Visiting Chartres cathedral, he fell deeply under the spell of medievalism. It struck him that the stately Gothic monument, with its richly colored stained glass, was built not by machine power but by spiritual power. The cathedral was a concrete expression of a worldview in which the universe was the creation of a loving God. Communities labored together to give back to God something of genuine beauty.

Adams then visited the 1900 Paris Exposition (a kind of World's Fair) to survey the technological achievements of the modern age. The Gallery of Machines included a huge, whirring steam turbine for generating electrical power. For Adams, the throbbing generator became a potent symbol of the Industrial Revolution and the new society it was creating—one where the central motivation was not to love God but to harness technological power to satisfy purely material

7-1 Chartres cathedral
Rose window, 1230

Spiritual power

wants. The ruthless efficiency of the machine seemed to speak of a universe governed by inexorable mechanical forces instead of God's will. As Adams put it, he began to see "lines of force all about him, where he had always seen lines of [divine] will." Feeling he had no choice but to accept the new worldview, Adams mentally "stepped into the mechanical theory of the universe."

Seduced by the Machine

Like every alternative to Christianity, the mechanistic worldview was essentially a substitute religion, a mental idol. Standing before the generator's huge, humming motor, Adams was overcome by a sense of awe—even worship. For worship is "the natural expression of man before silent and infinite force," as he put it. He even wrote a "Prayer to the Dynamo" warning that humans must either master technology or else be mastered by it.

7-2 Gallery of Machines,
Paris Exhibition, 1900

Machine power

Adams' struggle to adapt to modernity was chronicled in his 1918 book *The Education of Henry Adams,* which became a spectacular literary success. After winning a Pulitzer Prize, it was named the number one book on the Modern Library list of 100 Best Nonfiction Books of the Twentieth Century. Clearly the author's personal crisis touched a deep chord. Many readers shared his concern that Western culture had crossed a chasm. "What his ruminations point toward," said a reviewer, "is nothing less than the rapid collapse of Western culture as science replaces religion and dehumanized people increasingly pray to machines rather than to God."[1]

Adams was particularly sensitive to the change in worldviews because he was a Romantic. Romanticism arose as a reaction against Enlightenment worldviews, and it has remained a potent counter-stream to our own day. In chapters 5 and 6 we surveyed the family of worldviews that were heirs of the Enlightenment—the analytic tradition. Taking their inspiration from Kant's lower story of *nature,* these worldviews were reductionistic. They all tried to chop reality down to fit into a box: empiricism (box of the senses), rationalism (box of reason), naturalism (box of nature), materialism (box of matter), to name just the more influential ones. Now we turn to the family of worldviews that were heirs of Romanticism—the continental tradition. These were thinkers and artists who took their inspiration from Kant's upper story of *freedom.* Yet this tradition gave rise to reductionistic boxes of its own, which we must learn to identify, critique, and counter, in order to oppose the destructive power they continue to exert in our own day.

Sermons in Stones

To get our bearings, think back to the bird's eye view of the two traditions in chapter 4. As we saw there, the Enlightenment raised a serious challenge to the arts—and to the concept of truth itself. Classical physics seemed to suggest a world of sheer matter in motion—atoms bumping around in the void. The only things said to be real were mass, velocity, and extension—things that could be quantified and described in mathematical formulas. These were called *quantities*. By contrast, sensations such as color, sound, texture, taste, and smell were called *qualities.* They were not considered real in the same way. Instead they were said to be subjective effects produced by atoms impinging on our senses.

The term *quality* was extended to include anything that cannot be mathematically weighed, counted, and measured—such as moral ideals, purpose, love, and beauty. These too were said to be illusions produced by the human mind. They had no place in a mechanistic world. As historian Alexandre Koyré says, the mechanistic worldview rejected "our world of quality and sense perception, the world in which we live, and love, and die." In its place, science substituted "another world—the world of quantity, of reified geometry, a world in which . . . there is no place for man."[2] A world in which humans felt alienated.

We traced the outlines of this worldview in chapters 5 and 6. But to fully grasp the shock and alienation it produced, we need to back up further, to the medieval and Renaissance worldview it replaced. A common metaphor at the time was that creation is a book written by God. Therefore it seemed appropriate to interpret it the same way as God's other book, the Bible. This led to the idea that the creation is overlaid with multiple layers of moral and spiritual meanings.

Scholars call this the emblematic worldview because it conceived nature as a collection of emblems (signs or symbols) to be probed for moral and spiritual meaning. Understanding nature was like solving a puzzle or deciphering hieroglyphics. An example was Conrad Gesner's *History of Animals* from the 1500s. In Gesner's entry on *peacock,* for example, we read what ancient authors like Aristotle said about the bird. We learn that the peacock is associated with the goddess Juno. We encounter peacock proverbs, fables,

7-3 Conrad Gesner
History of Animals, 1558

Emblematic Worldview

legends, and even recipes. In other words, in the emblematic worldview, the goal was not to describe an organism physiologically or to classify it taxonomically (as science would do). What was most important was to probe a complex web of associations that linked the organism with history, mythology, religion, and culture.

Think of it as the Proverbs approach to nature: "Go to the ant, O sluggard." That is, learn from the ant to be diligent. For "without having any chief, officer, or ruler, she prepares her bread in summer and gathers her food in harvest" (Prov. 6:7–8 ESV). In short, nature taught spiritual and moral object lessons. "Animals were living characters in the language of the Creator," explains one historian. "And the naturalist who did not appreciate or understand this had failed to comprehend the pattern of the natural world."[3]

The emblematic view was captured in a line from Shakespeare's *As You Like It,* when a character says we find "tongues in trees, books in running brooks, sermons in stones." To the Renaissance mind, this was not anthropomorphism (ascribing human concepts to nature); nature *really did* have multiple layers of significance. The important thing to understand was not the natural causes of things but what they teach us.

The Imprisoned Mind

All this changed with the rise of the mechanistic worldview. It stripped nature of its moral and spiritual meanings, reducing it to nothing but a complex mechanism—cogs and gears. To the Romantics, this was a shocking reduction. It was almost as though the familiar world that humans had always known was now bisected into two separate, antagonistic worlds. The *real* world was said to be a vast machine running by inexorable mechanical laws—"hard, cold, colorless, silent, and dead," in the words of historian E. A. Burtt. Meanwhile, the world people *thought* they were living in—a world of colors and sounds, of morals and meaning—was reduced to purely mental status. The human mind became like a prisoner in a dark room, "a puny, irrelevant spectator" peering out at an alien universe that was starkly indifferent to human concerns.[4]

This worldview was attractive to physicists because it absolved them of the need to consider anything that could not be explained exclusively by their own discipline. Objective reality was limited to what was mathematically quantifiable (quantities). Things that were not quantifiable (qualities) were demoted to a creation of the human mind. As Randall puts it, modernists became adept at "shoving off these qualities, so inconvenient for the mathematical physicist, into a separate and totally distinct kind of thing, the mind." Put bluntly, the mind became "a convenient dumping ground for everything in experience which physics did not read in mechanical nature."[5]

Tragically, what was "dumped" was precisely what makes life worth living. As Sloan explains, "In the mechanistic view of nature, there are neither the qualities occasioned by sense experience—color, sound, and so forth—nor those qualities having to do with aesthetic and moral experience, with mind, meaning and purpose. *Yet these qualities constitute the most important experiences we have as human beings.*[6] No wonder the Romantics found the Enlightenment worldview alienating and dehumanizing.

Blake's Tree of Death

Qualities are also the very stuff of the arts. Essentially artists were being told that they trafficked in illusions—that the colors in a painting or the sounds of a symphony were not real, strictly speaking. The artist's role as a recorder of the natural world was challenged. In the words of historian Jacques Barzun, science had persuaded educated people that the universe was nothing but "the mechanical interaction of purposeless bits of matter." What impact did this have on aesthetics?

> Thoughtful people in the nineties [1890s] told themselves in all seriousness that they should no longer admire a sunset. After all, it was nothing but the refraction of white light through dust particles in layers of air of variable density.[7]

By the same token, why *paint* a sunset? It would only be painting an illusion. In the poignant words of philosopher Alfred North Whitehead, "The heavens had lost the glory of God."[8]

Many Romantic artists responded by treating science as an enemy. The poet John Keats complained that science would "unweave a rainbow" and "clip an angel's wings," relegating both to "the dull catalog of common things." William Blake expressed the same complaint more tersely: "Art is the Tree of Life. Science is the Tree of Death."

The application of science through technology seemed equally destructive. During the Industrial

7-4 Henry Gastineau
Nantyglo Iron Works, 1829
"Dark, Satanic Mills"

Revolution, green hillsides were blackened by coal mines. Cities were smothered by choking smoke from cotton mills. Blake famously denounced them as "dark, Satanic mills." Charles Dickens, in *The Old Curiosity Shop* (1841), gave voice to a lyrical lament:

[The] tall chimneys, crowding on each other, and presenting that endless repetition of the same dull, ugly form, which is the horror of oppressive dreams, poured out their plague of smoke, obscured the light, and made foul the melancholy air.

It was not really science itself that the Romantics opposed. What they objected to was the materialistic philosophy often presented as the inevitable *implication* of science. And they utterly rejected the Enlightenment view of nature as a vast machine to be controlled and exploited for profit. For many Romantics, art became a means of protest against the deadening world of rationalist science and industry—a means to recover a spiritualized view of nature.

Nature as the Language of God

Some Romantics remained within a Christian context. Caspar David Friedrich was an ardent Lutheran. He sought to rescue nature from naturalism by recovering its spiritual dimension. His *Cross on the Mountain* provoked controversy because it was the first altarpiece to consist primarily of a landscape. His goal, explains one art historian, "was to revitalize the experience of divinity in a secular world that lay outside the sacred confines of traditional Christian iconography."[9]

CHRISTIAN ROMANTICISM

7-5 Caspar David Friedrich
Cross in the Mountains, 1807

7-6 Caspar David Friedrich
Abbey Burial Ground, 1810

Rescuing nature from naturalism

Friedrich himself parsed the painting in these words: "The cross stands erected on a rock, unshakably firm like our faith in Jesus Christ. The firs stand around the cross, evergreen, enduring through all the ages, like the hopes of man in Him, the crucified." For Friedrich, rocks and evergreens were not just natural objects. They were symbols of divine communication.[10]

The "Two-Universe" Strategy

Many Romantics, however, felt that modern science had in some way discredited orthodox Christianity. Giving up the unity of truth, they embraced Kantian dualism. Their hope was that the Enlightenment worldviews they detested—empiricism, rationalism, materialism, utilitarianism—could be safely contained within Kant's lower story. At the same time, Kant's upper story would serve as an independent domain where humane and spiritual values could be protected. By this compromise strategy, the Romantics hoped to retain some cognitive territory for things that Enlightenment worldviews had wiped off the conceptual map—things like spirit, freedom, meaning, and beauty.

M. H. Abrams explains their two-story strategy in these words: "By the severance of the *poetic* universe from the *empirical* universe," the Romantics hoped to "achieve the logical distinction between two kinds, or 'universes,' of truth"—between "'rational truth' and 'imaginative truth.'"[11]

The Romantics' two-story truth

IMAGINATIVE TRUTH

Creative world (Art)

RATIONAL TRUTH

Deterministic world (Science)

The division was expressed in various ways. The poet Goethe called it *natural* versus *artistic* truth. But whatever phrase they used, the Romantics began to speak explicitly about a bifurcation of truth into two parallel tracks. As the external world was taken over by scientism, the Romantics retreated to the inner world of mind and imagination.

Metaphysics in Mind

Then they went on the offensive and elevated the mind and imagination to near godlike status. Here's how it worked. Prior to Kant, the empiricists had pictured the human mind as passive. They taught that sensations create impressions in the mind the way a mold pushes impressions into clay. This was the empiricist strategy for guaranteeing that human knowledge was objective, reliable, and trustworthy. For if the mind was passive, then it would not distort the data coming in through the senses in any way.

However, empiricism ran into several dilemmas. If knowledge is limited to sensation alone, then we no longer actually know a great many things we *thought* we knew—even such fundamental concepts as cause and effect. The person who recognized the problem was David Hume, whose name has grown familiar to us by now. Let's say we restrict our attention to information coming in directly through the senses, as empiricism decrees. Where in our sensations do we detect metaphysical concepts such as cause and effect? Nowhere, said Hume. No matter how thoroughly we winnow our sense perceptions, we never find any perception of a causal power. All we actually perceive are events following one another. In everyday language we might say, for example, that fire causes heat. But all we actually *perceive* is the sight of fire, followed or accompanied by a feeling of heat. Over time we develop a mental habit of expecting the two perceptions to appear together. Hume concluded that the concept of causality really refers only to our mental habits and expectations. We can know nothing about whether a causal order exists in the real world.

But if we know nothing about causality, then how do we know anything at all? We cannot trust scientific knowledge, because it depends on cause-and-effect relations. Other metaphysical concepts besides causality are likewise suspect, such as force and matter, time and space, the mind and the self. None of these are sense impressions. Thus, according to empiricism, they tell us nothing about the real world.

When Kant read Hume, it shook him deeply. Later he was to say that Hume awoke him from his "dogmatic slumbers." The scientific revolution had revealed the amazing power of the scientific method to explain nature. Yet here was Hume, logically demonstrating that science was impossible.

Kant set out to salvage science. But how? He decided that if causality is not something we perceive in the world *outside* the mind, then it must be something *within* the mind. Impressions flow in through the senses in a chaotic flux, and it is the mind that supplies the categories that shape, mold, and organize those impressions—the concepts of cause and effect, time and space, before and after. The mind is a grid that imposes form and order on our perceptions. You might say that the mind contains its own furniture into which the guests are forced to fit.

Thus Kant's legacy was the conviction that the mind does not passively receive impressions through the senses, as the empiricists had said. Instead it actively orders and arranges sensory impressions, like a cookie cutter imposing shapes onto dough. (We touched on this briefly in chapter 4.) Thus the order we *think* we discover in nature is actually imposed by our minds. The philosophical label for this is *idealism*. The philosopher Arthur Schopenhauer (himself an idealist) put it this way: Idealism takes the "eternal truths" that were the foundation of all previous philosophy, "investigates their origin, and then finds this to be in man's head."[12]

In other words, the world is not a beautiful, ordered complexity created by God. Instead it is a chaotic flux, and *humans* give it order and structure. Though Kant remained a theist of some stripe, he did not acknowledge God as the source of the natural order, or give thanks. Instead "the human mind took over the creative role from God."[13]

This was revolutionary and Kant knew it. He called it his own Copernican revolution. Copernicus had placed the sun at the center of the planetary system. Now Kant placed the human mind at the center of reality. According to idealism, the world as we know it is constituted by the human mind.

Art as Savior

Kant's Copernican revolution was seized on by the Romantics in their search for a way to overcome the Enlightenment's mechanistic view of nature. The answer seemed to lie in the godlike creative power that idealism granted to the human mind. The empiricist charge that qualities—colors, sounds, meanings—were created by the mind was no longer a liability. In a tour de force, the Romantics actually transformed it into *support* for the arts. For if qualities were created by the mind, then the artist was no longer just a craftsman but a creator. The poet Samuel Coleridge described artistic creation as "a repetition in the finite mind of the eternal act of creation in the infinite I AM." The poet Johann Gottfried Herder wrote, "The artist is become a creator God."

Idealism allowed the Romantics to argue that the imagination is actually superior to mere scientific reason. For it reenacts the very work of God in creating a new world from nothing. "Art is more Godlike than science," said the eighteenth-century painter John Opie, because "science discovers, art creates."

Thus was born the now-familiar notion of the artist as a prophet. William Wordsworth felt that his spirit had been "clothed in priestly robe" and singled out "for holy services." William Butler Yeats said that art became for him "a new religion, almost an infallible Church of poetic tradition."[14] Among the Romantics, says Barzun, "Art became the gateway to the realm of spirit for all those over whom the old religions have lost their hold."

In the process, he adds, art "inherits all the duties of the church."[15] And what were those duties? Every religion offers an interpretation of the world, a worldview, a counterpart to the biblical narrative of creation, fall, redemption. Translated into worldview terms, *creation* refers to a theory of origins: Where did we come from? What is ultimate reality? *Fall* refers to the problem of evil: What's wrong with the world, the source of evil and suffering? *Redemption* asks, How can the problem be fixed? What must I do to become part of the solution? These are the three fundamental questions that every religion, worldview, or philosophy seeks to answer.[16]

The answers offered by Romanticism were adapted from neo-Platonism.[17] In neo-Platonism, the counterpart to *creation,* or the ultimate source of all things, is a primordial spiritual essence or unity referred to as the One, the Absolute, the Infinite. Even thinking cannot be attributed to the One because thought implies a distinction between subject and object—between the thinker and the object of his thought. In fact, for the Romantics, thinking itself constituted the *fall,* the cause of all that is wrong with the world. Why? Because it introduced division into the original unity. More precisely, the fault lay in a particular kind of thinking—the Enlightenment reductionism that had produced the upper/lower story dichotomy in the first place. Coleridge wrote that "the rational instinct" posed "the original temptation, through which man fell." The poet Friedrich Schiller blamed the "all-dividing Intellect" for modern society's fragmentation, conflict, isolation, and alienation.

And what would redeem us from this fall? The creative imagination. Art would restore the spiritual meaning and purpose that Enlightenment science had stripped from the world. In 1820 Thomas Campbell wrote:

> When Science from creation's face
>   Enchantment's veil withdraws,
> What lovely visions yield their place
>   To cold material laws!

The task of art and poetry was to draw the veil of enchantment back over creation's face—just as mist and moonlight soften and transform a landscape, to use an analogy from Wordsworth. Coleridge even praised an artist who learned "to draw from Nature through gauze spectacles" (an early form of goggles).

In short, the artist's imagination would function like rose-colored glasses. It would re-enchant the world, heal the alienation between humans and nature, and usher in redemption. Coleridge borrowed (and distorted) the biblical image of a wedding feast between Jesus and the church: The creative imagination would bring about a "wedding" between the human mind and nature, a "Reconciliation from Enmity with Nature," thereby creating "a new Earth and a new Heaven."[18]

Romantic Despair

There was a fatal weakness in the Romantics' plan of salvation, however. If their re-enchanted vision of nature could be seen only through rose-colored glasses, was it really anything more than an illusion? Coleridge seemed to admit as much when he wrote,

> We *receive* but what we *give*
> And in our life alone does Nature live.

In other words, any sense of kinship we *get from* nature is only what we first *give to* nature. If we hope to perceive anything beyond the "inanimate cold world" of mechanistic science, Coleridge goes on, that vision must come from within:

> Ah! From the soul itself must issue forth
> A light, a glory, a fair luminous cloud
> Enveloping the Earth.
> And from the soul itself must there be sent
> A sweet and potent voice . . .

That is, from the human soul issues forth whatever light and glory we seem to find in nature, whatever sweet voice we seem to hear. For Coleridge, the imagination does not *discover* beauty so much as it exercises its own "beauty-making power."

This was Kant's Copernican revolution applied to the arts. Up until now, aesthetic theory had been grounded in the concept of creation: Art was beautiful because its design reflected God's design in nature.[19] But Kant no longer believed that nature was divinely designed. Thus he detached beauty from the concept of design. He argued that beauty in nature appears *as if* it were purposefully designed, but in reality it is not. In his words, nature exhibits "purposiveness without purpose." That phrase "as if" gives the game away. It says that we're fooling ourselves. In Kant's idealism, beauty is not actually a feature of natural objects themselves. It is merely a mental construct that we impose on nature. A product of the imagination's "beauty-making power."

This was the source of Romantic hubris—and ultimately of Romantic despair. For the truth is that artists are *not* godlike beings with the power to create from nothing. Finite beings like ourselves do not have the power to invest the world with beauty and purpose. And when the project failed, as it inevitably did, the Romantics experienced radical disillusionment and despair. Let's trace that tragic descent.

Spirits and Spells

In their search for a substitute religion, the Romantics recovered supernatural elements that had been banned from the arts by Enlightenment rationalism. They revived ancient myths, fairy tales, and folk legends. In poetry, Goethe was the leader of the *Sturm und Drang* movement (Storm and Stress), composing pieces full of stormy emotions and demonic forces. In his poem "Erlkönig," the title refers to an elf king who entices a dying boy to come live in the fairy world. Carl Maria von Weber stunned opera-goers with *Der Freischütz*, which reintroduced spooky supernatural elements such as magic, spells, ghosts, and a pact with the devil. No one had greater influence, however, than Richard Wagner and his Ring cycle based on Norse mythology, with its Valkyries, Rhinemaidens, Valhalla, and Götterdämmerung (the final downfall of the gods).

As the Romantic age came to a close, its vision was carried on by the symbolist movement. These poets and artists gave art the same two functions: to protest Enlightenment worldviews, while serving as an ersatz religion. As Barrett summarizes, on one hand, symbolism represented "a metaphysical revolt against the kind of world created by the positivism and scientism of the present age." On the other hand, the symbolists regarded poetry not as "an art merely of making verses, but a magical means of arriving at some truer and more real sphere of Being. Poetry becomes a substitute for a religion."[20]

PHILOSOPHICAL IDEALISM
SYMBOLISM

7-7 Carlos Schwabe
Death of the Gravedigger, 1895

7-8 Arnold Böcklin
Isle of the Dead, 1880

Art as a substitute religion

Like the Romantics, the symbolists mined mythology and dream imagery. The dramatist August Strindberg wrote plays with titles like *The Ghost Sonata* and *A Dream Play*. They believed that these dream-like symbols had immense power because they functioned as windows into a higher reality. Where did this conviction come from? It was derived from "the neo-Platonic concept . . . that natural forms were living symbols of a higher reality and that the artist's imagination was the key that could reveal these spiritual truths."[21]

That may sound abstract, but we can understand it better by focusing on that term *neo-Platonic*. Though we have touched on this philosophy a few times already, we must now dig more deeply, for it played an enormous role in the continental tradition. Neo-Platonism was founded in the third century by a Greek philosopher named Plotinus, who sought to imbue philosophy with the inspirational power of a religion. He patched together elements from the major Western thinkers—Pythagoras, Plato, Aristotle, the Stoics—then cast his net still further to include Eastern thought. From these diverse sources, Plotinus crafted a "big tent" worldview. You might think of neo-Platonism as the New Age movement of the ancient world because it combined elements from both East and West.[22] Its central concept, as we saw earlier, was that ultimate reality is the One, the Absolute. This was not a personal God who thinks, feels, wills, and acts. Instead it was a nonpersonal essence or substance.

But how does a nonpersonal essence create the world, since it cannot consciously will or act? Neo-Platonism answered that the One was so "full" of being that it simply emanated other beings automatically, without conscious intention, like the sun radiating light or a fountain spurting water. The world was thus an emanation or manifestation of the divine being. Just as a fountain may cascade down in successive waterfalls, so the world consisted of several levels of being—first a succession of spiritual entities (somewhat like the ranks of angels), then humans, animals, plants, and finally rocks and inanimate matter. And just as the sun's rays gradually fade into dark, so at each descending level, there was less spirit and more matter. The entire series of emanations was called the Ladder of Life or Great Chain of Being. The goal of life was to re-ascend the ladder and re-unite in mystical union with the One.[23]

Back in the Roman Empire when neo-Platonism was first proposed, its main appeal was that it offered an alternative to Christianity. During the first three centuries after Christ, the Christian church grew so rapidly that pagans began casting about for a philosophy attractive enough to counter it. Neo-Platonism seemed to fit the bill. It was not just a philosophy but also a mystical vision of spiritual ascent. Soon it was being wielded as a weapon by paganism in its battle against the church. When Roman emperors persecuted Christians, they often justified their harsh actions by citing the words of the neo-Platonic philosopher Porphyry, who was bitterly opposed to Christianity. In the fourth century, the emperor Julian tried to oust Christianity and restore paganism as the official religion of the Roman Empire. Though he did not succeed, the form of paganism he sought to reinstate was neo-Platonism.

Plato and Modern Science

Despite this hostility to Christianity, surprisingly the church fathers did not reject neo-Platonism outright. It did at least acknowledge the reality of a spiritual realm, in contrast to the materialist philosophers of the ancient world (such as Epicurus and Lucretius). Consequently many early Christian theologians—Clement, Origen, Augustine—reached over and borrowed philosophical arguments from neo-Platonism to defend doctrines such as the existence of the human soul. Augustine even said his conversion to Christianity was helped along by "certain books of the Platonists," which historians believe were works by Plotinus. (The more precise term *neo-Platonism* was not coined until the nineteenth century.)

The writer whose neo-Platonism had the widest influence on later times went by the name of Dionysius the Areopagite, a convert of St. Paul mentioned in Acts 17:34. He was later discovered to be a fraud who lived four hundred years later, so today he is known as Pseudo-Dionysius. Yet for centuries his work was thought to be genuinely apostolic, and was therefore highly revered. Translated into Latin in the ninth century by John Scotus Eriugena, it influenced virtually of all of medieval theology.

During the Renaissance, this neo-Platonized Christianity became quite popular among philosophers and artists (chapter 4). It also had a significant impact on the rise of modern science. Take heliocentrism, the idea that the sun, not the earth, is the center of the planetary system. Where did that idea come from? It was inspired by neo-Platonic dualism, in which God is the immanent soul of the material world. And what would be the most fitting place for the divine presence to be concentrated or localized? The sun. Just as God is the spiritual source of life, so the sun is the physical source of life on earth. And where should the sun be located? The most fitting place was the center of the universe, the only position compatible with its dignity as a divine symbol.

We detect a touch of this neo-Platonized Christianity in the writings of Copernicus, Kepler, and other champions of heliocentrism. In his writings, Copernicus quoted neo-Platonic literature hailing the sun as "the Visible God." He described the sun as "the Lamp, the Mind, the Ruler of the Universe [who] sits as upon a royal throne ruling his children the planets which circle around him." In a similar vein, Kepler wrote that the sun "alone appears, by virtue of his dignity and power, suited for this motive duty and worthy to become the home of God himself." Thus the concept of heliocentrism arose not so much for empirical reasons as for philosophical and spiritual reasons.[24]

Among the early chemists, neo-Platonic dualism led to the conviction that every natural substance consists of matter (called the *passive* element) combined with an internal divine spark or vital force (called the *active* element). The active element in any substance was thought to be the source of its potency—which is why the labels on medicine bottles still list the "active ingredients." Paracelsus, one of the founders of the chemical approach to medicine in the sixteenth century, decided that the active or spiritual ingredients could be discovered by heating and distillation. For example, alcohol was referred to as the "spirit of wine"—which is why alcoholic drinks are still sometimes referred to as *spirits*.

Even the great Isaac Newton retained elements of neo-Platonism, especially in his theory of gravity. The mechanistic scientists of his day taught that causes and effects must have direct physical contact—just as a billiard ball can cause another ball to move only by colliding with it. But Newton's concept of gravity works without any physical contact. The earth does not physically push and pull the moon to keep it in its orbit. Instead it exerts an invisible, intangible force. To mechanistic thinkers, that sounded like magic, not science. They reacted the way we might react to a movie scene when blue lightning zigzags out of a Jedi's finger and causes a spaceship to rise.

Where, then, did Newton get his idea of force? From a neo-Platonized Christianity which suggested that invisible spiritual forces—active elements—represented God's immanent power working in and through the created order. As one historian explains, the concept of force "served for Newton as a manifestation of the divine in the sensible world."[25]

Van Gogh's Starry Religion

Given this brief background, we can understand why the Romantics still considered neo-Platonism a live option for buttressing a spiritualized view of nature. They were especially enamored by the concept of creation as emanation, with its metaphor of a radiating sun or an overflowing fountain. They even applied the same metaphors to the *artist's* creativity. Art was a lamp radiating its own inner light onto the world, a fountain of overflowing emotions. Wordsworth defined poetry as "the spontaneous overflow of powerful feelings." The next major movement after symbolism came to be called expressionism.

The expressionists rejected the Impressionist dictum that the artist should paint only what the eye sees. The expressionist painter Alexej von Jawlensky said, "The artist expresses only what he has within himself, *not* what he sees with his eyes." Music historian Donald Grout summarizes the difference: Whereas impressionism "aimed to represent objects of the external world as perceived at a given moment," expressionism "sought to represent *inner* experience."[26]

Gauguin's *Vision after the Sermon*, featured on the next page, is not intended to show a realistic scene—note the flat perspective, the red background, the lack of any visible light source. Instead it depicts the *idea* in the women's minds as they pray. (They have just heard a sermon about Jacob wrestling with the angel.) As Rookmaaker explains, Gauguin wanted "to overcome the extreme naturalism of the impressionists," finding ways "to include *more* than the eye can see."[27]

In *Starry Night* Van Gogh's whirling stars and flame-like trees are likewise expressionistic. As a young man, Van Gogh wanted to become a preacher, but he was turned down by the theology school where he tried to enroll. Undaunted, he trained as a missionary and worked as an evangelist in a poor coal-mining district in southern Belgium. Determined to share the miners' poverty, he gave away his belongings and slept on the floor. Unfortunately, the missionary school did not appreciate his passion, and he was dismissed. Finally Van Gogh realized that art too can be a means of serving God. His swirling stars and writhing landscape express "a vision that ultimately belongs more to the realm of religious revelation than to astronomical observations."[28]

At times, Van Gogh said, he would try to paint in a more realistic style. But soon he would feel "a terrible need of—shall I say the word?—religion. Then I go out at night and paint the stars."

EARLY EXPRESSIONISM

7-9 Paul Gauguin
Vision after the Sermon, 1888

7-10 Vincent Van Gogh
Starry Night, 1889

The expression of inner experience

Sincerity über Alles

The definition of art as personal expression was a historical novelty. From the dawn of Western culture, art had been defined in terms of reflecting or representing reality in some way. During the Renaissance, artists liked to quote Cicero's maxim that art is "a copy of life, a mirror of custom, a reflection of truth." Leonardo da Vinci said, "The mind of the painter should be like a mirror." Given this definition, the main criterion of a work of art was its truthfulness. Did it offer a true representation? Was the mirror faithful to the original? The goal was not necessarily literal truth, but truthfulness to lived experience.

Beginning with the Romantics, however, the metaphor of a mirror reflecting the world was replaced by the metaphor of a lamp casting forth its *own* light to illumine the world. The artist's creative imagination would imbue the world with deeper meaning. Given this definition, the main criterion of art was not truth but sincerity. The question was not whether a work of art was true to the outer world but whether it was true to the inner world of the poet or artist. Did it match the artist's state of mind? Was it a genuine expression of his inner life? Art was no longer measured by standards of skill or craftsmanship, but by sincerity. Artists no longer recognized a responsibility to be true to nature, but true only to their inner self. This explains why they became willing to distort sense perception to express their inner vision. Gauguin paints the grass red. Van Gogh makes stars that swirl like cartwheels. Whatever helped convey meaning or emotion.

The Bankruptcy of Science

Around World War I, expressionism grew much darker. The war was taken as an indictment of Western science and rationality. Technological progress had not created the promised paradise on earth. Instead it had created grotesquely efficient killing machines—machine guns, tanks, bombs, poison gas. The resulting carnage was on a scale never witnessed before. Hundreds of thousands were slaughtered sometimes in a single battle. "Reason had become irrational and inhuman—soulless technique, technique without a conscience," Kuspit writes. It had also "become aggressively materialistic in this society, dehumanizing people and permitting the inhumanity that ran rampant in the First World War."[29]

Many felt that Europe had committed cultural suicide. "The science I pinned my faith to is bankrupt," laments a character in George Bernard Shaw's 1931 play *Too True to be Good*. "Its cruelties [were] more horrible than all the atrocities of the Inquisition . . . its counsels that were to have established the millennium have lead straight to European suicide."

Western culture seemed to have lost its unifying center. Ever since the Greeks, the arts had been informed by "the idea that a transcendent or unifying order governed the cosmos," says Walford. But now, "fragmentation, chance, chaos, and dissonance seemed more fitting artistic metaphors for human experience than the formal order of established art."[30] Artists began to distort their images even further to create a sense of a hostile, alienating world. They expressed themes of anger and anxiety through sharp angles, jagged lines, and harsh colors. In a line from T. S. Eliot, the world seemed to have collapsed into "a heap of broken images."

EXPRESSIONISM

7-11 **Ernst Kirchner**
Potsdamer Platz, Berlin, 1914

7-12 **Max Beckmann**
Hell of Birds, 1938

"A heap of broken images"

Many expressionist artists had first-hand experience of World War I, like Ernst Kirchner and Max Beckmann, who both suffered nervous breakdown while serving on the front. Later the Nazi regime denounced their paintings as "degenerate" and ordered hundreds of them destroyed. Kirchner committed suicide. Beckmann barely escaped and then painted *Hell of Birds*, which depicts a man being flayed alive by Nazis, some of whom are raising their arms in the Nazi salute.

In drama and film, the sense of alienation was conveyed by distortions in the set itself—walls that tilt precariously or jut into the air. *The Cabinet of Dr. Caligari,* a landmark expressionist film, featured skewed windows, crooked doors, and warped walkways.

7-13 **Robert Wiene**
The Cabinet of Dr. Caligari, 1919

Expressionism in film

Were these works beautiful? They were not intended to be. In the face of such cruelty and inhumanity, it seemed that one could create beautiful works of art only by indulging in Pollyanna sentimentality. "The Expressionists felt so strongly about human suffering, poverty, violence and passion, that they were inclined to think that the insistence on harmony and beauty in art was only born out of a refusal to be honest," writes Gombrich. "It became almost a point of honour with them to avoid anything which smelt of prettiness and polish, and to shock the 'bourgeois' out of his real or imagined complacency." [31]

Art Cries out for Spirit

In spite of their sensitivity to suffering—or perhaps because of it—the expressionists remained open to the spiritual realm. "Man cries out for his soul," wrote art critic Hermann Bahr in 1916. "Art also cries out in the dark, calling for help, appealing to spirit: that is Expressionism."[32]

RELIGIOUS EXPRESSIONISM

7-14 Emil Nolde
Pentecost, 1909

7-15 Georges Rouault
Christ Mocked by Soldiers, 1932

Art cries out for spirit

Many expressionists probed what the Christian gospel meant under such conditions. Emil Nolde was raised in a Protestant family that was intensely religious, but his mask-like faces and strident colors were too expressionistic for the Nazis. He was another painter denounced by the Nazi regime as "degenerate" and forbidden to paint any more.

Georges Rouault worked for a stained glass maker as a young man, an experience reflected in his strong black lines and luminous colors. A devout Roman Catholic, Rouault often portrayed the outcast and marginalized of society—criminals, prostitutes, circus clowns, refugees, and the poor. After the Great War, he devoted much of his work to images of suffering, including a series of prints titled *Miserere,* which means *Have Mercy,* from the Latin title for Psalm 51. The prints depict the horrors of war, interspersed with images of Christ's suffering. The last one is titled "by his stripes we are healed" (Isa. 53:5), conveying a profound message of redemption.

In these examples Christian artists were laboring to develop styles that were genuinely modern yet also genuinely biblical. The results were dramatically different from the sunny, sentimental, even cloying art that clutters most religious bookstores today. Christian expressionism was far more honest about the cruelty and corruption endemic in a fallen, sinful world. As a result, even today it can draw us into a far richer appreciation of the gospel's astonishing claim that God himself entered into the agony of the human condition and shared our suffering, in order to redeem us.

Painters and Pantheists

Some artists within the Romantic tradition decided that the only way to connect with spiritual realities was through abstract art. In chapter 5 we encountered geometric abstraction, with its straight black lines and blocks of primary color. But now we meet a different form of abstract art, often referred to as biomorphic abstraction. It was inspired by Romanticism and expressed a spiritual and organic worldview.

To understand the organic worldview, we must dip into the history of science again. The scientific revolution began in fields like physics and astronomy, but lagged behind in biology.[33] This is not surprising when you consider that physics is comparatively simple and universal. Galileo could drop cannonballs from the Leaning Tower of Pisa and extract generalized laws that apply universally. By contrast, plants and animals are different all around the globe. They are also far more complex than any physical system. As a result, a mechanistic account of living things was always more a promise than an actual accomplishment. For example, Descartes' clockwork metaphor for the organism was extremely influential, as we saw in earlier chapters. But his actual biological theories were exceedingly simplistic and crude, says zoologist Ernst Mayr. They offended "every biologist who had even the slightest understanding of organisms."[34]

By the nineteenth century, the stubborn refusal of living things to fit into any simplistic mechanistic explanation prompted a rebellion among biologists. They began to ask: Why should the machine be the metaphor for nature? Why not the organism? The Romantics decided that the world was not a static machine, but a growing and developing organism. From neo-Platonism they borrowed the idea that nature was permeated by a spiritual essence, soul, or Life Force. In Romanticism, says Randall, "the world was no machine, it was alive, and God was not its creator so much as its soul, its life."[35] In his *Essay on Man,* Alexander Pope described the "vast chain of being" in these words:

> All are but parts of one stupendous whole
> Whose body Nature is, and God, the Soul.

For the Romantics, explains theologian Ian Barbour, "God is not the external creator of an impersonal machine, but a spirit pervading nature."[36] And if matter was permeated with spirit, the implication seemed to be that matter itself has many of the qualities we normally associate with spirit or mind—will, perception, sensitivity, intelligence, and so on. The Romantics concluded that humans are not alone in an alien universe, after all. They enjoy a spiritual kinship with nature.

Long before Darwin

If nature has an inner spirit or life, then it is not static. For what is the central characteristic of life? Growth and development. Many Romantic biologists turned their attention to embryology. In the developing embryo they hoped to discover an internal Law of Development that would provide clues to the stages in the development of life itself.

This marked the beginning of historical consciousness, and it permanently altered the Western mind. For more than a millennium, the neo-Platonic image of a Ladder of Life or Great Chain of Being had been static—a fixed list or inventory of the things that exist in the universe, from spiritual beings to humans, animals, plants, and rocks. The individual might seek to rise up through the rungs to merge with the One (just as in Hinduism, the individual seeks to rise to higher levels of being in each reincarnation). But the ladder itself was static.

Then, in the nineteenth century, the Ladder of Life became dynamic. To picture the change, you might think of the ladder being tilted over to become an escalator—a series of stages through which the entire universe moves upward over time: first matter, then life, then consciousness.[37] And because God is the soul of the world, he evolves along with it. Everything is driven by a universal striving to ever-higher levels on the escalator.

The thinker who tilted the ladder over was Hegel. Writing in the early 1800s, Hegel taught that the Absolute Spirit or Mind unfolds dialectically over time. The Life Force became an immanent deity, a God-in-the-making. Thus, long before Darwin, the Romantics had already embraced a spiritualized form of evolution. This explains why Darwin's biological evolution was welcomed so quickly when it first appeared in 1859—not so much by scientists but by thinkers in fields like history, philosophy, theology, and the social sciences. It also explains, Randall remarks dryly, "why they pretty uniformly misunderstood him . . . and why they failed to see the real significance of his thought." That is, they thought they could use Darwin to support their own spiritualized version of evolution, failing to see that he was proposing a completely materialist version.[38]

To make sure *we* recognize the difference, consider an example. Jean Baptiste Lamarck proposed a theory of evolution in 1801 and is typically listed as a forerunner of Darwin. But the fact is that the two men lived in completely different conceptual worlds. Darwin's theory invokes a purely mechanistic process. Variations appear randomly and then are sifted by the blind, automatic process of natural selection. By contrast, Lamarck's theory invokes a vital power or Life Force progressing toward an end. As a giraffe strives and stretches to reach the upper foliage, its neck lengthens until, over several generations, a new species emerges. What drives evolution forward is the organism's will or internal striving—a biological version of the Romantic idea of a universal striving for higher levels of perfection. "In no serious sense, therefore, is Lamarck's theory of evolution to be taken as the scientific prelude to Darwin's," argues historian Charles Coulston Gillispie. Instead "it was one of the most explicit examples of the counter-offensive of Romantic biology" against scientific reductionism.[39]

Because history is written by the winners, we no longer realize how long Romantic versions of evolution remained popular. Darwin's theory was not elevated to the status of scientific orthodoxy until the 1930s, after Mendelian genetics was rediscovered. (Darwin's theory rests on random variations, but he did not know how they arose.) Until then, concepts of spiritually directed evolution were widely accepted because they seemed to support the concept of divine providence directing the process. "The idea of 'Evolution' proved a Godsend to the religious seekers," writes Randall, because it injected "God and Providence in the evolutionary process itself." It provided a version of evolution that was teleological (directed by a goal or purpose). Thus it assured people that "there is a Purpose in the world, man's ideals do matter to Nature, Heaven will be reached, in substantial form, on earth."

In other words, it assured people that, contrary to what materialism says, purpose and meaning were *not* strictly mental, located only in the human mind. They were embedded in nature as well. And humans were not aberrations painfully out of place in a mechanistic universe. Instead the deepest aspirations of the human mind found support and confirmation in an Absolute Mind permeating nature. Humans were joined to nature by a common spirit. "Everything has a life of its own," Coleridge wrote, and "we are all *One Life.*" Evolution became a process by which the Divine Life unfolds through history. As Randall concludes, "When science seemed to take God out of the universe, men had to deify some natural force, like 'evolution.'"[40]

Hegel and the Cut-and-Paste Bible

When evolution was deified, however, it had to find a way to depose its rival deity—namely, the biblical God. This was accomplished by making theology itself subject to the evolutionary process. If history was the progressive unfolding of the Absolute Spirit or Mind, then ideas themselves must evolve—law, ethics, philosophy, even theology. Hegel taught that no idea is true in an absolute or timeless sense. What is regarded as true in one stage of history will give way to a "higher" truth at the next stage. This radical relativism is called *historicism* because it says there is nothing that stands outside the ever-changing historical process.

The problem with historicism, of course, is that it undercuts itself. It commits suicide. For if everything is historically relative, then so is the idea of historicism itself.[41] In making his claims, Hegel had to presume that he had the power to stand above history and see it objectively as it really is. Yet historicism says that *nothing* stands outside history. Thus it is impossible for a historicist to assert that historicism is true. The only way to avoid suicide is to be logically inconsistent:

Hegel had to exempt his *own* views from the historicist categories that he applied to everyone else's views.

Despite this internal contradiction, historicism was soon imposed upon the Bible—with corrosive effects. Historicism asserts that Scripture is not divine revelation. It is merely a record of human conceptions of God, which evolve over time from simple to complex. The first stage in the evolution of religion is totemism or animism (which seemed simple to nineteenth-century thinkers). The next stage is polytheism (many gods), then henotheism (one main god, such as Zeus on Mt. Olympus), then monotheism (one god). The final stage is the ethical monotheism of prophets like Amos and Hosea, who taught that God is not only one but also holy.

Does the Bible exhibit this evolutionary progression? Clearly not. It teaches ethical monotheism from the opening pages of Genesis 1. Hegel's followers responded by saying, in essence, that just proves that the Bible is unreliable and riddled with errors. They took scissors and paste to the text and rearranged it until it *did* fit their preconceived sequence. Passages thought to express crude or primitive notions (such as verses describing God as angry) were dated earlier, while passages deemed sublime or advanced were dated later. To give the project a tone of scientific credibility, in 1878 Hegel's student K. H. Graf, along with *his* student Julius Wellhausen, proposed a method of "higher criticism" that broke up the books of the Old Testament and re-assigned the parts to different dates and authors. This became known as the Graf-Wellhausen hypothesis.[42]

The irony is that all this Hegel-inspired theorizing took place before archeology had even emerged as a modern discipline. As soon as it did, the claims of higher criticism ran aground on the facts. To give just one well-known example, critics had argued that Moses could not have written the Pentateuch because writing had not been invented yet in his day. But archeologists soon discovered that writing had been invented long before Moses. Today every schoolchild learns about the Code of Hammurabi, which preceded Moses by several hundred years. Even earlier, in Abraham's day, most towns and temples in Babylon had libraries containing dictionaries, grammars, and vocabulary lists in multiple languages for use by translators. The Old Testament writers lived in highly literate, complex, multi-ethnic societies.[43]

7-16 Code of Hammurabi
Babylon, ca 1790 BC

**Writing existed centuries
before Moses**

Nevertheless critics continue to insist that much of the Bible was composed long after the events it describes, so that the text is encrusted with myth and legend. And archeology continues to confound the critics. Several ancient texts have been unearthed: the Nuzi tablets, Mari tablets, Ebla tablets, the Shalmaneser obelisk, the Cyrus cylinder, the Lachish letters. Again and

7-17 Cyrus Cylinder
Persian Conquest of Babylon, 539 BC

Details that just happen to match the facts?

again, historical details mentioned in Scripture have proven accurate—nations, cities, rivers, trade routes, political leaders, customs, traditions. In many cases, these details were later completely forgotten. It is hardly credible that a writer living hundreds of years later would make up stories involving names, places, and customs that just happened to match facts that were unknown for centuries.

Importing Buddha

Hegel's philosophy appeared before any of these archeological facts were available, so it was entirely speculative. Yet it had enormous impact. Spiritualized versions of evolution became hugely popular, especially among artistic and literary figures. They began flocking to assorted spiritual and mystical techniques—astrology, mediums, séances, automatic writing, psychic research, and spirit guides. They embraced occult philosophies such as Theosophy, which had roots in neo-Platonism. In earlier ages, as we have seen, theologians had sought to make neo-Platonism compatible with Christianity. But now people tended to be more intrigued by its affinities with Eastern thought. Schopenhauer became the first philosopher to import full-blown Buddhism into the West.[44] (Nietzsche dubbed his philosophy "European Buddhism.") Because Schopenhauer also offered a highly influential aesthetic theory, his Eastern ideas penetrated deeply into the art world.

However, it was a Russian medium named Madame Blavatsky who had the greatest impact on artists. In the late nineteenth century she developed Theosophy into its modern form. It became a common-denominator mysticism that synthesized Eastern and Western thought, teaching that everything is part of an all-pervading divine essence. Through mystical experiences, the mind can evolve to higher levels of consciousness until it reaches a state of oneness with ultimate reality, the Absolute.[45]

Kandinsky's Spirituality

The most influential artist to fall under Madame Blavatsky's spell was Wassily Kandinsky, often credited with being the first abstract artist. In his highly influential book *On the Spiritual in Art* (1911), Kandinsky affirmed the neo-Platonic doctrine that "everything has a secret soul"— the stars, moon, woods, flowers. The pathology of modern society, he said, consists in its failure to discern the soul in all things: "In this era of the deification of matter, only the physical, that which can be seen by the physical 'eye,' is given recognition. The soul has been abolished."

The reason Kandinsky rejected realism in his art was that he associated it with materialism. If artists follow the rule to paint "only what the eye sees," then clearly they are limited to material objects. Kandinsky decided that the way to get rid of materialist *philosophy* was to get rid of material *objects* in favor of abstraction. Abstract art, he said was "less suited to the eye than to the soul." It would liberate the mind from "the harsh tyranny of the materialistic philosophy," becoming "one of the most powerful agents" of spiritual renewal.[46] Kandinsky's style is called biomorphic abstraction because its forms echo the curved lines of living things.

SPIRITUAL EVOLUTIONISM
BIOMORPHIC ABSTRACTION

7-18 Wassily Kandinsky
Yellow, Red, Blue, 1925

7-19 Franz Marc
Horses and Eagle, 1912

Art as an agent of spiritual renewal

To support his Theosophy-inspired spiritualism, Kandinsky appealed to the rise of atomic theory. Newton had presumed that the atom is a hard, solid mass, like a tiny billiard ball. The term *atom* literally means something that cannot be further divided (Greek: *a* = not, *tomos* = cut). But in 1911 Ernest Rutherford shot atomic particles at a paper-thin sheet of gold foil, and was amazed to discover that most of the particles went right through! Only a few zinged off in various directions—which told him that atoms consist mostly of empty space, with a tiny nucleus in the center. Suddenly, the world of ordinary experience seemed like an illusion. The floor beneath your feet, which seems so solid, is really mostly empty space. The quantity of matter it contains is miniscule. It holds you up mostly by fields of force within the atom.

Many seized on the new atomic theory as scientific support for philosophical idealism (the doctrine that reality is ultimately mental, not material). "The universe begins to look more like a great thought than like a machine," exulted physicist James Jeans in 1931. "Mind no longer appears to be an accidental intruder into the realm of matter . . . we ought to rather hail it as the creator and governor of the realm of matter."[47]

Kandinsky likewise heralded the new physics as the end of materialism. "The collapse of the atom model was equated, in my soul, with the collapse of the whole world," he wrote. "Suddenly the stoutest walls crumbled. . . . Science seemed destroyed: its most important basis was only an illusion." Indeed, is there even "such a thing as matter?"[48]

The world seemed to be dissolving into invisible forces, which seemed akin to spiritual forces. Franz Marc, whose *Horse and Eagle* is shown on the previous page, used lines of force in his paintings to suggest those invisible energies, which he incorporated into a pantheistic view of nature. In his words, "I want a style [expressing] a sensitivity for the organic rhythm of all things, a pantheistic empathy with the vibration and flow of blood in nature."

Historians often lump together all forms of abstraction. Yet geometric abstraction, with its straight lines and right angles, was formalist (lower story). Biomorphic abstraction with its rounded organic shapes, was expressive (upper story). As Gene Edward Veith notes, even as art grew abstract, it continued to show the same bifurcation into "the formalistic and the expressive" modes.[49]

We can recognize the same divide in architecture (see facing page). Whereas formalist architecture had produced austere glass-and-steel boxes, inspired by ideals of geometry and balance, expressionist architecture produced organic or biomorphic shapes, with a sense of movement.[50]

Cloud of Unknowing

Kandinsky is also considered an early representative of a broader movement called abstract expressionism. With its spiritual overtones, it clearly carries on the Romantic tradition of art as a substitute religion. But what *kind* of religion? Many art critics suggest that abstract expressionism has parallels to negative theology (Latin: *via negativa),* an approach that describes God not in

EXPRESSIONIST ARCHITECTURE

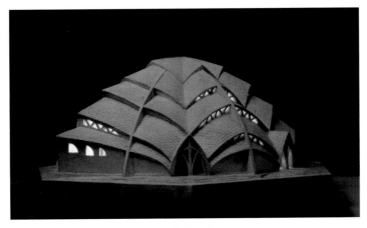

7-20 Otto Bartning
Sternkirche (Model), 1922

7-21 Erich Mendelsohn
Einstein Tower, 1921

Organic or biomorphic shapes

terms of what he *is* but what he is *not*. God is not material; God is not limited; God is not within time; and so on. Historians trace negative theory back to Plotinus, the founder of neo-Platonism, who taught that the One is beyond all human concepts. Therefore any human concept of the One must be false and misleading. The only way to approach the divine is to negate any conception we might have. As Plotinus wrote, "Our thought cannot grasp the One as long as any other image remains active in the soul." Thus "you must set free your soul from all outward things and turn wholly within yourself, lay your mind bare."

Christian mystics have sometimes used negative theology, mostly as a tool to drive out inadequate views of God. A well-known example is the fourteenth-century classic *The Cloud of Unknowing.* It teaches that the way to reach God is to leave behind everything we thought we knew about him, to enter into the darkness and silence of "unknowing." Yet negative theology has never been a major thread in Christianity simply because the Bible makes so many positive statements about God—about his character and his mighty acts in history.

The religions that make the greatest use of negative theology are in the East. In Hindu and Buddhist meditation, the most popular mantra is the syllable *Om*. The purpose of repeating a single monosyllable over and over is to clear the mind—to free it from its preoccupation with the material world until at last thought itself is transcended, inner silence is achieved, and the meditator merges with the Infinite or the Void.

In the same way, an abstract painting is intended to free the mind from its preoccupation with material objects and draw the viewer up to the spiritual realm. You might think of *monochromatic* art (a canvas painted a single color) as a visual parallel to the *monosyllabic* Om. Both are paths to the inner silence or darkness of negative theology—to a unity beyond thought, beyond reason.

7-22 Ad Reinhardt
Painting, 1958

Art as negative theology

Consider, for example, the twentieth-century abstract expressionist Ad Reinhardt, who was deeply influenced by Theosophy. He "developed a religious perspective that blends Eastern and Western mysticism to form what is, in effect, an artistic *via negativa*," says postmodern theologian Mark Taylor. Reinhardt is best known for a series of black paintings that represent, in his own words, a "mystical ascent." The mind leaves behind "the world of appearances" composed of separate images until it reaches an "undifferentiated unity." In this state, there is "no consciousness of anything" and "all distinctions disappear in darkness." The mind attains "the divine dark."[51] It has immersed itself in the cloud of unknowing.

We might borrow a label from Francis Schaeffer and call this a form of "mysticism with nobody there."[52] An experience like this may lift us out of the mundane world, but to connect with what? Not with a transcendent person who loves us, but with sheer silence and emptiness. Novelist Susan Sontag calls it a mysticism that ends "in a *via negativa*, a theology of God's absence, a craving for the cloud of unknowing beyond knowledge and for the silence beyond speech." In the same way, Sontag says, abstract art tends toward "the elimination of the 'subject' (the 'object,' the 'image'), the substitution of chance for intention, and the pursuit of silence."[53]

John Cage and Zen

Both of those themes—chance and silence—became trademarks of composer John Cage. In 1946 an Indian student told him that back home, the purpose of music was to quiet the mind, making it susceptible to divine influences. Cage immediately decided that Western artists had made a terrible mistake in defining art as self-expression. He began to study Zen Buddhism, which teaches that the way to quiet the mind and attain enlightenment is to free oneself of all desires. The implication, Cage decided, was that the composer should not impose his own likes and dislikes on tones. Instead he should treat every sound as an equally valid form of music. To eliminate his power of choice and control, Cage began to compose music using chance methods, such as tossing dice and consulting the Chinese I Ching, to decide what

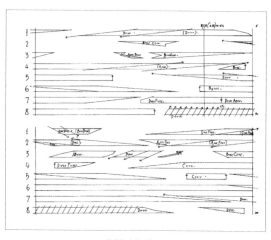

7-23 John Cage
Williams Mix, 1952, composed for tape recorder using I Ching

Buddhism in music

the next note should be. Or he might instruct performers to bang randomly on chairs, tables, and windowsills—whatever happened to be close by—as in his piece "Living Room Music."

As you might predict, a chance collection of notes and sounds typically ends up in chaos and cacophony. The commitment to a worldview has once again trumped considerations of beauty and aesthetics. As a university student, I was invited to play violin in a concert inspired by Cage. In place of musical notes, the composer had drawn loops, whorls, and wiggly lines ascending and descending. The score was written on a long strip of paper, wrapped around several music stands arranged in a circle. The performers walked around the circle playing their violins, oboes, French horns, and so on. Because the music was indicated only roughly by squiggly lines, the musicians had the freedom to improvise. The composer had relinquished his control of the music. Though I was one of the performers, I have to admit that the result was not a piece anyone would want to listen to.

Eveunally Cage descended into complete silence. In his infamous 1952 silent piece titled *4'33"* the musician sits at the piano and suspends his hands above the keyboard, but does not play a single note for four minutes and thirty-three seconds. The "music" consists of the random background noises in the room. The point was to eliminate the artist's creative choice and intention, in order to let the universe itself "speak."

The problem with this approach, observes Begbie, is that it "represents a virtual denial of any human transcendence over nature."[54] In fact, it expresses the Eastern idea that human transcendence over nature is an illusion. In Hindu thought, your sense of being a separate individual is *maya,* illusion. It is even the source of evil—the cause of greed, selfishness, war, and oppression. Thus the goal of meditation is to dissolve all sense of being a separate self by merging with the cosmic One, the undifferentiated All. A poem by Li Po, an eighth-century Chinese poet ends with these words:

We sit together, the mountain and I
until only the mountain remains.

This poem is frequently quoted in books on meditation. *Such peace! Such oneness with nature!* But what is the poet really saying? That a person's goal should be to dissolve into the rock of the mountainside. It's a radically dehumanizing message. The poem implies that the human being has less value and dignity than a rock. So little, in fact, that it is best to dissolve away and disappear into the rock—until only the mountain remains.

The reason Eastern pantheism leads to such a low view of the person is that it has a non-personal starting point. Its deity is not a personal God who thinks, acts, and feels, but a non-cognitive spiritual essence or substance. That's why, surprising as it may sound, pantheism is not really all that different from materialism. It is the flip side of the same coin. Materialism states that everything consists of material stuff. Pantheism states that everything consists of spiritual stuff. Both are non-personal. As a result, both worldviews fail to account for human personhood.

Just as water cannot rise above its source, so a nonpersonal force that does not think, act, or feel is incapable of producing personal agents who *do* think, act, and feel. Thus neither materialism nor pantheism is up to the task of accounting for the origin of human beings. Inevitably they end up denying and denigrating those features in humans that they cannot account for—those features that make a person essentially different from a rock.

It is puzzling that these worldviews are at all popular. After all, what we long for most of all is to be known and loved for who we are as unique persons—a longing that can be met only if the divine is a personal being. The God of Christianity does not erase our individual identity but actually affirms it, calling us to become ever more fully the unique individuals we were created to be. Contrary to Eastern mysticism, the goal is not to *suppress* our desires, but to *direct* our desires to what truly satisfies—to a passionate love relationship with the ultimate Person.

As created beings, of course, we do sense at times our unity with the rest of creation, and these can be powerful and moving experiences. The brilliance of snow-capped mountains, or the calm of a sunny summer day, can lift us beyond the superficial demands of daily life. This might be called a biblical form of nature mysticism. Yet as personal beings, we are also invited to a deeper mysticism—to share in the life and love between the three persons of the divine Trinity, in whose image we were made. In communion with the personal yet infinite God, we actually get in touch with our own personality at deeper levels than we ever thought possible.

Tree-Hugger Art

The tradition of Romantic nature mysticism lives on in land art. Seeking to escape the pressure to commodify their work, artists have abandoned the white-walled galleries of Soho to create abstract artworks in deserts, lakes, and mountains. Using bulldozers and caterpillars, they have constructed huge ramps and spirals, or stretched out fabric gauze across the landscape. These projects are "saturated in nostalgia," says Hughes. They express "the Romantics' awe in the face of nature."[55]

Many of these art works were temporary by intention and continue to exist only as photographic documents. They are a poke in the eye to the Western monumental tradition that once featured marble structures designed to last forever. These works implicitly state that the impact

LAND ART

7-24 Christo and Jeanne-Claude
Running Fence, Sonoma and Marin Counties, California, 1976

7-25 Robert Smithson
Spiral Jetty, Great Salt Lake, Utah,1970

Revival of Romantic nature mysticism

of humans on the planet will not last; that the land will eventually return to its natural state; that Nature will win in the end. *Only the mountain remains.*

Rothko's God that Failed

The art-as-religion movement came to a tragic end in the work of Mark Rothko. His trademark paintings consist of hovering, billowy clouds of color. They are produced by a build-up of numerous thin layers of paint, creating a subtle sense of depth and texture. They are also huge, which is intended to give the viewer a sense of being engulfed by the painting. At first sight, Rothko may seem a lot like the Color Field painters (chapter 6), who were interested only in formal relationships of color and line. But Rothko's motivation was diametrically opposed. "I am not interested in relationship of color or form," he insisted. If you "are moved only by their color relationships, then you miss the point!"

NEGATIVE THEOLOGY
ABSTRACT EXPRESSIONISM

7-26 Mark Rothko
Earth and Green, 1955

7-27 Mark Rothko
Orange and Yellow, 1956

No positive idea of the divine

What *was* the point then? In the same passage, Rothko says people often "break down and cry when confronted with my pictures." Why is that? "The people who weep before my pictures are having the same religious experience I had when I painted them."

What kind of religious experience did Rothko have in mind? In earlier paintings, Rothko had explored Christian symbols, along with images from ancient Greek and Egyptian mythology. But eventually he became convinced that every *particular* concept of the divine is too limited and must be transcended. Thus the huge, almost undifferentiated color fields were intended to suggest that ultimate reality cannot be identified with any definite or specific image of the divine. In negative theology, we can make no positive statements about who or what the divine is. We can approach the truth only through the negation of images.

Yet if you cannot identify the divine in any positive way, how do you even know it is real? How do you know there really *is* a spiritual presence that you are experiencing, and not just an illusion or wish fulfillment?

Toward the end of his life, Rothko worked on several large canvases for a chapel in Houston. The chapel's octagonal shape is the conventional structure of Eastern Orthodox churches, and Rothko's canvases are variations on the triptych format typical of an altarpiece. But instead of containing Christian narratives, the canvases are hauntingly blank, painted in dark, somber colors.

What was Rothko saying with these dark panels? The person who commissioned the paintings said they express "the silence of God, the unbearable silence of God."[56]

7-28 The Rothko Chapel
Houston, 1971

"The unbearable silence of God"

After completing the panels, before the chapel even opened, Rothko committed suicide. An undefined "mysticism with nobody there" is not enough. It does not fill the hunger in the human heart for connection with a personal God who knows and loves us.

Rothko's work reveals the tragedy of the divided concept of truth. The things that give life its deepest meaning, that give us a purpose and reason for living, have all been placed in the upper story, where they are reduced to merely subjective experiences—private, non-rational, and ultimately unknowable. This is artistic alienation at its deepest and most painful. The Romantic hope that art could replace religion by giving meaning to life inspired incredible artistic creativity. But inevitably it failed. As art historian Robert Rosenblum writes, Rothko's "passionate belief in art's magical power to save souls and to open transcendental vistas" now seems remote, its promise empty.[57] All that is left is the unbearable silence of God.

Fujimura and Bomer

Clearly artists like Rothko were struggling with ideas that have life-and-death consequences—ideas they were willing to stake their lives on. We must never treat worldview analysis simply as a way to slap a label on a work of art and pigeonhole it into some neat schema. Historically, artists were not just making pretty pictures but were wrestling with profound questions about life—not through words but through color, texture, tone, and composition. Art is a visual language, and Christians have a responsibility to learn that language.

All worldviews contain some grains of truth, simply because all people are made in God's image and live in God's world. Christians are called to identify what is good, and pour it into biblical wineskins (to adapt Jesus' metaphor). This explains why Christian artists are able to employ many of the same stylistic elements as secularist artists—taking what is true and pouring it into the much richer, fuller wineskin of a biblical worldview.

Among contemporary Christian artists, one of the best known is New York City painter Makoto Fujimura who merges abstract expressionism with an ancient Japanese technique called *nihonga*. In lieu of paint, Fujimura uses ground-up precious stones—gold leaf, lapis, and malachite. The results are works of shimmering color that communicate a sense of grace and hope. I am honored to say that Philadelphia Biblical University (where I have served as a research

CHRISTIAN ABSTRACTION

7-29 Carol Bomer
Weep for the Wiping of Grace, 1998

7-30 Makoto Fujimura
Zero Summer, 2005

Abstract patterns *are* realistic

professor) was the first Christian institution to commission a painting by Fujimura. Many evangelicals are suspicious of any art that is non-representational. But Fujimura responds, "Shall we be suspicious of fireworks spreading their abstraction over a summer sky? Or wave patterns created on the sand? What about classical music, or jazz? Life is full of abstraction."[58] To paint abstract patterns *is* to paint from life.

Asheville artist Carol Bomer combines elements of both abstraction and realism. "I believe that the Incarnation explains and resolves all dichotomies of artistic imaginative work," Bomer says, citing Colossians 1:18 ("in him, all things hold together"). "Christ is both God and man, Spirit and flesh, as well as Word and image. Through Christ and his Word, I attempt to join the tangible world and the spiritual world apprehended through the eyes of faith." Thus she seeks to overcome "the perceived dichotomy between abstraction and realism, form and content, and representation and non-representation."[59]

Bomer uses collage to juxtapose text and image, alluding to Christ as the Word made flesh. *Weep for the Wiping of Grace*, from her Prodigal Series, uses an architectural blueprint as background, which is meant to recall the Scriptural principle that we look forward to the city "whose architect and builder is God" (Heb. 11:10). From this heavenly home, grace descends to the body of the prodigal, who is curled up like a buried seed. The prodigal is following Christ, who descended into the darkness of the earth for us, thus fulfilling his own metaphor of the seed that must fall to the ground and die in order to produce fruit (John 12:24).

Tolkien and Lewis

Turning to writers, some of the world's favorite twentieth-century Christian authors were virtually unreconstructed Romantics. After all, the Romantics were right to protest the reductionism and materialism of the Enlightenment worldview. They were right to keep alive the conviction that humans are more than machines. They were right to search for a worldview that would defend the reality of mind, morals, and meaning. Back in the early church, when the church fathers expropriated what was true from Greek philosophy, they justified it by the biblical metaphor of "plundering the Egyptians." They were alluding to the book of Exodus, where we read that as the Children of Israel left Egypt, they asked the local inhabitants for food, clothing, money, and jewelry—thus "plundering the Egyptians." We might say that some of the best-loved Christian writers have plundered the Romantics, taking what is best and showing that it makes sense only within a biblical narrative.

7-31 J. R. R. Tolkein
Lord of the Rings, 1955

Plundering the Romantics

J. R. R. Tolkien was a Romantic at heart who drank deeply from Old Norse literature and mythology. Through the *Lord of the Rings* film trilogy, Americans have grown familiar with his great saga of good and evil, and its elves, dwarves, ents, and hobbits. Tolkien was revulsed by the machine age. In a letter he once wrote that all his works were about "the fall, Mortality, and the Machine."[60] At the same time, he was fascinated by medievalism. Enlightenment thinkers had denigrated the entire Middle Ages as "the dark ages." But Romantic thinkers, because of their historicism, believed that each stage in history makes a unique contribution to the evolution of consciousness. Thus they rehabilitated the Middle Ages, celebrating knights and armor, castles and quests, magic and mysticism. Tolkien was a major force in rendering these medieval motifs popular among twentieth-century readers.

C. S. Lewis likewise echoed themes from the Romantics. He criticized scientific materialism for "reducing Nature to her mathematical elements." In the process, he says, "the world was emptied first of her indwelling spirits . . . and finally of her colours, smells, and tastes." Having read this chapter, you know what he means: Nature was no longer seen as permeated with life, and qualities were no longer considered objectively real. The result, Lewis says, "was dualism." Humans stood over against a mechanized universe from which they felt alienated. "Man with his new [scientific] powers became rich like Midas but all that he touched had gone dead and cold."[61]

Lewis' passion to overcome this dualism was the force that fueled his own spiritual search. As a young man, Lewis studied under a tutor who was a stringent atheist. Impressed by the tutor's intellectual rigor, Lewis abandoned whatever scraps of childhood faith he had left. Modern worldviews like materialism and rationalism seemed so fashionable and sophisticated. And yet they left his imagination hungry. As Lewis later wrote, "The two hemispheres of my mind were in the sharpest contrast." On one side was "a glib and shallow 'rationalism'," which exhorted him "to believe in nothing but atoms and evolution." It was a worldview he found "grim and meaningless." On the other side was the imagination with its enchanted world of "poetry and myth," "gods and heroes." But that was a worldview he believed to be strictly "imaginary."[62]

Lewis called the two-story division "reason" versus "Romanticism." His close friend Owen Barfield struggled with the same inner tension. Western thought had become segregated into two "prison cells," Barfield wrote. Science was "locked and bolted" in one cell, while the arts and humanities were locked in the other. Both prisoners needed to be liberated before it would be possible to live a unified, integrated life.[63]

This explains why Lewis was "surprised by joy" when he discovered that Christianity provided the unity he longed for. Christ's life, death, and resurrection were events that occurred in the physical world, testable by the same means as any other historical event. Yet they were also the fulfillment of the ancient myths that Lewis had always loved. He used the term *myth* not to mean a story that is false but one that answers the deep human longing for transcendence. In his own words, "The heart of Christianity is a myth which is also a fact. The old myth of the Dying God, without ceasing to be myth, comes down from the heaven of legend and imagination to the earth of history."[64]

In other words, the great events of the New Testament have all the wonder and beauty of a myth. Yet they happen in a specific place, at a particular date, and have empirically verifiable historical consequences. The realm of empirical *fact* is imbued with profound spiritual *meaning*. Christianity unifies the two realms. The biblical worldview fulfills both the requirements of human reason and the yearnings of the human spirit.

When Lewis became a Christian, he did not give up his Romanticism. He merely subverted Romantic imagery to Christian purposes. In *That Hideous Strength* the main character, Ransom, marvels that space is no longer "the black, cold vacuity, the utter deadness, which was supposed to separate the worlds." Indeed "he could not call it 'dead'; he felt life pouring into him from it every moment." Lewis used fantasy to imaginatively portray a world where divine life and divine reason—the Logos—permeate the material universe.

In every age, the gospel fulfills people's most profound aspirations. In New Testament times, the Greeks sought wisdom, while the Jews looked for signs of spiritual power (1 Cor 2:21–25). Christianity fulfilled both. If people were willing to look beyond their normal definitions of those terms, they would discover that "Christ is the power of God and the wisdom of God." In modern times, some people are driven by a hard-headed "reason," while others are motivated by a soft-hearted "Romanticism." Again, Christianity offers fulfillment to both. Biblical truth is rich enough to satisfy all the hungers of the human personality.

Yet the Romantic tradition on the whole did not take Lewis' route back to Christianity. Its pantheism was eventually secularized, giving rise to movements like postmodernism and deconstructionism. To evaluate these movements intelligently and resist their radical impact, we must continue our journey through the upper story. In the next chapter, we will follow the path of continental philosophy up to our own day.

Chapter 8

Art is "the nearest thing to a sacramental activity
acknowledged by our secular society."
—*Susan Sontag*

Escape from Nihilism
(The Romantic Heritage)

"He is a nihilist!"

"What?" asked Nikolai Petrovich, while Pavel Petrovich lifted his knife in the air with a small piece of butter on the tip and remained motionless.

"He is a nihilist," repeated Arkady.

"A nihilist," said Nikolai Petrovich. "That comes from the Latin nihil, nothing, as far as I can judge; the word must mean a man who . . . who recognizes nothing?"

"Say, who respects nothing," interposed Pavel Petrovich and lowered his knife with the butter on it.

"A nihilist is a person who does not bow down to any authority, who does not accept any principle on faith, however much that principle may be revered". . . .

Pavel Petrovich was sipping his cocoa; suddenly he raised his head. "Here is Mr. Nihilist coming over to visit us," he murmured.

Bazarov was in fact approaching through the garden, striding over the flower beds. His linen coat and trousers were bespattered with mud; a clinging marsh plant was twined round the crown of his old round hat, in his right hand he held a small bag in which something alive was wriggling. He walked quickly up to the terrace and said with a nod, "Good morning, gentlemen; sorry I was late for tea; I'll join you in a moment. I just have to put these prisoners away."

"What have you there, leeches?" asked Pavel Petrovich.

"No, frogs."

"Do you eat them or keep them for breeding?"

"For experiments," answered Bazarov indifferently, and went into the house.

"So he's going to cut them up," observed Pavel Petrovich; "he has no faith in principles, but he has faith in frogs."

—Ivan Turgenev, *Fathers and Sons*, 1862

Monks and Beasts

When Turgenev published *Fathers and Sons*, it ignited instant controversy. The book is typically regarded as a fictional account of the generation gap, with the "sons" represented by Arkady and his friend Bazarov, and the "fathers" represented by Arkady's father and uncle, Nikolai and Pavel Petrovich. Yet Turgenev's goal was not just to probe the perennial tension between the generations. His aim was to portray the emergence of a genuinely novel personality type: the new "scientific man."

Turgenev's creative insight was that worldviews form character—and that the modern science-based worldview was actually producing a new personality type, represented by Bazarov. Deliberately curt and abrupt (good manners are a sign of aristocratic snobbery), Bazarov rejects anything not established by the methods of natural science. Art, music, poetry, beauty—all of it he dismisses as "Romantic rubbish." The philosophy of empiricism has taught him that the most exalted ideals and moral principles derive ultimately from sense perceptions. "All principles are reducible to mere sensations," he declares. As a result, "a decent chemist is twenty times more useful than any poet."

The two "sons" eagerly devour books by the most widely read science popularizers of Turgenev's own day, an emerging breed of materialists including Ludwig Büchner, Jacob Moleschott, and Karl Vogt.[1] When Bazarov discovers that Arkady's father still reads Romantic poets like Pushkin, he is disgusted.

"It's something astonishing," went on Bazarov, "these old Romantic idealists! . . . Please explain to him how utterly useless that is. After all he's not a boy. It's high time he got rid of such rubbish. And what an idea to be Romantic in our times! Give him something sensible tread."

"What should I give him?" asked Arkady.

"Oh, I think Büchner's Stoff und Kraft [Matter and Force] to start with."

Clearly Turgenev was using a story about generational conflict to flesh out the broader antagonism between the Romantics and a new breed of Enlightenment thinkers. By the end of the nineteenth century, Romantic literature had come to seem soft and foppish. We saw this in chapter 6, when the literary naturalists rejected Romanticism as insufferable Victorian sentimentalism. Many young people reacted by adopting a hard, doctrinaire materialism. They rejected Romanticism's concept of a Life Force as too vague and metaphysical to be accessible to scientific study. And they challenged the older generation to face up to the materialistic implications of Darwinism.

The greatest scientific advances of the day were occurring in the physical sciences, where successes seemed to be chalked up daily. The only way for biology to match that success rate, it seemed, was to borrow its methodology from the physical sciences. Many began to insist that life processes could be subject to scientific explanation only if they were reduced to physics and chemistry. When Bazarov is asked why he collects frogs, he responds that humans themselves are little more than glorified frogs: "I shall cut the frog open and see what's going on in his inside, and then, as you and I are much as frogs (only we walk on two legs), I shall know what's going on inside us too."

The upshot is that at the end of the nineteenth century, the successors to Romanticism faced a newly energized opposition from Enlightenment materialism and even outright nihilism (the denial of all moral or metaphysical truths). Turgenev's novel made *nihilism* a household word in Russia. Even Nietzsche, the best-known philosopher of nihilism, picked up the term by reading the novel. The historical figures whose names appear in the story—Büchner, Moleschott, and Vogt—were aggressively using their scientific credentials to attack religion and promote a materialistic worldview, somewhat like the New Atheists in our own day.

By this time, materialism had moved beyond the simple Cartesian clockwork image of the organism to include new developments in electricity and thermodynamics. Yet it was, if anything, even more doctrinaire. Biologists began to picture the body as an electrical machine, with nerves acting as wires. "In the 1860s and 70s, at a time when electrical machines such as the telegraph seemed a great marvel, physicians and the public alike came to understand the brain as an electrical machine," operating by input/output mechanisms.[2] The tension between Enlightenment and Romantic worldviews was growing acute.

Nor was it merely a philosophical tension. The two conflicting views of human nature often waged war within people's hearts and minds. In *Howards End* (1910) E. M. Forster laments that people are painfully divided between the "passion" side of their character (artistic, spiritual) and the "prose" side (scientific, material). "We are meaningless fragments, half monks, half beasts," longing to find "the rainbow bridge" that will connect the two. The best-known line from the novel is, "Only connect! . . . Only connect the prose and the passion." Forster literally calls this a "sermon" pointing the way to "salvation."

In this chapter we will continue to follow the post-Romantics' quest for salvation to our own day. We will see how their false promises of salvation turned out to be just as harmful and dehumanizing as the Enlightenment reductionism they were hoping to counter.

Salvador's Salvation

In the late nineteenth and early twentieth centuries, the Romantic concept of an Absolute Mind or Life Force was reinterpreted in a form more suitable for a psychological age. It became identified with a universal or collective Mind that could be tapped via the unconscious forces in the subterranean levels of the human mind. The concept of an unconscious mind was given a quasi-scientific interpretation by Sigmund Freud. To probe its depth, he proposed a toolbox of psychotherapeutic techniques, such as dreams and free association. In the original German, Freud did not write about the *mind* but the *soul (Seele)*. Thus, in Europe, many regarded Freud's techniques as methods for uncovering the inner depths of the soul.

Carl Jung recast the Life Force as a Collective Unconscious containing the accumulated wisdom of the human race throughout its entire evolution. He taught that we can tap that wisdom through myths, dreams, legends, and symbols. Jung even used religious language, urging artists to draw upon "the healing and redeeming forces of the collective psyche."[3]

COLLECTIVE UNCONSCIOUS
SURREALISM

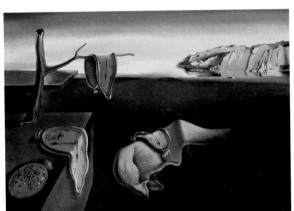

8-1 Salvador Dali
The Persistence of Memory, 1931

8-2 Giorgio de Chirico
Love Song, 1914

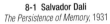

Irrationality as salvation

These ideas gave rise to surrealism, with its dream-like images. Objects were portrayed with hard-edged realism but dislocated in random associations, somewhat like the free association used in psychoanalysis. In fact, the surrealists practiced a host of psychoanalytic techniques—including hypnotism and dream analysis—in an effort to overcome the control of reason and connect with the unconscious. They might admit that reason can give us science, but insisted that only *unreason* can give us art. Why? Because analytical reason employs concepts that are fixed and stable; therefore it is not capable of capturing the evolving flux of the Life Force. Only by transcending reason can we immerse ourselves in the concrete flow of existence. Dali wrote that his ambition was to "materialize images of concrete irrationality."

Irrationality was elevated to a means of liberation—even salvation. As Barzun explains, "The wish to be saved was recast as the hope that through art the barrier between the conscious mind and the unconscious would be broken down."[4] This was not salvation by a personal God who knows and loves us, but salvation by immersing oneself in the Life Force. Once again, it is a mysticism with nobody there.

Klee at Play

If the surrealists portrayed objects realistically but in random juxtapositions, the next step was to submit objects themselves to random or chance processes. This step was taken by abstract expressionism, which began with Kandinsky (chapter 7) but came to prominence in the mid-twentieth century. It suggested that the way to let the Life Force create through the artist was to eliminate all conscious control. The artist should not plan his work ahead of time but simply let it "grow" organically according to its own laws.[5] For example, abstract expressionists used a kind of automatic drawing (*automatism*), in which they would simply doodle random lines, or play with shapes and colors, until images emerged. They also used chance processes such as dripping or pouring paint, letting it flow and pool on the canvas. "I prepare the ground for a picture by cleaning my brush over the canvas," Joan Miro said playfully. "Spilling a little turpentine can also be helpful."

The resulting style featured organic shapes that look a bit like jellyfish or amoebas floating across the canvas. This is biomorphic abstraction and it is exemplified in the paintings by Miró and Arshile Gorky on the next page. Note how different it was from the straight lines and sharp right angles of geometric abstraction. Alfred H. Barr, Jr., founding director of the Museum of Modern Art, offered a snappy summary of the difference between the two forms of abstract art. He quipped: "The shape of the square confronts the silhouette of the amoeba."[6]

The rejection of conscious control led to the overthrow of traditional standards for evaluating art. Ever since the ancient Greeks, it had been assumed that art was a craft involving skill. It must follow certain rules and methods. And those rules were thought to be rooted in the objective order and harmony of the universe. As Walford explains, "Artists were expected to discover the timeless, underlying principles of beauty in nature," in much the same way that "an Enlightenment scientist or philosopher sought to uncover fundamental principles in nature."[7]

Beginning with the Romantics, however, artists began to renounce rules and methods as nothing but dead conventions. Their goal was the free unleashing of inner energies and impulses from the unconscious. Looking at a work of art, you were no longer supposed to ask, Is it a good example of the rules of the craft? but only, Does it express the artist's inner vision? Artists "focused more on the process of externalizing consciousness than on the resultant work of art."[8] What counted was not aesthetic quality, but how well the image embodied the artist's consciousness.

ABSTRACT EXPRESSIONISM

8-3 Joan Miró
People at Night, Guided by the Phosphorescent Tracks of Snails, 1947

8-4 Arshile Gorky
Garden in Sochi, 1940

Using chance to tap the unconscious

The Outsiders Inside

The idea that true wisdom could be found by tapping the unconscious led to an interest in children and primitives, even the insane. They seemed less "spoiled" by civilization, more in touch with natural impulses, closer to the Life Force. This was a typical Romantic theme, of course. Rousseau had glorified the Noble Savage, free from the restraints of civilization. Wordsworth had elevated the child to divine status: "Infancy is the perpetual Messiah, which comes into the arms of fallen men, and pleads with them to return to paradise." The idea arose that deep within each person is an inner child, which is purer and more genuine than the rule-bound outer self.

This explains why many artists adopted a childlike style. Paul Klee is known for his whimsical, toy-like images. He said he wanted to paint "as though newborn." Jean Dubuffet tried to imitate the art of children, and was fascinated by the art created by inmates of an insane asylum. He said he wanted to "replace Western art with that of the jungle, the lavatory, the mental institution." Dubuffet coined the term *outsider art* to describe works created by self-taught artists who were completely outside the mainstream world of art schools and museums. In his view, these outsiders had a fresh, raw perspective that had escaped the contamination of Western civilization and was therefore pure and authentic. He hoped that by eliminating rules and conventions, he could imitate that raw perspective and create art with a more direct emotional impact.

NATURAL AND UNSPOILED

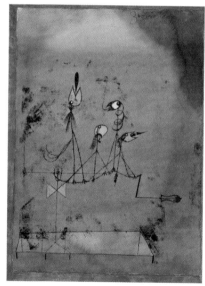

8-5 Paul Klee
Twittering Machine, 1922

8-6 Jean Dubuffet
The Cow with a Subtile Nose, 1954

Imitating children and savages

Today we are far more skeptical of the Romantic notion that humans have an inner core that is naturally good. Logically it hardly makes sense: If humans are intrinsically good, then how did cultures become evil and corrupt? Cultures can only reveal the character of those who created them. In addition, we are far more aware today of the ineradicable power of evil, having witnessed the horrors of two world wars, Nazi concentration camps, the Gulag, the killing fields of Cambodia, the Ugandan genocide, the Rwandan genocide, and on and on. The biblical concept of sin now seems to yield a more credible view of human nature. As G. K. Chesterton observed, the doctrine of original sin—that something is radically awry at the heart of human nature—has been verified by thousands of years of human history.

Sartre and Silence

The Romantic tradition's interest in the irrational and the unconscious had the effect of increasing its conflict with the Enlightenment tradition. Eventually the tension between the two was stretched to the breaking point. It seemed a person had to choose one or the other. Historian Henry Steele Commager wrote that people were confronted with a choice "between a 'brute,' tough-minded philosophy which banished idealism and mysticism in the name of science," and a "tender-minded philosophy which banished science in the name of mysticism and idealism."[9] In other words, the upper and lower stories had been isolated and exaggerated past the possibility of reconciliation. Kant's gap between nature and freedom was now an uncrossable chasm.

This explains the rise of existentialism. The existentialists took a clear, unflinching gaze into that uncrossable chasm and voiced their agonizing sense of alienation. No longer was there any Cosmic Spirit to give humans a connection with the cosmos. Instead the individual stood alone vis-à-vis a cold, alien, non-personal world.

That cosmic loneliness was expressed poetically by the Nobel Prize-winning biochemist Jacque Monod in *Chance and Necessity* (1971). "Man must at last wake out of his millenary dream and discover his total solitude, his fundamental isolation," Monod wrote. "He must realize that, like a gypsy, he lives on the boundary of an alien world; a world that is deaf to his music, and as indifferent to his hopes as it is to his sufferings or his crimes."[10] This melodramatic portrait goes far beyond anything that can properly be called science.[11] Monod was portraying the scientist as an existentialist hero facing an alien, absurd universe.

The existentialist concept of the absurd was a direct consequence of the idea of the death of God. For if God does not exist, then there is no way to fulfill human aspirations for ultimate truth, justice, love, and meaning. As the existentialist philosopher Albert Camus writes, "the absurd is born of this confrontation between the human need and the unreasonable silence of the world."[12] To live authentically (in the existentialist definition of the term) we must put on a brave face and act *as if* life had meaning, all the while knowing that it does not.

In the 1970s existentialism was wildly popular among university students, especially in Europe. I was studying in Germany at the time, and all my classmates were avidly reading Albert Camus and Jean Paul Sartre—then trying to live by the existentialist creed. It was a tragic example of the way philosophies filter down to shape the thinking and lives of ordinary people, especially the young.

Condemned to be Pollock

If you have ever taken Philosophy 101, you probably heard existentialism summed up in the phrase, "Existence precedes essence." What does that mean? An essence is a pre-existing ideal. If I say "I am a mother" or "I am a teacher," I am defining my identity in terms of an ideal of what it means to be a mother or teacher. Our most fundamental identity is derived from the ideal of human nature itself, which provides a universal moral guideline telling us what it means to live as a full human being.

The existentialists denied that there is any ideal or universal human nature. In Sartre's words, "There is no human nature because there is no God to have a conception of it."[13] As a consequence, they denied that there are any universal moral guidelines. We simply make our choices day by day (existence), inventing our identity (essence) as we go along.

For the existentialists, humans are caught up in the ceaseless flux of evolution. Just as species are constantly changing and evolving, so too individuals must leave behind all stable concepts of right or wrong, and immerse themselves in the flux of life. In Sartre's famous phrase, they are "condemned to be free"—condemned to act in a complete vacuum, making choices grounded in nothing beyond their own will, with no way of knowing whether those choices are right or wrong. In the absence of any God-given identity, individuals must create their own identity moment-by-moment through their actions.

These ideas inspired the action painters (next page). They did not plan their paintings ahead of time. They made no preliminary studies. Instead they created their paintings through unpremeditated, spontaneous action. They defined art not in terms of its end result (the painting itself) but in terms of the action of creating it (the physical gesture of slinging paint on canvas). As art critic Harold Rosenberg says, for the action painters, a canvas was not a space on which to reproduce images or express feelings but "an arena in which to act." The artist literally sought to create his personal identity through the act of artistic creation. He "gesticulated upon the canvas and watched for what each novelty would declare him and his art to be."[14]

The best-known action Painter was Jackson Pollock. He adopted the abstract expressionist technique of automatism—dripping, pouring, and flinging paint to eliminate conscious choice and control. But then he went further by abandoning all compositional conventions. He was the first "all-over" painter: There is no central motif, no focal point, no discernable relationships between the parts, no distinction

EXISTENTIALISM
ACTION PAINTERS

8-7 Jackson Pollock
Number 33, 1949

8-8 Pollock at work

Creating personal identity through action

between figure and ground—in fact, no bounded figure at all, whether representational or abstract.

While flying across the country, I once saw a trailer for *Mona Lisa Smile* flash on the movie screen. I snatched up the headphones. Here was an opportunity to discover how a movie would probe the meaning of art. The plot proved to be dismally predictable. Julie Roberts' character wants to shake up her pampered, privileged students, so she takes them to New York City to view a Jackson Pollock drip painting in a Greenwich Village loft.

"See past the paint," she intones. "Let us open our minds to a different idea."

I sighed. Is that the best a screenwriter could do to explain the action painters? A more instructive approach is to ask what worldview influenced Pollock. The action painters were expressing "the refusal of values," explains Rosenberg. "The gesture on canvas was a gesture of liberation from Value—political, esthetic, moral." By giving up all compositional conventions, consciously or not they were conveying the existentialist theme that there are no binding moral or intellectual ideals. There is only the endless flux of life.

No Alpha or Omega

At the same time, modernist writers were proclaiming their own liberation by giving up literary conventions—the idea that a novel needs to have a well-constructed structure. Think back to what you learned in high school literature class: that a novel should have a beginning, a development, a climax, and finally a denouement, in which all plot lines are resolved. The structure is an intelligible whole. Everything in the story has some logical connection to the overall plot.

As Barrett points out, this standard for literature arose when Western thinkers still held to the idea that reality itself "is a system in which each detail providentially and rationally is subordinated to others and ultimately to the whole itself."[15] The Bible teaches that history is linear, moving in a definite direction toward a future in which all wrongs will be righted and all wounds healed. Every event has meaning within this overarching goal or purpose.

But when Western intellectuals declared the death of God, they lost the concept of purpose-driven history. After all, most cultures do *not* have a linear view of history. The ancient Chinese, Babylonians, Hindus, Greeks, and Romans all thought of history as cyclical—an endless flow without beginning or end, like a circle. This seems to be the default position of the human mind apart from biblical revelation. What was the effect on literature? In Taylor's words, the death of the biblical God meant "the death of the Alpha and Omega." It became "impossible to locate a definite beginning and a decisive end" to history. "The narrative line is lost and the story seems pointless."[16] Life was reduced to an endless, meaningless present.

Writers began to experiment with non-linear structure to convey that sense of an unintelligible and pointless present. As Camus put it, modern people are "deprived of the memory of a

NON-LINEAR NARRATIVE

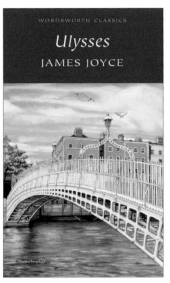

8-9 William Faulkner
The Sond and The Fury

8-10 James Joyce
Ulysses

8-11 Franz Kafka
The Complete Stories

An endless, meaningless present

lost home or the hope of a promised land."[17] That is, they no longer know where they came from or where they are going—their origin or their destiny. Why write coherent stories if the universe itself is no longer thought to have a coherent story line? Modernist writers like James Joyce and William Faulkner also experimented with stream-of-consciousness style, plunging readers into the fluid, shifting free-flow of evolving experience. The flux of life.

The most consistent expression of existentialism was Theatre of the Absurd. In Samuel Beckett's *Waiting for Godot,* two characters engage in meaningless dialog while waiting for someone who never shows up. Earlier existentialists like Camus and Sartre had composed carefully ordered dramas and novels to communicate their philosophy that the world has no meaningful order. But Beckett took the next logical step. "If confusion and chaos are the human condition," explains one literary critic, "then the form of the play itself must make use of interruption, discontinuity, incongruity, and senseless logic and repetition."[18] The style itself expressed an existentialist worldview.

Escape from Reason

Like visual artists, writers began to embrace irrationality as a form of liberation. The problem was that the concept of reason had been so deflated that it no longer seemed to be the means for discovering any really important truths. Prior to the modern age, reason had been regarded as a powerful tool for knowing truth, goodness, and beauty. But the split between facts and values had locked reason into the lower story, reducing it to nothing but cause-and-effect calculations—sometimes called *instrumental* reason. That is, reason gives us tools to control nature. But it cannot indicate which uses of nature are good or humane. Reason shows us how to achieve our goals. But it cannot determine which goals are right to pursue in the first place. It ascertains what we *can* do, but not what we *should* do. What works, but not what is good. Facts, but not values. As a result, many people concluded that the only way to plumb the Big Questions was to "escape from reason" (the title of one of Schaeffer's books). That is, to leave reason behind and take a leap of faith from the lower story to the upper story.

"Leap of faith" was the trademark phrase of existentialist theology. The seeds of existentialism were planted by Søren Kierkegaard, a passionate Danish Lutheran.[19] Later an entire school of existentialist theology grew up called neo-Orthodoxy (which included Karl Barth, Paul Tillich, Reinhold and Richard Niebuhr). Because reason had been narrowly defined as a tool for predicting and controlling nature, it no longer seemed appropriate to apply *that* kind of reason to the spiritual realm. After all, God is not subject to human control. As a result, however, the neo-Orthodox concept of the spiritual realm was fundamentally non-rational. As Sloan says, it amounted to little more than "a Romantic mood of wonder and awe."

Like their secular counterparts, religious existentialists embraced "the two-realm theory of truth," Sloan explains. They accepted "the dichotomy between science as fact and religion as meaning." As a result, they treated religious statements as "assertions that demanded arbitrary, existential decisions" with "no rational grounding." Faith became an "existential leap"[20] to the upper story.

This was a far cry from the biblical definition of faith, which is a commitment of the whole person, including the mind. No irrational leap is required because there is no dichotomy that limits reason to the lower story. God himself created human reason, and he expects us to use it. When Paul writes, "We live by faith, not by sight" (2 Cor. 5:7), many readers seem to think he is speaking metaphorically and means "by faith, not *reason*." But Paul is speaking literally: His point is that the spiritual realm is unseen, invisible. It takes tremendous faith to act on the basis of realities we cannot see. He does not mean that Christianity is opposed to reason.

Tragically, the high dignity accorded to reason as part of the image of God has been so thoroughly lost that even theologically orthodox Christians often hold the mistaken notion that biblical faith is irrational. This is a major reason they are ineffective in addressing the contemporary world. They have absorbed the same faith/reason dichotomy that lies at the core of contemporary worldviews. Thus they have no genuine alternative to offer.

Sex, Drugs, and D. H. Lawrence

Among literary figures, the escape from reason was often achieved through drug use and sexual libertinism. The trend started in the Romantic age when poets like Coleridge and De Quincy used opium to stimulate their imagination (then suffered the consequences of addiction and enslavement). Some were even fascinated by insanity. A friend of Coleridge spent time in a mental hospital and later wrote, "Dream not of having tasted all the grandeur and wildness of Fancy, till you have gone mad." Madness was treated as a source of artistic inspiration, a state that "escaped the mechanical and blind workings of rationalism."[21] Drugs and alcohol were simply handy ways of achieving temporary insanity.

These themes were picked up in the late nineteenth century by movements like the symbolists and the decadents, who focused on morbid subjects such as death, depression, and deviance, especially sexual deviance. In 1871 the poet Arthur Rimbaud turned addiction and self-destruction into a holy calling, a form of martyrdom on behalf of art. "Now I am debauching myself as much as I can," he wrote. "The poet makes himself a *seer* by a long, immense, and calculated *derangement of all the senses.* All the forms of love, of suffering, of madness." Rimbaud popularized the idea that the artist, in pursuit of some fresh insight, must distort his senses and violate social conventions through drugs, alcohol, sex, and a dissipated lifestyle. Much of Rimbaud's poetry was written while he was in a homosexual relationship.

In his 1927 novel *Steppenwolf,* Herman Hesse likewise portrayed drugs and sexual encounters as the means for re-connecting with one's authentic self. In his 1954 book *The Doors of Perception,* Aldous Huxley recounted his personal experiment with drugs. To explain how hallucinogenic drugs work, Huxley revived the Jungian concept of a collective consciousness, which he called Mind at Large. "Each one of us is potentially Mind at Large," capable "of perceiving everything that is happening everywhere in the universe," he wrote. However, so much knowledge would quickly overwhelm us. Thus in order "to make biological survival possible, Mind at Large has to be funneled through the reducing valve of the brain and nervous system. What comes out at the other end is a measly trickle of the kind of consciousness which will help us to stay alive on the surface of this particular planet." For those dissatisfied with such a measly trickle, Huxley suggested that hallucinogenic substances could widen the reducing valve and give access to the wisdom of the Mind at Large. They could open "the doors of perception."[22] These ideas penetrated deeply into the counter culture of the 1960s, and were even reflected in the names of rock bands such as Steppenwolf and The Doors.[23]

As secular, materialist worldviews closed off traditional forms of spiritual transcendence, artists were searching for alternative avenues of transcendence. Virtually any means to distort the senses and disrupt ordinary consciousness might be tried as a technique to escape from reason and break through to the upper story.

TECHNIQUES OF FALSE TRANSCENDENCE

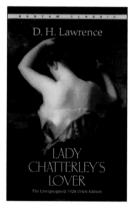  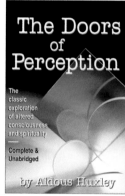 

8-12 D. H. Lawrence	8-13 Hermann Hesse	8-14 Aldous Huxley	8-15 Alan W. Watts
Lady Chatterley's Lover	*Steppenwolf*	*The Doors of Perception*	*The Joyous Cosmology*

Breaking through to the upper story

This explains the stereotype of the artist, writer, or musician as someone living a dissolute, bohemian life, hooked on alcohol or drugs, and drifting from one sexual relationship to another, as often as not driven to suicide in the end. These tragic lives are testaments to the power of the assumption that the artist must be alienated from mainstream society—that it is from his wounds, his outcast position, that he draws his creative power (even when the wounds are self inflicted through addiction). Christians should weep for people so hungry for transcendence that they are willing to destroy their bodies and minds in the search for some higher meaning to life.

Postmodern Science

The idea that life's higher meaning is essentially non-rational leads us to postmodernism, a term that is widely used but widely misunderstood. To get a handle on it, we need to step back and trace how it arose. It is no exaggeration to say that all the philosophical schools within the continental tradition have shared one major motivation: to carve out a space for human freedom in a world conceived as a vast machine. To defend Kant's *freedom* from Kant's *nature*. To protect the upper story from the intellectual imperialism of the lower story. To resist the reductionism of scientism and positivism.

For example, in the late nineteenth century, the German philosopher Wilhelm Dilthey proposed that there are two different forms of science—a science of nature and a science of mind—each with its own distinctive methodology. The science of nature searches for universal regularities. It explains natural events in terms of causal connections. It requires an attitude of detached observation. And it yields knowledge that is objective and universally valid.

The science of mind requires a completely different methodology. Under this label, Dilthey included what we might call the human sciences—ethics, theology, the humanities, the social sciences. Here the source of information consists mostly of literary texts. And to interpret a text, you must enter empathetically into another person's thinking. You must seek to get "inside the person's skin" and understand how the world appears to him or her. You are not looking for universal regularities so much as unique, individual perspectives. Explanations are couched not in terms of natural causes but in terms of motivations, goals, purposes, beliefs. For Dilthey, the knowledge this method yields is subjective and culturally relative. He accepted Hegel's concept of cultural evolution—that each culture produces its own "truth" suitable for the current stage of the evolution of consciousness.[24]

This was Dilthey's version of the lower/upper story divide. Downstairs were the natural sciences; upstairs were the human sciences. This division had enormous impact on continental thinkers because it seemed to provide a means of resisting reductionism. Over against natural science there stood another science, which was definable and defensible in its own right.

Eventually some thinkers even came up with a counter-reductionism to the old Enlightenment reductionisms. They began to question whether there was really such a thing as *natural* science. After all, it is a product of human culture just as much as literature or the arts. Scientific theories are not simply factual observation reports. They involve mental constructions such as interpretation, inference, conjecture, and generalization. Even fundamental scientific concepts such as mass, force, and energy are mental abstractions. (We observe individual objects, but we never observe "mass.") Moreover, scientists are ordinary people driven by the same economic interests, social pressures, and worldview commitments as everyone else—all of which play into the scientific theories they construct. In short, natural science does not consist solely in empirical discoveries. It is a rich network of ideas intricately connected to the other parts of culture.

Some drew the conclusion that the natural sciences are really no different from what Dilthey had called the human sciences. Both are social constructions. Both are products of human culture. To picture it visually, we might say science was pulled up into the upper story. There *was* no lower story any more. Everything was in the upper story. This was the birth of postmodernism.

Move Over, Euclid

Postmodernism seemed plausible because of changes within science itself. In the late nineteenth and early twentieth centuries, Western thought was shaken to the core by two scientific revolutions, which raised questions about the very nature of scientific truth: non-Euclidean geometry and the new physics (relativity and quantum physics).

For nearly two thousand years after Euclid, geometry had been regarded as the most reliable and universally valid form of human knowledge. Just as children might use a few simple blocks to build an entire play city, so mathematicians could use a few simple axioms to create the thousands of theorems that make up Euclidean geometry. "Every two points determine one line." "Any straight line can be extended indefinitely." "All right angles are congruent." The resulting system was consistent internally, while externally it seemed to correspond perfectly to the physical world. As one philosopher explains, geometric theorems "seem to have a double truth: *formal* truth that originates in the coherent logic of discourse, and *material* truth originating in the agreement of things with their object."[25] As a consequence, geometry was held up as the exemplar for all other fields of knowledge to imitate.

Then, in the nineteenth century, the academic world was rocked by the discovery that Euclidean geometry was not universal after all—that alternative forms of geometry could be generated. That is, you could begin with different axioms from the ones Euclid chose, and reason from them to produce different geometric systems—ones that were just as logically consistent as Euclid's geometry. Suddenly mathematicians were no longer sure *which* version of geometry was true to the physical universe. As an analogy, you might think of a complex computer game with a game universe that is internally consistent, but has nothing to do with the real world.

After the initial shock, it was eventually decided that different geometries could be equally valid, depending on the context. Euclidean geometry works when dealing with surfaces that are ordinary planes. It applies most of the time in ordinary experience because surfaces are small enough that you can discount the curvature of the earth and treat them essentially as planes. But a different geometry—Riemannian geometry—works when dealing with surfaces that have a positive curvature (such as a sphere). Einstein popularized this form of geometry when he applied it to his concept of curved space. There is also a geometry called Lobatchevskian, which works when dealing with surfaces that have a negative curvature.

The discovery that that logical truth (exemplified by geometry) could be separated from physical truth was devastating. Ever since the ancient Greeks, most Westerners had assumed that reality is ultimately rational—that what is *logically* true is also *really* true. The new geometries challenged that conviction. Here were several systems that were all internally consistent, yet incompatible with one another—which meant they could not all be true. For the first time a chasm opened between what is rational and what is true.[26] It seemed as though truth itself had shattered.

The fall of Euclidean geometry was too esoteric to affect popular culture, but it shook the foundations of academia. Far from being universally true, Euclidean geometry was now relegated to the status of one of many possible truths, relative to the context in which it was applied. The crisis in geometry became a metaphor for the shattering of established truths across the board. In the words of mathematician E. T. Bell, it encouraged "disbelief in eternal truths and absolutes" in all subject areas.[27]

For example, moral philosophy begins with universal, unchanging principles and then reasons from those principles to real-world applications. "Too Euclidean!" critics charged. A non-Euclidean approach recognizes that different cultures begin with different moral axioms, resulting in different moral systems—all of them equally valid, relative to the cultural context. Likewise in legal theory, Jerome Frank of Yale Law School argued that the traditional understanding of law was too Euclidean. In political theory, Charles Beard dismissed foundational American institutions, such as the balance of powers, as Euclidean. In economics, John M. Clark argued for different economic systems—systems "with axioms as far removed from each other as the geometry of Euclid and the non-Euclideans." In anthropology and sociology, the vast variety of human societies was said to be akin to the diverse forms of non-Euclidean geometry.[28]

In virtually every field, parallels were drawn between geometry and human cultures. Both, it was said, rest on axioms chosen arbitrarily from an indefinite number of possibilities. And in both, different axioms would give rise to different systems, all equally valid. Non-Euclidean geometry was invoked to sweep away any claim of a single, overarching truth. And thus it opened the door to postmodernism.

Beyond Einstein

Another door to postmodernism was the new physics—relativity theory and quantum mechanics. Just as geometry toppled Euclid, so now physics toppled Newton, whose work was the capstone of the scientific revolution. Newton had treated time and space as absolutes at the foundation of physics. Kant had treated them as universal categories of the human mind. But Albert Einstein decided they were neither. Time and space, he said, are relative to the observer's frame of reference.[29]

The public had little idea what relativity meant scientifically, but they eagerly interpreted it as support for moral and cultural *relativism*, the denial of all absolute truths. Einstein emphatically denied that his theory implied relativism. He even wanted to label it *invariance theory*, because his calculations show that physical laws *do not vary* from one reference frame to another.

To capture the basic concept, imagine that you are walking forward on the deck of a ship at a rate of 2 miles per hour, while the ship moves through the water at 20 miles per hour. How fast are you moving? Relative to the ship, you are moving 2 mph. Relative to the shore, you are moving 22 mph. Anything relativistic about that? Of course not. The laws of motion remain the same in both frames of reference. This was an early form of relativity theory, developed by Galileo. Einstein simply applied the same principle to electromagnetic phenomena such as light. Even though he had to make time slow down for the theory to work, his goal was to show that the laws of electromagnetism remain the same (invariant) across all frames of reference.

Nevertheless, Einstein's theory was greeted with a barrage of newspaper articles interpreting it as an attack on "absolutism." Even artists and writers applied it to their work. William Carlos Williams defended free verse (poetry without rhythm or rhyme) by saying that because of Einstein, poets can now employ "a *relatively* stable foot, not a rigid one."[30] In his 1921 poem "St. Francis Einstein of the Daffodils," Williams presents Einstein as a savior bringing freedom from "dead" and "old-fashioned knowledge." Despite Einstein's protests, the public got his theory exactly backward.

Physics and Mysticism

The rise of quantum theory was even more puzzling to the public. It demonstrated that, on the subatomic level, the laws of Newtonian physics do not apply. For example, classical physics assumed that an objective world exists, which we can observe and measure without essentially changing. But on the quantum level, it is impossible to observe reality without changing it. The classical distinction between subject and object seems to have collapsed. If we observe an atomic particle under one set of conditions, it functions as a wave. But if we observe it under different conditions, it functions as a particle. The wave/particle duality seems to destroy the ideal of scientific objectivity.

Some physicists go even further in their interpretation. If the experiment determines which properties an atomic entity has, they say, then the act of observation is essentially an act of creation. The observer *creates* what he observes. This seems to harmonize with the occult worldview of Eastern religion, which teaches that reality is ultimately mental or spiritual—that the material world is a creation of consciousness. Many popular books on quantum physics offer an Eastern interpretation, such as Fritjof Capra's now classic *The Tao of Physics: An Exploration of the Parallels between Modern Physics and Eastern Mysticism*.

But there is more. Another unsettling result of quantum theory is the uncertainty principle. The centerpiece of classical physics was its theory of motion. If we know where an object is to begin with (position) and we know its velocity (which in physics includes both speed and direction), then we can plot its course—whether the trajectory of a football or a planet. Hypothetically, if we knew the position of every particle in the universe, along with all the forces acting on it, we could predict the entire future. The implication seemed to be that every event in the universe is completely determined.

On the quantum level, however, it turns out that we cannot know both position and velocity at the same time. In ordinary life, I can shine a flashlight on someone and the photons of light hitting him do not knock him over. But if I flash a beam of light to investigate subatomic particles such as electrons, they are so minute that the photons *do* knock them off course. Thus we cannot determine a particle's position without knocking it off course and changing its velocity. We can never get an accurate read on both position and velocity at the same time.

The implication is that complete determinism is impossible. Quantum theory recognizes a realm of indeterminacy within the atom, at the very heart of matter.

Losing Faith in Physics

For those who had pinned their hopes on formulating a fully deterministic worldview, the new physics was deeply disconcerting. "Newton's universe was the stronghold of rational determinism," says a character in Shaw's *Too True to Be Good*. "Everything was calculable. . . . Here was my faith: Here I found my dogma of infallibility." But that faith had splintered on the rocky shores of the new physics. "And now—now—what is left of it? The orbit of the electron obeys no law," Shaw's character laments. "All is caprice, the calculable world has become incalculable."

Even stolid scientists threw up their hands. Physicist Percy Bridgman wrote, "Whenever the physicist penetrates to the atomic or electric level in his analysis, he finds things acting in a way for which he can assign no cause. . . . This means nothing more or less than that the law of cause and effect must be given up."[31] To be sure, in everyday experience, objects still behave according to classical Newtonian physics—which means engineers can still use it to construct bridges and buildings. But that is only because of the statistical averaging of large numbers of atoms. Scientists can no longer appeal to classical determinism to explain *why* physics works. J. C. Polkinghorne, a physicist turned Anglican priest, says it is "rather like being shown an impressively beautiful palace and being told that no one is quite sure whether its foundations rest on bedrock or shifting sand."[32]

For many Western thinkers, it seemed that the bottom had fallen out of any attempt to construct an intelligible model of the universe. How could human rationality be trusted when its most stellar achievement, classical physics, could crumble so suddenly? Up until now, it had been assumed that science advances steadily upward, with new facts gradually added to an ever-expanding pool of knowledge. But relativity and quantum physics did *not* simply add to Newtonian physics. They razed it to the ground and started over again.

To describe this sudden and dramatic shift, science historian Thomas Kuhn coined the phrase "paradigm shift," which was seized on by postmodernists. They took it to mean that science proceeds not so much by rational inquiry but by intuitive leaps. Rationality was not the hallowed path to truth, as the Enlightenment had claimed. The escape from reason now seemed to have support from science itself.

The Fall of Atom

The new physics was welcomed as a godsend by defenders of the upper story. For three centuries, the determination of classical physics had been protested by artists, poets, theologians, ethicists, and idealist philosophers. Yet because they were not scientists, their criticisms had dismissed as merely anti-scientific. With the rise of the new physics, for the first time a critique arose from *within* science. "For the first time," writes social theorist Floyd Matson, "the image of the great machine came under direct attack by science itself."[33]

Gone was the image of the universe as a machine determined by mathematical laws. Gone was the image of humans as mere cogs in the mechanism. No longer could science be invoked to deny human moral and creative freedom. Many hailed the new physics as a great emancipator, opening the door once again to free will and human dignity. "The old physics showed us a universe which looked more like a prison than a dwelling place," wrote James Jean. "The new physics shows us a universe which looks as though it might conceivably form a suitable dwelling-place for free men."[34]

Even miracles seemed possible again. In classical physics, the world was ordered not by the faithfulness of a personal God but by inexorable natural laws. Nothing was permitted to intervene in nature's fixed order. Theologians were pressured to abandon concepts like miracles and providence. Liberal theologians, caving in to the pressure, urged Christians to "de-mythologize" the Bible—which meant to eliminate any reference to the supernatural. For example, Rudolf Bultmann wrote, "Modern man acknowledges as reality only such phenomena or events as are comprehensible within the framework of the rational order of the universe. He does not acknowledge miracles because they do not fit into this lawful order."[35] For Bultmann, what "modern man" does not acknowledge, Christians must give up.

But the new physics showed that the "lawful order" which so impressed Bultmann was not fixed after all. As a result, it could no longer be used to eliminate the supernatural. A powerful barrier to accepting miracles crumbled to the ground. Physics could no longer be used to rule out biblical accounts of God's mighty acts in history.

Today the euphoria of the new physics has worn off, and we can assess its implications more soberly. What exactly does it mean for moral and theological issues? Quantum physics does not actually offer any *positive* evidence for either free will or miracles. All it really does is remove a long-standing *barrier* erected by classical physics, albeit a very powerful barrier. In the place of determinism, quantum theory recognizes a realm of indeterminacy—chance or randomness. But is chance the same thing as choice? Certainly not. As theologian Ian Barbour writes, "We would hardly attribute freedom to a roulette wheel simply because its stopping point is not predictable."[36] Nor would we invoke a miracle and say God stopped the wheel. Quantum physics does not offer a loophole for mind or spirit in the universe (though you can still find books and articles making that claim). It merely limits the range of classical physics.

Why did the revolution in physics have such far-reaching impact? Because many people had turned science into an idol. In analytic thought, the essence of anything is discovered by slicing it down to its smallest component. The old physics said: If the atom is determined, so are human beings. The new physics said: If the atom is *in*determinate, so are human beings. But why should we define people by the characteristics of atoms? Why should we accept such a radical reductionism? Both conclusions treat the atom virtually as a mini-god.

Every worldview must identify something as the final reality, the cause of everything else. Historically, as Western thinkers turned *away* from God as the ultimate cause, many turned *to* matter. They dissected it down to its smallest building blocks, hoping to discover what was fundamentally real. "Since the Renaissance," Koestler writes, "the Ultimate Cause had gradually shifted from the heavens to the atomic nucleus."[37] The atom, not God, determined our destiny. But with the development of quantum physics, that Ultimate Cause seemed to dissolve into chance. The modernist idol crumbled. For many people, science itself now seemed to point to a postmodern worldview.

From Prophet to Parody

We are now prepared to focus on that postmodern worldview—to diagnose both its possibilities and its perils. Though postmodern thinkers staunchly opposed the reductionism of Enlightenment worldviews, tragically, their own theories often proved just as reductionistic.

Consider the postmodern view of the self. On one hand, postmodern thinkers firmly rejected the modernist concept of the autonomous self—the self-sufficient, sovereign ego of the Cartesian cogito (I think, therefore I am). But many postmodernists fell off the other side of the horse by dissolving the self into a network of social forces—race, class, gender, and sexual orientation.

The reasoning goes back to Hegel. If history is the unfolding of an Absolute Spirit or Mind, as Hegel taught, then the real actor in history is not the individual but Mind itself—an immanent mental force unfolding through history. Any given culture is the expression of Mind in its current stage of evolution. The culture's laws, customs, religion, art, morality, and language are not the product of individual creativity but of the pantheistic Mind working in and through the members of the community. The implication is that individuals do not really have any unique or original ideas. Most of their thoughts are products of factors they did not choose or create, but merely absorbed.[38]

Hegel's pantheism eventually eroded away, but it left behind the assumption that individuals are not *producers* of culture so much as *products* of it. This view has been labeled *anti-humanism* because it is radically dehumanizing. It denies that humans are genuine moral or creative agents. This goes far beyond toppling the Cartesian self off its pedestal. It is the denial that there *is* such a thing as the self. (It also commits suicide: Who originated the idea that humans have no original ideas?) Those who deny the concept of God as Creator end up ultimately denying human creativity.

The impact on the arts was dramatic. The artist was no longer held up as a prophet who offers original cutting-edge insights, because *no one* has original insights. The artist was merely a mouthpiece for the larger social forces that produced him. This explains why so much postmodern art consists of mockery and parody. The prophets of old had two functions: to proclaim God's truth and to denounce the sins of society. Postmodern artists had lost the first function. They no longer revealed any higher truths. But they could still enjoy a sense of prophetic edge by denouncing society's sins—its consumerism, triviality, and superficiality.

POSTMODERNISM
POP ART

8-16 Roy Lichtenstein
The Melody Haunts My Reverie, 1965

8-17 Andy Warhol
Black Bean, 1968

Parody and caricature

This explains why much Pop Art was little more than caricature. It held up the products of a consumer society in order to parody them. Pop artists often enlarged commercial items, such as soup cans or comic strips, to mock-heroic size, as though to hit viewers in the face with their sheer banality. (The comic strip featured on the cover of this book is a painting by Roy Lichtenstein.) If artists were merely mouthpieces for society, they seem resolved to embrace that role with a vengeance. They would mirror its most trite and vapid elements.

Death of the Artist

In literary theory, the loss of the idea of creativity was encapsulated in the phrase "the death of the author." Literary critic Roland Barthes argued that writers are akin to the bards or shamans of old, who were not inventors of their own stories so much as transmitters of the stories of their clan or tribe. A literary text is not a product of original creativity, he said, but merely "a tissue of quotations" absorbed from the surrounding culture and historical period.

Of course, every community harbors conflicting interests and beliefs—which means every author will unconsciously reflect conflicting cultural messages. As Barthes puts it, a text does not have a single meaning but is a mix "in which a variety of writings, none of them original, blend and clash."[39] Sorting out those contradictory meanings is called *deconstructing* the text.[40] Hence the term *deconstructionism.*

Traditionally, the goal of the literary critic was to discern what the author intended to say. But if a text was not actually the author's creative product, then it no longer made sense to ask what he or she meant. Readers were free to assign their *own* meanings to the text. Deconstructionists hailed this as liberating, because it freed literary texts from any fixed or stable meaning. As Barthes put it, to discern the author's intention "is to impose a limit on that text, to furnish it with a final signified." Deconstructionism refused to impose any limit on its meaning.

Not surprisingly, postmodern thinkers do not apply the same principles to their *own* writings. They hope their own work will be treated as a serious contribution from a creative intellect, not merely a replay of cultural messages. And they certainly want readers to care about what the author himself means. Thus ironically, postmodernists contradict their own views every time they write a book or present a paper.

Let us engage in a little deconstruction of our own. When someone embraces a position that is internally inconsistent, typically that indicates a deeper motivation at work. Barthes' motivation comes clear if we continue reading in the passage previously quoted. After explaining that deconstructionism denies any definitive meaning to text, Barthes adds a very strange sentence: This "liberates what may be called an anti-theological activity, an activity that is truly revolutionary since to refuse to fix meaning is, in the end, to refuse God."[41]

Wait a moment: What does God have to do with it? Barthes is suggesting that God is the ultimate source of meaning. After all, Christians have always treated the world itself as a kind of text or writing or story. Psalm 19 says, "The heavens declare the glory of God." Augustine wrote, "These heavens, these books, are the works of God's fingers." Throughout history, Christians have employed the metaphor of two books—the book of God's Word (the Bible) and the book of God's world (creation). And because God is the author of both, he has *author*-ity over the right way to interpret them. There is an objective standard of truth.

By the same token, human beings, created in God's image, are genuine authors of their own works. If you want to know what a text means, you ask the author.

All this changed when Nietzsche declared the death of God. To use one of Nietzsche's favorite metaphors, all previous philosophies were attempts to uncover a transcript of the book of the universe. That is, the universe is like a play unfolding on a stage, and philosophers were trying to find the transcript so they could understand the plot line. According to Nietzsche, however, there *is* no author of the book of the universe—no one in a position to give an authoritative transcript. Thus there is no objective or universally valid truth about the universe. As Mark Taylor says, "The death of God was the disappearance of the Author who had inscribed absolute truth and univocal meaning in world history."

And because humans are made in the image of God, Taylor concludes, "the death of God implies the disappearance of the author."[42] Once again, those who deny the divine Creator end up denying human creativity as well.

Metanarratives and Death Camps

Postmodernists welcomed the implication of the death of God—that there is no "absolute truth and univocal meaning in world history." Any attempt to explain the meaning of history they called a *metanarrative,* a master narrative that connects the dawn of the universe to its final destiny in one grand system.[43] And what did they have against metanarratives? They viewed them as the source of brutal, oppressive political systems.

Most of the founders of postmodernism were Europeans who had witnessed oppressive political systems up close—Nazism and Communism. Both these systems were organized around a single principle: race (Nazism) or economic class (Communism). Both embraced a grand vision of history moving inexorably toward some ideal society. And both ended up becoming totalitarian, using their utopian visions to justify secret police and death camps.

After World War II, many European thinkers who had suffered under totalitarian regimes decided that the source of totalitarianism lay in "totalizing" metanarratives. By "totalizing" they meant any metanarrative that focuses on a single dimension of human experience and elevates it to a false absolute. The Nazis put all social relations into the box of race. If you were Aryan or Jewish or Slavic, *that* was said to determine your views, your character, your worth. The Communists put all social relations into the box of economics. If you were a member of the capitalist class or the proletarian class, *that* was the all-determining factor. The lesson postmodernists drew from these totalitarian systems was that attempts to unify society artificially according to some grand totalizing theory leads to coercion, oppression, and violence.

Of course, ever since the pre-Socratics, philosophers have tried to find a single principle that would unite all reality within a coherent explanatory system. What postmodernists pointed out is that no matter which unifying principle you choose, it is invariably reductionistic—too narrow and limited to account for the real world. The resulting worldview will end up denying the complexity and diversity of actual life. It will become totalizing. And when a totalizing worldview is linked to political power, the state will seek to impose unity by squashing those who cannot or will not adhere to its official, state-sanctioned metanarrative—anyone who does not fit into its prescribed box. The Soviet Communists killed roughly 60 million people, the Chinese communists killed about 35 million, the Nazis, 21 million. The Maoist Khmer Rouge in Cambodia massacred more than a quarter of the nation's population.[44] Political ideology has a bloody and barbarous track record.

Postmodern thinkers concluded that the best way to challenge claims to absolute *power* was by challenging claims to absolute *truth*. They rejected the search for a single, unified truth. Instead they celebrated diversity and multiplicity. Because worldviews are transmitted through language, postmodernists often refer to them as "language games." They claim that there is an irreducible plurality of language games, each with its own rules for playing the game. Just as baseball and football are two entirely different games with virtually no rules in common, so worldviews are different language games with no overlap or common ground. Postmodernists believe the way to prevent absolute state power and support democracy is for societies to remain divided into smaller groupings based on their language games. They reject any metanarrative that would unify all groups across a society.

A Christian would agree with much of the postmodern critique of reductionism. In fact, we have critiqued several forms of reductionism in earlier chapters. But does the postmodern solution work? Should we abandon all claims to a unified truth? The flaw in this solution is that it is self-refuting. In the very act of stating that there is no universally valid truth, the postmodernist is asserting his *own* view as true. This is not so much a logical contradiction as what philosopher Jürgen Habermas calls a "performative contradiction." The phrase means that in the very act of stating a position, a person is implicitly claiming that it is true. Thus every time the postmodernist *states* his own view, he *contradicts* it.[45] Postmodernism commits suicide. It self-destructs in the process of being asserted.

Just as important, without some kind of transcendent truth, there is no way to stand against social and political evil—the very things that postmodernists were so concerned about. Without a moral absolute, we cannot say, "That is wrong" or "That is unjust." Lived out consistently, postmodernism leads to complicity with evil and injustice.

No Visual *Metanarratives*

Despite its flaws, postmodernism has permeated deeply into the arts community. And how can you give visual expression to the idea that there is no metanarrative, no larger story line to give coherent meaning to life? By refusing to give a work of art any coherent overall design. This explains why deconstructionist artists favor the pastiche or collage—a patchwork of disconnected images that defy any attempt at interpretation. As Gablik explains, "Because the unifying presence of a belief in a transcendental cosmic order no longer exists in our culture, the implication is that works of art can no longer offer the sort of unified vision of the world that existed" in earlier ages. For example, David Salle offers random images that "slide past one another, disassociated and decontextualized, failing to link up into a coherent sequence." They are "images that no longer narrate, but in their detached free-floatingness actually obstruct any attempt at decipherment."[46] In other words, the collage was intended to obstruct the natural human attempt to find some logical connection or coherence.

Similarly, Robert Rauschenberg "juxtaposed images in ways to suggest random incoherence, to which the artist—and viewer—can bring no meaningful order." What was he saying with these collages? That "life's random occurrences . . . cannot be made to fit in any inherent hierarchy of meaning."[47]

DECONSTRUCTIONIST PAINTING

8-18 David Salle
Angels in the Rain, 1998

8-19 Robert Rauschenberg
Retroactive I, 1963

No transcendent cosmic order

Classical music composers created a kind of auditory collage by incorporating ironical quotations from Bach, Beethoven, or Monteverdi into scores that were otherwise abstract and discordant. For example, Harrison Birtwistle's 1966 opera *Punch and Judy* assimilates aspects of Greek tragedy, Baroque opera, and Bach's *St. Matthew Passion* into the score.

Postmodern architecture has its own version of the pastiche or collage. As one journalist puts it, postmodernism "has brought us girders hanging unfinished out of the edges of buildings, archways cut off in space, and walls which don't meet walls."[48] In contrast to the international style, with its geometric order and balance, postmodern architecture suggests disequilibrium and instability. Often classic elements are stitched into the structure, but exaggerated out of proportion in ironical incongruities, like the oversized Ionic column in the building on the right below. As though to flout the modernist love of functionalism, this column is deliberately non-functional (it does not support anything).

DECONSTRUCTIONIST ARCHITECTURE

8-20 Frank O. Gehry
Case Western Reserve University, 1997

8-21 Kengo Kuma
M2 building, Tokyo, 1991

Irony and disequilibrium

Deconstructionist architecture can be quite disorienting, and once even had life-and-death consequences. In Cleveland in 2003, a gunman who had shot three people led SWAT teams on a maddening cat-and-mouse chase through a building designed by Frank Gehry (on the left). The avant-garde design, with its undulating steel walls, led to a seven-hour chase over several floors. "There are no right angles in the building," the chief of police said in exasperation, explaining why the SWAT teams had such difficulty tracking down the killer. The teams had trained intensively, he said, but in a conventional warehouse, "a very rectangular building."[49]

Politicizing the Classroom

One consequence of postmodernism that people often encounter in ordinary life is the ubiquitous pressure for political correctness. Rules for politically correct behavior are now *de rigueur* in most social institutions—schools, newspapers, law, politics. How did postmodernism give rise to political correctness? It stems from the postmodern aversion to totalizing metanarratives. If coercion was the result of imposing unity, then it seemed that the way to protect liberty was to celebrate difference. This explains the popularity of buzzwords like *diversity* and *multiculturalism*.

The glaring flaw in political correctness is that only select groups are singled out to represent "diversity"—certified victim groups based on race, class, gender, and sexual orientation. And the analysis of the problem is typically derived from Marxism. Some group is said to be victimized and oppressed, and the path to liberation is to revolt against the oppressors.

This explains why art and literature departments on the university campus have become thoroughly politicized. Literary criticism no longer deals with issues of aesthetics such as style, structure, content, and composition. Instead it focuses on issues of race, class, gender, and the environment. Writing in the *Chronicle of Higher Education,* an English professor defined the goal of literary study in strictly Marxist terms: Its goal is to help students decide "which side of the world-historical class struggle they take: the side of the owners of the means of production, or the side of the workers. This and only this is the real question in textual literacy."[50]

Classic Marxism may have been discredited in economics. But Marxist knock-offs are still alive and well in English and humanities departments.

To adhere to the dictates of politically correctness, students often have to master a complex new vocabulary. One father was stunned to find that he could not understand his daughter's textbook on film studies—despite the fact that he was a professional film critic. The book was densely packed with terms such as *heterogeneity, narratology,* and *symptomology.* The father picked two of them—*fabula* and *syuzhet*—and asked his daughter if she knew what they meant.

"They're the Russian formalist terms for 'story' and 'plot'," his daughter replied.

"Well then, why don't they use 'story' and 'plot'?"

"We're not allowed to. If we do, they take points off our paper."[51]

The jargon is so thick, jokes Andrew Delbanco of Columbia University, that eventually people talking about *Romeo and Juliet* will not be able to say, "They fell in love and got married." Instead they might say something like this: "Privileging each other as objects of heterosexual desire, they signified their withdrawal from the sexual marketplace by valorizing the marital contract as an instrument of bourgeois hegemony."[52]

In fact, a physicist named Alan Sokal *did* say something like that in a notorious hoax. In 1996 he composed a paper made up entirely of nonsense phrases couched in postmodern jargon. Under the title "Transgressing the Boundaries: Toward a Transformative Hermeneutics of Quantum Mechanics," he submitted the piece to a humanities journal. Completely taken in, the editors published the piece. They have yet to live down the infamy.

If art theory once imitated religion, it is now a parody of science, generating its own arcane specialized jargon.[53]

In the process, sadly, it tends to discourage the love of art and literature for its own sake. Frank Lentricchia, a critic so radical that he was once dubbed the Dirty Harry of literary theory, grew disenchanted when he observed that his own students developed a suffocating sense of moral superiority. They would pass judgment on authors as racist or sexist or capitalist or impe-rialist or homophobic *before even reading their works*. In dismay, Lentricchia said, "Tell me your [literary] theory, and I'll tell you in advance what you'll say about any work of literature, espe-cially those you haven't read."[54]

Clearly, critical theories are being used not to gain a deeper understanding of works of lit-erature but to dismiss them out of hand. Politically correct regimes are not liberating students to think for themselves. They are turning students into cadres of self-absorbed reactionaries ready to take orders from the faddish theorist of the moment.

Postmodernism started out seeking to unmask the implicit imperialism of modernist worldviews. But it has itself become imperialist, insisting that postmodernists alone have the ability to see through everyone else's underlying interests and motives—to deconstruct and debunk them. Thereby it effectively silences every other perspective.

Marxism Goes to Church

The same neo-Marxist worldview has filtered down to theology, where it has inspired black, feminist, and liberation theology.[55] During the 2008 presidential campaign, the American public was stunned to discover how radical some versions of black theology can be. For some twenty years, then-candidate Barack Obama had attended a Chicago church pastored by Reverend Jeremiah Wright, who asked God not to bless America but to "damn" it. Wright is a follower of theologian James Cone, who condemns white churches as "the racist Antichrist" and advocates "destruction of the white enemy."[56]

Marxist-inspired theologians typically say, I'm not a Marxist, I merely use Marxist tools of analysis. Thus Cone writes, "The Christian faith does not possess in its nature the means for analyzing the structure of capitalism. Marxism as a tool of social analysis can . . . help Christians to see how things really are."[57] Cone is tragically mistaken. A Christian world-view does have the resources to analyze economic structures like capitalism. But because he does not recognize those resources, Cone reaches over to the Marxist toolbox to borrow its conceptual tools. The problem with this strategy is that the conceptual tools we use change the way we think—just as practical tools, like the car or the computer, have changed the way we live. Liberation theology often ends up as little more than theological frosting on a Marxist cake.

Most secular worldviews contain elements of truth, and Marxism can sometimes high-light genuine social problems. It echoes biblical themes in its concern for the poor, the oppressed, and the alienated. But history has rendered repeated examples of what Marxism looks like when welded to political power, and its solutions are invariably coercive and inhumane.

Schaeffer's Sources

Our survey of the Enlightenment heritage (chapter 6) ended with an inspiring account of Christians employing elements of analytic philosophy to support biblical truth. Are Christians working within the continental tradition as well? Absolutely.

The most widely known is Francis Schaeffer, who first introduced many evangelicals to the problem of the two-story dichotomy. Schaeffer was influenced by philosopher Herman Dooyeweerd, a Dutch Calvinist who died in 1977.[58] Why did Dooyeweerd identify the central problem of the modern age as dualism? Because as a Dutchman, he was influenced by continental thought—which, as we have seen, has wrestled with the two-story dualism ever since the Romantic era.[59]

By the end of the nineteenth century, the tension between the two stories had grown so acute that many thinkers experienced a sense of intellectual schizophrenia. Here in America, for example, the founders of philosophical pragmatism were constantly declaring war on dualism, especially the fact/value split. William James said he wanted to create "a system that will combine both things, the scientific loyalty to *facts* . . . but also the old confidence in human *values*." As one historian explains: "The noble goal of pragmatism, in James's own terms, was the bridging of fact and value, science and religion."[60]

The pragmatists did not succeed, but in Europe the same noble goal was pursued by Edmund Husserl, founder of phenomenology. This philosophy is not as well known as existentialism or postmodernism. But it was the precursor to both.

How did Husserl propose to bridge the upper/lower story divide? By diagnosing how it arose in the first place. The entire dialectical process was triggered by the mistake of elevating one limited realm of human experience to the status of ultimate reality. Enlightenment materialism, which absolutized matter, evoked the reaction of Romantic idealism, which absolutized the free consciousness. In the ensuing tug of war, the Western mind was torn in two.[61]

Of course, the very nature of scholarship requires us to abstract some aspect of experience—to bracket it, isolate it, and investigate its properties. The danger is that we can easily forget to return it to its real-world context. A physicist focuses on mathematical patterns in matter, but may then elevate matter to the sole reality—materialism. A biologist focuses on natural process, but may then insist that nature is all that exists—naturalism. And so on. As Husserl said, false absolutes arise when we forget that our concepts are "really no more than abstractions divorced from their original genesis in our life-world."[62]

The solution, then, is to reverse the process—to return abstract, specialized knowledge to its larger context in the matrix of human experience. As Husserl put it, we must re-connect *theoretical* thought with our *pre-theoretical* experience of the world, which is integral and unified.

The Blind Men and the Elephant

According to Dooyeweerd, the tendency to absolutize some part of creation is the source of all non-biblical worldviews—"the source of all isms."[63] Like the famous poem of the blind men and the elephant, each thinker is sure that the part of reality he has grabbed hold of is the interpretative key to everything else. The man who caught hold of the trunk insists that the entire elephant is like a snake; the one who grasped the tusk argues that the animal is like a spear; the one who found the tail insists that the beast is like a rope. And so on. As Hegel put it, all philosophies are born out of the tendency for each thinker to absolutize his own limited horizons of experience.

This can be translated into theological terms as the human tendency to create mental idols. Those who reject the transcendent Creator will build their worldview on something within creation. They will worship and serve "created things rather than the Creator" (Rom. 1:25). Philosophers are no different from everyone else in this regard. They, too, select some aspect of created reality that appeals to them. *That* becomes for them the key that will unlock the universe, the set of conceptual categories that will explain all of human experience, the ultimate truth that conditions every other truth claim, the fulcrum at the center of reality. In short, it becomes a mental idol.

But of course, no matter *which* part of reality is absolutized, it is still *only* a part. Therefore the worldview built on that foundation will always be partial, incomplete, one-sided, and off balance. There will always be some things that fail to fit its categories of explanation, that fall outside its grid, that stick out of the box.

What then? Anything that sticks outside of the box is simply dismissed or denied. For example, materialism insists that anything beyond matter is not real. Empiricism says anything beyond the senses is not real. Naturalism says anything beyond the natural is not real. Pantheism says anything besides the all-encompassing One is not real. These are all forms of reductionism because they *reduce* the complex, many-leveled reality that God created down to one level. Reductionism is like a kid who argues that whatever does not fit into his toy box is not a toy. Or to borrow a metaphor from G. K. Chesterton, reductionism is like a mental prison, "the prison of one thought."[64] Whatever does not fit inside that prison is denied and suppressed.

No wonder postmodern thinkers referred to this as *totalizing*. And it has ramifications far beyond the realm of ideas. People who adopt a lopsided, totalizing worldview often seek to gain political power and impose it across an entire society. And when they succeed, those who disagree will be marginalized, oppressed, left out, silenced, dominated, co-opted, controlled, and coerced. They will be stigmatized as different, perceived as "the other." All must be made to bow to the state-enforced idol—or burned in the fiery furnace of oppression.

The study of worldviews is not merely an abstract subject to be discussed hypothetically in the classroom. It has life and death consequences.

To create a humane society, we must "unmask the temporal idols"[65] (Dooyeweerd's phrase) to show how dangerous an unbalanced, lopsided worldview really is. The only basis for genuine human rights and dignity is a fully biblical worldview. Because Christianity begins with a transcendent Creator, it does not idolize any part of creation. And therefore it does not deny or denigrate any other parts. As a result, it has the conceptual resources to provide a holistic, inclusive worldview that is humane and life affirming. This is good news indeed. It is the only approach capable of healing the split in the Western mind and restoring liberty in Western society.

By adapting elements of phenomenology, thinkers like Dooyeweerd have once again "plundered the Egyptians." Other Christians influenced by phenomenology include Paul Ricoeur, Gabriel Marcel, Jean-Luc Marion, and the former pope John Paul II.[66] In fact, so many religious thinkers have embraced phenomenology that secularists complain about a "theological turn" within the movement. Just as Christians have found ways to work within the analytic tradition, so they have found ways to work within the continental tradition, adapting those elements that are compatible with a biblical worldview.

Beasts and Lunatics

Over the past few chapters, we have explored several worldviews within the analytic and continental traditions. Worldviews are not disconnected systems of thought. They cluster into on-going traditions related by family resemblances.

Two streams, many schools

CONTINENTAL

Idealism, marxism, phenomenology, existentialism
postmodernism, deconstructionism

ANALYTIC

Empiricism, rationalism, materialism, naturalism
logical positivism, linguistic analysis

Recall some of the connecting themes: Facts/values. Box of things/box of mind. Machine/ghost (Descartes). Nature/freedom (Kant). Formalism/expressionism. And so on. In the nineteenth century, John Stuart Mill noted the antagonism already separating the two traditions: The lower story, with its materialism, "is accused of making men beasts" while the upper story, with its irrationalism, is accused of making men "lunatics."[67] Read any contemporary book by analytic philosophers talking about continental philosophers, or vice versa, and you will find similar accusations still being hurled across the divide.

Most people are attracted by temperament to one side of the other. An analytical person (scientist or engineer) is likely to hold lower-story worldviews. A creative person (artist or writer) is likely to be sympathetic to upper-story worldviews. A Christian is called to make the gospel credible to each type. As Paul says, "Let your conversation be always full of grace, seasoned with salt, so that you may know how to answer each person" (Col. 4:6). The study of worldviews provides the tools to individualize our approach in presenting the gospel.

Over the course of history, these two traditions have not remained watertight. At times, they have overlapped or borrowed from one another. In fact, most people actually hold elements of both (as we saw in chapter 2): Their views are shaped by Romantic thinking in the *value* realm and by Enlightenment thinking in the *fact* realm. The same is true of society as a whole, says philosopher Charles Taylor. Romantic subjectivism permeates in the private realm of personal relationships, leisure, and entertainment. But Enlightenment utilitarianism dominates in the public realm of business, academia, medicine, and politics.[68]

Two Cultures

In 1959 C. P. Snow published a book called *The Two Cultures,* warning that Western culture had split in two. In his words, a "gulf of mutual incomprehension" and "hostility" divides the sciences (chemists, engineers, physicists, and biologists) from the humanities (painters, poets, novelists, and philosophers—whom he called "literary intellectuals").[69] Over the course of the past few chapters, we have seen how right he was.

Since Snow wrote those words, the gulf has widened into a grand canyon. Back in the 1950s, explains Wendy Steiner, "the opponents in the 'Two Cultures' debates were evenly matched: on both sides they were tweedy men who believed in truth and thought their path toward it was the right one." As a result, "they felt equally entitled to a place in the university."[70] Since then, however, the two groups have become *unevenly* matched. Science and technology have continued their forward march, confident that all problems can be solved by scientific methodology. By contrast, artists and writers no longer believe that they have any significant truth to offer. As literature professor Daniel Ritchie writes, "The common academic-in-the-ivory-tower is no longer persuaded that literature has something unique to teach us about life."[71] Snow's literary intellectuals may still be tweedy men, but they no longer believe in truth or think their path toward it is the right one.

Chinese theologian Carver Yu describes the problem as a "gulf between technological optimism and literary pessimism."[72]

These developments call for some tough questions for Christians. Motivated by compassion and love of neighbor, they must ask themselves: Where were they when this gulf was growing? Where were they when artists began to cry out in despair for alternatives to the dehumanizing impact of scientific reductionism? Were they paying attention? Were they reading the cultural signposts? Did they know how to interpret the language of their most immediate mission field—the people living all around them? Did they communicate thoughtful, compassionate answers? As Calvin Seerveld writes, "God's people must become aware of *our* guilt in the plight of those caught in cultural dead ends."[73]

Sadly, when Christians do pay attention to modern art, they often condemn or even ridicule it. When I show slides of modern art in my classes, students often make jokes about *soi-disant* artists laughing all the way to the bank. Admittedly, the rejection of skill has sometimes allowed unscrupulous people to claim the prestige and status of art for inferior work. But serious art must be taken seriously. We may not personally like certain art forms or find them beautiful. Nevertheless we have an obligation to pay attention to what they tell us. We should give artists the respect of asking what *they* intended in their works, not only how we react to them. As Rookmaaker once said, "Many works would be senseless, real junk, but for the fact that, being art, they are exhibited because they have a message of almost religious importance, interpreting man and his world."[74]

Christians are responsible for learning how to read that message—just as missionaries are responsible for learning the language of the culture where they live. They must also show empathy and understanding to those who are captured by destructive and nihilistic worldviews. As Schaeffer once wrote, there is nothing uglier than theological orthodoxy without understanding or compassion.[75] Only by demonstrating genuine compassion will Christians earn the right to offer a biblical alternative.

The same worldviews filter down to popular culture, where they are absorbed by teens and children. That's why it is crucial for even young people to learn how to recognize and resist secular worldviews. Turn to the next chapter for some disturbing examples, along with pointers on how to build resistance skills.

Chapter 9

"Through modern art, our time reveals itself to itself."
—*William Barrett*

Morality at the Movies

With the progressive dawn, the outlines of an immense camp became visible: long stretches of several rows of barbed wire fences; watch towers; search lights; and long columns of ragged human figures, grey in the greyness of dawn, trekking along the straight desolate roads . . . .

We did not realize the meaning of the scene that was to follow presently. We were told to leave our luggage in the train and to fall into two lines—women on one side, men on the other—in order to file past a senior SS officer. . . .

The officer had assumed an attitude of careless ease. His right hand was lifted, and with the forefinger of that hand, he pointed very leisurely to the right or to the left. . . .

The significance of the finger game was explained to us in the evening. For the great majority of our transport, about 90 percent, it meant death. Those who were sent to the left were marched from the station straight to the crematorium. . . .

We who were saved, a minority of our transport, found out the truth in the evening. I inquired from prisoners who had been there for some time where my colleague and friend P—had been sent.

"Was he sent to the left side?"

"Yes," I replied.

"Then you can see him there," I was told.

"Where?" A hand pointed to the chimney a few hundred yards off, which was sending a column of flame up into the grey sky of Poland. It dissolved into a sinister cloud of smoke.

—Viktor Frankl, *Man's Search for Meaning*

God of the Gas Chambers

We live in an age of ideology. It was in the name of an ideology that millions of people were sent to their death in a sinister cloud of smoke in Nazi Germany. It was in the name of an ideology that even greater numbers of people perished in hard labor camps in Stalinist Russia and Maoist China. Of course, beliefs have always shaped history. In the past, however, beliefs tended to take the form of tacit, taken-for-granted assumptions that filtered down organically through a society's religion, customs, and traditions. Most people paid little attention to formal philosophy. In fact, they "wrote philosophy off as utterly impractical and useless," observes the Polish poet Czeslaw Milosz. It was only in the middle of the twentieth century that Westerners discovered "that their fate could be influenced directly by intricate and abstruse books of philosophy."[1]

Both Communism and National Socialism (Nazism) had their birth in abstract philosophical systems, discussed by university professors in classrooms and faculty lounges. Both were eventually imposed politically through a coercive state orthodoxy. And both were used by totalitarian regimes to justify the mass murder of their of their own citizens. Though cruelty and oppression have been endemic to human society since the fall, the role played by speculative philosophies or worldviews to *justify* oppression is a modern phenomenon. The state-sponsored violence of the twentieth century reveals the power that ideological idols wield in the modern age.

Viktor Frankl was a psychotherapist who endured years of imprisonment in Nazi concentration camps. The account above describes his first day, as it came crashing in on him that these were not work camps but death camps. Later he would write that a worldview is not just an innocuous abstraction, but actually has the power to corrupt people. Totalitarianism is the ultimate result of a materialist worldview: "When we present man as an automaton of reflexes, as a mind-machine, as a bundle of instincts, as a pawn of drives and reactions, as a mere product of instinct, heredity and environment, we feed the nihilism to which modern man is, in any case, prone." And nihilism paved the way to the gas chambers. Frankl ends with these compelling words: "I am absolutely convinced that the gas chambers of Auschwitz, Treblinka, and Maidanek were ultimately prepared not in some Ministry or other in Berlin, but rather at the desks and in the lecture halls of nihilistic scientists and philosophers."[2]

Historians often wonder why some of the most advanced nations of Europe succumbed to such appalling inhumanity. Frankl is right: A major reason was the acceptance of a materialist worldview that denied human freedom and dignity, thus leading to nihilism. Government policy merely followed where the universities led. As J. Gresham Machen once observed, "What is today a matter of academic speculation begins tomorrow to move armies and pull down empires."[3]

The gas chambers disproved once for all any misguided notion that ideas are neutral. Today ideologies determine how the state governs, how the economy is managed, how the news is framed in the media, and how the education system shapes the next generation. Wrestling with worldview questions is no mere intellectual exercise. It should always be done with an overwhelming sense that we are dealing with questions of life-and-death importance.

Zombie Jesus?

As ideas filter down from the university classroom to popular culture, they inform the thinking of ordinary people who will never read a philosophy book or visit an art gallery. Let me illustrate with the story of two teenage boys. Both were raised in committed Christian families and attended church regularly. Yet in high school, both rejected their Christian upbringing.

One teen, who I'll call Todd, was drawn to the New Atheism, today's most aggressive version of Enlightenment thought. As one journalist points out, the arguments of the New Atheists are "cribbed in most particulars from the heyday of Enlightenment skepticism."[4] Todd began to mimic the fierce satire of Christianity that he read on Internet web sites—like one that mockingly called Jesus a zombie. After all, isn't that what we call someone who comes back from the dead? One Easter, Todd decorated his Facebook page with a grotesque illustration of "Zombie Jesus" copied from a web site—a Victorian Sunday school image of the Savior with his face rotting away. The caption read, "Jesus died for our sins, he was reborn for our brains" (an allusion to the myth that zombies eat people's brains).

The other teen, who I'll call Tom, was drawn to a creative, artistic trend called emo (short for *emotional),* inspired by Romantic themes. Emo fashion includes black clothing, skinny jeans, eyeliner (for both sexes), and hair dyed black, covering one eye. Emo bands feature lyrics of sadness, loneliness, and despair. It is considered emo to be fascinated by death, suicide, and self-harm (cutting). Seemingly overnight, Tom went from being a responsible, high-achieving teen to being a poster-child for emo, almost as though he were following a script. Who wrote the script? Emo culture exaggerates themes inherited from the Romantics, especially the symbolists and the decadents, which have now filtered down to the popular level.

What these examples make clear is that young people are confronted not only by moral temptations but also by *philosophical* temptations—fleshed out in the idiom of pop culture. For young people, learning the skills of worldview awareness can literally mean the difference between spiritual life or death. Ideas exert enormous power when set to music in a YouTube video or translated into glowing images on the theater screen.

Do you have the skills to confront that power and harness it for good? Let's take out our worldview detectors and practice on several movies. Many of the following films are not suitable for children. Some are mediocre in quality. However, I have selected movies whose worldview themes are relatively obvious, because that is where we can best hone our worldview skills.

Breaking the Cider House Rules

Susan is a committed Christian working on Capitol Hill as a policy analyst for a member of Congress. In the past when Susan took time off from her high-powered job to go to the movies, she treated it as sheer entertainment—a chance to sit back and enjoy a good story. Until she watched *The Cider House Rules*.

"What did you think of it?" a friend asked afterward.

"It was a good movie," Susan replied. "I enjoyed it."

"How can you say that?" her friend burst out. "It's one of the most pro-abortion movies ever made!"

Susan was jarred into the realization that movies are far more than entertainment. *The Cider House Rules* is based on a novel by John Irving. As he explains, the book is about "a woman's right to an abortion," and the movie is about "the history of illegal abortion." The filmmakers even held several screenings for Planned Parenthood groups. "I'm as active as I can be for Planned Parenthood and the National Abortion Rights League," Irving told the *LA Times*. "That's my politics and people know that."[5]

9-1 An apologetic for abortion

But did people know that before buying their tickets and popcorn? Did they realize that the purpose of the movie was to promote Irving's liberal position on abortion? The main character is a young man named Homer Wells who was raised in an orphanage. Though medically trained by the resident doctor, Homer refuses to perform abortions, haunted by the fact that *he* could have been aborted. Later, however, when Homer encounters a teenager who is a victim of incest by her father, he decides that giving her an abortion is the only compassionate course—even though it means discarding his moral convictions.

The lesson is obvious: Rules stand in the way of compassion. The doctor says his policy is to give women whatever they want—a baby or an abortion. Nothing is ever said about moral principles or obligations. The film reduces morality to desires and feelings. It is David Hume at the movies.

All through the movie, rules are broken constantly. The characters lie at the drop of a hat, whether to cover up a painful truth or advance a good cause. The cider house in the title refers to a bunkhouse for migrant workers located on an apple farm. Nailed to the wall is an old yellowed sheet of paper proclaiming rules ranging from obvious safety principles like not smoking in bed (which the workers violate daily) to puzzling rules like not sleeping on the roof. But the actual content of the rules is irrelevant. The workers object vehemently to the idea of following any rules at all. Homer tears the paper off the wall and burns it in the fire. The leader of the work crew declares, "We're the ones who are supposed to make our own rules. And we do, every day." Later he adds, "Sometimes you got to break some rules to put things straight."

Those two lines encapsulate the movie's theme. Yet the filmmakers do not seem to sense the ugly paradox they contain. For the work crew leader who utters them is also the father who is raping his daughter. In essence he is saying that *he* is free to make up *his* rules and do whatever *he* wants—to her.

Most reviewers missed the paradox entirely, praising the film as a beautiful coming-of-age tale. And it *is* a beautifully produced film. The characters are sympathetic. That's precisely what makes the movie so destructive. Audience members find themselves *wanting* Homer to perform an abortion to free the daughter from the result of her victimization. But if you think about it rationally, in the real world, the one who benefits most from abortion is the perpetrator. By eliminating the evidence of his crime, it leaves him free to continue victimizing the girl. (In the movie the daughter stabs her father and runs away, but in reality of course many girls are too young and dependent to escape ongoing abuse.)

When you go to the theater, do you simply let the story wash over you? Or do you have the skills to analyze what a film is saying? A movie generally communicates its perspective through the lead character. What the main character learns or discovers is what the filmmakers want the audience to learn. In this movie, Homer learns that his opposition to abortion is misguided and naïve, a product of his sheltered life at the orphanage. Life is too complex for any predetermined moral rules. It is better to make up our own rules as we go along.

Yet if objective moral rules do not exist, then there is no way to stand up to bullies, tyrants, users, and exploiters. One of the movie's most chilling scenes shows the orphanage incinerator, where the tiny bodies of the aborted babies are burned. Gray smoke curls up from the tall brick chimney into the sky. It is the same "sinister cloud of smoke" that Frankl witnessed in a Nazi death camp.

James Spiegel, professor of philosophy at Taylor University, writes that "every film offers a worldview, a set of beliefs and values for understanding how the world is and how it should be."[6] When watching a movie, we should be asking: What worldview is the movie communicating? Are there elements that are true? Are there elements that are false and destructive? If Christians do not learn to ask those questions, they may well absorb nonbiblical ideas without even being aware of it. T. S. Eliot once noted that the serious books we read do not influence us nearly as much as the books we read for fun (or the movies we watch for entertainment). Why? Because when we are relaxing, our guard is down and we engage in the "suspension of disbelief" that allows us to enter imaginatively into the story. As a result, the assumptions of the author or screenwriter may go unnoticed and seep all the more deeply into our consciousness.[7] When we "suspend disbelief," we must take care not to suspend our critical faculties.

Zany Zen

Like *Cider House Rules*, some films contain a message so obvious that it is virtually an apologetic or propaganda piece. *Million Dollar Baby* is an apologetic for euthanasia. *Brokeback Mountain* is an apologetic for homosexual rights. *V for Vendetta* says the church is thoroughly corrupt, the government is thoroughly oppressive, and so obviously, bloody revolt is justified.

Other movies portray worldviews in conflict. *I Love Huckabees* is practically a philosophy lesson, taught through humor. Two of the characters are "Existential Detectives" who offer their services for hire to investigate the meaning of their client's life. They preach a kind of fuzzy Eastern philosophy mixed with quantum physics, brandishing a blanket to explain how all the particles in the universe interconnect like threads in the fabric. They intone supposedly profound principles such as, "Everything is connected and everything matters."

9-2 Do we have to ask those questions?

The antagonist is a French philosopher who opposes the detectives' cheery Zen with dark nihilism. She preaches an atomistic philosophy: Nothing is connected so nothing matters. Life is a meaningless accident, littered with misery and chaos. "Existence is a cruel joke."

It's a movie treatment of the clash between upper/lower story worldviews. Yet the themes are treated in a light-handed way—a kind of metaphysical slapstick. The movie is full of lines like, "Have you ever transcended space and time?" One reviewer called the movie a "mishmash of screwball Sartre and zany Zen."[8] In the end, both sides are said to be right, even though they are contradictory.

Along the way, the movie pauses to take pot shots at Christianity. A Christian family is portrayed as self-righteous, hostile, and foul-mouthed. They have adopted a Sudanese orphan, but only, it seems, to give them more-charitable-than-thou bragging rights. The most telling exchange occurs when the main character has dinner with the family and asks, "If the forms of this world die, which is more real, the me that dies or the me that's infinite? Can I trust my habitual mind, or do I need to learn to look beneath those things?"

The daughter looks blankly at her mother and says, "We don't have to ask those questions, do we, Mom?"

"No, honey," Mom answers.

Sadly, the caricature contains some truth. Christians are paying the price for adopting the fortress mentality over the past century and not paying attention to the questions people are asking. A better approach was suggested by C. S. Lewis when he said that in every subject area, it is Christians who should think the most deeply and be the most creative—until people wonder why it is that all the best books and movies are by Christians.[9]

Woody Allen Does It Again

In *Crimes and Misdemeanors,* Woody Allen portrays the conflict of worldviews in a much more serious vein. The main character is a wealthy eye doctor who hires a killer to murder his mistress when she threatens to reveal their affair. The film then essentially walks us through an extended argument about the murder, carried on among three worldviews: a theistic worldview, an upper-story worldview (existentialism), and a lower-story worldview (empiricism).

Theism is represented by a rabbi. He insists that the universe has "a moral structure, with real meaning." Yet the rabbi suffers from an eye disease and is rapidly going blind. In an interview Allen explained what the metaphor means: "I feel that his faith is blind. . . . it requires closing your eyes to reality."[10] Allen drives the point home in the movie by having the rabbi's father say that if his religion ever turned out to be false, "I'll always choose God over the truth." Blind faith indeed.

The existentialist worldview is represented by a philosopher. "The universe is a pretty cold place," he says. "It is only we with our capacity to love that give meaning to the indifferent universe." This notion goes back to the Romantics, who said that it is humans who confer meaning on meaningless universe. Before the end of the movie, however, the philosopher commits suicide—symbolizing Allen's conviction that existentialism does not work.

The movie also puts existentialist themes into the mouth of Allen's own character, a film producer. At the movie's climax, the eye doctor and the film producer discuss the murder in hypothetical terms. The producer, thinking that they are discussing a movie plot, says the story should end with the murderer turning himself in: "In the absence of God or something, he is forced to assume that responsibility himself." But the doctor responds, "That's fiction . . . I'm talking about reality." In other words, the existentialist idea that humans alone, without God, have the capacity to imbue their actions with moral significance is a fiction.

CRIMES AND MISDEMEANORS

9-3 Reality is only what the eye sees

Finally, an empiricist, materialist worldview is represented by the ophthalmologist. He helps people to see the world as it really is—and the implication is that the world consists *only* in what we can see. As a boy, the doctor had been taught that "the eyes of God see all." But the message of the film Allen states bluntly, is that "there's no God" and therefore no one to see. "If you're willing to murder and you can get away with it, and you can live with it, that's fine."[11] The theme of the movie is that there is no transcendent justice, no final balancing of the books, no ultimate moral consequence to our actions. As long as you don't get caught, you're home free.

But (what the film does *not* say) in that case, your actions are also meaningless. Humans face a fundamental dilemma. Either there *is* an objective morality, in which case we fall short and are guilty. Or there is *no* morality, in which case our actions have no ultimate significance. To avoid guilt, Allen has chosen insignificance.

Seven Deadly Sins

Another film that questions the existence of transcendent justice is the thriller *Seven*—but it ends by suggesting an existentialist answer. Morgan Freeman's character is a cop who laments that human justice is painfully inadequate: "So many corpses roll away unavenged." Is there any cosmic justice that will ultimately avenge those deaths and balance the books? The movie's answer is no.

In fact, the premise of the movie is that *if there were* such a thing as divine justice, it would be repulsive. Going through the traditional seven deadly sins one by one, the movie depicts what is taken to be a Christian view of justice based on Dante's *The Inferno*—that the punishment fits the

9-4 An existentialist leap of faith

crime. How is the sin of gluttony punished? When an obese man is force-fed until his stomach bursts. How is the sin of greed punished? When an unscrupulous lawyer (who "bled" his victims) is literally bled to death. And so on. If there *were* such a thing as divine justice, the movie is saying, God would be a cosmic sadist. The world would be a Dante-esque hell. Therefore there is no divine justice. There are only the partial, imperfect attempts at human justice.

At the end of the film, Morgan Freeman's character quotes a line from Hemingway's *For Whom the Bell Tolls*: "Ernest Hemingway once wrote, 'The world is a fine place and worth fighting for.' I agree with the second part." In other words, the world is *not* a fine place, but I will fight for it anyway. This is existentialism: Objectively speaking, we face a dark world with no cosmic justice, no transcendent morality, no hope that evil will ultimately be set right. Life is absurd. But we can take a leap of faith to the upper story and continue to fight for justice—without any objective basis, driven solely by our personal, subjective sense of right and wrong.

Camus Goes to the Movies

The movie *eXistenZ* expounds existentialism far more explicitly. You might say that instead of taking a leap of faith, it stays in the upper story throughout the entire movie. The title is the German word for existentialism, and writer/director David Cronenberg calls himself a "card-carrying existentialist." He calls the movie "existentialist propaganda"—"a kind of philosophical illustration of existentialist principles."[12] He even had the actors bone up on Sartre, Kierkegaard, Nietzsche, and Camus so they could communicate the worldview more clearly.

9-5 Thou art God of your own little universe

How does Cronenberg preach his existentialism creed? In the story, "eXistenZ" is the name of a highly advanced virtual reality game. Throughout the movie, the characters drop in and out of the game—only to discover that there is ultimately no exit from the maze of games. At the end of the movie, what we thought was reality turns out to be yet another game, called "Transcendenz" (another term borrowed from existentialism).[13] In the final scene, a character asks, "Tell me the truth: Are we still in the game?" Fade to black.

The philosophical point is that there is no such thing as objective reality. In Cronenberg's words, "All reality is virtual. It's all invented." The virtual reality games symbolize the idea that all worldviews are invented. They are like games that we make up and then live in. To quote Cronenberg, every view of reality "expresses a creative act of will among humans. We are masters of the universe."[14] In one scene, a character plays a game called "Art God" with the tag line, "Thou, the player of the game, art God."

According to existentialism, to be authentic, the individual must make sure that he really *is* the God of his own universe. What makes this difficult is that we are all raised in a family, society, culture, nation, and religion. Other people's ideas and expectations are constantly pressing on us, forcing us into their molds. In existentialism, when you live by prescribed roles and rules, that is inauthentic.

In the movie, this is illustrated when pre-destined "game urges" take over and force the characters into a certain roles. The designer of "eXistenZ," Allegra, is playing the game with Ted when suddenly he asks, "What happened? I didn't mean to say that."

"It's your character who said it," Allegra explains. "There are things that have to be said to advance the plot and establish the characters, and those things get said whether you want to say them or not."

Later after doing something offensive, Ted says, "That wasn't me. That was my game character." Finally he is even compelled to kill a man. Ruefully he comments, "Free will is obviously not a big factor in this little [game] world." Existentialism teaches that we must become aware of how much we are trapped by other people's standards and expectations, then work to free ourselves. In an interview, Cronenberg quotes Sartre's phrase that humans are "condemned to be free"—condemned because, as we saw in chapter 8, it is a dizzying freedom with no objective yardstick to measure right or wrong.

Reviewers typically described *eXistenZ* as a movie about a game designer who gets trapped in her own game. But that is only a literary device. Clearly Cronenberg is wrestling with questions of truth, reality, and human freedom—all within the context of a celluloid story.

Making the Matrix

A movie with a strikingly similar theme is *The Matrix,* which appeared at about the same time. Written and directed by the Wachowski brothers, once again the world that the characters *think* is real turns out to be a virtual reality, akin to a computer game. The theme is summed up in a question asked raised by one of the characters: "Have you ever had a dream, Neo, that you were so sure was real? What if you were unable to wake from that dream? How would you know the difference between the dream world and the real world?"

9-6 A supermarket
of religious wares

Christian moviegoers were at first intrigued by the film because it is littered with biblical names and terms. But scattered alongside them are names from ancient Greek Gnosticism, Egyptian mythology, Hinduism, and Buddhism. It's a supermarket of religious wares, and the underlying assumption seems to be that all religions are nothing more than symbolic projections of some underlying spiritual experience. Therefore the differences between them do not matter; we are free to choose whichever symbols we prefer.

The Wachowski brothers credit Nietzsche as the source of their existentialist creed. They also required the actors to read books by Jean Baudrillard, who has been called the "high priest" of postmodernism.[15] Like *eXistenZ,* the movie wrestles with philosophical questions of truth and reality, free will and determinism—though unlike *eXistenZ* it is a glossy, hyped-up, big-budget action movie with crowd-pleasing special effects and MTV-style editing.

Ethan Hawke Dreams

Waking Life is just the thing if you're going to the movie theater for a lesson in continental philosophy. The movie does not even have a story line. Instead it consists entirely of snippets of philosophical musings by philosophers, scientists, filmmakers, and actors. The characters are rendered in a wavy, paint-by-numbers style of animation that imparts a dreamlike quality to everything. The main character appears to be in a dream, floating off to various locations and listening as people ponder the meaning of life. The only coherent theme that emerges is that dreams can be avenues to a collective unconscious that is evolving to ever-higher levels. Carl Jung, call your office.

In one scene, two actors (Julie Delpy and Ethan Hawke) speculate on the possibility that humans are connected telepathically through a "collective memory"—a "telepathic thing going on that we're all a part of, whether we're conscious of it or not." In another scene, African-American writer Aklilu Gebrewold states that the collective mind is the main force in history, constantly breaking through to new states of consciousness. Chemistry professor Eamonn Healy tries to give the idea scientific plausibility by suggesting that evolution is accelerating to the point where it will "produce a neo-human with a new individuality and a new consciousness."

9-7 Carl Jung, call your office

And the way to tap that consciousness is through dreams. The film's title is taken from a maxim by George Santayana: "Waking life is a dream controlled." The film's message seems to be summed up by an unnamed character, who expounds on "the venerable tradition of sorcerers, shamans and other visionaries who have developed and perfected the art of dream travel, the so-called lucid dream state where, by consciously controlling your dreams, you're able to discover things beyond your capacity to apprehend in your awake state."

What is the rationale for thinking that dreams give us the power to "discover things"? The answer given is remarkably similar to Aldous Huxley's rationale for using psychedelic drugs (chapter 8). "In the waking world, the neural system inhibits the activation" of most of the brain, says singer/songwriter Guy Forsyth. This "makes evolutionary sense" because to function in ordinary life, we require only a narrow range of consciousness." Dreams are a way to expand the range of consciousness—without Huxley's drugs.

All this begs the question why expanded consciousness is a good thing. If life is meaningless and purposeless, why would we find it fulfilling to become more conscious of that fact? Expanded consciousness is not the panacea it is often presented to be. The prior question is *what kind* of reality exists for us to be conscious of. Unless there is a God who created and loves us, enhancing awareness would merely sharpen our sense of life's meaninglessness.

Elvis and the Meaning of Life

For other movies that give an upper-story perspective, think of virtually any movie that deals with spirituality. In *Finding Graceland* the plot revolves around an Elvis impersonator who is traveling to participate in a concert for Elvis impersonators—people who have built their entire sense of identity and purpose around imitating the famous singer. In one scene, a young man asks the female lead, "Why do you guys all sound like philosophers?" That's a signal that she is about to deliver a philosophical idea.

She responds, "Everybody needs guidance. What difference does it make whether you get it from Jesus, Buddha—or Elvis?" In other words, the *content* of belief doesn't matter, as long as it gives you a sense of purpose and identity. As long as it helps you get through the night.

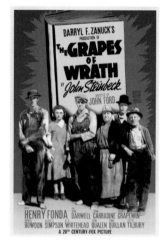

9-8 The gospel according to Emerson

One of the most popular spiritual messages Hollywood preaches is New Age-style pantheism. It appeared as early as 1940 in the classic film *Grapes of Wrath*. At the movie's climax, Henry Fonda's character, Tom Joad, says, "A fellow ain't got a soul of his own, just little piece of a big soul, the one big soul that belongs to everybody." Tom is about to leave his family to become a political activist, and he is explaining to his mother why she should not grieve his absence. It doesn't matter if I leave, he explains, "'cause I'll be all around . . . I'll be everywhere." Of course, that explanation would not fly with any real mother. But Steinbeck is delivering a mini-sermon on pantheism. As one reviewer wrote, this is "the gospel according to St. Walt"[16]—referring to Ralph Waldo Emerson's philosophy that we are all part of the Oversoul.

The pantheistic theme is often connected to environmentalism and Noble Savage primitivism. Even if you never watched *Pocahontas*, you probably saw the trailer in which the lithe Indian princess sings, "I know every rock and tree and creature has a life, has a spirit, has a name." It's the same doctrine taught by the Jedi in *Star Wars,* where Obi-Wan Kenobi describes the Force as "an energy field [that] surrounds us, penetrates us and binds the galaxy together."

9-9 An apologetic for pantheism

The same basic theme is promoted in *Dances with Wolves, Fern Gully, Battle for Terra, Balto II, Avatar*, and many others. *Avatar* features the mythical planet Pandora where all the flora and fauna are connected by a vast neural network—a kind of collective unconscious. It is personified by a Gaia-like goddess called Eywa, who is beyond good and evil. As one of the natives explains, "Our great mother does not take sides. She protects only the balance of life." Yin yang. A *New York Times* review called Avatar a "long apologia for pantheism—a faith that equates God with nature and calls humanity into religious communion with the natural world."

Rebels against No Cause

Let's move now to films with lower-story worldviews. The classic *Rebels without a Cause* (1955) was one of the first adolescent-angst films. The adults in the film preach a bleak, nihilistic vision of reality—and then seem nonplussed when young people actually live out what they have been taught.

Toward the beginning, a scientist at a planetarium tells an audience of students that ultimately the earth and everything on it "will disappear into the blackness of the space from which we came—destroyed, as we began, in a burst of gas and fire. The heavens are still and cold once more." The implication is that human life has no ultimate significance. "In all the immensity of our universe and the galaxies beyond, the earth will not be missed," the

9-10 When adult culture preaches nihilism

scientist continues. "Through the infinite reaches of space, the problems of man seem trivial and naive indeed. And man, existing alone, seems himself an episode of little consequence."

This is outright preaching for a lower-story worldview: Human life is trivial, temporary, and meaningless. The planetarium show ends with a dramatic red burst of gas and fire, signifying the end of the world.

The young people in the movie are angry and impatient at their parents' failure to give them any cause worth living for. The main characters, played by James Dean and Natalie Wood, cling to one another as though their love might create a small enclave of warmth and light in the face of a dark and meaningless world. Yet the film ends with a shot of the scientist arriving at the planetarium the next morning to continue his work. The image suggests that the scientist's bleak message will prevail in the end. The young people's rebellion, like all of human life, is ultimately pointless.

Star Trek and AI

A common theme in lower-story worldviews is to explore whether humans are really qualitatively different from robots. Typically the story involves robots endowed with human consciousness and feelings, in order to raise the question whether they really *are* human. Examples include *2001: A Space Odyssey, Blade Runner, Bicentennial Man,* and *AI: Artificial Intelligence.* In *I, Robot,* the chief robotics designer suggests that in his most advanced robot, there could well be "a ghost in the machine."

The question raised by these movies is hotly debated by scientists working in the field of artificial intelligence as well. If intelligence is merely a form of calculating or information-processing, then some computers are indeed "smarter" than humans. In these cases, some scientists conclude, computers can be said to have minds in the same sense that human beings have minds. The implication, of course, is that humans themselves are merely advanced machines.

This was a frequent theme in *Star Trek*. In an episode titled "The Measure of a Man," a cyberneticist named Commander Maddox wants to reverse-engineer an android named Lieutenant Commander Data to learn more about the workings of his positronic brain. A debate breaks out over whether this would mean dismantling a machine or killing a sentient life form.

At a formal hearing, a reluctant Commander Riker is pressed into service as prosecutor on behalf of Commander Maddox. He makes a persuasive case that Data is in fact a machine.

Even if that is true, Captain Picard retorts, "it is not relevant. We, too, are machines, merely machines of a different type."

Ultimately, Captain Louvois rules in favor of Data: "You want me to try and prove that Data's a mere machine. I can't. I don't believe it."

Commander Riker responds, "Then I'll rule summarily based upon my findings. Data is a toaster. Have him report to Commander Maddox immediately for experimental refit."

In the end, Data was not dismantled. But the debate over whether humans are anything more than complex toasters continues today, not only in the rarefied atmosphere of academia but also in the movie theater and on the television screen.

Pulp and Other Fictions

Of course, not every film is intentional about conveying a worldview. Many focus on telling a warm human story or offering sheer spectacle and entertainment. Even then, however, the story is told from a certain perspective that shapes the tone and theme. "A movie story when 'told' has an informing vision . . . a frame of reference," writes Robert K. Johnston in *Reel Spirituality*. "In fact, no story can develop without some more-or-less coherent perception of reality, some fundamental opinion about life." Thus "any film, as a product of human creativity, contains hints on the worldview of the moviemaker."[17]

Those hints often are encapsulated in a movie's theme—what we might call its message, or the moral of the story. The theme of *Fatal Attraction* is that infidelity can have dangerous consequences. *Jurassic Park* suggests that control of nature through technology is often an illusion—that "life will find a way" out of human attempts to control it. *Lion King* is a movie about living up to your responsibilities. Simba's father tells him, "You *are* more than what you have *become*." (That is, you are a child of the king, but you are not living like one.) *The Apostle* grudgingly admits that even a fire-breathing country evangelist with moral failings can still do some good. The theme of *Minority Report* is that even if we could foretell the future, we would not be determined but could still make genuine moral choices. *Fight Club* warns that men who grow up without fathers to teach them how to face pain and danger often end up as repressed cubicle slaves who define themselves by their paychecks and consumer items—and their suppressed masculinity may break out in dangerous ways.

Sometimes the surface theme of a movie is not its real theme. In reading reviews of *The Truman Show,* you might think it was a science fiction movie. The premise is a television set so advanced that a character could mistake it for reality and live his entire life in it. But the movie is not really about advanced technology. The real theme is exploitation. At the climax of the movie, the producer Christof (note the religious allusion) tries to prevent the main character Truman (True Man) from escaping out of the television set to the real world. The dialogue makes it clear that the producer does not care about Truman for his own sake. He only wants to continue exploiting him to enhance his own professional status and financial gain. The TV set is a metaphor for the way exploitive people seek to control others by controlling their definition of reality.

9-11 Get your life under (my) control

Pulp Fiction is another unpredictable movie. Many reviewers labeled it postmodern because of its nonlinear structure. Other reviewers gave it bad ratings for its violence. But the most striking plot element is that a hit man, Jules, undergoes a religious conversion. When a criminal fires a gun at him six times at point blank range without hitting him, Jules concludes that he has experienced a miracle. It is a sign from God that he should leave the life of crime. Throughout the rest of the movie, he and his partner debate what really happened. When Jules refers to "the miracle we just witnessed," his partner protests: "The miracle *you* witnessed. *I* witnessed a freak occurrence."

9-12 A sign from God?

At the end, Jules demonstrates his change of heart by refusing to shoot two amateur thieves, a young couple, who have held him up. Instead he sends them on their way with the bag of loot they have stolen. With this money, Jules tells them, "I am buying your life." The implicit message is that they too should leave their life of crime and start new life. (The biblical term *redeem* literally means "buy back.") Having been saved himself, Jules is now becoming an agent of salvation for others. A *TV Guide* review concludes: "Without its commitment to an idea of salvation, *Pulp Fiction* would be little more than a terrific parlor trick; with it, it's something far richer and more haunting."[18]

Worldview for Our Generation

Of course, a movie is more than the worldview it expresses. Because filmmakers are made in God's image, their art is often better than their worldview, bringing universal themes to life. For example, historically based films can transport us to a different time and place. *Gladiator* movingly portrayed the ancient Roman warrior's ethic of honor. *Schindler's List* was a powerful protest of Nazi inhumanity. *Braveheart* was an inspiring account of the Scottish fight for independence. *Saving Private Ryan* invoked World War II so powerfully that it reduced many veterans to tears. *Hotel Rwanda* tells the true story of a hotel manager who saved more than a thousand lives when the Hutus massacred a million people in Rwanda in 1994. (What the film did not clearly depict is that the real hotel manager is a strong Christian.) *Blood Diamond* is a compelling portrayal of the savagery of civil war in Sierra Leone in 1999.

Movies can also offer genuine insights into the human condition. *Spitfire Grill* tells a story of a young woman from prison who brings unexpected reconciliation to a small town. *The Shawshank Redemption* is a finely drawn portrait of the relationship between two prison inmates, one white and the other African American. *Driving Miss Daisy* portrays the relationship between two even more disparate characters, a wealthy, acerbic, old Jewish woman and her elderly black driver. *Tender Mercies* tells the story of a down-and-out country singer who discovers that the simple pleasures of ordinary life—family and church—outweigh fame, money, and klieg lights.

Many of these movies portray religion sympathetically, as a normal part of life. *Places in the Heart* is a story about an unlikely group of people who grow stronger by facing adversity together in a small Texas town during the Great Depression. In a surprise ending, the movie closes with the scene of a church service where all the characters are reconciled and united as they pass the communion elements from person to person. The camera first focuses on an adulterous husband and his wife, who forgives him and takes his hand. The camera then moves on to several white Klansmen, and to a black farmhand whom they had brutally assaulted, now healed and whole, sitting beside them. Suddenly, with a jar, we notice that the congregation even includes characters who died during the movie—a sheriff who was shot and the black teenager who accidentally shot him and was lynched. All the while, the preacher is reading 1 Corinthians 13, the well-known passage about love, and you realize that the movie is creating a vision of heaven, when those who are alienated will be reconciled, reunited, and healed by divine love.

Movies made by Christians with an explicitly evangelistic message have grown more sophisticated in recent years as well. *Facing the Giants* and *Fireproof* were produced by Sherwood Baptist Church in Albany, Georgia. The protagonist of *Fireproof* is a firefighter named Caleb, played by Kirk Cameron (of TV's "Growing Pains"), who is a hero at work but not at home. To quote a film review by Rick Pearcey, "On the job, he lives and breathes a heroic code: 'Never leave your partner behind.' But at home, he leaves his partner behind on a regular basis."[19] The problem is that Caleb is a regular porn user, which is killing his marriage. His father challenges him to read *The Love Dare,* a book outlining fotty days of practical, one-day-at-a-time steps toward learning how to love his wife and restore their marriage.

Caleb's struggle toward recovery is not sugar coated. His wife does not immediately respond to his overtures. The film makes it clear that rebuilding a marriage requires effort and risk—that the path to healing is through suffering. To quote Pearcey again, "Because we live in a moral universe that has been spoiled, every act of redemption involves a kind of death." After all, "The cross is not a piece of shiny jewelry; it's a symbol of brutality about a tortured Messiah." The film's spiritual realism clearly struck a chord: *The Love Dare,* which started out as a plot device, was later turned into a real book and instantly rocketed to the top of the bestseller lists.

9-13 No quick fixes

This is only a quick sampling of movies, with no attempt to be comprehensive but only to suggest strategies for discerning worldviews in movies. While it's fine to enjoy film as art and entertainment, we should also watch for the ways it reveals the thinking of our generation—not primarily so we can launch protests and boycotts, but so we can respond to the people in our lives more intelligently and compassionately. Learning to "read" pop culture provides tools to connect with people better and communicate the life-giving truths of Scripture in language and concepts they will understand.

In *Fight Club,* Tyler Durden says of his generation, "We've got no great war to fight, no Great Depression. Our great war is a spiritual war." Yet every age has its spiritual war—one that is waged in the church and on the campus, in the movie theater and on the television set, in the concert hall and in the White House. Are you equipped to engage that struggle? Do you recognize the enemy? Do you know where the front line is? Christians are called to have the mind of Christ in everything they do, to think as he did and act as he did, in our modern pluralistic society.

But it is not enough to critique secularism. Christians must also create their own cultural contributions. How can churches once again become seedbeds of creativity, as they were in earlier ages? To learn positive principles for cultural creation, turn to the epilogue.

Epilogue

*"No great radical idea can survive unless it is
embodied in individuals whose lives are the message."*
—Erich Fromm

Bach School of Apologetics

Bach is taking Japan by storm. The eighteenth-century Baroque composer is inspiring not only a musical trend but also a spiritual revival.

"A veritable Bach boom has been sweeping that country for the past 16 years," reports journalist Uwe Siemon-Netto. Its driving force is Masaaki Suzuki, founder and conductor of the Bach Collegium Japan, which has spawned hundreds of similar societies throughout the country. Suzuki's performances of Bach's *Christmas Oratorio* during Advent and *St. Matthew Passion* during Lent are always sold out—even though tickets cost more than $600. The printed programs give audiences an opportunity to read Japanese translations of the lyrics, which convey the gospel message.

"Bach works as a missionary among our people," Suzuki said in an interview. "After each concert people crowd the podium wishing to talk to me about topics that are normally taboo in our society—death, for example. Then they inevitably ask me what 'hope' means to Christians." He concluded: "I believe that Bach has already converted tens of thousands of Japanese to the Christian faith."

The Fifth Gospel

The Bach concerts have even inspired scores of young Japanese to go on pilgrimages to Leipzig, Germany, where he worked for twenty-seven years until his death in 1750. There they sit in the church where Bach was once cantor, "following with shining eyes the rich Lutheran liturgy," writes Siemon-Netto. For example, a Japanese musicologist named Keisuke Maruyama traveled to Leipzig to study the daily Scriptural readings that were part of the Lutheran lectionary cycle. His academic goal was to analyze the impact these Scriptural passages had on Bach's cantatas. But he discovered far more than he had bargained for. After completing his scholarly work, Maruyama sought out the bishop of Bach's old church and said, "It is not enough to read Christian texts. I want to be a Christian myself. Please baptize me."

And so the saying is once again proved correct that Bach's cantatas are the "fifth Gospel."

Amazingly, even his purely instrumental music can have a spiritual impact. One famous convert is Masashi Masuda, who started out as an agnostic. He dates the beginning of his spiritual journey to hearing the *Goldberg Variations* performed by Glenn Gould, which have no Scriptural words at all. Masuda now teaches systematic theology at Sophia University in Tokyo.

Organist Yuko Maruyama likewise attributes her conversion to the music of Bach. Once a devout Buddhist, Maruyama says "Bach introduced me to God, Jesus and Christianity." She adds, "When I play a fugue, I can hear Bach talking to God."

Conductor Robert Bergt, who worked in Japan, says Bach's music has brought musicians and audiences into contact with the Word of God. "Some of these people would then in private declare themselves as 'closet Christians,'" Bergt told *Christian History* magazine. Though only one percent of Japan's population is officially Christian, Bergt estimates that if secret believers were included, the real figure could be three times as high.[1]

Roll Up Your Sleeves

Where are today's counterparts to Bach? Where is the music and art that expresses biblical truths so eloquently that it invites people to embark on a search for God? Christians must go beyond criticizing the degradation of American culture, roll up their sleeves, and get to work on positive solutions. The only way to drive out bad culture is with good culture. After all, Jesus called his disciples *salt* and *light*. The metaphor of light means Christians must seek out places of darkness and despair, and enter into those places to illuminate them with the splendor of God's truth. And because salt was used in biblical times as a preservative—to prevent food from spoiling and decaying—the salt metaphor means that Christians must seek out places where society is corrupt and falling apart, and enter into those places with God's power to preserve and renew.

The church must once again become a place with a reputation for nurturing artists, those with a special gift for giving visual and imaginative expression to biblical truth.[2] The arts are not just window-dressing on a didactic message—a candy coating to help the teaching go down more easily. Scripture itself is made up of a wide variety of literary forms: poetry, proverbs, prophecy, historical narrative, commands, parables, love songs, practical admonition, and hymns of praise. In fact, only a fraction of Scripture is devoted to straightforward didactic teaching. The writers of Scripture used artistic and literary forms to convey truths too profound for straightforward propositional statements.

Jesus himself taught many of his most powerful lessons through story, metaphor, and imagery. He could have just commanded us to take care of those who are victimized and oppressed. Instead he told the parable of the good Samaritan. He could have assured us that God forgives sins. Instead he told the parable of the prodigal son. "The Kingdom was far too deep and rich a truth to entrust to merely rational abstract propositions," writes Hollywood screenwriter Brian Godawa. Jesus "chose stories of weddings, investment bankers, unscrupulous slaves, and buried treasure" instead of speaking in logical syllogisms or abstract axioms.[3] The Bible's literary form underscores the importance of the arts for nourishing the human spirit.

Biblical theology itself can be understood as a narrative. The story line has three fundamental turning points—creation, fall, and redemption (leading to a final glorification). The account begins with creation, which means that even today, the world continues to bear signs of the beauty and wonder of its original creation. But its perfection was shattered by the tragedy of the fall into sin, erupting into war, injustice, and oppression. Throughout history, the forces of good and evil have engaged in cosmic battle—until, finally, history reached its climax in the incarnation, death, and resurrection of Jesus Christ. In Christ, God himself entered the space/time world to share the human condition. By suffering injustice and death himself, he broke their power over us. Ever since that great turning point, God has been applying the effects of salvation to liberate captives and regain territory. Now we look forward to the final denouement—the *Last Battle*, as Lewis calls it in the Narnia tales—when evil and suffering will end. In God's wondrous new creation, there will be neither death nor tears. This is a great epic story that captures the moral imagination. Indeed, all good stories echo it in some way.

Missionaries at Home

People were created with an imagination to need inspiring stories and images just as much as they need good food to eat and clean air to breathe, says John Erickson. "The opening chapter of Genesis tells us that God's first act of creation was to impose structure on the primeval chaos, separating the dry land from the water, day from night, earth from sky, and male from female." In the same way, "a structured story says, without saying it, that there is order in the universe. And in this crazy world, that becomes a profoundly religious statement, an affirmation of the divine act of creation." A well ordered story "affirms divine order in the universe and justice in human affairs."

And yet, Erickson notes, today's "popular culture offers just the opposite: frantic television images that have no coherence, movies that cannot distinguish between heroes and villains, art that seems to have lost all vision of form and beauty, books with characters we would never invite into our homes, and jagged 'music' that offers neither a melody nor harmony."[4]

Think of it this way: Parents are less worried about their children taking philosophy courses in college than about their children being sucked into the morass of pop culture. They are looking for guidance to help their children navigate through an increasingly decadent world of music and entertainment. Christian parents cannot protect their children from ever encountering opposing worldviews. But they *can* help them develop resistance skills, by giving them the tools to recognize false ideas and counter them with a solid grasp of biblical concepts.

Christians are called to adopt the mentality of a missionary, even if they never set foot in a foreign country. A missionary has to sift the indigenous culture carefully, deciding which aspects of the society can be redeemed and which must be rejected. It has been that way ever since the early church, when the first Christians faced a highly developed Greco-Roman culture. Some parts of that culture they rejected as unbiblical. But other parts they saw as consistent with biblical teaching and thus adapted and embraced—so much so that ever since, Western culture has consisted of a blend of the classical and the Christian heritage.

The same sifting must be done in every era. On one hand, much of human culture is good, because all humans are made in the image of God and must live within the structures of the world God created. They benefit from God's common grace, the gifts that God bestows on all creation. As Matthew 5:45 puts it, God causes his rain to fall on the just and the unjust alike. The implication is that non-Christians can be creative artists, successful businessmen, skillful doctors, and loving parents. As Jesus said, even "you who are evil know how to give good gifts to your children" (Matt. 7:11). On the other hand, Scripture also teaches that sin and evil are pervasive. No part of life is untouched by corruption and falsehood. Nothing is theologically neutral. Christians are responsible for evaluating everything against the plumb line of scriptural truth.

Taken together, these two themes give Christians a balanced approach to culture—affirming and supporting what is good, while resisting anything that conflicts with Scripture. To use Jesus' metaphor, we are to be innocent as doves but wary as serpents (Matt. 10:16).

Spiritual Junk Food

What does this balance imply for the arts? On one hand, it gives Christians the liberty to enjoy any work of art for its beauty and aesthetic power. As Gene Edward Veith writes, "We may acknowledge the artistic skill of a work, possibly even finding great value in its aesthetic dimension, while disagreeing with its overt message."[5]

On the other hand, a work of art may be solidly biblical in content, yet have little or no artistic merit. Christians should not allow themselves to develop sloppy aesthetic judgment by accepting low-quality religious kitsch just because they agree with the message. When I was growing up, the typical religious art exhibited a saccharine Victorian sentimentalism.

10-1 Cicely Mary Barker
'Jesus, tender shepherd, hear me,
Bless Thy little lamb to-night,' 1929

10-2 Anonymous
Jesus, Good Shepherd,

Christian sentimentalism

What makes this sentimentalized art and music so insipid? It equates Christianity with sugar and spice and everything nice. The poet Paul Claudel pilloried the sweet-and-light style by asking, "If the salt hath lost its savour, wherewith shall it be salted? With sugar!"[6]

When generations of children are nourished on these sugary images, they lose a sense of Jesus' true character. In the words of Dorothy Sayers, "We have very efficiently pared the claws of the Lion of Judah," turning Jesus "into a household pet for pale curates and pious old ladies." Yet in the first century, this so-called "gentle Jesus, meek and mild" was so adamant and inflammatory "that He was thrown out of church, stoned, hunted from place to place, and finally gibbeted as a firebrand and a public danger."[7] How will the church portray *that* Jesus in its art?

Today's parallel to Victorianism would include praise music that mirrors the vapid emotionalism and egocentrism of pop culture. I once visited a church where I was startled to hear the congregation sing lines like "You are my all desire," and "I want to feel the warmth of your embrace." The lyrics made no mention of God or Jesus. No reference to salvation or justification or any other theological theme. Nothing to suggest that the song was anything but a love song to someone's girlfriend. The lyrics were such an extreme example of the Jesus-is-my-girlfriend genre that I wondered how any man could sing it with a straight face—though as I looked around the room, I saw several men with their eyes closed, arms raised.

Why are evangelicals attracted by such superficial emotionalism? Because they have absorbed a two-story dualism of their own. We call it the sacred/secular split. The problem is that when spiritual things are moved to the upstairs, then worship is reduced to little more than an emotional buzz. Church becomes a brief escape that does little to equip people to deal with the real world of sin, sorrow, conflict, and alienation. The sacred/secular dualism isolates God's truth in the upstairs, away from the ordinary world—which implicitly denies God's power to *redeem* the ordinary world. "It capitulates to the banishment of the arts and of worship from a materialist world," says theologian and literary critic Amos Wilder. And in the process it "abandons the actual life of men as unredeemable."[8]

Christian art should grow out of the robust confidence that nothing is unredeemable— that Jesus himself entered into the darkest levels of human experience and transformed them into sources of life and renewal. A full-orbed work of Christian art should include all three elements of the biblical worldview: creation, fall, redemption. It should allude to the beauty and dignity of the original creation. But it should also be transparently honest about the reality of sin and suffering. Finally, it should always give hints of redemption. No matter how degraded or corrupt a character may be, he or she should be portrayed with the dignity of being redeemable. Some ray of hope should penetrate the darkness.

10-3 William H. Johnson
Mount Calvary, 1944

Christian primitivism

Art that conveys the complexity and beauty of a biblical worldview will attract people to the gospel, just as Bach's work continues to do. One model is the work of William H. Johnson, whose paintings were selected by President Obama to hang on the walls of the White House. Johnson adopted a form of primitivism to express "what I feel both rhythmically and spiritually, all that has been stored up in my family of primitive tradition."[9] The bright happy colors in this painting suggest that Christ's crucifixion is not the end—that the tragedy will lead to resurrection.

Re-Moralizing Culture

How can the church nurture new generations of artists to give visual and verbal expression to a Christian worldview? First, it must get past the mentality of negative protest. Here's a quick test: What is the name of the chairman of the National Endowment for the Arts? A few years ago, many Christians could snap out the answer immediately. In the 1990s the NEA was the most controversial department in the U.S. government. It was funding projects like the infamous crucifix in a jar of urine, and sexual exhibitionism offered as "performance art" (Annie Sprinkle's "Sluts and Goddesses: How to Be a Sex Goddess in 101 Easy Steps").

But how many Christians kept up with the NEA afterward? How many knew that under the Bush administration its chairman was a Christian? Dana Gioia is a poet who rose from a blue-collar background to become a leader in a movement called neo-formalism, which aims to restore rhythm and rhyme to poetry. (Imagine that!) As chairman of the NEA, Gioia's first major initiative was called "Shakespeare in American Communities." It funded the production of Shakespeare plays across the nation, especially in lower income neighborhoods where students might not otherwise be exposed to the bard.

Sadly, during Gioia's tenure, most Christians had no clue he existed. Many ministries and activist groups pay no attention to the arts unless it is politically expedient—unless it gives them an opportunity to mount a public protest, rally the troops, and raise money. But where were those same groups when they had an opportunity to applaud a Christian for using his government post to work positively for cultural renewal? Where is their ongoing support for creative people who are gifted to lead culture in positive directions?

In *Dynamics of Spiritual Life,* Richard Lovelace makes a compelling case that the best defense is a good offense. "The ultimate solution to cultural decay is not so much the repression of bad culture as the production of sound and healthy culture," he writes. "We should direct most of our energy not to the censorship of decadent culture, but to the production and support of healthy expressions of Christian and non-Christian art." [10] Public protests and boycotts have their place. But even negative critiques are effective only when motivated by a genuine love for the arts. The long-term solution is to support Christian artists, musicians, authors, and screenwriters who can create humane and healthy alternatives that speak deeply to the human condition.

Exploiting "Talent"

The church must also stand against forces that suppress genuine creativity, both inside and outside its walls. In today's consumer culture, one of the greatest dangers facing the arts is commodification. Art is treated as merchandise to market for the sake of making money. Paintings are bought not to exhibit, nor to grace someone's home, but merely to resell. They are financial investments. As Seerveld points out, "Elite art of the New York school or by approved gurus such as Andy Warhol are as much a Big Business today as the music business or the sports industry." [11] Artists and writers have been reduced to "talent" to be plugged into the manufacturing process.

That approach may increase sales, but it will suppress the best and highest forms of art. In the eighteenth century, the world nearly lost the best of Mozart's music because the adults in the young man's life treated him primarily as "talent" to exploit. His domineering father

Leopold kept urging him to compose light, easy music that would sell well and make a lot of money (to enrich his own coffers). At the same time, Mozart's Salzburg boss, the Archbishop, treated him as his personal court property, a servant whose talents could be used to enhance the Archbishop's own status and prestige. At one point he forbade Mozart to concertize *even on his own time* to earn extra money and develop his professional reputation. As a result of these constraints, Mozart knew that he was not fulfilling his potential as a serious composer. Other people were putting his lamp under a bushel. If he had not broken away from these exploitive relationships, the world might have been robbed of his artistic genius.[12]

Today those involved in the production of Christian books, music, and films sometimes fall into similarly exploitive patterns. I once talked to a prominent figure in the evangelical world who acknowledged that he used ghostwriters for various writing projects, which he then presented to the public under his own name. When I suggested that this practice could be considered dishonest and unethical, he replied, "Isn't it *my* work if I paid the writers who researched and wrote it?" Of course, saying it is "his" work is supposed to mean that he wrote it, not that he paid for it. Like Mozart, the writers were being treated essentially as personal property to enhance a celebrity's own status and prestige. As a result, their talents were being hidden, absorbed into the oversized ego of the so-called leader. Yet in *Art for God's Sake* Philip Ryken says, "God's gifts are never to be hidden; his calling is never to be denied."[13]

On the other side, I also interviewed a writer who had worked as a ghostwriter on the staff of a Christian ministry. While there, he had been forbidden to write his own articles *even on his own time* to earn extra income and develop his professional reputation. The head of the ministry told him, "I pay your salary, so I'm the one who owns your ideas." Clearly no thinkers or writers will create their best work under such exploitive wage-slavery. As a result, the church is being deprived of their gifts.

A few years ago, veteran journalist David Aikman wrote a column arguing that ghostwriting is unethical and deceptive to the public.[14] The reader response was one of the largest he ever received—much of it from writers who felt exploited. They told of Christian publishers asking them to produce high-quality work to sell under the name of prominent pastors or ministry leaders who "didn't have the time" to do their own thinking and writing—but who enjoyed the fame and money that the books brought in, while the writers who did the actual work struggled to support their families.

When Christians accept such exploitive practices, they are broadcasting to the world that they do not value creative or intellectual work, no matter what they may say. As Makoto Fujimura says, the church shows that it devalues creativity when it asks artists to give of their talents without "proper credit and honor."[15]

The solution is to develop a biblical theology of work that fleshes out the cultural mandate given in Genesis. Just as God's work in creation reflects his nature and character, so too the products we create reflect our character. As philosopher Alexandre Kojève writes, "the man who works" reveals his deepest self in his product; "in it he discovers and reveals to others the objective reality of his humanity."[16] Thus when a celebrity claims the work of others as his own, he violates their very humanity. John Milton, the poet of *Paradise Lost*, once wrote that books "preserve as in a vial the purest efficacy and extraction of the living intellect that bred them." How can anyone take the extraction of someone else's living intellect and market it to the public as his own?

To obey the cultural mandate, Christians must take a hard look at practices within the church that suppress the creation of culture. According to television producer Mark Joseph, a major force stifling creativity is the paradigm of "superstar" pastors and ministry leaders. "If you go to a pastor's church where he's a star, you're really there as a member to uphold his arms and help him make a bigger impact for the world." A more biblical model is the reverse, where the leader's role is teaching and equipping lay people to go out and work on the front lines. As Joseph puts it, the pastor should be "holding up the arms of the people of his congregation, who are then empowered to go and do good things for the world," whether in music, art, politics, law, science, or business.[17]

The Dogma Is the Drama

Instead of living vicariously through the achievements of superstar leaders, all Christians are called to see themselves as artists, conveying the beauty of salvation through their work. There is an artistry of management, an artistry of entrepreneurship, an artistry of scientific discovery. In every walk of life, we have an opportunity to draw people to the gospel through the beauty of a life shaped by God's saving truth.

For God's truth is indeed beautiful—a drama so exciting and intense that we can hardly bear to consider it directly, just as we cannot look at the sun directly. Dorothy Sayers once said, "The dogma *is* the drama." That is, biblical doctrine is itself the gripping plot line of universal history. "We are constantly assured that the churches are empty because preachers insist too much upon doctrine—'dull dogma,' as people call it. The fact is the precise opposite. It is the neglect of dogma that makes for dullness. The Christian faith is the most exciting drama that ever staggered the imagination of man." No other religion teaches that the highest divinity, the one who created the universe, entered the human condition, shared its sufferings, and was condemned by his own creatures. "That man should play the tyrant over man is the usual dreary record of human futility; but that man should play the tyrant over God . . . is an astonishing drama indeed," Sayers writes. "Any journalist, hearing of it for the first time, would recognize it as news; those who did hear it for the first time actually called it news, and good news at that."[18]

Even more astonishingly, we ourselves have the opportunity to participate in that drama through our own lives. The Bible's doctrines are inseparably rooted in the history of ordinary human beings—in the Old Testament, people like Abraham, Isaac, and Jacob, and in the New Testament, Peter, Paul, and John. As Erich Auerbach points out, these were people so humble that they would never have been main characters in a Homeric poem or a Greek drama. Yet in the Bible, their encounters with God are treated with "the importance of world-revolutionary events."[19] The implication is that every one of us, though we too are ordinary people, can lead lives imbued with the same world-revolutionary significance as we participate in the unfolding of God's redemptive plan.

The church's artists and writers are those specially gifted to convey the drama and excitement of the gospel. They should not be tamed or exploited, but nurtured and supported in their vital mission. Through their ministry, they help everyone to recognize the beauty and cosmic purpose of their own lives.

The Church as Work of Art

Sociologists tell us that every worldview requires a social base where it can be fleshed out in concrete ways. Ideas are very difficult to accept if they are solely abstract and theoretical. We need to see them lived out practically—made visible and tangible. To use a sociological label, we need a "plausibility structure," which means a social structure that renders an idea more plausible or believable. And what is the plausibility structure for the gospel? The church, the corporate life of the Christian community. Writing to the Corinthian church, St. Paul said, "You show that you are a letter from Christ . . . written not with ink but with the Spirit of the living God" (2 Cor. 3:3). Every local church is a letter from Christ to the world. Outsiders will be drawn in when they see the beauty of relationships marked by grace and forgiveness, the beauty of justice for the oppressed, the beauty of creativity in every field of human endeavor.

As Dennis Hollinger puts it, the church itself is the best apologetic. "Postmoderns can best understand a holy, loving, just, forgiving, life-giving God of grace when they see a holy, loving, just, forgiving, life-giving community founded on the grace of God." The Christian community is the concrete reality where the transcendent reality of the gospel is made manifest—"a visible, corporate expression of the Christian worldview."[20]

This is a sobering thought, because the other side of the coin is that the gospel is also most easily *discredited* through the church. What happens when nonbelievers hear preachers proclaim the importance of the family, but see churches full of workaholic parents with little time for their own children? When they see power relationships that are as exploitive as anywhere else? When they see Christians trapped in the same sexual addictions as the rest of society? When they see evangelical celebrities using the same dishonest spin tactics as the secular advertising world? Christians may preach passionately about the need for a biblical worldview, but unless they are submitting themselves to a continual process of sanctification, they will not have the power to live out that worldview—and they will discredit the very message they are seeking to communicate.

The ancient Greeks thought virtue and truth were so interconnected that without virtue, a person could not even see the truth clearly. Scripture teaches a similar principle when it says that sin leads to a kind of blindness. Self-interest and personal ambition can so cloud our perception that we literally do not recognize certain spiritual truths. That's why Jesus said that we must be willing to act right as a precondition to even recognizing what is right. "If anyone chooses to do God's will, [then] he will find out whether my teaching comes from God" (John 7:17). In order to develop a biblical worldview, each person must first make a searching inventory of his or her own areas of sin, temptation, and weakness, and embark on a process of sanctification in every area of life.

Post-Conservatives

Without that kind of personal transformation, talking about *worldview* can become just another cover for pride and self-assertion. A woman I'll call Amy was married to a man who appeared to be a committed Christian. Both husband and wife had grown up in Christian families. Both were active in their church. They were homeschooling their children to give them a biblical worldview education.

Then Amy's world fell apart. In her husband's truck she uncovered a hidden cache of love letters from several women—undeniable evidence that her husband had engaged in multiple affairs. Confronted with the evidence, her husband decided to stop leading a double life. He abandoned his family, along with his Christian faith, to take up with his current flame.

This tragic story illustrates what can happen when Christians pick up the idea of a biblical worldview merely as an intellectual system, or as the latest fad in the evangelical world, without allowing it to transform their own deepest motivations. Those who aspire to a Christian worldview must remember that when St. Paul talks about "the renewing of our minds" (Rom. 12:1), that verse is in the context of a call to lay our entire lives on the altar as a "living sacrifice." In other words, the path to intellectual renewal is to offer up one's entire self—mind, body, heart, and spirit—in solidarity with the sacrifice of Christ. Anything less can become pride and empty intellectualism.

J. Gresham Machen once said the church is called to advance the kingdom of God in two ways: *extensively* by attracting ever more people but also *intensively* by consecrating our lives ever more deeply to God. As Machen put it, "The Church must seek to conquer not merely *every* man for Christ, but also the *whole* of man." Thus he says we look forward to the end of time when "every knee shall bow and every tongue confess that Jesus is Lord." But we must also be inspired to work for a time "when all of science converges to one great conviction, when all of art is devoted to one great end, when all of human thinking is permeated by the refining, ennobling influence of Jesus, when every thought has been brought into subjection to the obedience of Christ."[21] This should be the revolutionary vision that draws the church forward.

Let me end with a trademark quotation from Francis Schaeffer, which is as surprising today as it was back in 1974: "One of the greatest injustices we do to our young people is to ask them to be conservative. Christianity is not conservative, but revolutionary." The technical meaning of *conservative* is to *conserve* the status quo. But "we must teach the young to be revolutionaries, revolutionaries against the status quo."[22] We are called to revolt against false idols and the power they exert over minds and hearts. Christians should be on the front lines fighting to liberate society from its captivity to secular worldviews.

And who is better equipped than artists to communicate that liberating message—to jar the church out of its complacency, tear away the veil of religious euphemism, expose hypocrisy and self-righteousness, and create works that reveal the breath-taking beauty of salvation?

Like Bach, today's artists could well inspire a spiritual revival, and in turn spark a global cultural revolution.

Acknowledgments

Those who have read my earlier books, especially *Total Truth,* know that I owe a profound debt to Francis Schaeffer. It was through visiting L'Abri, and then reading his books, that I first came to Christianity. In graduate school at the Institute for Christian Studies in Toronto, I studied the works of Herman Dooyeweerd. It was Phillip E. Johnson's *The Wedge of Truth* that gave me a clearer understanding of the way the fact/value split functions in secular strategies to discredit and marginalize Christian perspectives in the public square.

As a college student I had the opportunity to meet Hans Rookmaaker, the Dutch art historian who introduced so many Christians, including Schaeffer, to the formative role played by worldviews in the arts. I met Rookmaaker at a L'Abri conference in 1972, when I joined a group of questioners gathered around him after his lecture. Not entirely satisfied with his answer to my question, I shrugged, turned around, and left the building. Moments later, I heard footsteps behind me. I was astonished to discover that Rookmaaker had searched me out to ensure that he had adequately addressed my concerns. I was just a long-haired, hippie college student (I had hitchhiked with a friend across several states to attend the conference). Yet Rookmaaker addressed me with the same focused attention he would have given a professional colleague. As we talked, he related the story of meeting Schaeffer in the early days of L'Abri Fellowship and their shared passion to recover the culture-forming role that Christianity once had—and is intended to have. Through Rookmaaker's influence, the arts became an influential theme in Schaeffer's books, helping to persuade evangelicals that it is not only acceptable but even imperative to engage with art and culture.

Another important turning point was the opportunity to meet Martha Bayles at the Ethics and Public Policy Center in Washington DC in the late 1990s. Bayles is the author of a book on the history of popular music, *Hole in Our Soul*, and her brief but insightful discussion of the relationship between art and truth spurred my initial research for this book. I gave the subject a preliminary treatment in "Soli Deo Gloria," one of the chapters I authored in *How Now Shall We Live?* (coauthored by Chuck Colson and Harold Fickett), where I analyzed Romanticism under the categories of creation, fall, and redemption.

An opportunity to develop these themes further came when I was invited to speak at a 2004 symposium organized by Phillip Johnson at Biola University. The material has since benefited from interaction in the classroom and the conference hall, with lectures given to professional artists in New York City, hosted by the International Arts Movement; to actors and screenwriters in Hollywood, hosted by ActOne and InterMission at Hollywood Presbyterian Church; to university faculty at the National Faculty Leadership Conference, hosted by the Christian Leadership Ministries of Campus Crusade; to Capitol Hill staffers, hosted by Faith and Law; to Christian secondary and elementary teachers, especially those with the Association for Christian Schools International; and to students and faculty at several universities, both secular and religious, especially Biola University's Torrey Honors Institute, Philadelphia Biblical University, and Patrick Henry College. I taught the material over several summers for the World Journalism Institute. Finally, when the manuscript was complete, I used it as a textbook in two homeschool high school classes. Many thanks to the families of WHEAT (We Home Educate and Train) and STARS (Springfield Teaching and Resource Services).

I owe a special debt of gratitude to the president of Philadelphia Biblical University, Todd Williams, for a three-year research professorship starting in the fall of 2007, which gave me the opportunity to write the book while enjoying the stimulating intellectual fellowship of PBU colleagues and students. Todd's creative and forward-looking perspective in his support for original scholarship is rare and exemplary.

I am grateful to friends and colleagues who gave generously of their time to read and comment on part or all of the manuscript, including Jim Colman, John R. Erickson, Makoto Fujimura, David Koyzis, Tim McGrew, Karen Mulder, Dorothy Randolph, Calvin Seerveld, and Gene Edward Veith. Their insights were invariably stimulating and informative.

My agent is, without a doubt, one of the best in the business. Curtis Yates, of Yates & Yates, is unfailingly professional, supportive, and diplomatic.

It has been a joy to work with B&H Publishing Group. When Yates & Yates sent out an initial inquiry regarding this book, president Brad Waggoner responded all but instantaneously. As a former seminary professor, he had taught *Total Truth* in the classroom. Likewise, when I met my editor Jennifer Lyell, she expressed her appreciation for Total Truth and the genuine impact it had on her thinking. All I can say is that every writer should have an editor as creative and energetic as Jennifer to shepherd the book project through all the twists and turns of the editorial process. I appreciate her passionate commitment to excellence. A book filled with images presents special challenges in design and production, and those challenges were met with grace and goodwill by everyone at B&H, especially Managing Editor Kim Stanford and Art Director Jeff Godby.

Standing behind all my efforts are my parents, who made enormous sacrifices to provide all six of their children with a musical education. When I was twelve years old, my father took a one-year research position at the University of Heidelberg in Germany. While there, our family traveled to Salzburg, Austria, to purchase musical instruments directly from a violin maker. But there was a problem: Even though the price was a fraction of what it would have been in the U.S., my parents did not have enough money to buy instruments for our large family and still pay for tickets for the trip home. They would have to choose one or the other.

Well, we did not go home. Instead my father found another job (in Oslo, Norway) that enabled us to remain in Europe so that the entire family could be outfitted with musical instruments. A violin for me, a cello for my older brother, a viola for my older sister, a small-sized cello for my younger sister, a harpsichord for the family, and recorders (a Baroque wind instrument) for everyone. Two brothers later went from the recorder to the bassoon and the French horn. My mother, a professional violinist, used to joke that she had always wanted to play in a string quartet, but she didn't know she would have to grow her own. Even my father, a mathematician, bought an alto recorder and learned to play Renaissance and Baroque music. After the children grew up and left home, he and my mother formed an ensemble to perform concerts of early music on the violin, recorder, viola da gamba, and harpsichord.

This rich musical heritage remained a formative part of my life, which included music camps and state orchestras in high school, and music scholarships in college. I also had the opportunity to return to Germany and study violin at the Heidelberg conservatory. I am deeply grateful for the opportunity my parents provided not only to study the arts but to be a practitioner as well. What a privilege to have actually played some of the great masterpieces of the Western musical tradition.

My most enthusiastic supporter and promoter is my husband Rick, whose sharp editorial eye and savvy suggestions have improved the book immensely. His experience as an editor at various Capitol Hill publications, including *Human Events,* affords him penetrating insights into political and cultural issues (see The Pearcey Report, www.pearceyreport.com). Rick's own musical talent also refreshed and sustained me in the writing process. Many evenings as I pounded on the computer keyboard, he was pounding on the piano keyboard nearby, playing blues, Beatles, and his own compositions, the notes washing over my mind as I worked. It is to him that I dedicate this book.

Notes

Introduction: Why Americans Hate Politics

1. William Galston, "An Old Debate Renewed: The Politics of the Public Interest," *Daedelus*, 22 September 2007.

2. Adam Wolfson, "Public Interest Lost?," *Daedelus*, 22 September 2007.

3. Lionel Robbins, *An Essay on the Nature and Significance of Economic Science* (London: Macmillan and Company, 1952 [1932]), 150.

4. E. J. Dionne, *Why Americans Hate Politics* (New York: Simon & Schuster, 1991), 332.

5. Colin Hay, *Why We Hate Politics* (Cambridge, UK: Polity Press, 2007), 155.

Chapter 1: Are You An Easy Mark?

1. Personal interview with John R. Erickson, 31 January 2007. See also John R. Erickson, "Outrage: CBS Injected Feminist Virus into 'Hank the Cowdog' Program," on the Pearcey Report, http://www.pearceyreport.com/archives/2006/12/outrage_cbs_inj.php.

2. Robert K. Johnston, *Reel Spirituality* (Grand Rapids, MI: Baker, 2000), 119–20.

3. Peter Berger, "The Desecularization of the World," *The National Interest,* 46:8, emphasis in original. For a good description of the forces of modernization, see Berger's "Four Faces of Global Culture," *The National Interest,* Fall, 49:23. The impact of urban culture is growing partly because cities themselves are growing. In 2007 for the first time in human history, the

earth's population became more urban than rural. In the United States, the tipping point was in the late 1910s. North Carolina State University (May 25, 2007). "Mayday 23: World Population Becomes More Urban than Rural," reported in *ScienceDaily*, 25 May 2007.

4. Benjamin R. Barber, "Jihad vs. McWorld," *Atlantic Monthly*, March 1992.

5. Timothy Keller, "Advancing the Gospel into the 21st Century, Part IV: City-Focused Strategy," http://www.theresurgence.com/ tim_keller_2004-02_advancing_the_gospel_into_the_21st_century_part_4.

6. Ken Boa, "How Accurate Is the Bible?," *Knowing & Doing*, the C. S. Lewis Institute, Winter 2009. In the second half of the twentieth century there was a revolution in scholarly opinion regarding the New Testament documents, from widespread skepticism to widespread respect for their historical reliability. See William Lane Craig, "Contemporary Scholarship and the Historical Evidence for the Resurrection of Jesus Christ," *Truth* 1 (1985): 89–95.

7. William Barrett, *Irrational Man: A Study in Existentialist Philosophy* (Garden City, New York: Doubleday, 1958), 63.

8. Todd Gitlin, *The Twilight of Common Dreams: Why America Is Wracked by Culture Wars* (New York: Metropolitan Books, 1995), 147.

9. James Davison Hunter, "Is There A Culture War?" transcript of a conference hosted by the Ethics and Public Policy Center, 23 May 2006.

10. Michael Hirsch, "Brains Are Back," *Newsweek*, 7 November 2008. Chris Mooney, "Hail to the Intellectual President," *New Scientist*, 12 May 2009. Lewis H. Lapham, "Achievetrons," *Harper's*, March 2009. The term was coined to describe the Obama administration by David Brooks in "The Insider's Crusade," *New York Times*, 21 November 2008. Obama prevailed among white voters with college or postgraduate degrees, while McCain enjoyed a plurality among non-college-educated whites (who were 53 percent of the electorate in 1992 but are now only 39 percent). Peter Wehner and Michael Gerson, "The Path to Republican Revival," *Commentary*, 1 September 2009.

11. "New UK research shows significant decline in institutional Christianity," *Ekklesia*, 17 December 2009. "European data show that the religious have had a demographic advantage over their secular counterparts for several generations, but also that this advantage has been balanced out by the secularisation of many of the children of Europe's faithful. . . . Surely many of the children of the religious in the US will become secular, as they have in western Europe for generations." Eric Kaufmann, "Breeding for God," *Prospect*, Issue 128, November 2006.

12. The church fathers vigorously criticized materialistic schools of philosophy (such as Epicureanism), with the result that those schools virtually fell off the philosophical map for more than a millennium—until they were revived during the scientific revolution. By contrast, the church fathers found Plato and Aristotle far more congenial and adapted

many of their philosophical concepts. For a summary, see my book *Total Truth: Liberating Christianity from Its Cultural Captivity* (Wheaton, IL: Crossway, 2004), appendix 3.

13. J. Gresham Machen, "Christianity and Culture," *The Princeton Theological Review*, vol. 11, 1913.

14. Lillian Kwon, "Survey: High School Seniors 'Graduating from God'," *The Christian Post*, 10 August 2006.

15. Alex and Brett Harris, *Do Hard Things* (Colorado Springs: Multnomah, 2008).

16. Interview with Becky Garrison, "John Marks' *Reasons to Believe*," *God's Politics*, 30 April 2008.

17. Voddie Baucham, *Family-Driven Faith* (Wheaton, IL: Crossway, 2007), 69.

18. Philip Jenkins, *The Next Christendom: The Coming of Global Christianity* (Oxford University Press, 2002). See also Philip Jenkins, "A New Christendom," *Chronicle of Higher Education*, 29 March 2002; Philip Jenkins, *The New Faces of Christianity: Believing the Bible in the Global South* (Oxford University Press, 2006). For a summary, see Robert Bruce Mullin, *A Short World History of Christianity* (Louisville, KY: Westminster John Knox Press, 2008). "For the first time since the start of the second millennium of the Christian era, the face of Christianity has again become brown. The great historic churches of Europe and North America are not only minorities within the Christian world, but they are static or declining in the face of real expansion in Asia, Africa, and South America" (276).

19. John Micklethwait and Adrian Wooldridge, "God Still Isn't Dead," *The Wall Street Journal*, 7 April 2009. See also Lamin Sanneh, *Whose Religion Is Christianity? The Gospel Beyond the West* (Eerdmans, 2003), 15.

20. Sanneh, *Whose Religion Is Christianity?*, 69–70.

21. Michael Parris, "As an atheist, I truly believe Africa needs God," Timesonline, 27 December 2008.

22. Philip Jenkins, "Europe's Christian Comeback," *Foreign Policy*, June 2007.

23. Daniel Wakin, "In New York, Gospel Resounds in African Tongues," *New York Times*, 18 April 2004.

24. "Anti-evolutionists raise their profile in Europe," *Nature*, 23 November 2006, 444, 406–7.

25. Joshua Livestro, "Holland's Post-Secular Future," *The Weekly Standard*, vol. 012, issue 16, 1 January 2007.

26. Timothy Samuel Shah and Monica Duffy Toft, "Why God Is Winning," *Foreign Policy*, (July/August 2006), reprinted in *Dallas Morning News*, 16 July 2006. According to Freedom House, the number of "free" and "partly free" countries jumped from 93 in 1975 to 147 in 2005, http://www.freedomhouse.org/uploads/pdf/Charts2006.pdf.

27. Harvey Cox, *The Secular City* (New York: Macmillan, 1965), 1.

28. Rodney Stark and Roger Finke, *Acts of Faith* (Los Angeles: University of California Press, 2000), 64.

29. Christian Smith, *American Evangelicalism: Embattled and Thriving* (Chicago: University of Chicago Press, 1998), 111, 151. Finke and Stark, *The Churching of America 1776–1990: Winners and Losers in Our Religious Economy* (New Brunswick, NJ: Rutgers University Press, 1992), 203–7.

30. Lisa Miller, "Harvard's Crisis of Faith: Can a secular university embrace religion without sacrificing its soul?" *Newsweek,* 22 February 2010.

31. Stanley Fish, "One University under God?" *Chronicle of Higher Education,* 7 January 2005.

Chapter 2: Truth and Tyranny

1. Dan Harris, "Are Young Evangelicals Skewing More Liberal?" ABC News, 10 February 2008.

2. Lorenzo Albacete, "For the Love of God," *New York Times,* 3 February 2006.

3. Francis Schaeffer discusses the divided concept of truth in *Escape from Reason* and *The God Who Is There,* in *The Complete Works of Francis A. Schaeffer* (Wheaton, IL: Crossway, 1985).

4. Martin Luther King, Coretta Scott King, *The Words of Martin Luther King, Jr.,* 2nd ed. (Newmarket Press, 2001), 48. Albert Einstein, "Science and Religion," an address at Princeton Theological Seminary on 19 May 1939.

5. John Horgan, "Clash in Cambridge: Religion and Science Seem as Antagonistic as Ever," *Scientific American,* 12 September 2005.

6. Quoted by Brett Kunkle, "Relativism is Alive and Well in Our Youth," 30 July 2007, Stand to Reason Blog, http://str.typepad.com/weblog/2007/07/relativism-is-a.html.

7. Ernst Gellner, *Legitimation of Belief* (New York: Cambridge University Press, 1974), 193–95.

8. Kunkle, "Relativism Is Alive and Well in Our Youth."

9. Tim Sweetman, "*Total Truth . . . Versus Real Citizenship?*" 13 February 2006, http://agenttimonline.com/2006/02/13/total-truthversus-real-citizenship.

10. Brett Kunkle, "Relativism: Alive & Well," 8 May 2008, Stand to Reason Blog, http://str.typepad.com/weblog/aabrett/index.html.

11. Josh McDowell, "Reaching Youth Today," a speech delivered at the Assemblies of God 1998 Ministerial Enrichment Conference.

12. Francis Schaeffer, *The God Who Is There* (Downers Grove, IL: InterVarsity, 1968), 13.

13. Alvin Plantinga, *Warranted Christian Belief* (New York: Oxford University Press, 2000), 62.

14. Lee Siegel, "Do We Need Faith? Believe It," *The Los Angeles Times,* 7 October 2007.

15. I am paraphrasing a sermon given by Timothy Keller of Redeemer Presbyterian Church in New York City. Similarly, Ian Barbour says any power that religion has to motivate people morally depends on "the assumption that certain propositions are true. It would be

unreasonable to adopt or recommend a way of life unless one believes that the universe is of such a character that this way of life is appropriate." *Myths, Models and Paradigms: A Comparative Study in Science and Religion* (San Francisco: Harper and Row, 1974), 58.

16. J. S. Bezzant, *Objections to Christian Belief,* cited in Francis Schaeffer, *The God Who Is There* (Downers Grove, IL: InterVarsity, 1998), 120.

17. C. S. Lewis, "Man or Rabbit?" *God in the Dock: Essays on Theology and Ethics* (Grand Rapids, IL: Eerdmans, 1970), 110.

18. Gerald L. Zelizer, "Where did we come from? (And what can we teach our kids?)," *USA Today,* 6 February 2005.

19. Michael Heller, "Statement on Winning the 2008 Templeton Prize," *The Global Spiral,* 12 March 2008.

20. Cited in "Protestant Baby Boomers Not Returning to Church," unsigned article, *New York Times,* 7 June 1992.

21. Dean R. Hoge, Benton Johnson, and Donald A. Luidens, *Vanishing Boundaries: The Religion of Mainline Protestant Baby Boomers* (Louisville, KY: Westminster/John Knox Press, 1994). The study was a follow-up to a 1972 book by Dean Kelley titled *Why Conservative Churches Are Growing.*

22. Smith, *American Evangelicalism,* 57–58, 61.

23. John Stott, *Your Mind Matters: The Place of the Mind in the Christian Life* (Downers Grove, IL: InterVarsity, 2006), 18.

24. Julie Reuben, *The Making of the Modern University* (Chicago: University of Chicago Press, 1996), 17. J. P. Moreland, *Kingdom Triangle* (Grand Rapids, IL: Zondervan, 2007), 69.

25. Reuben, *The Making of the Modern University*, 112. See also Phillip E. Johnson, "How the Universities Were Lost," *First Things,* March 1995.

26. Cited in Subroto Roy, *Philosophy of Economics* (Routledge, 1991), 23.

27. Robert Proctor, *Value-Free Science? Purity and Power in Modern Knowledge* (Cambridge, MA: Harvard University Press, 1991), 80.

28. Stanley Fish, "The Trouble With Tolerance," *Chronicle of Higher Education,* 10 November 2006.

29. Quoted in Nicholas Wade, review of *Discoverer of the Genetic Code* by Matt Ridley, *New York Times*, 18 July 2006.

30. Stephen Carter, *The Culture of Unbelief: How American Law and Politics Trivialize Religious Devotion* (New York: Doubleday, 1993), 22.

31. Mark Henderson, "Cells from 'cytoplasmic hybrids' won't make it into humans," *The Times,* 20 May 2008.

32. Lisa Miller, "Arguing Against the Atheists," *Newsweek,* 27 September 2008.

33. Johnson, "How the Universities Were Lost."

34. Christopher Hitchens, a presentation given at the University of Toronto, cited by Barbara Bradley Hagerty, "A Bitter Rift Divides Atheists," National Public Radio, 19 October 2009.

35. "Darwin's 'most dangerous idea' is that natural selection and other causal factors provide a more adequate explanation for the descent of humans than the postulation of divine fiat or design." Paul Kurtz, "Darwin Re-Crucified: Why Are So Many Afraid of Naturalism?" *Free Inquiry*, vol. 18, no. 2, Spring 1998.

36. Paul Kurtz, "Are science and religion compatible?" *Skeptical Inquirer*, March 2002.

37. H. Allen Orr, "Gould on God: Can religion and science be happily reconciled?" *Boston Review*, October/November 1999. Orr is reviewing a book by Stephen J. Gould, but his insight applies to more generally to other materialist views as well.

38. Dallas Willard, "New Age of Ancient Christian Spirituality," unpublished interview, 18 July 2002, http://www.dwillard.org/articles/artview.asp?artID=95.

39. Terry Eagleton, *Literary Theory: An Introduction* (Minneapolis, MN: University of Minnesota Press, 1983, 1996), 10, 14.

40. Nicholas Wade, "Scientist Finds the Beginnings of Morality in Primate Behavior," *New York Times*, 20 March 2007.

41. See Dallas Willard, "Moral Rights, Moral Responsibility and the Contemporary Failure of Moral Knowledge," a talk given at the first annual Human Rights conference hosted by the IPFW Institute for Human Rights at Purdue University, 10 December 2004.

42. Michael Ruse, *Research News*, May 2001.

43. Tamler Sommers and Alex Rosenberg, "Darwin's Nihilistic Idea: Evolution and the Meaningless of Life," Biology and Philosophy, 18 (2003): 653, emphasis added. See Nancy Pearcey, "Is Religion an Emotional Crutch? The Cultural Impact of Darwinism," NAMB, http://www.4truth.net/site/c.hiKXLbPNLrF/b.2903957/k.7515/Is_Religion_an_Emotional_Crutch_The_Cultural_Impact_of_Darwinism__Apologetics.htm.

44. Gordy Slack, "What neo-creationists get right," TheScientist.com, 20 June 2008.

45. Cited in Wayne Booth, *Modern Dogma and the Rhetoric of Assent* (Chicago: University of Chicago Press, 1974), 42, emphasis in original.

46. "Seeking Christian Interiority: An Interview with Louis Dupré," *The Christian Century*, 16–23 July 1997.

47. C. S. Lewis, *Mere Christianity* (New York: Macmillan, 1943, 1945, 1952), 58.

48. John Marks, *Reasons to Believe: One Man's Journey Among the Evangelicals and the Faith He Left Behind* (Ecco, 2008), 105.

Chapter 3: Sex, Lies, and Secularism

1. Anne Lamott, "At Death's Window," *The Los Angeles Times*, 25 June 2006.

2. Anne Lamott, "The Rights of the Born," *The Los Angeles Times*, 10 February 2006.

3. Miranda Sawyer, "I knew where I stood on abortion. But I had to rethink," *The Observer*, 8 April 2007.

4. John Herman Randall, *The Making of the Modern Mind* (New York: Columbia University Press, 1926, 1940), 276.

5. The term "Cartesian" came to refer to the irreconcilable contrast between an objectified nature and a free subject. Descartes himself may not have intended such an extreme polarization. See John W. Cooper, *Body, Soul, and Life Everlasting: Biblical Anthropology and the Monism-Dualism Debate* (Grand Rapids, IL: Eerdmans, 2000), 14–15.

6. T. Z. Lavine, *From Socrates to Sartre: The Philosophic Quest* (New York: Bantam Books, 1984), 128. See also Stephen Shapin, *The Scientific Revolution* (Chicago: University of Chicago Press, 1996), 30 ff.

7. Jacques Maritain, *The Dream of Descartes* (New York: Philosophical Library, 1944), 179.

8. J. V. Langmead Casserley, *The Christian in Philosophy* (New York: Scribner's Sons, 1951), 99.

9. David West, *An Introduction to Continental Philosophy* (Cambridge: Polity Press, 1996), 14-15. He adds: "Our knowledge of this disenchanted world no longer provides unequivocal or immediate support for either morality or religion."

10. David Schindler, "Biotechnology and the Givenness of the Good: Posing Properly the Moral Question Regarding Human Dignity," *Communio* 31 (Winter 2004), 617. "'Fact' is now an (empirically-accessed) mechanism whose intelligibility is elicited through human control, while 'value' is the human will's imposition on 'fact' of what is now only non-naturally 'good'—i.e., 'good' not as given first-intrinsically by nature, but only as posited, instrumentally-arbitrarily, by man." Similarly, John Paul II writes that nature is no longer regarded as *intrinsically* good, revealing the goodness of its creator, but only *instrumentally* good as it is used to achieve human purposes. See *Veritatis Splendor* (The Splendor of Truth), para. #46. The former pope analyzed the two-tiered view of the human person and its impact on ethical issues in *Evangelium Vitae*. See my essay, "*Evangelium Vitae:* John Paul Meets Francis Schaeffer," in *The Legacy of John Paul II,* ed. Tim Perry (Downers Grove, IL: InterVarsity, 2007).

11. N. T. Wright, *Surprised by Hope* (New York: HarperOne, 2008), 75.

12. Roger Lundin, *The Culture of Interpretation: Christian Faith and the Postmodern World* (Grand Rapids, IL: Eerdmans, 1993), 102.

13. Peter Berkowitz, "Rediscovering Liberalism," *The Boston Book Review,* March 1995, 14. The term "liberal" is useful because it allows us to speak of both secular and religious liberalism.

14. George Gaylord Simpson summed up Darwinian evolution in these words: "Man is the result of a purposeless and natural process that did not have him in mind." *The Meaning of Evolution* (New Haven: Yale University Press, 1967), 345.

15. Daniel Dennett, "The Origins of Selves," *Cogito*, 3, 163–73, Autumn 1989. Dennett himself does not believe there is any self or soul. The concept he describes goes back to Plato, who spoke of the soul *using* the body.

16. Küng is cited in "Hans Küng Joins Abortion Debate in Mexico," *California Catholic Daily*, 6 April 2007. The Peter Singer quotation is from his "The Sanctity of Life," *Foreign Policy*, September/October 2005. The Joseph Fletcher quotation is from his *Humanhood: Essays in Biomedical Ethics* (Buffalo, NY: Prometheus Books, 1979), 11, emphasis added. Leon Kass, chairman of President Bush's Council on Bioethics, summarizes by saying that contemporary bioethics "dualistically sets up the concept of 'personhood' *in opposition* to nature and the body." Leon R. Kass, *Life, Liberty, and the Defense of Dignity: The Challenge for Bioethics* (San Francisco: Encounter Books, 2002), 17, 286, emphasis in original.

17. From "FAQ" on Peter Singer's web site, http://www.princeton.edu/~psinger/faq.html.

18. John Harris, "Wrongful Birth," in *Philosophical Ethics in Reproductive Medicine*, ed. D. R. Bromham, M. E. Dalton, and J. C. Jackson (Manchester: Manchester University Press, 1990), 156–71.

19. James Watson, "Children from the Laboratory," *Prism: The Socioeconomic Magazine of the American Medical Association* 1:2 (1973), 12–14, 33–34. Singer is quoted in Mark Oppenheimer, "Who lives? Who dies? The utility of Peter Singer," *Christian Century*, 3 July 2002.

20. Stanley Fish, "Why We Can't All Just Get Along," *First Things*, 60 (February 1996):18–26.

21. Yuval Levin, "In the Beginning: The Democratic ticket confuses science and theology," *National Review Online*, 8 September 2008. The quotes by Obama and Biden are in this article.

22. Cited in Deborah Danielski, "Deconstructing the Abortion License," in *Our Sunday Visitor*, 25 October 1998.

23. Paul Bloom, "The Duel between Body and Soul," *New York Times*, 10 September 2004. For a response, see Patrick Lee and Robert P. George, *First Things*, 150 (February 2005), 5–7.

24. Jennie Bristow, "Abortion: Stop Hiding behind the Science," *Spiked*, 22 October 2007.

25. N. T. Wright, *Surprised by Hope* (New York: HarperOne, 2008), 50.

26. John Richard Pearcey, "Christmas Spirit in the Dirt," 30 December 2007, http://www.pearceyreport.com/archives/2007/12/christmas_spiri.php.

27. "Three Tales," a 2002 opera by Steve Reich.

28. Court TV, 24 March 2005.

29. Wesley Smith, "Dehydration Nation," *The Human Life Review*, Fall 2003. See also Robert Johansen, *National Review Online*, 16 March 2005.

30. Wesley Smith, "'Human Non-Person': Terri Schiavo, bioethics, and our future," *National Review Online*, 29 March 2005.

31. Wesley Smith, "Welcome to Our Brave New World," interview with John Zmirak, *Godspy—Faith At the Edge*, 15 December 2004.

32. John Gray, *Straw Dogs* (London: Granta, 2002), chapter one.

33. Nick Bostrom, "Transhumanist Values," http://www.nickbostrom.com/ethics/values.html.

34. Cited in Wesley Smith, "Biohazards: Advances in biological science raise troubling questions about what it means to be human," *San Francisco Chronicle,* 6 November 2005.

35. Brian Goodwin, interview by David King, *GenEthics News,* issue 11, March/April 1996, 6–8. Goodwin is author of *How the Leopard Changed Its Spots* (Princeton University Press, 1994, 2001).

36. Cited in E. O. Wilson, *The Diversity of Life* (New York: Norton, 1992, 1999), 302.

37. Adrian Woolfson, *An Intelligent Person's Guide to Genetics* (New York: Overlook Press, 2006), preface.

38. Richard Rorty, "Moral Universalism and Economic Triage," paper presented at the Second UNESCO Philosophy Forum, Paris, 1996. Reprinted in *Diogenes,* vol. 44, issue 173 (1996).

39. Smith, "Welcome to Our Brave New World."

40. Kathy Dobie, "Going All the Way: A reporter argues that young women are fooling around with their emotional health," *The Washington Post,* 11 February 2007. Benoit Denizet-Lewis, "Friends, Friends with Benefits and the Benefits of the Local Mall," *New York Times,* 30 May 2004.

41. Janet Reitman, "Sex & Scandal at Duke," Rollingstone.com, 1 June 2006.

42. Wendy Shalit, *Girls Gone Mild: Young Women Reclaim Self-Respect and Find It's Not Bad to be Good.* For an analysis of the worldview held by the architects of the sexual revolution, such as Margaret, Sanger, Alfred Kinsey, and Mary Calderone, see my article "Creating the 'New Man': The Hidden Agenda in Sex Education," *Bible-Science Newsletter,* May 1990. I updated that material in "Salvation through Sex?" chapter 25 in *How Now Shall We Live?* a book I coauthored with Charles Colson (Wheaton, IL: Tyndale, 1999), with contributions by Harold Fickett, who is credited in the book's acknowledgements with writing the ten chapters that consist of extended anecdotes (the "story chapters").

43. Kathy Dobie, "Going All the Way"; Nona Willis-Aronowitz, "The Virginity Mystique," *The Nation,* 19 July 2007.

44. "What Kids Want to Know about Sex and Growing Up," Children's Television Workshop, 1992, a "1-2-3 Contact Extra" special program.

45. John Francis Kavanaugh, S. J., *Following Christ in a Consumer Society: The Spirituality of Cultural Resistance* (New York: Maryknoll, Orbis Books, 1986; rev. ed. 1991), 56, emphasis added.

46. Judith Butler, *Gender Trouble* (New York: Routledge, 1999), 136.

47. Fred Bernstein, "On Campus, Rethinking Biology 101," *New York Times*, 7 March 2004. See also Gene Edward Veith, "Identity Crisis," *World,* 27 March 2004.

48. Bret Johnson, *In the Family,* July 1998. Cited in Laura Markowitz, "A Different Kind of Queer Marriage: Suddenly Gays and Lesbians Are Wedding Partners of the Opposite Sex, " *The Utne Reader*, no. 101, September/October 2000. See also Stephen F. Sternberg, "Can those identifying themselves as homosexual experience change?" Leadership U, http://dev.leaderu.com/stonewall/issues/change.html, updated 14 July 2002.

49. Carol Queen and Lawrence Schimel, eds., *PoMoSexuals: Challenging Assumptions about Gender and Sexuality* (San Francisco: Cleis Press, 1997).

50. For a much fuller treatment, see *Total Truth*, chapter 12. See also two of my articles, "A Plea for Changes in the Workplace," in *Pro-Life Feminism: Different Voices,* ed. Gail Grenier Sweet (Toronto: Life Cycle Books, 1985), "Why I Am Not a Feminist (Any More)," in the *Human Life Review*, Summer 1987.

51. Cited in John W. Kennedy, "The Transgender Moment: Evangelicals hope to respond with both moral authority and biblical compassion to gender identity disorder," *Christianity Today*, February 2008, vol. 52, no. 2.

52. Mary E. Hunt, "Grace—is a transgender person who loves women and men," *The Witness*, July/August 2001, vol. 84, no. 7/8.

53. Many educators take their lead from the Sexuality Information and Education Council of the United States (SIECUS). Its publication "Guidelines for Comprehensive Sexuality Education, 3rd edition: Kindergarten through 12th Grade" states that gender identity "refers to a person's internal sense of being male, female, or a combination of these" and "may change over the course of their lifetimes."

54. Peter Osborne and Lynne Segal, "Gender as Performance: An Interview with Judith Butler," *Radical Philosophy,* 67 (Summer 1994).

55. Cited in Avery Dulles, "John Paul II and the Mystery of the Human Person," *America,* vol. 190, no. 3, 4 February 2004, emphasis added.

56. The survey results are discussed in *unChristian: What a New Generation Really Thinks About Christianity . . . and Why It Matters*, by David Kinnaman (Grand Rapids, MI: Baker, 2007).

57. Dan Harris, "Are Young Evangelicals Skewing More Liberal?" ABC News, 10 February 2008; Laurie Goodstein, "Obama Made Gains among Younger Evangelical Voters, Data Show," *New York Times,* 6 November 2008; Venessa Mendenhall, "Are Young Evangelicals Leaning Left?" PBS Newshour, Generation Next, 21 November 2006.

58. Quoted in Wayne Slater, "Young evangelical voters diverge from parents," *The Dallas Morning News,* 15 October 2007.

59. The book is by Robert Putnam and David Campbell, and as this goes to press, it has not been published but initial findings have been reported on the book's blog: http://american grace.org/blog/?p=31.

Chapter 4: Crash Course on Art and Worldview

1. Menotti tells the story in an NPR interview, "All Things Considered," hosted by Robert Siegel, 24 December 2001. Some details were taken from a 1981 *Guideposts* story written by Richard H. Schneider and reprinted here: http://www.cantonsymphony.org/media/1/4/ Amahl%20StudyGuide%202009.pdf.

2. Gian-Carlo Menotti, *Amahl and the Night Visitors* (New York: G. Schirmer, 1986), 28–30.

3. Henry Pleasants, *The Agony of Modern Music* (New York: Simon & Schuster, 1955), 39–40.

4. Cited in Bernard Holland, "Gian Carlo Menotti, Opera Composer, Dies at 95," *New York Times,* 2 February 2007.

5. Richard Gilman, "Introduction," *The Playwright as Thinker* by Eric Bentley (New York: Harcourt, Brace, Jovanovich, 1987 [1945]) xix, emphasis in original.

6. Meyer Schapiro, "Style" in *Aesthetics Today*, ed. Morris Philipson (Cleveland, OH: World Publishing, 1961), 106. The essay was first published in 1953 in *Anthropology Today*. Finley Eversole, "Jackson Pollock Retrospective," *Theology Today*, vol. 24, no. 2, July 1967. Hans Rookmaaker, "Pondering four modern drawings," in *Modern Art and the Death of a Culture*, the Complete Works of Hans Rookmaaker, vol. 5, ed. Marleen Hengelaar-Rookmaaker (Carlisle: Piquant, 2003), 227. David Gobel, "Building Babel: Architecture and Worldview," presented at a conference hosted by Philadelphia Biblical University titled "Beauty, Art, and the Church," 8 November 2008. I discussed the relation of art and worldview in chapter 42 of *How Now Shall We Live?*

7. Dana Gioia, keynote address given at a conference titled "Artists as Reconcilers," International Arts Movement, February 2006. I have slightly condensed his comments.

8. John Walford, "On Writing *Great Themes in Art,*" presented at the Wheaton Women (Intercessors) Group, February 2006.

9. Louis Finkelstein, "New Look: Abstract-Impressionism," *Art News*, March 1956, in *Theories of Modern Art: A Source Book by Artists and Critics,* ed. Herschel B. Chipp (Los Angeles, CA: University of California Press, 1968), 572.

10. Jean-Paul Sartre, "On *The Sound and the Fury,*" in William Faulkner, *The Sound and the Fury,* ed. David Minter (New York: Norton, 1994), 265, 271. Francis Schaeffer makes a similar point: "If the artist's technical excellence is high, he is to be praised for this, even if we differ with his worldview." Yet even as we "recognize that he is a great artist in technical excellence and validity—if in fact he is—if we have been fair with him as a man and as an artist, then

we can say that his worldview is wrong." *Art and the Bible* (Downers Grove, IL: InterVarsity, 1973), 42, 44.

11. Philip J. Davis, "Mathematics and Art: Cold Calipers against Warm Flesh?" in *Mathematics, Education, and Philosophy: An International Perspective,* ed. Paul Ernest (London: Falmer Press, 1994), 168.

12. E. John Walford, *Great Themes in Art* (New Jersey: Prentice Hall, 2002), 72.

13. Kenneth Clark, *The Nude: A Study in Ideal Form* (New York: MFJ Books, 1956), 15, 25, 30, 38, 40–42.

14. Louis Dupré, *Passage to Modernity: An Essay in the Hermeneutics of Nature and Culture* (New Haven: Yale University Press, 1993), 36–38, 45–46.

15. Richard Kearney, *The Wake of Imagination* (Minneapolis, MN: University of Minnesota Press, 1988), 8–9, 132–36; William Dyrness, *Visual Faith: Art, Theology, and Worship in Dialogue* (Grand Rapids, MI: Baker, 2001), chapter 1; E. H. Gombrich, *The Story of Art* (New York, NY: Phaidon Press, 16th edition, 1995 [1950]), chapter 6. On the loss of realism in Christian art, see Michael Gough, *The Origins of Christian Art* (New York: Praeger, 1973).

16. Roger French and Andrew Cunningham, *Before Science: The Invention of the Friars' Natural Philosophy* (Brookfield, VT: Ashgate, Scolar Press, 1996). The Dominicans arose in the age of the Cathars, who taught that the material world is evil, and therefore there must be two gods—one good and the other evil. To counter this Manichean-style heresy, the Dominicans redefined the term "nature." Until then, it had been used mostly in the sense of essences—the "nature of things." Now the term became tied more directly to physical creation, God's good handiwork. "The Dominicans found a very simple way of proving that the material world was good: 'Nature' was equated with 'creation.'" That is, the nature of things is simply another way of saying how God created them. Over against the Cathars' teaching that the material world is evil, the Dominicans' "message was that God is good, His creation is good, the goodness and the causality of the creation are evidence of the goodness of God." (140, 202) This new interest in nature influenced not only art but also the earliest stages of modern science. See my essay, "Recent Developments in the History of Science and Christianity" and "Reply," Pro Rege 30, no. 4 (June 2002), 22.

17. Dupré, *Passage to Modernity*, 36–38, 45–46.

18. Charles R. Mack, *Looking at the Renaissance: Essays toward a Contextual Appreciation,* (University of Michigan Press, 2005), 27, 29.

19. Stephen A. McKnight, *The Modern Age and the Recovery of Ancient Wisdom: A Reconsideration of Historical Consciousness, 1450–1650* (Columbia, MO: University of Missouri Press, 1991), 73, 76.

20. Mack, *Looking at the Renaissance*, 94–103. The development of linear perspective itself had a theological origin. The Franciscans developed a complex mysticism of light as a sign of God's presence in the world. They studied the workings of the eye and the application of geometry and mathematics to light rays. Books on the history of science will typically include a number of Franciscans under the heading of The Development of Optics, including Robert Grosseteste and Roger Bacon. As one historian says, "linear perspective came about in the early Renaissance," because the Franciscans believed it was a model illustrating how "God spreads His grace through the universe." They believed that insight into optics would lead to insight into the very nature of God. See David C. Lindberg, review of *The Renaissance Rediscovery of Linear Perspective* by Samuel Y. Edgerton, Jr., Isis, vol. 68, no. 1 (March 1977), 150–52. See also French & Cunningham, chapter 10, "And There Was Light!" The main inspiration for the Franciscans was the mystic Dionysius, who taught a neo-Platonic concept of emanations. Thus for the Franciscans, light became a symbol of divine emanation: "Spiritual Light is what God is . . . Visible light is what He uses to carry out His purposes in the sensible world. Study of visible light therefore tells one most directly about God and His actions," 223–24, 230.

21. Stephen A. McKnight, *Sacralizing the Secular: The Renaissance Origins of Modernity* (Baton Rouge, LA: Louisiana State University, 1989), 57.

22. Mack, *Looking at the Renaissance*, 66.

23. Giovanni Gentile, "Leonardo's Thought," in *Leonardo da Vinci* (New York: Barnes & Noble, 1996), 174.

24. Jan Vermeer was baptized and raised in the Dutch Reformed Church, the dominant Protestant church of the Netherlands. When he married a Catholic woman, he converted to Catholicism and sometimes painted in the Caravaggio style typical of Catholic artists. "His more familiar domestic scenes, however, are suffused with a light that is surely both Protestant and secular." Patrick Collinson, *The Reformation: A History* (New York: Modern Library, 2003), 195.

25. E. John Walford, *Jacob van Ruisdael and the Perception of Landscape* (New Haven, CT: Yale University Press, 1991), 19–20.

26. See John M. King, *English Reformation Literature: The Tudor Origins of the Protestant Tradition* (Princeton, NJ: Princeton University Press, 1982), 140, 147. John Phillips, *The Reformation of Images: Destruction of Art in England, 1525–1660* (Los Angeles, CA: University of California Press, 1973); Carlos M. N. Eire, *War Against the Idols: The Reformation of Worship from Erasmus to Calvin* (New York: Cambridge University Press). Some Protestants, including Lutherans and Anglicans, retained things like candles, robes, and liturgy. Luther even came out of hiding in the Wartburg castle, at the risk of his own life, to stop the iconoclasts. See Gene Edward Veith, *State of the Arts: From Bezalel to*

Mapplethorpe (Wheaton, IL: Crossway, 1991), 62. And without Luther's love of music, there would have been no Bach, with his enormous impact on the entire Western musical tradition. Nevertheless, even in these churches there was a shift in emphasis from image to word.

27. Phillips, *The Reformation of Images*, 11. On earlier iconoclasm controversies, see Dyrness, 33–38. Iconoclastic tendencies surfaced within Catholicism as well. At the end of the fifteenth century, the city of Florence came under the influence of Savonarola, a spellbinding Dominican priest. "Paintings, along with other luxury items such as expensive clothes, were destroyed as 'vanities' in public bonfires." Robert Williams, *Art Theory, A Historical Introduction* (Oxford: Blackwell, 2004), 43.

28. Veith, *State of the Arts*, 69–70. Gene Edward Veith, *Painters of Faith: The Spiritual Landscape in Nineteenth-century America* (National Book Network, 2001), 59.

29. "At the heart of Emerson's transcendentalism can be found Plato and the Neoplatonists, especially Plotinus." Unsigned article, "Emerson's World Soul," *Harpers*, 7 June 2009.

30. Veith, *Painters of Faith*, 126.

31. Veith, *Painters of Faith*, 126. James F. Cooper, *Knights of the Brush: The Hudson River School and the Moral Landscape* (New York: Hudson Hills Press, 1999), 59.

32. Martha Bayles, *Hole in Our Soul: The Loss of Beauty and Meaning in American Popular Music* (Chicago, IL: University of Chicago Press, 1996), 33.

33. Walker Percy, *Signposts in a Strange Land* (New York: Picador, 1991), 278.

34. Immanuel Kant, *The Critique of Pure Reason*, trans. Kemp Smith (New York: Macmillan, 1929), 528–29, emphasis added.

35. David Goldston, "The Scientist Delusion," *Nature*, 452, 5 March 2008, 17; Gray, *Straw Dogs*, 120, 71; Steven Pinker, "The Mystery of Consciousness," *Time,* 19 January 2007.

36. Woolfson, *An Intelligent Person's Guide to Genetics.*

37. See Tim Adams, "The meaning of life," a review of *What We Believe but Cannot Prove,* ed. John Brockman, *The Observer*, 11 December 2005.

38. Robert Solomon and Kathleen Higgins, *A Short History of Philosophy* (New York: Oxford University Press, 1996), 215. E. L. Allen writes, "Kant has given us two worlds, one of freedom and the other of nature." *From Plato to Nietzsche* (Greenwich, CT: Fawcett Publications, 1962 [1957]), 129. Herman Dooyeweerd describes the Kantian division in these words: "Above this sensory realm of 'nature' there existed a 'suprasensory' ream of moral freedom which was not governed by mechanical laws of nature but by norms or rules of conduct which presuppose the autonomy of human personality." *Roots of Western Culture: Pagan, Secular, and Christian Options* (Toronto: Wedge, 1979; orig., Zutphen, Netherlands: J. B. van den Brink, 1959), 171.

39. Kant, *Introduction to Logic* (London: Longmans, Green, & Company, 1885), IX, 60, emphasis in original.

40. West, *An Introduction to Continental Philosophy*, 39. See Frederick Beiser, "Post-Kantian Philosophy," in *A Companion to Continental Philosophy*, ed. Simon Critchley and William Schroeder (Oxford: Blackwell, 1998).

41. Stanley Hauerwas, *With the Grain of the Universe* (Grand Rapids, IL: Brazos Press, 2001), 37–38.

42. From a 1954 essay on *The Tempest*, cited in *The Sea and the Mirror: A Commentary on Shakespeare's* The Tempest, ed. and intro. Arthur Kirsch (Princeton: Princeton University Press, 2003), xiii.

43. For a history of philosophical idealism, see Robert C. Solomon, *Continental Philosophy Since 1750: The Rise and Fall of the Self* (New York: Oxford University Press, 1988).

44. "Kant is often said to be the last point of contact between analytic and Continental philosophy. He is a common point of reference and influence for both traditions." Philip Stratton-Lake, "Introduction," *The Edinburgh Encyclopedia of Continental Philosophy*, by Simon Glendinning (Routledge, 1999), 23. "Kant, whose significance is acknowledged within both analytical and continental traditions, represents a decisive point of transition or even rupture." West, *An Introduction to Continental Philosophy*, 3. Kant "in many ways is both the final great figure common to both the analytic and Continental traditions and announces the parting of their ways. . . . It is arguable that much of the difference between analytic and Continental philosophy simply turns on *how* one reads Kant and on *how much* Kant one reads." Analytic thinkers focused on Kant's first *Critique*, while Continental thinkers focused on his second and third *Critiques*. Simon Critchley, "Introduction: What Is Continental Philosophy?," in *A Companion to Continental Philosophy*, 1, 11.

45. Brian Leiter, "'Analytic' and 'Continental'" Philosophy," *The Philosophical Gourmet Report*, Blackwell, 2009, emphasis in original, http://www.philosophicalgourmet.com/analytic.asp. "Without exception, the best philosophy departments in the United States are dominated by analytic philosophy, and among the leading philosophers in the United States, all but a tiny handful would be classified as analytic philosophers." John Searle, *The Blackwell Companion to Philosophy*, ed. Nicholas Bunnin and E. P Tsui-James (Blackwell, 2003), 1.

46. The survey also asked philosophers which dead philosopher they most identified with. The clear winner was David Hume. A report of the survey, along with a good summary of the two philosophical traditions, can be found in Anthony Gottlieb, "What Do Philosophers Believe?" *Intelligent Life*, Spring 2010.

47. In Kant's words, any question that goes beyond the empirical world is a question that reason "is not able to ignore, but which, as transcending all its powers, it is also not able to answer." *Critique of Pure Reason*, 7.

48. Anthony Quinton, cited in Simon Critchley, "Introduction," *A Companion to Continental Philosophy*, 7. Michael Dummett, *Origins of Analytical Philosophy* (Cambridge, MA: Harvard University Press, 1996), 193. Simon Critchley, "Introduction," *A Companion to Continental Philosophy*, 14.

49. Sociologist Christian Smith observes, "Those intellectuals most responsible for the historical secularization of American public life" came largely from two traditions—"they were scientific intellectuals and Romantic intellectuals." Introduction, *The Secular Revolution: Power, Interests, and Conflict in the Secularization of American Public Life,* ed. Christian Smith (Berkeley, CA: University of California Press, 2003), 33–34. Philosopher Alvin Plantinga offers a metaphor borrowed from Augustine, who described human history as a struggle between the City of God and the City of the World. Today, Plantinga says, the City of the World—the secular realm—has split into two subdivisions, which he labels naturalism (modernism) and anti-realism (postmodernism). "Christian Philosophy at the End of the Twentieth Century," in *The Analytical Theist* (Grand Rapids, IL: Eerdmans, 1998).

50. Robert Pirsig, *Zen and the Art of Motorcycle Maintenance* (New York: HarperCollins, 1974, 1999), 61, 70–71, 134, 433.

51. M. H. Abrams, *The Mirror and the Lamp: Romantic Theory and the Critical Tradition* (Oxford: Oxford University Press, 1953), 299, 301. See also Barbara M. Shapiro, *A Culture of Fact: England, 1550–1720* (Ithaca, NY: Cornell University Press, 2000). Ironically, the rationalist critics echoed many of the same criticisms of art made by the Puritans. See Russell A. Fraser, *The War against Poetry* (Princeton, NJ: Princeton University Press, 1970).

52. Ernest Lee Tuveson, *The Imagination as a Means of Grace* (Los Angeles, CA: University of California Press, 1960), 6, 80, 85. See also Basil Willey, *The Seventeenth Century Background: Studies in the Thought of the Age in Relation to Poetry and Religion* (Garden City, NY: Doubleday, 1953 [1934]), 93.

53. George Santayana, *The Sense of Beauty*, 16, cited in Tuveson, 9.

54. Calvin Seerveld, *Rainbows for the Fallen World: Aesthetic Life and Artistic Task* (Toronto: Tuppence Press, 1980), 84, 91, 93.

55. Percy, *Signposts*, 215–16, 192.

56. Jeremy Begbie, *Voicing Creation's Praise* (London: T & T Clark International, 1991), 196.

57. Donald Kuspit, "Revisiting the Spiritual in Art," presented at Ball State University, January 21, 2004, emphasis added. Kuspit is speaking of Kandinsky in particular, but his analysis applies to artists generally.

58. Kuspit, "Revisiting the Spiritual in Art."

59. Jacques Barzun writes of "two streams" in art: "idealist and naturalist." *Use and Abuse of Art* (Princeton NJ: Princeton University Press, 1974), 58. Rookmaaker writes: "Ever since the Enlightenment, man has dealt with reality in a double way: reason and Romanticism,

positivism and idealism, naturalistic reality and the realm of human freedom in the arts." *Modern Art and the Death of a Culture* (Wheaton, IL: Crossway, 1970, 1973, 1994), 203. Fritz Novotny writes: "Only with the development of a 'total' naturalism in the course of the nineteenth century was Western art at last secularized, and antagonism expressed in quarrels between 'idealists' and 'realists'—ultimately between 'idealists' and 'naturalists.'" "Naturalism in Art," *Dictionary of the History of Ideas*, vol. 3, 343.

60. "Aesthetics in the last hundred years has been dominated by expressionists and formalists." F. David Martin, "On the Supposed Incompatibility of Expressionism and Formalism," *The Journal of Aesthetics and Art Criticism*, vol. 15, no. 1 (September 1956), 94. Walford describes the "modern opposition between art stressing *formal* values and art which focuses more on *expression* of feeling and the inner life." *Great Themes,* 404, emphasis added.

61. Douglas Sloan, *Faith and Knowledge* (Louisville, KY: Westminster John Knox Press, 1994), 92.

62. Abrams, *Mirror,* 334. See also Willey, 92–93.

63. Gene Edward Veith, *Reading between the Lines: A Christian Guide to Literature* (Wheaton, IL: Crossway, 1990), 169.

Chapter 5: Beauty in the Eye of the Machine (The Enlightenment Heritage)

1. John Stuart Mill, *Autobiography*, http://www.efm.bris.ac.uk/net/mill/auto.

2. Ibid.

3. Simon Critchley, *Continental Philosophy: A Very Short Introduction* (Oxford: Oxford University Press, 2001), 42.

4. Abrams, *Mirror,* 321–23. In the 1940s C. S. Lewis offered a withering critique of this subjectivist view in *The Abolition of Man.* By then it had become the unquestioned perspective in public school textbooks.

5. Rodney Stark, *"For the Glory of God": How Monotheism Led to Reformations, Science, Witch-Hunts, and the End of Slavery* (Princeton, NJ: Princeton University Press, 2003), chapter 2. The two skeptics were Edmund Halley and Paracelsus. But many historians disagree about Paracelsus. See Christopher Kaiser, *Creation and the History of Science* (Grand Rapids, IL: Eerdmans, 1991), 116–20.

6. A. R. Hall, *The Scientific Revolution, 1500–1800: The Formation of the Modern Scientific Attitude* (Boston: Beacon Press, 1954), 171–72. Randall, *Making,* 274. For more on the contribution of Christian thought to the rise of science, see my article, "Christianity Is a Science-Starter, Not a Science-Stopper," *Areopagus Journal* 5:1 (January/February 2005). A slightly revised version can be read at http://www.pearceyreport.com/archives/2005/09/post_4.php. See also Nancy Pearcey, "How Science Became a Christian Vocation," *Reading*

God's World: The Scientific Vocation, ed. Angus Menuge (St. Louis, MO: Concordia, 2004); and my articles in the *Bible-Science Newsletter*, "The Birth of Modern Science," October 1982; "How Christianity Gave Rise to the Modern Scientific Outlook," January 1989. These articles became the basis for the opening chapter in *The Soul of Science*. I invited Charles Thaxton to join me in that project to provide scientific expertise and review. See Nancy Pearcey and Charles Thaxton, *The Soul of Science: Christian Faith and Natural Philosophy* (Wheaton, IL: Crossway, 1994).

7. Carl Becker, *The Heavenly City of the Eighteenth-Century Philosophers* (New Haven, NY: Yale University Press, 1932), 55.

8. Harvey Cox, *The Secular City*, rev. ed. (Toronto: Macmillan, 1966), 21.

9. Thomas Sieger Derr, *Ecology and Human Need* (Philadelphia, PA: Westminster Press, 1975), 20, 26.

10. Ernst Benz, *Evolution and Christian Hope* (Garden City, NY: Doubleday, 1975), 123–25. See also David F. Noble, *The Religion of Technology* (New York: Penguin, 1997, 1999); Nancy Pearcey, "The Nature of Nature Competing: Worldviews in the Environmental Debate," delivered at a conference held by Philadelphia Biblical University on March 27, 2010; Nancy Pearcey, "Technology, History, and Worldview," *Genetic Ethics: Do the Ends Justify the Genes?* (Grand Rapids, MI: Eerdmans Publishing,1997).

11. Lynn White, "What Accelerated Technological Progress in the Western Middle Ages?" *Scientific Change*, ed. A. C. Crombie (New York: Basic Books), 290–91.

12. Cited in Francis D. Klingender, *Art and the Industrial Revolution* (London: Noel Carrington, 1947), 24.

13. Richard Helgerson, *Self-Crowned Laureates* (Berkeley, CA: University of California Press, 1983), 226–27.

14. Fred Licht, *Goya: The Origins of the Modern Temper in Art* (New York: Harper & Row, 1979), 116–27. See also Penelope J. E. Davies, Walter B. Denny, Frima Fox, et.al., *Janson's History of Art*, 8th ed., vol. II (London: Prentice Hall, 2011), 824–25.

15. John Canaday, *Mainstreams of Modern Art* (New York, NY: Holt, Rinehart, & Winston, 1959), 75.

16. Mishoe Brennecke, "Double Début: Édouard Manet and The Execution of Maximilian in New York and Boston, 1879–80," *Nineteenth-Century Art Worldwide*, vol. 3, issue 2, Autumn 2004.

17. Canaday, *Mainstreams of Modern Art*, 167, 166, emphasis added.

18. Frederick Hartt, *Art: A History of Painting, Sculpture, and Architecture*, 4th ed. (New York: Harry N. Abrams, 1989, 1993), 830.

19. Williams, *Art Theory, A Historical Introduction*, 122–23.

20. See Richard Bauckham, *Jesus and the Eyewitnesses: The Gospels as Eyewitness Testimony* (Grand Rapids, MI: Eerdmans Publishing, 2006).

21. Roger Cotes, preface to the second edition of Newton's *Principia,* in *Newton's Philosophy of Nature: Selections from His Writings,* ed. H. S. Thayer (New York: Hafner, 1953). See Edward B. Davis, "Newton's Rejection of the 'Newtonian World View': The Role of Divine Will in Newton's Natural Philosophy," *Science and Christian Belief,* 3, no. 1, 117.

22. John Brooke and Geoffrey Cantor, *Reconstructing Nature: The Engagement of Science and Religion* (Oxford: Oxford University Press, 1998), 20, emphasis in original. For more detail on how voluntarist theology led to a contingent view of nature, see my articles, "Christianity Is a Science-Starter, Not a Science-Stopper," and "Recent Developments in the History of Science and Christianity." See also *Soul of Science,* 30–33, 81ff.

23. Richard Popkin, Preface, *The Problem of Certainty in English Thought, 1630–1690,* by Henry G. Van Leeuwen (The Hague: Martinus Nijhoff, 1963), xi. See also Richard Popkin, *The History of Scepticism: From Savonarola to Bayle,* 3rd ed. (Oxford University Press, 2003); Barbara Shapiro, *Probability and Certainty in Seventeenth-Century England* (Princeton, NJ: Princeton University Press, 1983).

24. Erich Auerbach, *Mimesis: The Representation of Reality in Western Literature* (Princeton, NJ: Princeton University Press, 1953, 2003), 555, 72. Significantly, the Old Testament had predicted that the coming Messiah would have "no beauty to attract us to him, nothing in his appearance that we should desire him" (Isa. 53:2). Adrienne Chaplin comments that Christ's humiliation "would have been in stark contrast to the worship of the Greek gods at Christ's time, whose muscled bodies—the idols of their time—could be admired in their sculpted images throughout the cities." "From Vision to Touch: Returning Beauty to Lived Experience," theotherjournal.com, 27 May 2009.

25. Hartt, *Art,* 908.

26. Alain Besançon, *The Forbidden Image: An Intellectual History of Iconoclasm* (Chicago, IL: University of Chicago Press, 2000)*,* 261.

27. Cited in J. Carter Brown, *Rings: Five Passions in World Art* (New York: Harry H. Abrams, 1996), 82.

28. Cited in Peter Fuller, "The Geography of Mother Nature," *The Iconography of Landscape,* ed. Denis Cosgrove and Stephen Daniels (Cambridge: Cambridge University Press, 1988), 18.

29. Cited in Ibid., 17.

30. Ibid.

31. Auerbach, *Mimesis,* 22–23.

32. For a description of how difficult it can be for the newly sighted to learn how to visually identify shape, size, height, and distance, see Annie Dillard, *Pilgrim at Tinker Creek* (Harper Perennial Modern Classics, 2007), 28 ff. Dillard draws from a 1932 book titled *Space and*

Sight by Marius von Senden, who collected dozens of cases of adults who received their sight for first time after cataract operations.

33. Williams, *Art Theory, A Historical Introduction,* 137.

34. Rookmaaker, *Modern Art and the Death of a Culture,* 85.

35. H. W. Janson, *History of Art* (Upper Saddle River, NJ: Prentice-Hall, 1969), 492. Starting with the 7th edition, Janson's chapter on realism and impressionism (chapter 25) is titled "The Age of Positivism."

36. Canaday, *Mainstreams of Modern Art,* 74, emphases added.

37. Licht, *Goya,* 135.

38. Bruce Cole and Adelheid Gealt, *Art of the Western World: From Ancient Greece to Postmodernism* (New York, NY: Summit Books, 1989), 149–50. See also Walford, *Great Themes,* 413–14; *Janson's History of Art,* 8th ed., 870.

39. Tom Lubbock, "Manet, Edouard: The Railway (1873)," Great Art series, *The Independent,* 18 April 2008.

40. Donald Grout and Claude Palisca, *A History of Western Music,* 6th ed. (New York: Norton, 2000), 664. See also Harold C. Schonberg, *The Lives of the Great Composers* (New York: Norton, 1970, 1981, 1997), 453, 462–63. On tonality, see Leonard Bernstein's lecture series "The Unanswered Question" delivered at Harvard University, 1973.

41. Peter Fuller, *Theoria: Art and the Absence of Grace* (London: Chatto & Windus, 1988), 125.

42. Edgar Allan Poe, "The Poetic Principle," in *The Complete Poetic Works of Edgar Allan Poe* (New York: Thomas Y. Crowell Co., 1902, 1922), 227.

43. Robert Hughes, *American Visions: The Epic History of Art in America* (New York: Knopf, 1997), 239, emphasis added.

44. Lionel Trilling, *Beyond Culture* (New York: Viking Press, 1965).

45. Suzi Gablik, *Has Modernism Failed?* (New York: Thames & Hudson, 1985), 24, emphasis added.

46. Rookmaaker, *Modern Art and the Death of a Culture,* 67, 75–77.

47. Rookmaaker, *Modern Art and the Death of a Culture,* 95.

48. Morris Kline, *Mathematics: The Loss of Certainty* (New York: Oxford University Press, 1980), 34–35. For a historical account of the relationship between Christianity and mathematics, see *Soul of Science,* chapters 1, 6, 7. These chapters are based on articles I published earlier in the *Bible-Science Newsletter,* "Mind Your Mathematics: A Two-Part Series on the Role of Mathematics in Science," March 1990; "The Rise and Fall of Mathematics," April 1990.

49. Dudley Shapere, *Galileo: A Philosophical Study* (Chicago, IL: University of Chicago Press, 1974), 134–36, emphasis in original. Even Aristotle, who taught that the ideal forms are *in* things, taught that the material world never fully conforms to the eternal forms. Thus he

expected actual biological organisms to exhibit a wide range of irregularity—to be erratic, unstable, variable. Conway Zirkle, "Species before Darwin," *Proceedings of the American Philosophical Society* 103, no. 5, (October 1959), 636–44.

50. C. F. von Weizsacker, *The Relevance of Science* (New York: Harper & Row, 1964), 163.

51. R. G. Collingwood, *An Essay on Metaphysics* (Chicago, IL: Henry Regnery, Gateway Editions, 1972 [1940]), 253–57, emphasis added.

52. Cited in Kline, *Mathematics*, 31.

53. Vincenzo di Grazia, cited in Michael R. Matthews, *Science Teaching: The Role of History and Philosophy of Science* (Routledge, 1994), 118, emphasis added. See also E. A. Burtt, *The Metaphysical Foundations of Modern Science,* rev. ed. (New York: Doubleday, 1954 [1932]), 38, 52; Richard Blackwell, "Galileo Galilei," *Science and Religion: A Historical Introduction,* ed. Gary B. Ferngren (Baltimore, MA: Johns Hopkins University Press, 2002). Not all Aristotelians rejected mathematical demonstration in principle; some simply thought Galileo's proofs were inadequate. See Steven Harris, *Roman Catholicism Since Trent* in Ferngren, 249, and William R. Shea and Mariano Artigas, *Galileo in Rome: The Rise and Fall of a Troublesome Genius* (Oxford University Press, 2004).

54. Collingwood, *An Essay on Metaphysics*, 250.

55. Kline, *Mathematics,* 52.

56. See Alexandre Koyré, *From the Closed World to the Infinite Universe* (Baltimore: Johns Hopkins University Press, 1957), chapter 5.

57. In England, the Newtonian system led to an image of the universe as a cosmic machine requiring a Maker—thus supporting religion. By contrast, in France, Newtonian physics was interpreted to imply "a self-sufficient world machine of matter and motion"—thus supporting materialism. See Henry May, *Enlightenment in America* (New York: Oxford University Press, 1978), 108, 110.

58. Rudolph Weingartner, "Historical Explanation," *The Encyclopedia of Philosophy,* vol. 4, ed. Paul Edwards (New York, NY: Macmillan), 7.

59. Lucy Adelman and Michael Compton, "Mathematics in Early Abstract Art," *Towards a New Art: Essays on the Background of Abstract Art, 1910–1920* (London: The Tate Gallery, 1980), 86.

60. Wendy Steiner, *Venus in Exile: The Rejection of Beauty in 20th-Century Art* (Chicago, IL: University of Chicago Press, 2001), 74, 94, 96.

61. Adelman and Compton, "Mathematics in Early Abstract Art," 87.

62. Others have suggested that cubism was influenced by Einstein's theory of relativity. Lynn Gamwell makes a persuasive case that this is incorrect: "Einstein's theory was unknown to the general public in prewar Paris because it had not been proven experimentally." Even after the theory was confirmed in a 1919 solar eclipse, Picasso and Braque saw no relevance

to their art. *Exploring the Invisible: Art, Science, and the Spiritual* (Princeton, NJ: Princeton University Press, 2002), 138.

63. Meyer Schapiro, *Worldview in Painting* (New York: George Braziller, 1999), 99, 102–3.

64. F. T. Marinetti, *Let's Murder the Moonshine: Selected Writings* (Los Angeles, CA: Sun & Moon Classics, 1991), 63, 98.

65. Francis Schaeffer, *The God Who Is There* in *The Francis A. Schaeffer Trilogy* (Wheaton, IL: Crossway, 1990), 54.

66. Cited in Roger Lipsey, *The Spiritual in Twentieth-Century Art* (Dover Publications, 2004), 71. See also *Janson's History of Art,* 8th ed., vol. 2, 1006.

67. Piet Mondrian, "Natural Reality and Abstract Reality," in Chipp, 323, originally published in *De Stijl,* 1919. Mark C. Taylor, *Disfiguring: Art, Architecture, Religion* (Chicago, IL: University of Chicago Press, 1992), 3–4.

68. Donald Kuspit, "A New Sacred Space," *Per Contra, The International Journal of the Arts, Literature, and Ideas,* Winter 2006–2007, issue 5.

69. Tom Wolfe, *The Painted Word* (New York: Bantam Books, 1975), 118–19.

70. Schonberg, *The Lives of the Great Composers,* 600.

71. Jeremy Begbie, *Theology, Music, and Time* (Cambridge: Cambridge University Press, 2000), 193.

72. Jeremy Begbie, *Resounding Truth: Christian Wisdom in the World of Music* (Grand Rapids, MI: Baker, 2007), 246.

73. Alex Ross, *The Rest Is Noise: Listening to the Twentieth Century* (New York: Farrar, Straus & Giroux, 2007), 426–27.

74. Anthony Tommasini, "Unraveling the Knots of the 12 Tones," *New York Times,* 14 October 2007.

75. Bayles, *Hole in Our Soul,* 16.

76. Cited in Begbie, *Theology, Music, and Time,* 192.

77. See Pearcey, *Total Truth,* 40–42.

78. Timothy Keller, "Talking about Idolatry in a Postmodern Age," April 2007, Gospel Coalition, http://www.monergism.com/postmodernidols.html.

79. See Nancy Pearcey, "The Creation Myth of Modern Political Philosophy," presented at the sixth annual Kuyper Lecture in Washington, DC, sponsored by the Center for Public Justice, 2000.

80. Cited in Michael Oakeshott, *Rationalism in Politics and Other Essays* (Methuen 1962, Liberty Fund, 1991), 15. See also A. W. Ward and A. R. Waller, ed. *The Cambridge History of English Literature* (New York: G. P. Putnam's Sons, 1919), 329.

81. Karl Popper, *Conjectures and Refutations: The Growth of Scientific Knowledge* (New York: Routledge, 2002 [1963]), 20–21, emphasis in original.

82. Randall, *Making,* 267, emphasis in original.

83. Writing about those who pride themselves on debunking traditional values, Lewis writes, "Their skepticism about values is on the surface: it is for use on other people's values; about the values current in their own set, they are not nearly skeptical enough." C. S. Lewis, *The Abolition of Man* (New York: HarperCollins, 1944, 1947), 29.

84. Alex Ross, "Revelations: Messiaen's Quartet for the End of Time," *The New Yorker,* 22 March 2004.

Chapter 6: Art Red in Tooth and Claw (The Enlightenment Heritage)

1. Cynthia Eagle Russett, *Darwin in America: The Intellectual Response 1865–1912* (San Francisco, CA: W. H. Freeman, 1976), 175.

2. Earle Labor and Jeanne Campbell Reesman, *Jack London*, rev. ed. (New York: Twayne Publishers, 1994) 13. See also Malcolm Cowley, "Naturalism in American Literature," *Evolutionary Thought in America,* ed. Stow Persons (New York: George Braziller, 1956).

3. Nikolas Kompridis, "Re-Inheriting Romanticism," *Philosophical Romanticism* (New York: Routledge, 2006), 1.

4. The genteel tradition had a distinct gender component. As Russett (174) writes, "Fiction labored under the burden of the genteel tradition, with its curious bifurcation of the American mind into a practical, aggressive male mentality and a genteel, moral, feminine one. There existed two worlds: the world of affairs, peopled by men of enterprise little given to intellectualism or fussy moral scrupulousness, and the world of higher culture, presided over by ladies, for whom one must write, Frank Norris protested, in such a way as not to 'call a blush to the cheek of the young.'" Similarly, Malcolm Cowley (301) writes: "On one side was religion; on the other, business. On one side was the divine in human beings; on the other, everything animal. On one side was art, on the other, life. On one side were women, clergymen, and university professors, all guardians of art and the ideal; on the other side were men in general immersed in their practical affairs." For more on the bifurcation between men and women in the nineteenth century, see *Total Truth,* chapter 12.

5. Cassandra Vinograd, "Humans Are on Display at London Zoo," *AP*, 26 August 2005.

6. "Scarlett Johansson: 'I'm Not Promiscuous'," *AP*, 9 October 2006; Jenny Eliscu, "Hot Actress: Sienna Miller; With a searing turn in 'Factory Girl,' she aims to leave the tabloids behind," *Rolling Stone,* 6 October 2006.

7. Ernst Mayr, *The Growth of Biological Thought: Diversity, Evolution, and Inheritance* (Cambridge, MA: Harvard University Press, 1982), 88–90. Max Delbrück, "How Aristotle Discovered DNA," in *Physics and Our World,* ed. Kerson Huang (New York: American Institute of Physics, 1976).

8. Mayr, *The Growth of Biological Thought,* 103–4.

9. Jerry A. Coyne, "Seeing and Believing: The never-ending attempt to reconcile science and religion, and why it is doomed to fail," *The New Republic,* 4 February 2009. Janet Browne, *Charles Darwin: Voyaging, A Biography* (Princeton, NJ: Princeton University Press, 1995), 542.

10. See Paul Conkin, *When All the Gods Trembled: Darwinism, Scopes, and American Intellectuals* (Lanham, MD: Rowman & Littlefiield, 1998), 42.

11. Stephen Jay Gould, *Ever Since Darwin: Reflections in Natural History* (New York: Norton, 1977), 12–13. "It is increasingly evident that moral standards, practices, and policies reside in our neurobiology." Patricia Churchland, "Moral Decision-Making and the Brain," in *Neuroethics,* ed. Judy Illes (Oxford: Oxford University Press, 2006), 3.

12. Greg Koukl, *Tactics* (Grand Rapids, MI: Zondervan, 2009).

13. Charles Taylor, *Hegel* (Cambridge: Cambridge University Press, 1975), 564.

14. Douglas J. Futuyma, *Evolutionary Biology,* 2nd ed. (Sunderland, MA: Sinauer, 1986), 3.

15. Balzac lived just before Darwin but "the Theory of Evolution was very much in the air at that time" and Balzac was quite interested in it. Marion Ayton Crawford, "Introduction," *Old Goriot* by Honoré de Balzac (New York: Penguin, 1951), 7. See also E. K. Brown, "Introduction," *Pere Goriot and Eugenie Grandet* (New York: The Modern Library, 1946, 1950), ix–x; Hippolyte Taine, "Balzac's Philosophy," *Pere Goriot* (New York: Norton & Co., 1998), 228–29.

16. Theodore Dreiser, *An American Tragedy.* For general treatments of literary naturalism, see Richard Lehan, *Realism and Naturalism: The Novel in an Age of Transition* (Madison, WI: University of Wisconsin Press, 2005); Donald Pizer, *Realism and Naturalism in Nineteenth-Century American Literature,* rev. ed. (Carbondale, IL: Southern Illinois University Press, 1984); Donald Pizer, *Twentieth Century American Literary Naturalism* (Carbondale, IL: Southern Illinois University Press, 1982).

17. Theodore Dreiser, *A Book about Myself,* cited in Charles C. Walcutt, "Theodore Dreiser: The Wonder and Terror of Life," in *Sister Carrie* by Theodore Dreiser, ed. Donald Pizer (New York: Norton, 1991), 487.

18. Martin Esslin, "Chekhov and the Modern Drama," in *Anton Chekhov,* ed. Harold Bloom (Philadelphia, PA: Chelsea House Publishers, 1999), 140.

19. Rookmaaker, *Modern Art and the Death of a Culture,* 79.

20. Emile Zola, *The Experimental Novel* (New York: Cassell, 1893), 125, 25, 12.

21. Emile Zola, preface, 2nd ed. *Therese Raquin* (New York: Penguin, 1962), 22–23.

22. John Caughie, *Television Drama: Realism, Modernism, and British Culture* (Oxford University Press, 2000), 96–97.

23. George and Portia Kernodle, *Introduction to the Theatre* (New York: Harcourt, Brace, Jovanovich, 1971), 13–14.

24. Russett, *Darwin in America*, 193. See also chapter 7, "Three Naturalist Writers."

25. Richard Dawkins, "Let's stop beating Fawlty's car," http://www.edge.org/q2006/q06_9. html.

26. The young man's name was Joe Manzari. See Logan Gage, "Who wrote Richard Dawkins's new book?" *Evolution News & Views,* 28 October 2006, http://www.evolutionnews. org/2006/10/who_wrote_richard_dawkinss_new.html. My account is slightly different because it is taken from an audio tape. Tom Wolfe makes a similar observation: "At a recent conference on the implications of genetic theory for the legal system—five distinguished genetic theorists are up on stage—I stood up in the audience and asked, 'If there is no free will, why should we believe anything you've said so far? You only say it because you're programmed to say it.' You've never heard such stuttering and blathering in response to anything in your life." Cited in Carol Iannone, "A Critic in Full: A Conversation with Tom Wolfe," *Academic Questions*, 11 August 2008.

27. Auerbach, *Mimesis,* 41–45.

28. Cited in George P. Landow, *Victorian Types, Victorian Shadows: Biblical Typology in Victorian Art and Thought* (Boston, MA: Routledge & Kegan Paul, 1980), 79. See also Earl Miner, ed., *Literary Uses of Typology: From the late Middle Ages to the Present* (Princeton, NJ: Princeton University Press, 1977); Sacvan Bercovitch, ed. *Typology and Early American Literature* (University of Massachusetts Press, 1972); Northrop Frye, *The Great Code* (New York: Harcourt, 1981, 1982).

29. Landow, *Victorian Types, Victorian Shadows,* 97–99, 112, 118.

30. Jonathan Rosen, "Missing Link," *The New Yorker,* 12 February 2007.

31. Zola, *The Experimental Novel,* 126, 123–4.

32. John Perreault, "Dada Perfume: A Duchamp Interview," *Review,* December 1996. Man Ray is cited in Robert Hughes, *The Shock of the New,* rev. ed. (New York: Knopf, 1980, 1991), 243.

33. For example, a philosopher of aesthetics named George Dickie writes: "But the *Fountain* has many qualities that can be appreciated—its gleaming white surface, for example. In fact, it has several qualities which resemble those of Brancusi and Moore." Dickie, along with Duchamp's response, are cited in Gablik, *Has Modernism Failed?,* 38–39.

34. Charles Darwin*, The Autobiography of Charles Darwin*, ed. Nora Barlow (New York: Norton, 1993), 86.

35. Neal Gillespie, *Charles Darwin and the Problem of Creation* (Chicago, IL: University of Chicago Press, 1979), 46, emphasis added. See also Nancy Pearcey, "You Guys Lost," in *Mere Creation: Science, Faith, and Intelligent Design,* ed. William A. Dembski (Downers Grove, IL.: InterVarsity, 1998).

36. Gillespie, *Charles Darwin and the Problem of Creation,* 146, 153.

37. David Hume, *Inquiry Concerning Human Understanding*, section XII, part 3, 173. Earlier rationalists held a significantly different conception of rationality. For example, Descartes held that true ideas are innate in us, and that intuiting them is the surest way to truth. The positivists rejected innate ideas. They believed that all knowledge begins with sensation, and reduced rationality essentially to logic (what Hume called "necessary connections").

38. John Cottingham, *Rationalism* (London: Paladin, 1984), 109.

39. See Peter Galison, "Aufbau/Bauhaus: Logical Positivism and Architectural Modernism," *Critical Inquiry*, vol. 16, no. 4 (Summer 1990).

40. Theo van Doesburg, cited in Bayles, *Hole in Our Soul*, 39.

41. Charles Jencks, "Postmodernism and the Revenge of the Book," in *This Is Not Architecture*, ed. Kester Rattenbury (New York: Routledge, 2002), 192.

42. Hughes, *Shock of the New*, 180.

43. James C. Scott, *Seeing Like a State: How Certain Schemes to Improve the Human Condition Have Failed* (New Haven, CT: Yale University Press, 1999), 116.

44. Galison, "Aufbau/Bauhaus: Logical Positivism and Architectural Modernism," 716–18

45. Cited in Hughes, *Shock of the New*, 165.

46. Fiona MacCarthy, "House Style," *The Guardian*, 17 November 2007.

47. Theodore Dalrymple, "Do Sties Make Pigs?" *City Journal*, Summer 1995.

48. Art historian Barbara Rose is credited with first using the term in "ABC Art," *Art in America*, October 1965.

49. Seerveld, *Rainbows*, 162, 176, 232.

50. Ian MacDonald, *The People's Music* (London: Pimlico, 2003), 176, 184.

51. Schonberg, *Lives of the Great Composers*, 14.

52. Calvin Seerveld, *Bearing Fresh Olive Leaves: Alternative Steps in Understanding Art* (Carlisle, UK: Piquant, 2000), 85, see also 70.

53. Hartt, *Art*, 1043. A PBS television series summarized minimalism as "anonymous, cold, indifferent, and seemingly mechanical forms that have at their core some mathematical relationship." Cited in Cole and Gealt, *Art of the Western World*, 317.

54. Cited in Gregory Battcock, ed. *Minimal Art: A Critical Anthology* (Los Angeles, CA: University of California Press, 1995), 107.

55. Carl Andre, *Cuts: Texts 1959–2004* (Cambridge, MA: MIT Press, 2005), 85.

56. Gablik, *Has Modernism Failed?*, 23.

57. Cited in Gablik, *Has Modernism Failed?*, 97.

58. Cited in Battcock, *Minimal Art*, 157–58. One justification offered for formalism was simply professional specialization. Each branch of the arts sought to identify what was distinctive about its particular medium, and then to "purify" itself by eliminating anything thought to belong to any other medium. Hence it was decreed that painting must eliminate

any story line or narrative because that supposedly belonged to literature. Painting must get rid of shaded modeling to make things look rounded because that belonged to sculpture. Painting must limit itself to its irreducible "two-dimensionality," or the flatness of the picture plane. "The history of art becomes a series of formal revisions and innovations in which painting is concerned with nothing other than itself." Obviously, this approach leaves "little room for religious and spiritual concerns." On the devaluing of individuality, see Mark C. Taylor, *Disfiguring*, 77.

59. Gablik, *Has Modernism Failed?*, 93, 97.

60. Ernest Gellner, *Words and Things* (London: Rutledge), 23. In the last line Gellner is quoting David Pears, *Wittgenstein* (London: Fontana/Collins, 1971), 184.

61. Barrett, *Irrational Man*, 49.

62. Gablik, *Has Modernism Failed?*, 22.

63. For more on common sense realism and its impact on American evangelicalism, see *Total Truth*, chapter 11.

64. Quentin Smith, "The Metaphilosophy of Naturalism," in *Philo* 4, no. 2 (Fall/Winter 2001). See also *Total Truth*, 58–59.

65. "Modernizing the Case for God," *Time*, 7 April 1980.

66. Ross, *The Rest Is Noise*, 125. See also Patrick Kavanaugh, *The Spiritual Lives of the Great Composers* (Nashville, TN: Sparrow Press, 1992), chapter 12.

Chapter 7: Romancing the Canvas (The Romantic Heritage)

1. Sanford Pinsker, "Henry Adams and Our New Century," *Partisan Review*, vol. LXVII, no. 2, 6 June 2000.

2. Alexandre Koyré, *Newtonian Studies* (London: Chapman & Hall, 1965), 24.

3. William B. Ashworth, Jr., "Natural History and the Emblematic Worldview," *Reappraisals of the Scientific Revolution*, ed. David C. Lindberg and Robert S. Westman (Cambridge: Cambridge University Press, 2000), 306–8. See also Pearcey, "Recent Developments in the History of Science and Christianity"; James Bono, *The Word of God and the Languages of Man: Interpreting Nature in Early Modern Science and Medicine* (University of Wisconsin Press, 1995), 174 ff; Peter Harrison, *The Bible, Protestantism, and the Rise of Natural Science* (Cambridge: Cambridge University Press, 1998), 17.

4. Burtt, *The Metaphysical Foundations of Modern Science*, rev. ed., 238–39.

5. Randall, *Making*, 268. Alfred North Whitehead complains of the "bifurcation of nature" into real quantities and unreal qualities. *The Concept of Nature* (Middlesex, UK: The Echo Library, 2006), chapter 2. See also William Barrett, *Death of the Soul: From Descartes to the Computer* (New York: Anchor Books, 1986), 36.

6. Sloan, *Faith and Knowledge*, 193, emphasis added.

7. Barzun, *Use and Abuse of Art*, 53.

8. Alfred North Whitehead, *Science and the Modern World* (New York: Free Press, 1967 [1925]), 195.

9. Robert Rosenblum, *Modern Painting and the Northern Romantic Tradition: Friedrich to Rothko* (London: Thames and Hudson, 1975), 14.

10. Besançon, *Forbidden Image*, 288–90.

11. Abrams, *Mirror*, 278–79.

12. Arthur Schopenhauer, *The World as Will and Representation*, vol. 1 (Mineola, NY: Dover, 1966), 421.

13. John B. Cobb, Jr., Introduction, *Back to Darwin: A Richer Account of Evolution* (Grand Rapids, MI: Eerdmans, 2008), 2. See also Abrams, *Mirror*, 62–63.

14. Samuel Taylor Coleridge, *Biographic Literaria* (1817), cited in Abrams, *Mirror*, 119. Herder is cited in Begbie, *Resounding*, 244. John Opie is cited in the Monthly Musical Recond (London: Augener & Co.), vol. 20, no. 238, 1 October 1890, 225. Wordsworth is cited in M. H. Abrams, *Natural Supernaturalism: Tradition and Revolution in Romantic Literature* (New York,: Norton, 1971), 169. Yeats is cited in J. W. Burrow, *The Crisis of Reason in European Thought, 1848–1914* (New Haven, CT : Yale University Press, 2000), 230.

15. Barzun, *Use and Abuse of Art*, 30, 39.

16. For more on how all worldviews offer a counterpart to creation, fall, redemption, see *Total Truth*, chapter 4.

17. Arthur Lovejoy says that a conspicuous aspect of Romanticism was "a revival of the direct influence of neo-Platonism." *The Great of Being* (Cambridge, MA: Harvard University Press, 1936, 1964), 297. Similarly, Paul Reiff writes: "If we are to speak of anyone at all as a 'key' to the understanding of Romanticism, one man only merits the term, Plotinus," the founder of neo-Platonism. Cited in Abrams, *Natural Supernaturalism*, 428.

18. Abrams, *Natural Supernaturalism*, 29, 268–69, 339.

19. See Jonathan Loesberg, *A Return to Aesthetics* (Stanford, CA: Stanford University Press, 2005).

20. Barrett, *Irrational Man*, 130.

21. Edgar Wind, *Symbolism: Great Artists of the Western World* (London: Marshall Cavendish, 1988), 9, 69.

22. See *Total Truth*, appendix 2, "Modern Islam and the New Age movement."

23. Does the Bible address neo-Platonism? Yes. Though neo-Platonism arose in the third century AD (the 200s), it incorporated many ideas that were current earlier when the New Testament was being written. For example, in neo-Platonism, the One creates automatically out of the "fullness" of its being; hence the realm of the One and all its spiritual emanations was called the "fullness" or *pleroma*—the totality of divine power. In Colossians 1:19

and 2:9 Paul tells us that the fullness (*pleroma*) of deity dwells in Christ. In addition, in neo-Platonism, the ranks of spiritual emanations were often personified as spiritual beings, somewhat like angels. Colossians 1:16 refers to them as thrones, dominions, principalities, and authorities, teaching that Christ reigns supreme over all of them.

24. Historians of science are more willing today than they were in the past to consider philosophical and religious influences on the rise of modern science. See *Soul of Science,* chapter 2. This chapter draws on earlier articles of mine in the *Bible-Science Newsletter,* "The Science of Science," August 1983; "From Tyrant to Tool: A New View of Science," April 1986.

25. P. M. Rattansi, "Reason in Sixteenth- and Seventeenth-Century Natural Philosophy," *Changing Perspectives in the History of Science,* ed. Mikulás Teich and Robert Young (London: Heinemann, 1973), 159.

26. Donald Grout and Claude Palisca, *A History of Western Music,* 6th ed. (New York: Norton, 2001), 715–16, emphasis in original.

27. Rookmaaker, *Modern Art and the Death of a Culture,* 89–90, emphasis added. The term *expressionism* was actually coined later by German artists and applied retrospectively to Gauguin and Van Gogh.

28. Rosenblum, *Modern Painting and the Northern Romantic Tradition,* 96. For more on Van Gogh, see Veith, *State of the Arts,* 77–79.

29. Donald Kuspit, "A Critical History of Twentieth-Century Art," chapter 2, part 2, *Artnet,* 17 February 2006.

30. Walford, *Great Themes,* 441, 455.

31. Gombrich, *The Story of Art,* 564, 566.

32. Cited in *Art: A World History* (New York, NY: Dorling Kindersley Adult, 2002), 570.

33. See *Soul of Science,* chapter 5, "The Belated Revolution in Biology."

34. Mayr, *Growth of Biological Thought,* 97.

35. Randall, *Making,* 419.

36. Ian Barbour, *Issues in Science and Religion* (New York: Harper & Row, 1966, 1972), 67. Neo-Platonism was not so much pantheism (all is God) as panentheism (all is *in* God). For scientific support, the Romantics fastened on the work of Leibniz, a contemporary of Newton. For Newton, everything was composed of atoms, tiny hard particles of matter. For Leibniz, everything was composed of monads, tiny centers of spiritual or mental energy. The term *monad* derives from neo-Platonism, and Leibniz employed it to say that nature is a vast organism imbued with a soul or spirit. "The whole nature of bodies is not exhausted in their extension, that is to say their size, figure, and motion," he wrote. Instead "we must recognize something that corresponds to soul." See *Soul of Science,* 84.

37. Lovejoy, chapter IX, "The Temporalizing of the Chain of Being," 242–87. The escalator metaphor comes from Mary Midgley, who calls the myth of progress the Escalator Myth, in *Evolution as a Religion?* (London: Methuen,1985). In *How Now Shall We Live?*, chapters 23–29, I show that many modern ideologies are variations on the Escalator Myth in areas as diverse as Marxism, sex education, New Age spirituality. These chapters draw on several earlier articles of mine published in the *Bible-Science Newsletter*, including, "What Do You Mean, Evolution Is a Religion?" April 1988, "Religion of Revolution: Karl Marx's Social Evolution," June 1986; "The Evolving Child: John Dewey's Impact on Modern Education," Parts 1 and 2, January/February 1991; "Creating the 'New Man': The Hidden Agenda in Sex Education," May 1990; "New Age for Kids," December 1988.

38. Randall, *Philosophy after Darwin* (New York: Columbia University Press, 1977), 12–13. The exception was America, where Hegelian evolutionary theology was rare, and therefore Darwin provoked greater controversy: "In America there was no large religious party to welcome Darwin; the full shock of his naturalization of man was felt there." (35).

39. Charles Coulston Gillespie, *The Edge of Objectivity* (Princeton, NJ: Princeton University Press, 1960), 276.

40. Randall, *Philosophy after Darwin*, 8.

41. As philosopher Roy Clouser writes, if all ideas are little more than stories we invent, then "historicism, too, according to historicism, is just one more story we invent without ever having any way to know that it does or doesn't correspond to reality." Thus historicism fails "because it is self-referentially incoherent." "A Critique of Historicism," *Contemporary Reflections on the Philosophy of Herman Dooyeweerd*, ed. D. F. M. Strauss and E. M. Botting (Lewiston, NY: Edwin Mellen Press, 2000), 4.

42. Lower criticism, or textual criticism, corrects copying errors and compares different versions of the Bible in order to reconstruct the original text. Higher criticism seeks to determine the date, authorship, literary structure, literary sources, and so on, of the biblical text. However, the term is often equated with theories like the Graf-Wellhausen hypothesis that treat the Bible as myth and legend.

43. See my articles in the *Bible-Science Newsletter*, "Interpreting Genesis: A Reply to the Critics," August 1984; "Real People in a Real World: The Lessons of Archaeology," June 1985; "Did It Really Happen? Genesis and History," March 1987.

44. Schopenhauer wrote: "With Plotinus there even appears, probably for the first time in Western philosophy, idealism that had long been current in the East." Cited in Solomon & Higgins, 224–26. On the Westernizing of Eastern pantheism, see my articles in the *Bible-Science Newsletter*, "East Meets West in Science," February 1985; "New Age for Kids," December 1988. See also Nancy Pearcey, "Spiritual Evolution? Science and the New Age Movement," presentation at the National Creation Conference, Cleveland, Ohio, August

14–16, 1985. For an update of the topic, see "The New Age Religion," chapter 28 in *How Now Shall We Live?*

45. See Maurice Tuchman, "Hidden Meanings in Abstract Art, in The Spiritual in Art: Abstract Painting 1890–1985 (New York: Abbeville Press, 1986), 19. Abstract art "reveals a deep immersion in multiple forms of Neoplatonic spirituality." Pamela Schaeffer, "Spirituality in Abstract Art," *Christian Century,* 30 September 1987.

46. *Kandinsky: Complete Writings on Art,* ed. Kenneth C. Lindsay and Peter Vergo (New York: Da Capo, 1994).

47. James Jeans, *Physics and Philosophy* (New York: Dover Publications, 1981 [1943]), 216. James Jeans, *The Mysterious Universe* (Gretna, LA: Pelican Books, 1938), 19. For a recent version of this view, see Richard Conn Henry, "The Mental Universe," *Nature,* vol. 436, 7 July 2005.

48. *Kandinsky: Complete Writings,* 101, 364.

49. Veith, *State of the Arts,* 84.

50. The terms *geometric abstraction* and *biomorphic abstraction* were coined by Alfred H. Barr, Jr., founding director of the Museum of Modern Art. He pointed out that modern art had split into "two main polarized currents," which he diagrammed in a famous flow chart. The geometric current ran from Cezanne to cubism to the Bauhaus—the same current we traced in chapter 5 and 6. The biomorphic current ran from Gauguin to Kandinsky—and then on to styles like surrealism, which we will discuss in the next chapter. See Sybil Gordon Kantor, *Alfred H. Barr and the Intellectual Origins of the Museum of Modern Art* (Cambridge, MA: MIT Press, 2002), 325–28. The flow chart is on page 23.

51. Mark C. Taylor, *Disfiguring,* 85. See also Giles Fraser, "Modernism and the Minimal God: On the Empty Spirituality of the God of the Philosophers," *Faith and Philosophical Analysis: The Impact of Analytical Philosophy on the Philosophy of Religion,* ed. Harriet A. Harris and Christopher J. Insole (Burlington, VT: Ashgate, 2005).

52. Francis Schaeffer, *Escape from Reason,* FAS Trilogy, 250, 256.

53. Susan Sontag, "The Aesthetics of Silence," *Aspen* nos. 5 & 6 (a multimedia magazine of the arts published from 1965 to 1971).

54. Begbie, *Resounding,* 251.

55. Hughes, *Shock of the New,* 386.

56. Dominique de Ménil, cited in Julia Goldman, "A Landscape for Contemplation," *The Jewish Week,* 11 July 2003.

57. Robert Rosenblum, "Isn't It Romantic?" *Artforum International,* 1 May 1998. Kuspit says "Rothko's paintings are perhaps the death throes" of the "mystically inclined" abstraction founded by Kandinsky. "A New Sacred Space," *Per Contra,* Winter 2006–2007.

58. Personal interview, 6 May 2009.

59. Personal interview, 9 June 2009.

60. Cited in Alan Jacobs, *The Narnian* (New York: HarperOne, 2005), 185.

61. C. S. Lewis, *English Literature in the Sixteenth Century* (London: Oxford University Press, 1954), 3–4.

62. C. S. Lewis, *Surprised by Joy: The Shape of My Early Life* (New York: Harcourt Trade, 1995), 164, 167. See also *Total Truth*, 120–21.

63. Owen Barfield, *The Rediscovery of Meaning* (Middletown, CT: Wesleyan University Press, 1977).

64. C. S. Lewis, "Myth Became Fact," *God in the Dock* (Grand Rapids, IL: Eerdmans, 1970 [1944]), 66.

Chapter 8: Escape from Nihilism (*The Romantic Heritage*)

1. Similar themes were probed by Fyodor Dostoyevsky in his novel about nineteenth-century Russian revolutionaries, *The Possessed.* Dostoyevsky uses the names of the same historical figures—Büchner, Moleschott, Vogt—to represent doctrinaire materialists. His characters dismiss the works of Pushkin and other Romantics as "nonsense and a luxury."

2. Gamwell, 68, 130.

3. Carl Gustav Jung, *Psychology and Literature,* in *Modern Man in Search of a Soul,* 3rd ed. (Orlando, FL: Harcourt Harvest, 1955 [1933]), 172. See also Burrow, *The Crisis of Reason in European Thought, 1848–1914,* 164–69.

4. Barzun, *Use and Abuse of Art,* 89.

5. Gombrich, *The Story of Art,* 578, 592

6. Cited in Kantor, *Alfred H. Barr and the Intellectual Origins of the Museum of Modern Art,* 326.

7. Walford, *Great Themes,* 354. Artistic rules were thought to conform "to that objective structure of norms whose existence guaranteed the rational order and harmony of the universe." See also Abrams, *Mirror,* 16–17.

8. Dyrness, *Visual Faith,* 111.

9. Henry Steele Commager, *The American Mind: An Interpretation of American Thought and Character Since the 1880s* (New Haven, CT: Yale University Press, 1950), 93. Similarly, Paul Conkin says a person could choose the realm of science and facts, but at the cost of accepting a determinism that denied "the validity of his ideals and his feelings of worth and purpose." Or he could choose the realm of moral and spiritual ideals, but "at the expense of logic [and] fact." *Puritans and Pragmatists* (Bloomington, IN: Indiana University Press, 1968), 275.

10. Jacques Monod, *Chance and Necessity* (New York: Alfred A. Knoft, 1971), 173.

11. See Midgley, *Evolution as a Religion?* I discuss this theme in greater detail in "What Do You Mean, Evolution Is a Religion?" *Bible-Science Newsletter,* April 1988, and in "The Drama of Despair," chapter 27 in *How Now Shall We Live?*

12. Albert Camus, *The Myth of Sisyphus* (New York: Knopf, 1955, Vintage, 1991), 28. As West writes (151), "The absurd is a direct consequence of the absence of God."

13. John Paul Sartre, "Existentialism and Humanism," in *The Modern Tradition: Backgrounds of Modern Literature,* ed. Richard Ellmann and Charles Fiedelson, Jr. (New York: Oxford University Press, 1965), 828.

14. Harold Rosenberg, "The American Action Painters," *Art News* 51 (September 1953): 344.

15. Barrett, *Irrational Man,* 51.

16. Mark C. Taylor, *Erring: A Postmodern A/Theology* (Chicago, IL: University of Chicago Press, 1984), 73.

17. Camus, *The Myth of Sisyphus,* 6.

18. Kernodle, *Introduction to the Theatre,* 187.

19. Kierkegaard is "now often regarded as the first existentialist." West, 81, 118, 126. For similar statements, see Solomon & Higgins, 227–28, 276–77, 279; Richard Kearney, *Modern Movements in European Philosophy,* 2nd ed. (Manchester: Manchester University Press, 1994), 54–55. David Cooper calls Kierkegaard "the father of existentialism" but explains how his thought differed from that of later existentialists. "Søren Kierkegaard," in *The Blackwell Guide to Continental Philosophy,* ed. Robert Solomon and David Sherman (Oxford: Blackwell, 2003). Merold Westphal offers an insightful analysis in his essay on Kierkegaard in *A Companion to Continental Philosophy.*

20. Sloan, *Faith and Knowledge,* 114, 121, 123, 126.

21. Charles Rosen, *The Romantic Generation* (Cambridge, MA: Harvard University Press, 1995), 647.

22. Aldous Huxley, *The Doors of Perception & Heaven and Hell* (New York: HarperCollins, 2004, [1954]).

23. Jim Morrison, lead singer for The Doors, read deeply in the works of Rimbaud and modeled himself after the poet's self-destructive philosophy. See Wallace Fowlie, *Rimbaud and Jim Morrison: The Rebel as Poet* (Durham, NC: Duke University Press, 1994).

24. See Wilhelm Dilthey, *Pattern and Meaning in History* (New York: Harper & Row, 1961), 5. I treat these issues in greater detail in *The Soul of Science,* chapter 2. To describe the methodology of the human sciences, Dilthey borrowed a term that until then had been used mostly in biblical interpretation: He called it *hermeneutics,* which has become a favored term among postmodernists.

25. Louis Rougier, cited in Philipp Frank, *Philosophy of Science* (Englewood Cliffs, NJ: Prentice-Hall, 1957), 83.

26. As E. T. Bell writes, a split emerged between "*mathematical* geometry," which was "a system of postulates and deductions from them," and *physical* geometry, which is a "practical science designed to give a coherent account of the world of sensory (and scientific) experience." *The Magic of Numbers* (New York: Dover Books, 1946), 373–76.

27. Bell, 331. I give a much fuller discussion of the philosophical implications of non-Euclidean geometry in *Soul of Science,* chapter 7.

28. These examples and many more can be found in Edward A. Purcell, *The Crisis of Democratic Theory: Scientific Naturalism and the Problem of Value* (Lexington, KY: University Press of Kentucky, 1973).

29. For a more thorough discussion of the new physics and its philosophical implications, see *The Soul of Science,* chapter 8, "Is Everything Relative? The Revolution in Physics," and chapter 9, "Quantum Mysteries: Making Sense of the New Physics." These chapters are expanded from earlier articles of mine published in the *Bible-Science Newsletter,* "The New Physics and the New Consciousness," parts 1 and 2, October/November 1986.

30. Cited in Alan J. Friedman and Carol C. Donley in *Einstein as Myth and Muse* (Cambridge, MA: Cambridge University Press, 1985), 70 (emphasis is Williams').

31. Percy Bridgman, *Reflections of a Physicist* (New York: Philosophical Library, 1950), 93.

32. J. C. Polkinghorne, *The Quantum World* (Princeton, NJ: Princeton University Press, 1984), 1.

33. Floyd Matson, *The Broken Image* (New York: George Braziller, 1964), 130.

34. Jean, *Physics and Philosophy,* 216.

35. Rudolf Bultmann, *Jesus Christ and Mythology* (New York: Charles Scriber's Sons, 1958), 37–38.

36. Barbour, *Issues,* 309.

37. Arthur Koestler, *Arrow in the Blue* (London: Hamish Hamilton, 1952), 258.

38. See Kearney, *Modern Movements in European Philosophy,* 92–96, 107, 288–89.

39. Roland Barthes, "The Death of the Author," in *Image—Music—Text* (New York: Hill and Wang, 1977).

40. The concept of deconstruction began with Heidegger, whose German term *Destruktion* was rendered in French by Derrida as *déconstruction.* Surprisingly, Heidegger was inspired partly by Luther, who spoke of the "destruction" of medieval Aristotelian scholasticism in order to recover an authentic scriptural Christianity. Kierkegaard spoke of the "destruction" of speculative Hegelian metaphysics to recover a living form of Christianity. Applying this meaning of the term to philosophy, Heidegger actually intended deconstruction to be a positive process of uncovering the underlying experiences of life that inspire philosophy in the first place. Charles B. Guignon, *The Cambridge Companion to Heidegger,* 2nd ed. (Cambridge, MA: Cambridge University Press, 2006), 328–29.

41. Barthes, "The Death of the Author."

42. Cited in Kevin J. Vanhoozer, "Special Revelation and General Hermeneutics," in *Disciplining Hermeneutics: Interpretation in Christian Perspective,* ed Roger Lundin (Grand Rapids, MI: Eerdmans: 1977), 136. Mark C. Taylor, *Disfiguring,* 261. Taylor is referring specifically to architecture, though his observation generalizes to any of the arts: "Inasmuch as the author-architect is made in the image of God, the death of God implies the disappearance of the author-architect."

43. West, *An Introduction to Continental Philosophy*, 197–98. "A metanarrative in Lyotard's sense is equivalent to a philosophy of history. The contingent events of history are understood in terms of an all-inclusive narrative, which is supposed to encapsulate 'the' meaning of history."

44. Numbers from R. J. Rummel, *Death by Government* (New Brunswick, NJ: Transaction Publishers 1994). See also first-hand accounts such as Aleksandr Solzhenitsyn's *The Gulag Archipelago* and Loung Ung's *First They Killed My Father,* about the Khmer Rouge.

45. Jürgen Habermas, *Philosophical Discourse of Modernity* (Cambridge, MA: MIT Press, 1987).

46. Gablik, *Reenchantment,* 30–32.

47. Walford, *Great Themes,* 488. See also 476.

48. Marc Porter Zasada, "Irrational Exuberance in the New Century," *Los Angeles Downtown News,* 21 December 2002. See Christopher Jencks, *The Iconic Building* (New York: Rizzoli, 2005).

49. Danny Hakim, "Ex-Employee Held in Campus Attack," *New York Times,* 11 May 2003.

50. Letters, *Chronicle of Higher Education,* June 27, 1997, cited in Carl P. E. Springer, "The Hermeneutics of Innocence: Literary Criticism from a Christian Perspective," updated July 13, 2002, http://www.leaderu.com/aip/docs/springer.html#text6.

51. David Weddle, "Lights, Camera, Action. Marxism, Semiotics, Narratology. Film School Isn't What It Used to Be, One Father Discovers," *Los Angeles Times,* 13 July 2003.

52. Andrew Delbanco, "The Decline and Fall of Literature," *The New York Review of Books,* vol. 46, no. 17, 4 November 1999.

53. Wendy Steiner, "Practice without Principle," *The American Scholar,* Summer 1999.

54. Frank Lentricchia, "Last Will and Testament of an Ex-Literary Critic," *Lingua Franca,* September/October 1996: 64. A critique of the politicizing of literature can be found in John Ellis, *Literature Lost: Social Agendas and the Corruption of the Humanities* (New Haven, CT: Yale University Press, 1997).

55. Classic works on liberation theology were published at about the same time: black theology (James Cone's *A Black Theology of Liberation,* 1970), feminist theology (Rosemary Ruether's *Liberation Theology,* 1972), and Latin American liberation theology (Gustavo

Gutiérrez's *A Theology of Liberation,* 1972). See my articles in the *Bible-Science Newsletter,* "Religion of Revolution: Karl Marx's Social Evolution," June 1986, and "Liberation, Yes . . . But How? A Study of Liberation Theology," July 1988. I condensed and updated the material in "Does It Liberate?" chapter 24 in *How Now Shall We Live?*

56. James Cone, *A Black Theology of Liberation* (Philadelphia, PA: Lippincott, 1970), 136.

57. James Cone, *For My People: Black Theology and the Black Church* (Maryknoll, NY: Orbis, 1984), 187.

58. Schaeffer critiques the two-story concept of truth in *Escape from Reason* and *The God Who Is There,* in *The Complete Works of Francis A. Schaeffer,* vol. 1 (Wheaton, IL.: Crossway, 1982). Dooyeweerd critiques dualism in *Roots of Western Culture: Pagan, Secular, and Christian Options* (Toronto: Wedge, 1979; orig., Zutphen, Netherlands: J. B. van den Brink, 1959). See also *In the Twilight of Western Thought* (Nutley, NJ: Craig, 1972; orig., Presbyterian & Reformed, 1960) and his four-volume set *A New Critique of Theoretical Thought* (Ontario, Canada: Paideia Press, 1984; orig. published in Dutch in 1935). Hans Rookmaaker writes: "In the course of the years Schaeffer and I discussed many things, among which philosophy and particularly Dooyeweerd's philosophy were favourite topics. Dooyeweerd's ideas have had an influence on Schaeffer and L'Abri in that way. Of course Schaeffer incorporated these ideas in his own thinking. . . . I make quite an effort not to use his difficult terminology, which in a way belonged to the style of the 1930s. So you will not find Dooyeweerd's vocabulary in our discussions at L'Abri, but his thoughts are there just the same." Hans Rookmaaker 'A Dutch view of Christian philosophy,' *The Complete Works of Hans Rookmaaker,* ed. Marleen Hengelaar-Rookmaaker (Piquant, 2005), vol. 6, part III, The L'Abri Lectures.

59. Dooyeweerd argues that *every* nonbiblical worldview ultimately splits into some form of dualism. He identified three major examples in Western thought: the Greek form/matter dualism; the scholastic nature/grace dualism; Kant's nature/freedom dualism. A twentieth-century Catholic school of theology known as *nouvelle theologie* has been credited with overcoming the scholastic nature/grace dualism. Dooyeweerd welcomed this movement: "It is a gladdening symptom of a re-awakening biblical consciousness, that under the influence of Augustinianism an increasing number of Roman Catholic thinkers, belonging to the movement of the so-called *nouvelle theologie,* have begun to oppose this dualistic view. They agree with the Reformed philosophical movement in the Netherlands in advocating the necessity of a Christian philosophy." *The Twilight of Western Thought,* 141.

60. William James, *Pragmatism: A New Name for Some Old Ways of Thinking* (Indianapolis, IN: Hackett Publishing, [1907] 1981), 13. Conkin, *Puritans and Pragmatists,* 324. Today pragmatists continue to insist that they have succeeded in overcoming the fact/value split—for example, Hilary Putnam's *The Collapse of the Fact/Value Dichotomy and Other Essays* (Harvard

University Press). For a fuller discussion of philosophical pragmatism, see *Total Truth*, chapter 8.

61. As philosopher Richard Bernstein explains, "The various forms of dualism that arise in modern philosophy can be traced back to a conviction that the world of mathematical, objectized nature is the measure of all that is genuinely real." Richard Bernstein, *The Restructuring of Social and Political Theory*, (Philadelphia, PA: University of Pennsylvania Press, 1976), 129.

62. Kearney, *Modern Movements in European Philosophy*, 2nd ed., 18, 22. A handy way to summarize continental thought is that it began with the 3 Hs: Hegel, Husserl, Heidegger.

63. Dooyeweerd, *New Critique*, I:46. For example, the mechanistic materialism of the Enlightenment resulted from "an absolutization of the mechanical phenomena." Dooyeweerd, *Roots*, 172–73. See also J. M. Spier, *An Introduction to Christian Philosophy*, (Philadelphia: Presbyterian and Reformed Publishing Co., 1954), 67–69. Examples of thinkers influenced by Dooyeweerd include Roy Clouser, who offers a Dooyeweerdian analysis of various philosophies of science, showing how each one absolutizes some aspect of creation, in *The Myth of Religious Neutrality* (Notre Dame, IN: University of Notre Dame Press, 1991). David Koyzis applies a Dooyeweerdian analysis to political philosophy: "Liberalism idolizes the individual, socialism the economic class, and nationalism the nation-state or ethnic community." *Political Visions & Illusions: A Survey and Christian Critique of Contemporary Ideologies* (Downers Grove, IL: InterVarsity, 2003).

64. G. K. Chesterton, *Orthodoxy* (a BiblioBazaar reproduction, 2008), 66.

65. Dooyeweerd, *New Critique*, I:58.

66. John Paul II "points out that the radical separation between the two great currents in the Western philosophy [which he calls realism versus idealism] originated in the absolutization of one of the two aspects of human experience"—either inner experience (of the self, the subject) or outer experience (of the world, the object). Jaroslaw Kupczak, *Destined for Liberty: The Human Person in the Philosophy of Karol Wojtyla/John Paul II* (Washington, DC: Catholic University Press, 2000), 76. See also Rocco Buttiglione *Karol Wojtyla: The Thought of the Man Who Became Pope John Paul II* (Grand Rapids, MI: Eerdmans, 1997), 68, 72.

67. John Stuart Mill, *Dissertations and Discussions* (Honolulu, HI: University Press of the Pacific, 2002), 332.

68. Modern society is "Romantic in its private and imaginative life" but "utilitarian and instrumentalist in its public, effective life." Charles Taylor, *Hegel*, 541.

69. C. P. Snow, *The Two Cultures and the Scientific Revolution* (London: Cambridge University Press, 1959).

70. Steiner, "Practice without Principle."

71. Daniel Ritchie, *Reconstructing Literature in an Ideological Age* (Grand Rapids, MI: Eerdmans, 1996), 3.

72. Carver Yu, "Truth and Authentic Humanity," in *The Gospel as Public Truth: National Consultation Organized by British and Foreign Bible Society and The Gospel and Our Culture,* National Consultation held 11–17 July 1992, published by Gospel and Our Culture, 27–28.

73. Seerveld, *Rainbows*, 177, emphasis in original.

74. Rookmaaker, *Modern Art and the Death of a Culture,* 18.

75. Schaeffer, *The God Who Is There,* 36.

Chapter 9: Worldview at the Movies

1. Czeslaw Milosz, *The Captive Mind* (New York: Random House, Vintage Books, 1951, 1953), 3.

2. Viktor Frankl, *The Doctor and the Soul: From Psychotherapy to Logotherapy* (New York: Random House, 1986 [1955]), xxvii.

3. Machen, 'Christianity and Culture."

4. Chris Lehmann, "Among the Non-Believers: The tedium of dogmatic atheism," *Reason,* January 2005.

5. John Irving, *My Movie Business: A Memoir* (Random House, 2000), 29, 54. See also *Margaret Michniewicz,* "A Conversation with Novelist John Irving," *Vermont Woman,* April 2006. Lorenza Munoz, "The Intention of John Irving," *Los Angeles Times,* excerpts posted in a review by David Bruce for Hollywood Jesus.com, http://hollywoodjesus.com/cider_house.htm.

6. James P. Siegel, "Introduction," *Film, Faith, & Philosophy* (Downers Grove, IL: InterVarsity, 2007), 9.

7. See Dyrness, *Visual Faith,* 141.

8. Dennis Lim, *Village Voice,* 29 September–5 October 2004.

9. I am paraphrasing C. S. Lewis' observation that it would be much more difficult for secularists to dismiss Christianity if, whenever they wanted a good book to some subject, "the best work on the market was always by a Christian." "Christian Apologetics," *God in the Dock,* 93.

10. Cited in Mark Conard, "The Indifferent Universe: Woody Allen's *Crimes and Misdemeanors,"* in *Movies and the Meaning of Life: Philosophers Take on Hollywood,* ed. Kimberly Blessing and Paul Tudico (Chicago, IL: Open Court, 2005), 117–18.

11. Cited in Ibid., 120.

12. Cited in Jack Vermee, "World Premier of eXistenZ," *Take One,* Spring 1999; Chris Rodley, "Game Boy," *Sight and Sound,* April 1999.

13. The existentialist philosopher Martin Heidegger stated that humans are constantly reaching beyond themselves to new understandings of life, constantly transcending their current condition. In his words, *"Existenz is Transcendenz."* See Kearney, *Modern Movements in European Philosophy*, 32.

14. Cited in Richard von Busack, "Pod Man Out," *Metroactive*, 22–28 April 1999.

15. For a more detailed review, see Brian Godawa, "The Matrix: Unloaded Revelations," *Christian Research Journal*, vol. 27, no. 1, 2004.

16. Martin Shockley "Christian Symbolism in the Grapes of Wrath," *College English*, vol. 18, no. 2, November 1956.

17. Johnston, 119–20. Johnston adds: "Movie stories offer a pattern; they make a claim; they challenge or proclaim; they seek to make a difference in their viewers." In short, "a movie is built on someone else's view of reality."

18. "Pulp Fiction: Review," an unsigned review, http://movies.tvguide.com/pulp-fiction/review/130222.

19. Rick Pearcey, "Fireproof—Reel Rebel Upsets Tinseltown Stereotypes," http://www.pearceyreport.com/archives/2008/10/fireproof_reel.php.

Epilogue: Bach School of Apologetics

1. Compiled from articles by Uwe Siemon-Netto: "Bach in Japan," in *Christian History*, issue 95, Summer 2007; "Where Bach was jailed, Asians pay homage," *The Asia Pacific Times*, January 2008. "Why Nippon Is Nuts About J. S. Bach," *The Atlantic Times*, December 2005.

2. See my interview with Calvin Seerveld, "Christianity and the Arts," *Perspective* 18, no. 3, June 1984.

3. Brian Godawa, *Hollywood Worldviews*, 2nd ed. (Downers Grove, IL: InterVarsity, 2009), preface.

4. John R. Erickson, "Stories as Nourishment," posted on the Pearcey Report, copyright John R. Erickson, 2004. See also John Erickson, *Story Craft* (Perryton, TX: Maverick Books, 2009).

5. Veith, *State of the Arts*, 43.

6. Cited in Amos Wilder, *Theology and Modern Literature* (Cambridge, MA: Harvard University Press,1958), 21.

7. Dorothy Sayers, *Creed or Chaos* (Manchester, NH: Sophia Institute Press, 1995 [1949]), 6.

8. Wilder, *Theology and Modern Literature*, 46.

9. Bruce Weber, *Paintings of New York, 1800–1950* (Petaluma, CA: Pomegranate Communications, 2005), 56.

10. Richard Lovelace, *Dynamics of Spiritual Life* (Downers Grove, IL: InterVarsity, 1979) 353–54.

11. Seerveld, *Bearing Fresh Olive Leaves*, 56.

12. A good source on the life of Mozart is Robert Greenberg's course, "Great Masters: Mozart—His Life and Music," 2000, from the Teaching Company's Great Courses series.

13. Philip Ryken, *Art for God's Sake* (Phillipsburg, NJ: P & R Publishing, 2006).

14. David Aikman, "A Christian Publishing Scandal," *Charisma,* July 2002. Ironically, the secular world is more ethical in this area than the Christian world. Aikman writes: "For many years, the secular U.S. publishing industry has all but insisted that celebrities who publish their stories include on the cover of the book the name of the actual writer or writers. In this respect, secular publishing houses have shown themselves to be more ethical than some Christian houses."

15. Makoto Fujimura, personal e-mail, 11 June 2009.

16. Alexandre Kojève, *Introduction to the Reading of Hegel* (Ithaca, NY: Cornell University Press, 1980), 27.

17. Interview with Mark Joseph, "Author and Filmmaker Mark Joseph Discusses *Sarah Barracuda,*" Christian Cinema.com, 3 November 2008.

18. Dorothy Sayers, "The Greatest Drama Ever Staged," in *Creed or Chaos?,* 3–9.

19. Auerbach, *Mimesis,* 14–15, 22–23, 41–43.

20. Dennis Hollinger, "The Church as Apologetic: A Sociology of Knowledge Perspective," *Christian Apologetics in a Postmodern World,* ed. Timothy R. Phillips and Dennis L. Okholm (Downers Grove, IL: InterVarsity, 1995), 191, 183.

21. Machen, "Christianity and Culture."

22. Francis Schaeffer, *The Church at the End of the Twentieth Century,* in *The Complete Works of Francis Schaeffer,* vol. 4, 70.

List of Images

4-11- *Windmill by a River (oil on canvas)*, Ruisdael, Jacob Isaaksz. or Isaacksz. van (1628/9-82) / Private Collection / Courtesy of Thomas Brod and Patrick Pilkington / The Bridgeman Art Library International

4-12- *The Denial of St. Peter, 1660 (oil on canvas)*, Rembrandt Harmensz. van Rijn (1606-69) / Rijksmuseum, Amsterdam, The Netherlands / The Bridgeman Art Library International

4-13- *Deposition, 1602-4 (oil on canvas)*, Caravaggio, Michelangelo Merisi da (1571-1610) / Vatican Museums and Galleries, Vatican City, Italy / The Bridgeman Art Library International

4-14- *The Raising of the Cross, 1610-11 (oil on panel)*, Rubens, Peter Paul (1577-1640) / Onze Lieve Vrouwkerk, Antwerp Cathedral, Belgium / Peter Willi / The Bridgeman Art Library International

4-15- *Mr and Mrs Andrews, c.1748-9 (oil on canvas)*, Gainsborough, Thomas (1727-88) / National Gallery, London, UK / The Bridgeman Art Library International

4-16- Recreation Galante, 1717-18 (oil on canvas), Watteau, Jean Antoine (1684-1721) / *Schloss Charlottenburg, Berlin, Germany / Giraudon / The Bridgeman Art Library International*

4-17- *Lake George*, John Fredrick Kensett/Image copyright © The Metropolitan Museum of Art / Art Resource, NY

4-18- *Kauterskill Clove, in the Catskills, 1862 (oil on canvas)*, Gifford, Sanford Robinson (1823-80) / Digital Image © 2009 Museum Associates / LACMA / Art Resource, NY

4-19- *Autumn on the Hudson River, 1860-* Jasper Francis Cropsey/ Copyright © National Gallery of Art, Washington, DC

4-20- *Zen and the Art of Motorcyle Maintenace-* Robert Pirisig

5-1- *Interior of a mill; carding and drawing, 19th century (print)*, Anonymous / Private Collection / The Bridgeman Art Library International

5-2- *Execution of the Defenders of Madrid, 3rd May, 1808, 1814 (oil on canvas)*, Goya y Lucientes, Francisco Jose de (1746-1828) / Prado, Madrid, Spain / The Bridgeman Art Library International

5-3- *Assassinations of Five Monks from Valencia, engraving-* Miguel Gamborino

5-4- *The Execution of the Emperor Maximilian, 1867-8 (oil on canvas)*, Manet, Edouard (1832-83) / Stadtische Kunsthalle, Mannheim, Germany / The Bridgeman Art Library International

5-5- *Burial at Ornans, 1849-50 (oil on canvas)*, Courbet, Gustave (1819-77) / Musee d'Orsay, Paris, France / The Bridgeman Art Library International

5-6- *Three Women in Church, 1882 (oil on panel)*, Leibl, Wilhelm Maria Hubertus (1844-1900) / Hamburger Kunsthalle, Hamburg, Germany / The Bridgeman Art Library International

5-7- *The Sower, 1850 (oil on canvas)*, Millet, Jean-Francois (1814-75) / Museum of Fine Arts, Boston, Massachusetts, USA / Gift of Quincy Adams Shaw through Quincy Adams Shaw, Jr. and Mrs Marian Shaw Haughton / The Bridgeman Art Library International

5-8- *The Banjo Lesson*, 1893- Henry Tanner/ Hampton University Museum, Hampton, Virginia

5-9- *The Hireling Shepherd, 1851 (oil on canvas)*, Hunt, William Holman (1827-1910) / © Manchester Art Gallery, UK / The Bridgeman Art Library International

5-10- *The Scapegoat, 1854 (oil on canvas)*, Hunt, William Holman (1827-1910) / © Lady Lever Art Gallery, National Museums Liverpool / The Bridgeman Art Library International

5-11- *Regatta at Argenteuil, c.1872 (oil on canvas)*, Monet, Claude (1840-1926) / Musee d'Orsay, Paris, France / Giraudon / The Bridgeman Art Library International

5-12- *The Boulevard Montmartre at Night, 1897 (oil on canvas)*, Pissarro, Camille (1831-1903) / National Gallery, London, UK / The Bridgeman Art Library International

5-13- *Ballerina and Lady with a Fan, 1885 (pastel on paper)*, Degas, Edgar (1834-1917) / Philadelphia Museum of Art, Pennsylvania, PA, USA / The Bridgeman Art Library International

5-14- *The Virgin of the Rocks (with the Infant St. John adoring the Infant Christ accompanied by an Angel), c.1508 (oil on panel)*, Vinci, Leonardo da (1452-1519) / National Gallery, London, UK / The Bridgeman Art Library International

5-15- *The Rehearsal, c.1877 (oil on canvas)*, Degas, Edgar (1834-1917) / Burrell Collection, Glasgow, Scotland / © Culture and Sport Glasgow (Museums) / The Bridgeman Art Library International

5-16- *Gare St. Lazare, 1872-3 (oil on canvas)*, Manet, Edouard (1832-83) / National Gallery of Art, Washington DC, USA / The Bridgeman Art Library International

5-17- *Symphony in White No. 1*, 1862- James Whistler/© Board of Trustees, National Gallery of Art, Washington

5-18- *In a Cafe, or The Absinthe, c.1875-76 (oil on canvas)*, Degas, Edgar (1834-1917) / Musee d'Orsay, Paris, France / Giraudon / The Bridgeman Art Library International

5-19- *Dressage des Nouvelles, par Valentin le Desosse (Moulin-Rouge), 1890*, Toulouse-Lautrec, Henri de (1864-1901) / Philadelphia Museum of Art, Pennsylvania, PA, USA / Peter Willi / The Bridgeman Art Library International

5-20- *Newton, 1795/circa 1805*- William Blake- Tate, London/Art Resource, NY

5-21- *Woman Playing a Guitar, 1913 (oil on canvas), Braque, Georges (1882-1963) / Musee National d'Art Moderne, Centre Pompidou, Paris, France / © DACS / Giraudon / The Bridgeman Art Library International* /© 2010 Artists Rights Society (ARS), New York / ADAGP, Paris

5-22- *Man with a Guitar, 1912*- Pablo Picasso/The Philadelphia Museum of Art/Art Resource, NY/© 2010 Estate of Pablo Picasso / Artists Rights Society (ARS), New York

5-23- *Les Demoiselles d'Avignon, 1907 (oil on canvas)*, Picasso, Pablo (1881-1973) / Museum of Modern Art, New York, USA / Giraudon / The Bridgeman Art Library *International* /© 2010 Estate of Pablo Picasso / Artists Rights Society (ARS), New York

5-24- *Descending a Staircase, No.2, 1912 (oil on canvas)*, Duchamp, Marcel (1887-1968)/Philadelphia Museum of Art, Pennsylvania, PA, USA/© DACS /The Bridgeman Art Library International /© 2010 Artists Rights Society (ARS), New York / ADAGP, Paris / Succession Marcel Duchamp

5-25- *The Knife Grinder, 1912*- Kasimir Malevich/Yale University Art Gallery / Art Resource, NY

5-26- *Simultaneous Counter Composition*- Theo van Doesburg

5-27- *Neo-plastic Composition*- César Domela/Bridgeman Art Library/Artists Rights Society (ARS), New York / ADAGP, Paris

5-28- *The Rite of Spring, 1913*- Igor Stravinsky/© National Endowment for the Arts

5-29- *Serialism*- Anonymous

5-30- *Quartet for the End of Time, 1941*- Olivier Messiaen

6-1- *Jungle Tales of Tarzan*- Edgar Rice Burroughs

6-2 *The Call of the Wild*- Jack London

6-3- *An American Tragedy*- Theodore Dreiser

6-4- *The Octopus*- Frank Norris

6-5- *Madame Bovary*- Gustave Flaubert

6-6- *Thérèse Raquin*- Emile Zola

6-7- *The Three Sisters, 1901*- Anton Chekhov

6-8- *Jane Eyre*- Charlotte Bronte

6-9- *A Farewell to Arms*- Ernest Hemingway

6-10- *Gift*- Man Ray/Digital Image © The Museum of Modern Art/Licensed by SCALA / Art Resource, NY/© 2010 Man Ray Trust / Artists Rights Society (ARS), NY / ADAGP, Paris

6-11- *Fountain, 1917/64 (ceramic)*, Duchamp, Marcel (1887-1968) / The Israel Museum, Jerusalem, Israel / © DACS / Vera & Arturo Schwarz Collection of Dada and Surrealist Art / The Bridgeman Art Library International /© 2010 Artists Rights Society (ARS), New York / ADAGP, Paris / Succession Marcel Duchamp

6-12- *Bauhaus Building, Dessau, Germany, 1926*-Walter Gropius

6-13- *Seagram Building, New York City, 1958*-Mies van der Rohe & Philip Johnson

6-14- *Opera House, from 'Souvenirs De Paris - Monuments Vues en Couleurs' (colour litho)*, French School, (20th century) / Private Collection / The Bridgeman Art Library International

6-15- *Laccio Table, 1925*- Marcel Breuer

6-16- *Schroeder Table, 1923*- Gerrit Rietveld

6-17- *Brandt Teapot Replica-* Anonymous

6-18- *Paris City Plan, 1925-* Le Corbusier/Banque d'Images, ADAGP/Art Resource, NY/© 2010 Artists Rights Society (ARS), New York / ADAGP, Paris / F.L.C

6-19- *Pruitt-Igoe housing development, St. Louis, 1972*

6-20- *Red Yellow Blue 1, 1963-* Ellsworth Kelly, © 1963 Ellsworth Kelly

6-21- *Red Yellow Blue Painting No. 1, 1974-* Brice Marden/Albright-Knox Art Gallery/Art Resource, NY/© 2010 Brice Marden / Artists Rights Society (ARS), New York

6-22- *Untitled, 1965-* Donald Judd- Digital Image © The Museum of Modern Art/Licensed by SCALA/Art Resource, NY/Art © Judd Foundation. Licensed by VAGA, New York, NY

6-23- *Two Open Modular Cubes/Half-Off, 1972-* Sol Le Witt/Tate, London / Art Resource, NY/© 2010 The LeWitt Estate / Artists Rights Society (ARS), New York

6-24- *Equivalent VIII, 1966-* Carl Andre/Tate, London/Art Resource, NY/Art © Carl Andre/Licensed by VAGA, New York, NY

6-25- *The Prince Patutszky-Red, 1962-* Jules Olitski/Art © Estate of Jules Olitski/Licensed by VAGA, New York, NY

6-26- *Number One, 1958-* Kenneth Noland/Art © Estate of Kenneth Noland/Licensed by VAGA, New York, NY

6-27- *Shipping on the Kil with `Oude Wachthuis' and the Grote Kerk, Dordrecht beyond,* Goyen, Jan Josephsz. van (1596-1656) / Private Collection / Photo © Christie's Images / The Bridgeman Art Library International

6-28- *Single Consentric Squares, 1974-* Frank Stella/Art Resource, NY/© 2010 Frank Stella / Artists Rights Society (ARS), New York

7-1- *Rose and lancet windows from the north wall (stained glass),* French School, (13th century) / Chartres Cathedral, Chartres, France / Giraudon / The Bridgeman Art Library International

7-2- *The French Electrical Machinery Gallery at the Universal Exhibition of 1900 (engraving) (b/w photo),* French School, (20th century) / Bibliotheque Nationale, Paris, France / Giraudon / The Bridgeman Art Library International

7-3- *History of Animals, 1558-* Conrad Gesner

7-4- *Nantyglo Ironworks, c.1829 (w/c on paper),* English School, (19th century) / © National Museum Wales / The Bridgeman Art Library International

7-5- *The Cross in the Mountains, 1808 (oil on canvas),* Friedrich, Caspar David (1774-1840) / Erich Lessing / Art Resource, NY

7-6- *Abbey Burial Ground, 1810-* Caspar David Friedrich/Bildarchiv Preussischer Kulturbesitz / Art Resource, NY

7-7- *The Death and the Gravedigger, 1900 (gouache, watercolour and pencil),* Schwabe, Carlos (1866-1926) / Louvre, Paris, France / Peter Willi / The Bridgeman Art Library International

7-8- *The Isle of the Dead, 1880 (oil on canvas),* Bocklin, Arnold (1827-1901) / Kunstmuseum, Basel, Switzerland / Peter Willi / The Bridgeman Art Library International

7-9- *The Vision after the Sermon (Jacob wrestling with the Angel) 1888 (oil on canvas),* Gauguin, Paul (1848-1903) / © National Gallery of Scotland, Edinburgh, Scotland / The Bridgeman Art Library International

7-10- *The Starry Night, June 1889 (oil on canvas),* Gogh, Vincent van (1853-90) / Museum of Modern Art, New York, USA / The Bridgeman Art Library International

7-11- *Potdamer Platz, Berlin, 1914-* Ernst Kirchner/Bildarchiv Preussischer Kulturbesitz / Art Resource, NY

7-12- *Hell of Birds, 1938-* Max Beckmann/© 2010 Artists Rights Society (ARS), New York / VG Bild-Kunst, Bonn/© 2010 Artists Rights Society (ARS), New York / VG Bild-Kunst, Bonn

7-13- *The Cabinet of Dr. Caligari, 1919*

7-14- *Pentecost, 1909 (oil on canvas), Nolde, Emil (1867-1956)* / Private Collection / The Bridgeman Art Library International

7-15- *Crucifixion, 1934 (gouache on canvas),* Rouault, Georges (1871-1958) / Private Collection / © DACS / The Bridgeman Art Library International /© 2010 Artists Rights Society (ARS), New York /

ADAGP, Paris

7-16- *Code of Hammurabi (Replica)*

7-17- *Cyrus Cylinder*

7-18- *Yellow, Red, Blue, 1925 (oil on canvas)*, Kandinsky, Wassily (1866-1944) / Musee National d'Art Moderne, Centre Pompidou, Paris, France / © DACS / Peter Willi / The Bridgeman Art Library International

7-19- *Horse and Eagle, 1912 (oil on canvas)*, Marc, Franz (1880-1916) / Sprengel Museum, Hanover, Germany / Peter Willi / The Bridgeman Art Library International

7-20- *Sternkirche (Model Replica), 1922-* Otto Bartning

7-21- *The Einstein Tower, Potsdam, 1921 (photo), / Potsdam, Germany /* © Edifice / The Bridgeman Art Library International

7-22- *Painting, 1958-* Ad Reinhardt/© 2010 Estate of Ad Reinhardt / Artists Rights Society (ARS), New York

7-23- *Williams Mix, 1952-* John Cage

7-24- *Running Fence, Sonoma and Marin Counties, California, 1972-75/* CNAC/MNAM/Dist. Réunion des Musées Nationaux / Art Resource, NY/ Photo: Jeanne-Claude/© 1976 Christo

7-25- *Spiral Jetty, 1970-* Robert Smithson/Art © Estate of Robert Smithson/Licensed by Vaga, New York, NY/Art © Estate of Robert Smithson/Licensed by VAGA, New York, NY

7-26- *Earth and Green, 1955-* Mark Rothko/© 1998 Kate Rothko Prizel & Christopher Rothko / Artists Rights Society (ARS), New York

7-27- *Orange and Yellow, 1956-* Mark Rothko/Albright-Knox Art Gallery / Art Resource, NY/© 1998 Kate Rothko Prizel & Christopher Rothko / Artists Rights Society (ARS), New York

7-28- *The Rothko Chapel, Houston, TX*

7-29- *Weep for the Wiping of Grace, 1998-* Carol Bomer/© Carol Bomer

7-30- *Zero Summer, 2005-* Makoto Fujimura/© Makoto Fujimura

7-31- *Lord of the Rings-* J.R.R Tolkien

8-1- *The Persistence of Memory, 1931 (oil on canvas)*, Dali, Salvador (1904-89) / Museum of Modern Art, New York, USA / © DACS / The Bridgeman Art Library International /© 2010 Salvador Dali, Gala-Salvador Dali Foundation / Artists Rights Society (ARS), New York

8-2- *The Song of Love. Paris, June-July 1914-* Giorgio de Chirico/Digital Image (c) The Museum of Modern Art/Licensed by SCALA / Art Resource, NY/© 2010 Artists Rights Society (ARS), New York / SIAE, Rome

8-3- *People at Night, Guided by the Phosphorescent Tracks of Snails, 1947-* Joan Miró/ Philadelphia Museum of Art

8-4- *Garden in Sochi, 1940-* Arshile Gorky/© 2010 The Arshile Gorky Foundation / The Artists Rights Society (ARS), New York

8-5- *Twittering Machine-* Paul Klee, 1922/Digital Image © The Museum of Modern Art/Licensed by SCALA / Art Resource, NY/© 2010 Artists Rights Society (ARS), New York / VG Bild-Kunst, Bonn

8-6- *The Cow with a Subtile Nose, 1954-* Jean Dubuffet/Digital Image (c) The Museum of Modern Art/ Licensed by SCALA / Art Resource, NY/© 2010 Artists Rights Society (ARS), New York / ADAGP, Paris

8-7- *Number 33, 1949 (enamel and aluminium painted gesso ground on paper and board)*, Pollock, Jackson (1912-56) / Private Collection / © DACS / James Goodman Gallery, New York, USA / The Bridgeman Art Library International /© 2010 The Pollock-Krasner Foundation / Artists Rights Society (ARS), New York

8-8- *Pollock at Work*/ National Portrait Gallery, Smithsonian Institution / Art Resource, NY/Hans Namuth © Hans Namuth Ltd.

8-9- *The Sound and the Fury*- William Faulkner

8-10- *Ulysses*- James Joyce

8-11- *The Complete Stories*- Franz Kafka

8-12- *Lady Chatterley's Lover*- D.H. Lawrence

8-13- *Steppenwolf*- Hermann Hesse

8-14- *The Doors of Perception*- Aldous Huxley

8-15- *The Joyous Cosmology*- Alan W. Watts

8-16- *The Melody Haunts My Reverie, 1965*- Roy Lichtenstein/ Digital Image © The Museum of Modern Art/Licensed by SCALA / Art Resource, NY/ Estate of Roy Lichtenstein

8-17- *Campbell Soup, 1968*- Andy Warhol/ Albright-Knox Art Gallery / Art Resource, NY /© 2010 Andy Warhol Foundation for the Visual Arts, Inc./ARS, New York/Trademarks, Campbell Soup Company. All rights reserved

8-18- *Angels in the Rain, 1998*- David Salle/Art © David Salle/Licensed by VAGA, NY, NY. Courtesy of Mary Boone Gallery, NY

8-19- *Retroactive 1, 1963*- Robert Rauschenberg/Wadsworth Atheneum Museum of Art / Art Resource, NY/Art © Estate of Robert Rauschenberg/Licensed by VAGA, New York, NY

8-20- *Case Western Reserve University, 1997*- Frank O. Gehry

8-21- *M2 Building, Tokyo, 1991*- Kengo Kuma

9-1- *The Cider House Rules*

9-2- *I Heart Huckabees*

9-3- *Crimes and Misdemeanors*

9-4- *Seven*

9-5- *eXistenz*

9-6- *Matrix*

9-7- *Waking Life*

9-8- *The Grapes of Wrath*

9-9- *Avatar*

9-10- *Rebel Without a Cause*

9-11- *The Truman Show*

9-12- *Pulp Fiction*

9-13- *The Love Dare*

10-1- *Jesus, tender Shepherd, hear me; Bless Thy little lamb to-night. Illustration from The Children's Book of Hymns by Cicely Mary Barker. Copyright © The Estate of Cicely Mary Barker, 1929. Reproduced by kind permission of Frederick Warne & Co. www.flowerfairies.com* / Private Collection / The Bridgeman Art Library International

10-2- *Jesus The Good Shepherd*- Anonymous

10-3- *Mount Calvary (oil on paperboard), 1944*- William H. Johnson/ Smithsonian American Art Museum, Washington, D.C., Gift of the Harmon Foundation